PUNCHED CARD DATA PROCESSING

PUNCHED CARD DATA PROCESSING

JOSEPH LEVY
International Business Machines Corporation
Account Representative
Data Processing Division
Nassau Community College, Evening Division

McGRAW-HILL BOOK COMPANY
New York San Francisco Toronto London Sydney

PUNCHED CARD DATA PROCESSING

 Library of Congress Catalog Card Number 67-29394.

37386

1234567890HDBP75432106987

This book is dedicated to my wife and my mother

FOREWORD

For a long time there has been a need for one comprehensive textbook covering punched card equipment and basic data processing.

Mr. Levy's book, "Punched Card Data Processing," adequately fills this need and should be a very valuable aid to the student of this subject. He places each topic in its proper perspective and presents it very logically in a step-by-step treatment of both theory and application.

Despite Mr. Levy's obvious technological background, he manages to set forth his explanations in layman's language. He establishes problems, discusses how to solve them, and leads the reader to a clear understanding of machine functions and problem solving.

Among the many vivid and meaningful illustrations to be found in this book are machine schematics, simple electromechanical drawings, control-panel wiring diagrams, and arithmetic examples to explain how each machine functions.

Mr. Levy has also included practice problems and questions designed to reinforce the student's knowledge and to extend his thinking.

While the book will have great meaning for new students, it should also be valuable to those who are already familiar with these machines. The extent to which Mr. Levy delves into the technical aspects of each machine might be quite illuminating to those who already know the "how" but not the "why."

And finally, any person involved in the intricate business of business should find the book very helpful in learning how to apply machines to business problems. Mr. Levy draws extensively upon both his technical knowledge and business experience, and his book contains many testiments thereto.

Lemuel Jones
International Business Machines Corporation
Data Processing Division
Newark Education Center

PREFACE

The text of this book is divided into ten sections. The first section deals with the IBM* punched card, the Hollerith Code of punched holes, and the means of representing data in the form of punched holes.

The second section concerns the IBM Key Punch. This machine is the primary device for coding information from a document into the IBM punched card.

The third section describes the IBM 82 Sorter. The Sorter's function is to arrange IBM punched cards in a logical sequence by individual cards or by groups of cards.

The fourth section covers some basic principles applied to all the control-panel machines, control-panel hubs, connecting wires, and diagramming conventions.

The fifth section is devoted to describing the 548 Interpreter. The Interpreter is able to read the punched holes and print their graphic representation on the face of the card.

The sixth section deals with the IBM 514 Reproducing Punch. The Reproducing Punch can reproduce all or certain punches from a card or cards into another card or cards.

The seventh section covers the IBM 85 Collator, a filing machine that arranges cards into a predetermined pattern for subsequent processing.

The eighth section describes the 402 Accounting Machine. This machine is capable of producing a variety of reports as the result of arithmetic calculations or directly from the information punched in the card.

The ninth section explains the 557 Alphabetic Interpreter which performs the same functions as the 548 Interpreter features that enable it to accomplish many other operations, such as the posting of ledgers.

The tenth and final section describes the 519 Document-Originating Machine which not only performs the same functions as the 514 Reproducing Punch but also has the ability to perform end printing of data punched in the card or to end print data that are punched in another card.

It is suggested that the problems be done as they are encountered and that every aspect of this book be understood before continuing, since any confusion will cause difficulties in learning the succeeding functions. Blank wiring diagrams appear at the back of the book.

At the beginning of each section dealing with a wired machine, the first diagram is that of the machine's control panel. The shaded areas represent special-feature hubs.

Portions of the text and some of the diagrams and photographs contained in this volume are reprinted with the permission of International Business Machines Corporation.

This book is an outgrowth of the author's experience as an evening instructor at Nassau Community College and should not be taken as an official IBM publication.

The author would like to acknowledge the assistance of the following people in the preparation of this text: James McGrath, Assistant Dean of New York City Community College; Dr. Melvin Morgenstein, Chairman and faculty member of the Business Department at Nassau Community College; Professor Charles Barta of the Business Department at Suffolk Community College; and Charles and Katherine Bovino.

* Registered Trademark of International Business Machines.

In the event that the student wishes to examine any of the concepts contained in this volume in greater detail, reference may be made to the following IBM manuals (with copyright dates noted) which also contain the diagrams and photographs used herein.

TITLE	FORM NUMBER	
IBM Operator's Guide	A24-1010-0	(1951)
IBM Functional Wiring Procedures	A24-1007-0	(1956)
An Introduction to IBM Punched Card Data Processing	F20-0074-0	
An Introduction to IBM Data Processing Systems	F22-6517-2	(1960)
The IBM Card and Its Preparation	320-1443	(1961)
The IBM Sorter	320-1444	(1961)
IBM 24 Card Punch, 26 Printing Card Punch	A24-0520-1	(1949)
IBM 82, 83 and 84 Systems	A24-1034-2	(1949)
IBM 548, 552 Interpreters	224-6384-2	(1946)
IBM 513, 514 Reproducing Punches	A24-1002-2	(1945)
The IBM Reproducer	320-1445	(1961)
Automatic Punches	D24-1014-0	(1959)
Collators	D24-1012-0	(1959)
IBM 85 and 87 Collators	A24-1005-2	(1958)
402, 403 and 419 Accounting Machines	A24-5654-0	(1949)
Basic Machine Operation Education Guide	R25-1612-2	(1964)
Functional Wiring Principles Education Guide	R25-1077-3	(1964)
IBM 557 Alphabetic Interpreter	A24-0516-1	(1954)
IBM 519 Document-Originating Machine	A24-1017-1	(1946)
557 Alphabetic Interpreter Examination	229-0178-1	(1964)
519 Document-Originating Machine Examination	R29-0168-0	(1964)

CONTENTS

Section 1

THE IBM PUNCHED CARD

The processing of data has been in existence since man first had the ability to record transactions (Fig. 1-1). The first mechanical means available were key-driven machines that can be seen today, such as the typewriter, cash register, and adding machine. These machines had the advantages of legibility, accuracy, and some degree of standardization. Also, no extensive training was required to operate these machines. Yet these machines still had disadvantages. Since there were no mechanical checking facilities, there was still the possibility of machine errors or human errors and, more important, there were no common media between machines, thereby necessitating a duplication of effort. The typewriter cannot read the paper tapes from the adding machine or the cash register, just as the cash register and adding machine are not able to read the typewritten forms. This deficiency was resolved when the IBM Corporation introduced punched card business machines which had the common medium of the IBM punched card. They have the following advantages:

Fig. 1-1. Data processing systems (Courtesy of International Business Machines.)

1. Once the transaction is accurately recorded, subsequent reports usually will be correct.
2. Mechanical classification of cards permits transmission of data to many reports without attendant posting.
3. The compatible feature of the punched card can be used on many specialized machines, some of which can transmit data over telephone lines.
4. The machines have preprogrammed decision-making capabilities.
5. Many machines provide incorporation of checking features without reduction of speed.
6. A growth in volume can be accommodated by obtaining a faster model of the machine, adding features, or acquiring additional machines without affecting the overall system.

The punched card is 7-3/8 in. by 3-1/4 in. by 0.007 in. It consists of 80 vertical columns numbered 1 to 80 from left to right. Each of the 80 columns is divided into 12 punching rows. From top to bottom these rows are numbered 12, 11, 0, 1, 2, 3, 4, 5, 6, 7, 8, 9. The 12, 11, and 0 rows are referred to as zone-punching positions. The 0 to 9 rows are referred to as digit-punching positions. Notice that the 0 can be either a zone or digit position. The cards are fed into the machines either 12 edge first or 9 edge first, face up (the printed side of the card is the face), or face down.

Some cards have ***corner cuts.*** These cuts have no effect on the machines; their only function is to enable you to see visually that the cards are properly aligned.

Some cards are colored or have colored stripes which permit easy visual recognition by the operator. Different types of cards may have different colors. For example, a name and address card may have a red stripe, while an accounts receivable card may have a blue stripe, and an accounts payable card may have a yellow stripe.

HOLLERITH CODE

The card is known as a ***unit record*** because the card is read or punched as a unit of information. The data is represented in the card by a code of punched holes called the ***Hollerith Code.*** These holes enable the data to be converted automatically to electronic language used by the machine. A code is a means of representing alphameric characters or special symbols such as *, $, ., or , . (The Morse Code is an example of a means of representing characters to enable mechanical devices to recognize the character.) The machines recognize the characters by allowing electric current to flow from a magnetized roller to a metal reading brush whenever there is a hole in the card column. At other times, the card acts as an insulator (Fig. 4-1). The Hollerith Code allows representation of a digit, an alphabetic character, or a special symbol in any of the 80 card columns.

The digits 0 to 9 are represented by a punch in the corresponding row. The specific card columns used would depend on the card design and the type of data represented.

The representation of an alphabetic character requires two punches in a card column. To code the letters A to I requires a punch in the 12-zone row plus a digit punch of 1 to 9. A is coded as a 12 and 1 punch, B as 12 and 2, C as 12 and 3, and so on, until I which is 12 and 9. Since we have ex-

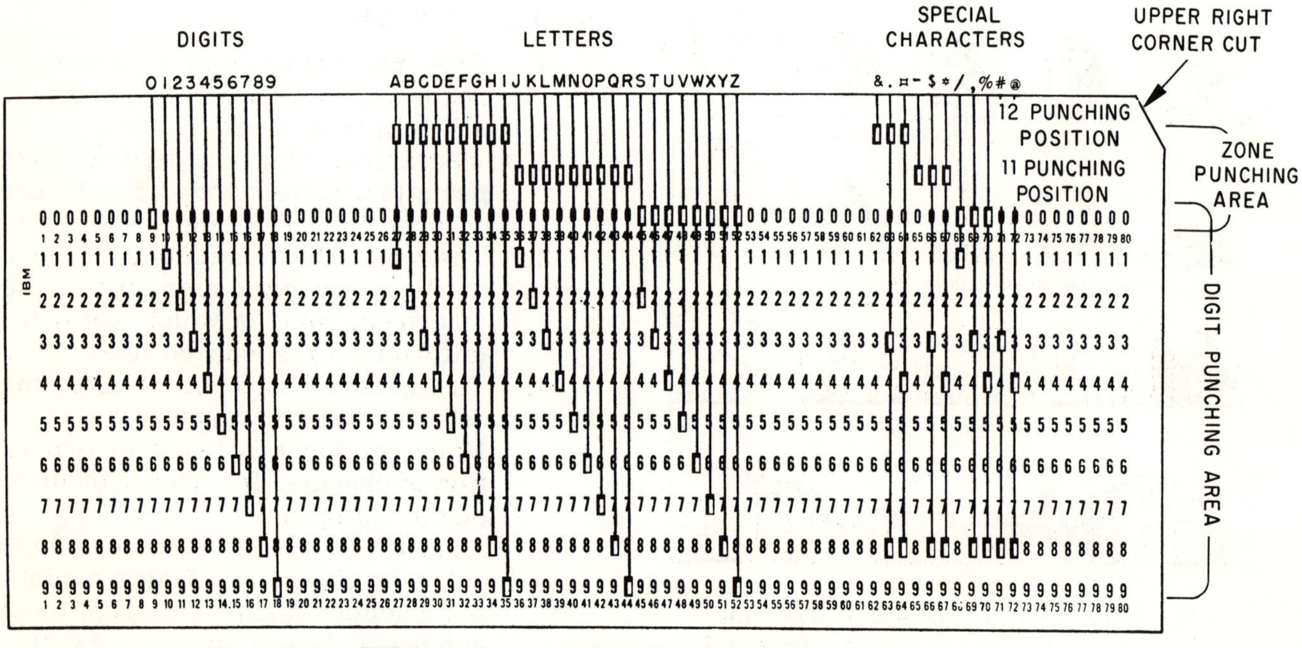

Fig. 1-2. IBM card containing the Hollerith Code (Courtesy of International Business Machines.)

hausted the digit rows, we now use a different zone row for the letters J to R. They are coded with an 11-row punch plus a 1 to 9 punch. For example, the letter J is 11 and 1 punches, K is 11 and 2, and so on, until R which is 11 and 9. To represent S to Z, we use the 0 row plus the digit rows 2 to 9. You will notice that this time we start with the 2 row and not the 1 row. The letter S is a combination of 0 and 2; the letter Z is a combination of 0 and 9. The entire Hollerith coding is shown in Fig. 1-2. The holes in the card can be interpreted and the graphic representation of the punches printed in the card.

PROBLEM 1: Show how the telephone number JE 6-6809 would look punched in a card.

CARD CODES

There are other types of codes used when working with IBM punched cards. We use codes to represent data that would take many card columns. For example, instead of having to use several card columns to represent the different states, we could code each of the 50 states with a two-digit number. By assigning two card columns to be used for states, we could code a maximum of 100 states (00 to 99). There are many examples of such codes:

1. An employee's I.D. number instead of his entire name.
2. A student's I.D. number instead of his entire name.
3. An item number in lieu of an item description.

There are four primary reasons for using these codes. First, they save keypunching time; second, they enable better utilization of the 80 available card columns; third, they save sorting time, as you will see later, and fourth, they conserve printing space in producing reports.

Another type of code commonly encountered is a *card code.* Most installations use several different cards such as name and address cards, accounts receivable cards, accounts payable cards, and item cards. We can assign a unique punch for each different card by setting aside at least one card column, for example, a 1 punch for all name and address cards, a 2 punch for all accounts receivable cards. These punches will enable the machines to distinguish between the different cards.

Another necessary code is the *debit or credit, plus or minus code.* In a scientific installation we might have the need to represent positive or negative numbers, whereas in a commercial installation we may have to code debit or credit transactions. For example, a bank will show deposits as positive transactions and withdrawals as negative transactions. The common standard is to show a negative transaction with an 11 punch over the rightmost digit of the amount. This is known as *overpunching,* because you have punched the 11 over the digit punch in that card column. If you look at Fig. 1-2, you will see that an 11 punch in column 65 prints as a dash. The 11 punch is usually referred to as an X punch, not to be confused with the letter X which is a 0 and 7 punch. For example, a withdrawal of $27.61 would look like 27.6J. The column with the 1 would have an 11 and 1 punch (this is also the letter J). The lack of the 11 punch signifies a positive transaction.

The last type of code to be discussed is an *X-punch control code.* The 11 punch is used to allow the machine to distinguish between two different types of cards, usually referred to as *master cards* and *detail cards.* There are devices on most machines which have the ability to recognize only the X punch and therefore to perform different functions for either an X-punched card or a non-X-punched card. This control punch can appear in any of the 80 card columns.

PROBLEM 2: Using card columns 1 to 4, show what a negative 1252 would look like in a card.

PROBLEM 3: Using card columns 11 to 17 show what the word COLLEGE would look like in a card.

FIELDS

The types of data contained in a card are dependent on the *input* (source documents) and the *output* (desired reports). The sequence of information in a card normally follows the sequence of the source document. This is done for ease of keypunching. Keypunching throughput is reduced if the key punch operator must skip all over the source document for the next data to be keypunched. Sometimes in order to achieve proper card design the source document must be revised.

The card columns assigned to specific items of data are called *Fields.* A field is a column or consecutive columns reserved for the punching of data of a specific nature. A field may be 1 to 80 columns in length, depending on the length of information to be punched. Examples of fields are: a name, an item number, a license plate number, or a person's age.

Certain fields are *left-justified.* For instance, if you have designed a card with a name field in card columns 1 to 24, you would start punching the name in card column 1. The unused card columns would be left blank. An example of a *right-justified* field would be a payroll card containing a gross-pay field in card columns 1 to 7, inclusive. This would mean that the most an employee could be paid would be $99,999.99. (Decimal points, $, and commas are rarely punched in the card, since you will know which card columns contain the cents.) If you were punching a salary of $126.00, you would punch it in card columns 3 to 7 and punch zeros in columns 1 and 2. In right-justified fields it is recommended that you fill unused high-order card columns of the field with zeros. In general, alphabetic fields are left-justified and numeric fields are right-justified.

There are accepted terms in referring to the different card columns in a field and also to either end of a field. The left side of a field is referred to as the *high-order position,* which is the lower numbered card column. The right side of a field is referred to as the *low-order position,* which is the higher numbered card column. The rightmost position is referred to as the *units position,* the second column from the right is the *tens position*, and so on (Fig. 1-3). Remember that the highest numbered card column contains the lowest value in a numeric field. Once a field is assigned a specific card column or columns, these card columns

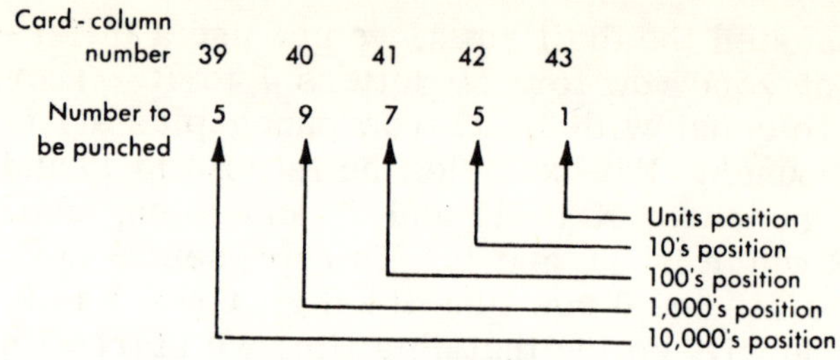

Fig. 1-3. Card-field positions (Courtesy of International Business Machines.)

should not be used for any other data. A simple way of counting the number of columns in a field is to subtract the lowest numbered column from the highest numbered column, then adding 1. For example, an item field in columns 8 to 13, inclusive, would be six columns in length.

We have discussed the terminology and codes of the punched card. Next we will describe the machine, which is the primary means of transferring the pertinent data from the source document to the punched card. It would be an arduous task to remember the alphabetic zone and digit combination and have to punch each character separately. The IBM Key Punch is available to perform this function with speed and flexibility. The key punch has the ability to punch any of the alphameric and special characters with the same ease as with a typewriter. In addition the key punch has the ability to perform many functions automatically.

IBM Punched Card Questions

Answer briefly

1. How many columns are there in a card?
2. How many rows are there in a card?
3. How are the rows designated?
4. Why is it necessary to represent alphabetic characters with two holes?
5. How many holes are necessary to represent special symbols?
6. If an amount field is designated as being in columns 18 to 23 and you punch 4613 into this field, what should be punched in card columns 18 and 19?
7. If a gross-amount field is in card columns 36 to 41, inclusive, how many columns does this field contain?

Section 2

THE KEY PUNCH

There are a number of machines which have the ability to punch holes in an IBM card. The first one that we will discuss is the ***key punch*** (Fig. 2-1), also known as a card punch. There are two types of key punches in wide use - the IBM 24 and the IBM 26. The only difference between them is that the 26 has the ability to print the character immediately over the card column as the character is being punched. The 24 Key Punch does not print; it can only punch. The key punch is the usual means of initially coding the data from the source document.

CARD PATH

After turning on the main-line switch, which supplies power to the machine, you

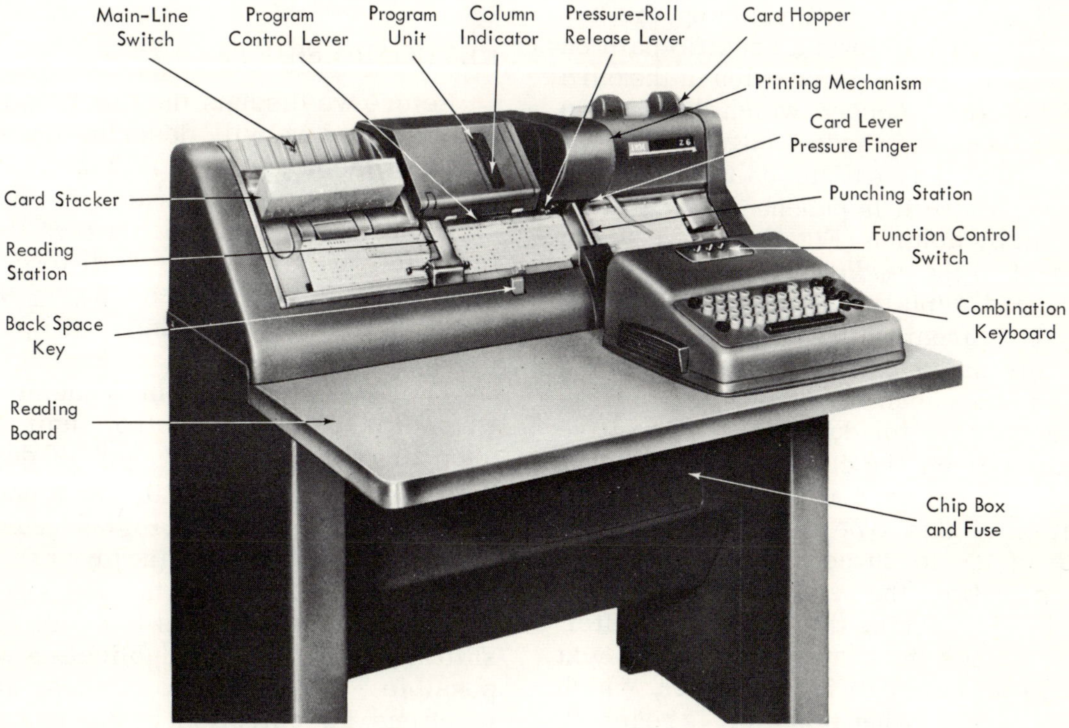

Fig. 2-1. The IBM 26 Key Punch (Courtesy of International Business Machines.)

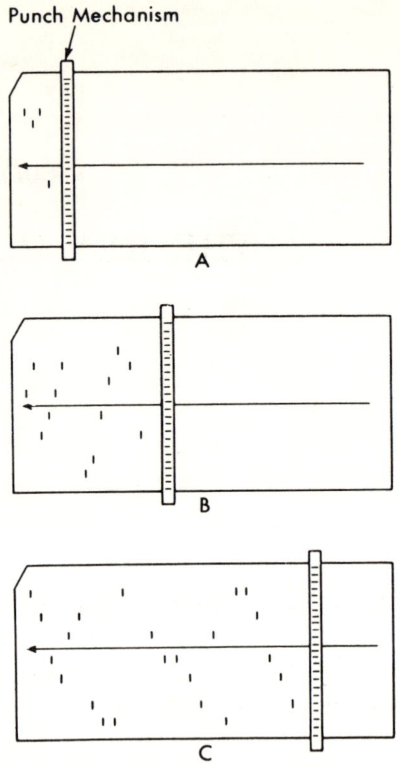

Fig. 2-2. Column-by-column punching (Courtesy of International Business Machines.)

must wait one minute before using the key punch. The card follows a specific path on the key punch. The first position in the card path is the ***card hopper*** which holds 500 cards and feeds the cards 9 edge down, face forward. Next the card moves to the ***punching station***, where it is punched ***serially***, that is, column by column (Fig. 2-2). The card moves next to the ***reading station***, where the card is read serially. This station is internally synchronized to the punch station so that the same card columns are being both read and punched. This synchronization is necessary for duplicating repetitive information from the card at the read station back into the card at the punch station. Duplication of this type is accomplished at the rate of 18 to 20 columns per second. When duplicating, the reading station is activated by depressing the DUP key. After the card passes the reading station its next position in the card path is the ***stacker,*** which holds 500 cards. When this limit is reached, the cards themselves turn the main-line switch off.

There are two other noticeable features near the card path. One is the backspace key (Fig. 2-1), which is located below the card bed between the reading and punching stations. Each depression of this key causes the card to be backspaced one card column. (The automatic program unit, which will be discussed later, is also backspaced.) The other feature is the ***column indicator*** which indicates the next column to pass the punch and read stations.

KEYBOARD

The keyboard is similar to that of a typewriter, in that the alphabetic keys are in the same position (Fig. 2-3). While upper-case letters can be typed on a typewriter by shifting, there are no lower-case characters on the key punch. When the key punch is in a shifted position special characters and digits can be punched. The key punch can have one of two different keyboard arrangements - commercial or scientific - the difference between them being that certain punches will have different graphics on the keys and print different graphics on the card. Some of these graphics are the %, #, =, (, and the).

KEYBOARD SHIFTS

Before we discuss the functional keys of the keyboard we will describe the different shifts of the key punch. When the keyboard is in alphabetic shift, which is the normal shift, and the operator depresses the L key, the letter L and not the digit 6 will punch. Similarly, if you depress the % key, the punch combination for the % will punch, not the comma.

The key punch is in a numeric shift when the program-control unit is being used or when the NUM key is depressed. When in a numeric shift, the 6 and comma would be punched. The ***program-control unit*** is activated by lowering the program-control lever (Fig. 2-1). The purpose of the program-control unit is to cause automatic shifting, skipping, and duplicating wherever possible. The sequence of these automatic functions is controlled by the use of a prepunched program-control card which is wrapped around the ***program drum*** (Fig. 2-4).

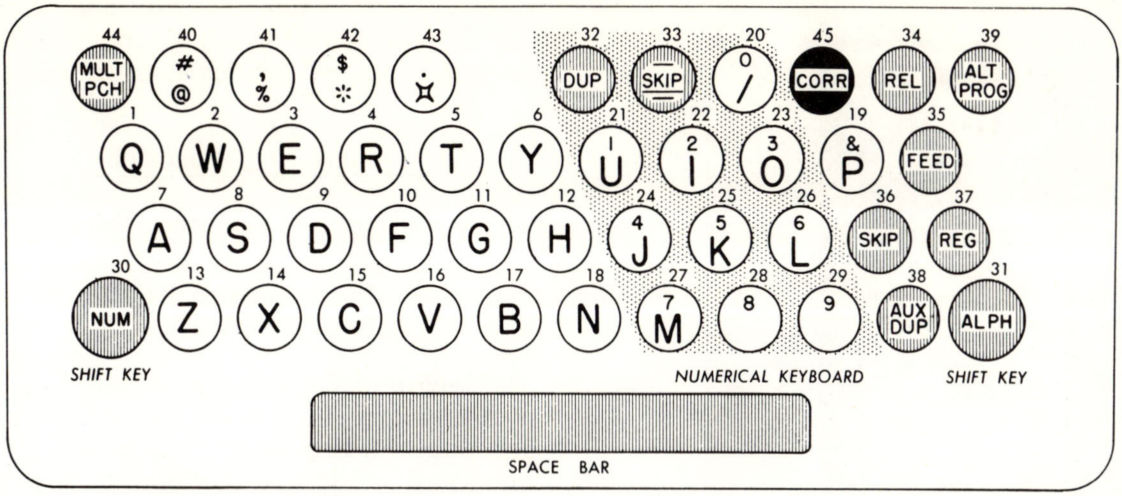

Character Keys Key Number	SHIFT Alphabetic	SHIFT Numeric
1.	Q	Depressing any of these keys while in numerical shift will cause the keyboard to lock up.
2.	W	
3.	E	
4.	R	
5.	T	
6.	Y	
7.	A	
8.	S	
9.	D	
10.	F	
11.	G	
12.	H	
13.	Z	
14.	X	
15.	C	
16.	V	
17.	B	
18.	N	

Character Keys Key Number	SHIFT Alphabetic	SHIFT Numeric
19.	P	& *
20.	/	0
21.	U	1
22.	I	2
23.	O	3
24.	J	4
25.	K	5
26.	L	6
27.	M	7
28.	8	8
29.	9	9
33.	– *	– *
40.	@ *	# *
41.	% *	, *
42.	* *	$ *
43.	*	. *

Control Keys Key Number	Function
30	Numeric shift
31	Alphabetic shift
32	Duplication
34	Releases card from its station
35	Feeds card from hopper
36	Initiates a skip
37	Registers card at station
38, 39	Special Devices
44	Suppresses card movements after punching a hole in card.

* Special character

Fig. 2-3. The keyboard chart (Courtesy of International Business Machines.)

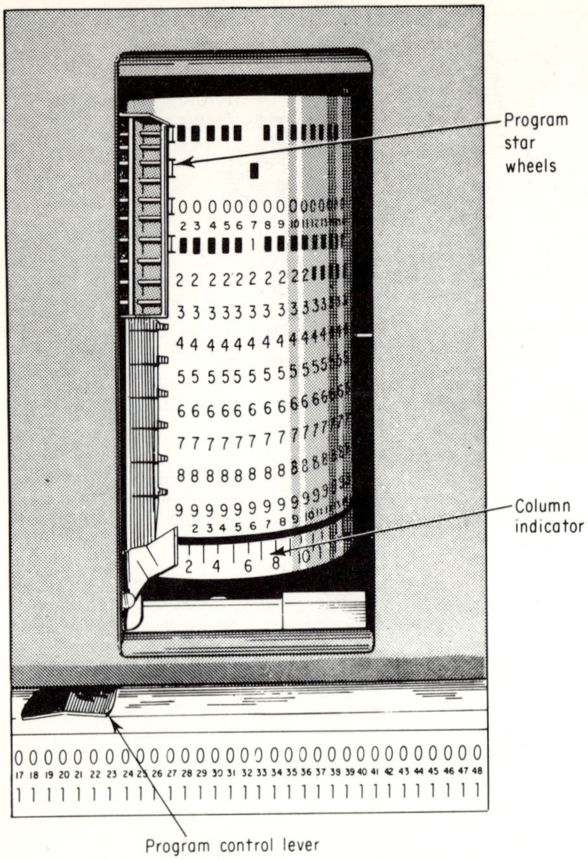

Fig. 2-4. The program drum (Courtesy of International Business Machines.)

For example, let us say that a number of identically formatted cards are to be keypunched as follows:

Columns	Function
1 to 3	Numeric shift
4 to 8	Skip
9 to 14	Numeric shift
15	Skip
16 to 33	Alphabetic shift
34 to 38	Numeric shift
39 to 44	Numeric shift
45 to 51	Numeric shift
52 to 58	Numeric shift
59 to 64	Numeric duplication
65 to 69	Numeric shift
70	Numeric duplication
71 to 80	Skip

The program card to accomplish this is shown in Fig. 2-5. The first card column of each field is punched with one of the following punches which indicates the function to be performed automatically:

Punch	Function
Blank	Numeric shift
1	Alphabetic shift
0	Duplication
11	Skip

The length of the field is defined by punches in the 12 zone. Since the use of the program unit puts the key punch in numeric shift, we must use an additional punch in the program card to put the key punch back in alphabetic shift. Shifting to alphabetic mode is accomplished by detecting a 1 punch in the program-control card. Therefore an alphabetic-field definition is a 12 and 1 punch. In order to duplicate a blank card column or columns from a field in the previous card, the program-control card must define the field as alphabetic. After the program-control card is fastened around the program drum, the drum is inserted into the program-control unit. The ***starwheels*** (Fig. 2-4), when lowered by the program-control lever, senses the holes in the program-control card, and the necessary automatic functions are performed.

KEYS

We will now discuss the functional keys shown in Fig. 2-3. NUM is the numeric shift key that allows you to put the key punch in a numeric shift manually when program-control is off. It is used either when the key punch is in its normal state (program-control unit not in use) or when you are using the program-control unit in an alphabetically defined field and want to keypunch a digit. For example, you may have defined an address field as an alphabetic field, but have to punch the house number. By depressing the NUM key, you will be able to punch a digit in any card column of the alphabetically defined field.

The ALPH key is the alphabetic shift key which allows you to keypunch an alphabetic character in a field defined as numeric in the program-control card. For instance,

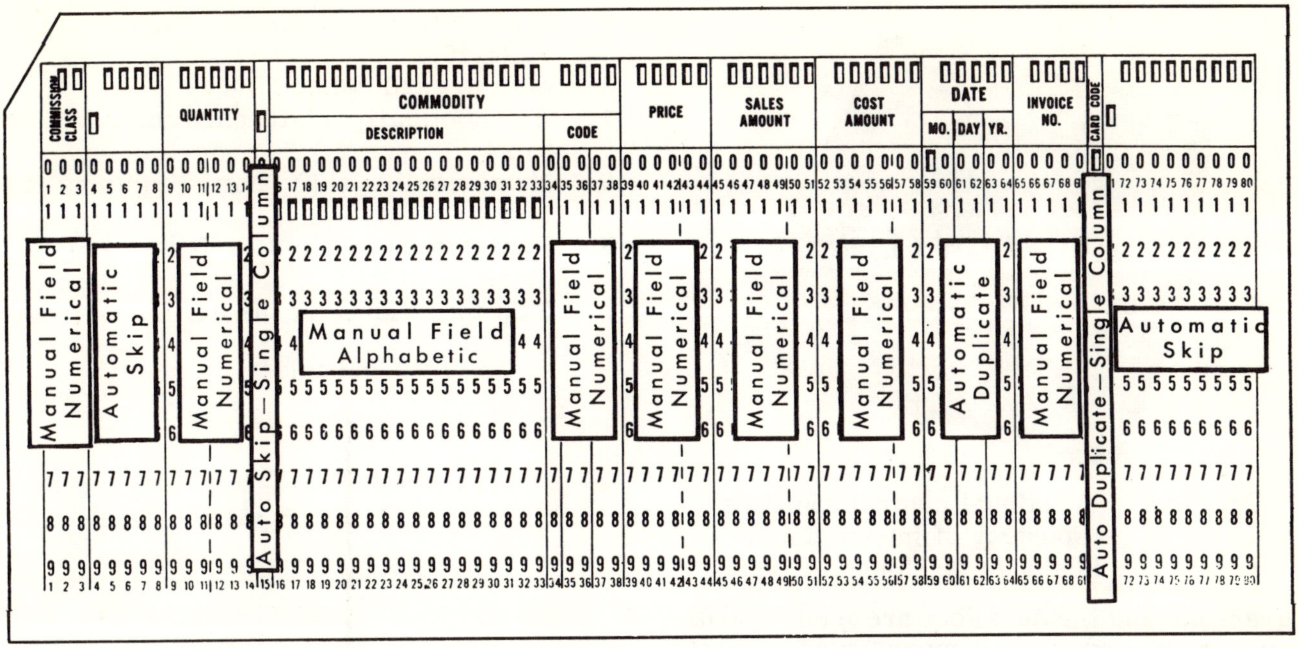

Fig. 2-5. Program card (Courtesy of International Business Machines.)

if you have defined a part number field as numeric, but which may contain an alphabetic character in any card column of the field, you can punch the letter by first depressing the ALPH key. The DUP key allows you to duplicate any or all of the card columns from the card at the read station, as long as you depress the key. When the program-control unit is active you can automatically duplicate the field or the balance of the field as defined in the program-control card from the card at the read station by pressing the key once. The field could have been defined as numeric or alphabetic.

The -SKIP key acts differently when in alphabetic shift from when in numeric shift. In alphabetic shift it punches an 11 punch; when in numeric shift, it punches an 11 and then skips the balance of the field as defined in the program-control card. The REL or ***release key*** moves the cards that are at the punching and reading stations forward one station. Depression of the FEED key will cause a card to be fed from the card hopper. Depressing the SKIP key will cause skipping past the unused right-hand portion of an alphabetic field as defined by the program-control card without punching. The REG key is the ***register key*** which, when depressed, will properly position cards at the punch and read stations.

The MULT PCH stands for multiple punch. As long as this key is held down, the card at the punch station will not advance, allowing you to keypunch any combination of punches or even all 12 punches in one card column.

AUX DUP and ALT PROG are special features. ALT PROG allows the key punch operator to select one of two program setups. AUX DUP permits duplication from data in the program card.

FUNCTIONAL CONTROL SWITCHES

The functional switches (Fig. 2-6) consist of three switches - Print, Auto Feed, and Auto Skip and Auto Dup. The ***Print switch*** pertains only to the 26, the printing key punch. If it is on, the character punched is printed over the same card column; if it is off, there will not be any printing. When on, the ***Auto Feed*** will cause a card to feed at the time that card column 80 of the card at the punching station passes the punching station. ***Auto Skip*** and ***Auto Dup*** work in conjunction with the program unit to allow automatic skipping and/or duplication as defined by the program card. The type and amount of keypunching determine whether the pro-

Fig. 2-6. Functional control switches (Courtesy of International Business Machines.)

gram unit and the Auto Feed are used. Cards must be placed in the hopper under any circumstances. The program unit, Auto Dup, and Auto Feed will most likely be used if the card design and volumes justify their use.

THE 56 VERIFIER

The 56 Verifier looks similar to the key punch, the difference being that instead of a punching station, the verifier has a verifying station which is used to verify the accuracy of the data punched by the key punch operator. The keypunched cards and the source documents are given to a verifier operator, preferably not the same operator who did the original key punching. The verifier operator tries to key the data using the same source document (Figs. 2-7 and 2-8). The verification station consists of thin metal plungers. If the key depressed corresponds to the holes in the card column, the metal plungers will pass through the holes, allowing the card to advance one card column. If the holes differ from the depressed key, the machine will lock and a red light will go on. The operator can unlock the machine and depress a key two more times. If this is still wrong, the card will be notched over the card column in error. If the card is verified to be correct, the card will be notched on the end (Fig. 2-9).

PROBLEM 1: Make up a program card to do the following:

1. Skip card columns 1 to 10.
2. Alphabetically duplicate card columns 11 to 15.
3. Skip to card column 20.
4. Alphabetically shift card columns 20 to 24.
5. Numerically shift card columns 25 to 30.
6. Duplicate numeric data from card columns 31 to 35.
7. Skip the balance of the card.

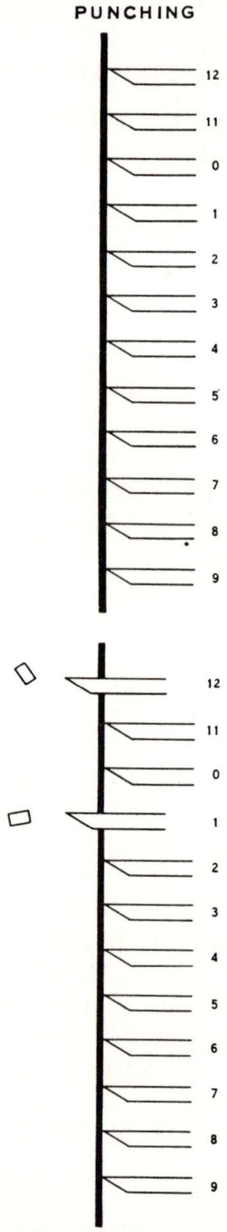

Fig. 2-7. Schematic of punch dies if the letter A is being punched (Courtesy of International Business Machines.)

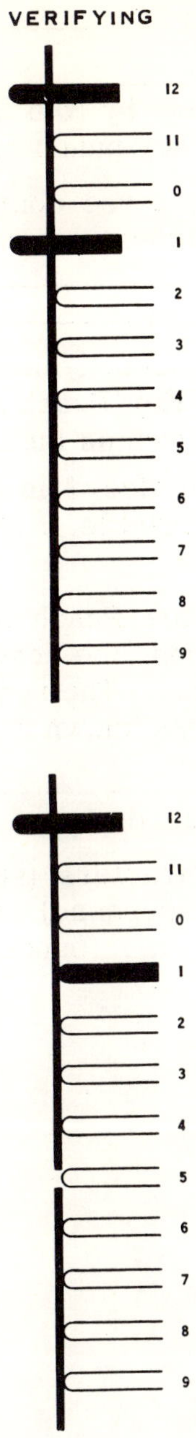

Fig. 2-8. Schematic of sense pins verifying the letter A (Courtesy of International Business Machines.)

Key Punch Questions

Answer briefly

1. The key punch contains a reading station and a punch station. What is the purpose of each? Which station is also on the 56 Verifier?

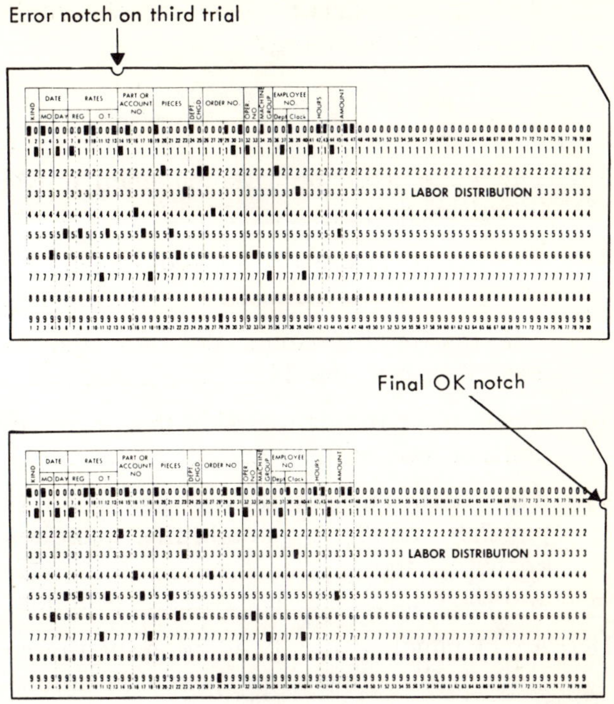

Fig. 2-9. Error and correct card notches (Courtesy of International Business Machines.)

2. After the main-line switch is turned on, how soon can operations begin?
3. How many multiple punches can be punched in one column of a card?
4. What is the purpose of the DUP key with program control? Without program control?
5. What occurs when the -SKIP key is used in alphabetic shift? In numerical shift?
6. What punch in the program card starts skipping? What punch continues skipping?
7. What punch in the program card starts numeric duplication? Alphabetic duplication?
8. What punch continues alphabetic duplication?
9. What punch continues numeric duplication?
10. What is the function of the Auto-feed switch?
11. What is the purpose of the verifier?

12. How are the error cards and the verified cards indicated?

Fill in blank spaces

13. The code used on IBM punched cards is called the ________________ code.
14. The program card is locked around the program ____________.
15. The major difference between the 24 and 26 is that the 26 ______________.
16. The column indicator below the program control unit shows ______________.
17. Alphabetic information is recorded in punched cards by combining punches known as the ________________ and the ________________ punches.
18. An 11 punched in a predetermined card column for control purposes is sometimes referred to as a ____________ punch.
19. A column or a group of columns set aside to receive specific information is referred to as a ______________.
20. The ________________ are raised and lowered by the program-control lever on a key punch machine.
21. Two of the three control switches (or toggle switches) on an IBM 26 are the ________________ switch and the ________________ switch.
22. Cards prepared from source documents on an IBM Key Punch are checked on a machine known as the ______________.
23. The printed side of an IBM card is generally referred to as the ____________ of the card.
24. The IBM Key Punch machine has two card stations, the read station and the punch station. The read station is used for a process known as ______________.
25. There are ____________ actual punching rows on a card.
26. Special characters (such as the dash, comma, ampersand) are usually made of from 1 to ____ punches in a column.

Section 3

THE 82 SORTER

Sorting is the rearranging of documents into an ascending or descending, numeric or alphabetic sequence. There are three primary reasons for sorting. The first is the grouping or classification of information. The arranging of cards by class of merchandise or by customer class is an example of this. You may want to arrange a file by grouping salesmen in the same territory. Second, sequencing of data allows you ease of reference. Think how difficult it would be to find a telephone number in the telephone directory if the names were not in alphabetic order. Third, sorting of information in a meaningful manner aids the neatness and legibility of reports.

The use of a mechanical sorter not only permits faster sorting, since sorter speeds range from 450 to 2,000 cards per minute, but also lends accuracy to this chore since manual sorting of documents is often a slow and tedious process and is consequently prone to human error.

There are only two keys on the 82 Sorter - the start and stop keys (Fig. 3-1). As in all other unit record machines, it has a main-line switch to supply current to the machine, and as the key punch, the sorter requires a 60-second warm-up period. The card hopper has a capacity of 1,200 cards. Each of the 13 pockets contains a pocket-stop lever which will automatically stop card feeding when a pocket reaches its capacity of approximately 550 cards. In order to resume operation, you must remove the cards from the pocket and press the start key.

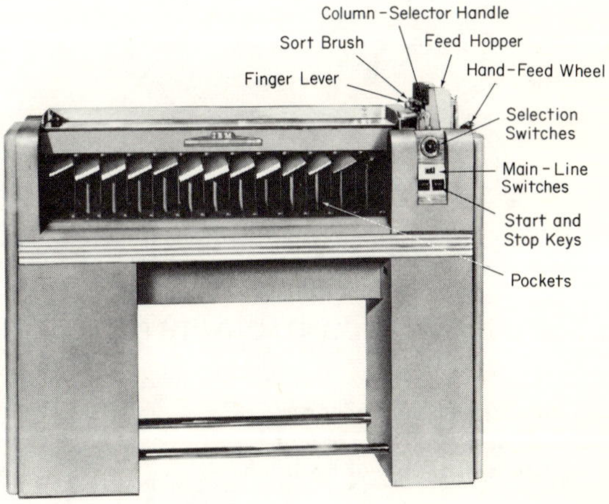

Fig. 3-1. The IBM 82 Sorter (Courtesy of International Business Machines.)

The ***hand-feed wheel*** on the right side of the sorter is used when either testing the machine or removing a card jam. To do this, you push in the wheel and then turn it manually. Cards are fed into the machine 9 edge first, face down. The card passes between the roller and the brush at a specific time in the cycle of the machine. Therefore, the differences in impulses created by the holes are recognized as a timed electrical impulse (Fig. 3-2).

The sorter has only one reading brush, which can be positioned over any one of the

80 card columns.

The *column-selector* handle moves the sort brush to the desired card column. Each turn of the handle moves the sort brush one card column. If you want to position the sort brush several card columns away, it is not necessary to turn the handle several times, since you can station the handle in its upper position, pull down the *finger lever*, and move the finger lever and the attached column indicator to the desired card column.

Cards are selected to one of 13 pockets. There are pockets for each of the 12 possible punches in a card column plus the thirteenth pocket, the R or *reject pocket*. Cards that contain blank card columns in

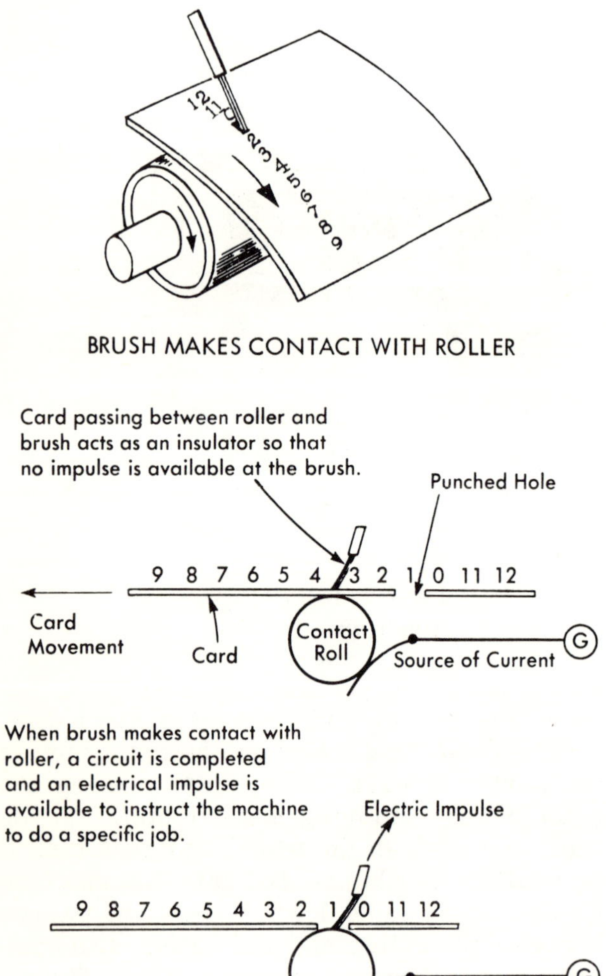

Fig. 3-2. Brush making contact with roller (Courtesy of International Business Machines.)

the column being sorted will fall into the reject pocket. In addition, as you will learn shortly, you can suppress sorting on any or all rows. As a result, any cards with the corresponding suppressed row punch will be selected to the reject pocket.

SELECTION SWITCHES

The *selection switch* (Fig. 3-1) consists of 12 small prongs, each representing one of the 12 possible row punches, and the thirteenth prong a larger red one which is equivalent to the 1 to 9 prongs. These 13 prongs are either in the inward or outward position. During regular sorting, all of the prongs are in the outward position, thereby allowing the selection of all possible row punches. When performing a regular sort, cards go to one of the 13 pockets, depending on the punch in the card column. For example, a card with a 3 punch will fall in the 3 pocket.

SUPPRESSION SORTING

Suppression sorting is the ability to select one or any combination of punches in a card column. This is accomplished by pushing the prong or prongs, corresponding to the row punches that you do not want to select out, toward the center. An illustration would be if you had a personal habits card for each of the students at a college, and in card column 15 you had keypunched the following coded information:

A 1 punch means a male nonsmoker.
A 2 punch means a male cigarette smoker.
A 3 punch means a male pipe smoker.
A 4 punch means a male cigar smoker.
A 5 punch means a female nonsmoker.
A 6 punch means a female cigarette smoker.

Now suppose that in order to determine the number of ashtrays required in the cafeteria and in the men's and women's lounges you would sort to determine how many smokers there were and how many of these were males and females. You would position the sort brush over card column 15. Next suppress prongs 1 and 5, and press the start key. Cards will fall into pockets 2, 3, 4, and 6. The balance of the cards will fall into the reject pocket in the same order that they were fed into the machine. The total number of cards selected would be the number of students at the school who smoke. The total number of cards selected to pockets 2, 3, and 4 equals the number of male smokers at the school. The cards in pocket 6 equal the number of female smokers.

PROBLEM 1: Card column 6 contains the types of cars owned by the employees of a plant. The following is the established code:

1 = two-door sedans
2 = four-door sedans
3 = two-door hardtops
4 = four-door hardtops
5 = convertibles
6 = two-door sedans, foreign make
7 = four-door sedans, foreign make
8 = two-door hardtops, foreign make
9 = four-door hardtops, foreign make
10 = two-door, sunroof, foreign make
11 = four-door, sunroof, foreign make
12 = convertibles, foreign make

If you were asked to select out all of the four-door cars, which prongs would you push toward the center to suppress sorting?

To see how sorting is accomplished, look at Fig. 3-3. You will notice that the card passes under the chute blade corresponding to the card rows. When a hole is encountered, the armature plate is drawn to the roller, attracting all the chute blades not insulated by the card, forcing the card up against the chute blades and over the lip of the blade corresponding to the punched row in the card. The card then passes to the proper pocket. You can check the accuracy of the sort either by eye or with a sorting needle (Fig. 3-4).

PROBLEM 2: If you were sorting on a column that contained the double punch 8 and 4, which pocket would the card select to?

NUMERIC SORTING

Numeric sorting is the sorting of a numeric field containing only 0 through 9 punches. To arrange the cards in ascending numeric order, you must sort each column of the field separately, starting with the units position first (high card column), and sort each lower numbered column consecutively until you sort the high-order position. After each column is sorted, remove the cards

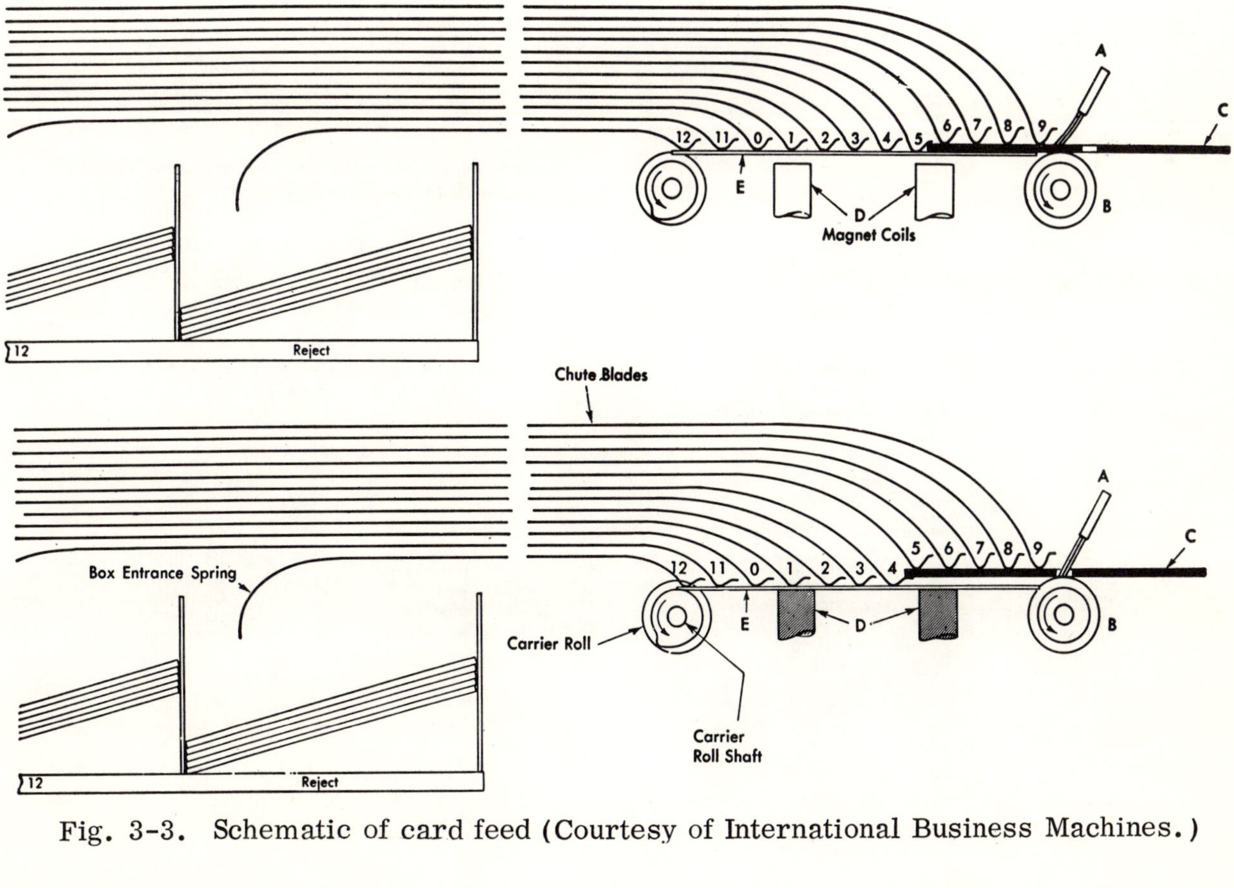

Fig. 3-3. Schematic of card feed (Courtesy of International Business Machines.)

from the pockets, going from right to left, keeping the cards face down and stacking them on top of the previously removed cards, thereby keeping the cards in ascending order.

You must remember to move the sort brush for each card column; otherwise you will just repeat the previous column sort (Fig. 3-5).

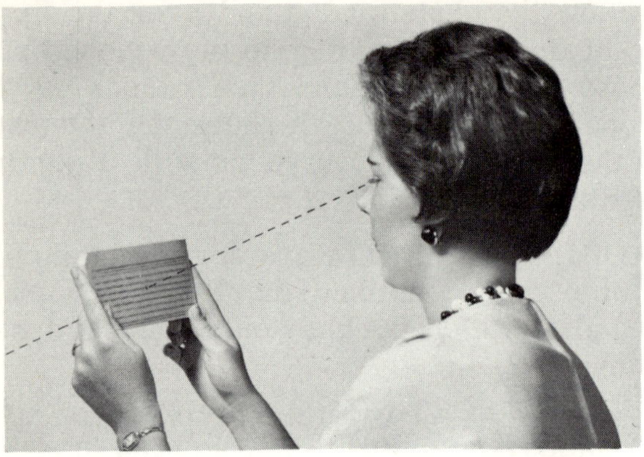

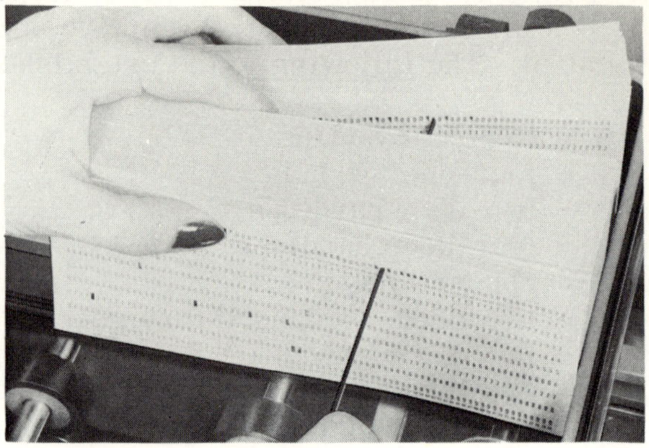

Fig. 3-4. Sorting and sight checking (Courtesy of International Business Machines.)

(a) Indicating the original sequence of cards before first sort on a 2 column field.

66, 90, 63, 65, 01, 38, 17, 81, 32, 79, 30, 14, 25, 61, 17, 83, 40, 91, 47, 18, 22, 31, 50, 10, 59, 19, 21, 47, 63

(b) At the end of the first sort which was made on the units position, the cards are in the pockets as follows:

9	8	7	6	5	4	3	2	1	0	11	12	R
								01				
								81	90			
		17						61	30			
79		17				63		91	40			
59	38	47		65		83	32	31	50			
19	18	47	66	25	14	63	22	21	10			

These cards are removed so that the 0 cards are on the bottom, the 1 cards on top of the 0 cards, etc. This may be done by removing the cards from the 0 pocket first, placing the cards from the 1 pocket on top, etc.

(c) Cards as removed from the pockets after the first sort.

79, 59, 19, 38, 18, 17, 17, 47, 47, 66, 65, 25, 14, 63, 83, 63, 32, 22, 01, 81, 61, 91, 31, 21, 90, 30, 40, 50, 10

OBSERVE THE NUMERICAL SEQUENCE OF THE RIGHT-HAND COLUMN!

(a) Indicating the sequence of the cards as removed from sorter pockets after first sort on a two-column field.

79, 59, 19, 38, 18, 17, 17, 47, 47, 66, 65, 25, 14, 63, 83, 63, 32, 22, 01, 81, 61, 91, 31, 71, 90, 30, 40, 50, 10

(b) At the end of the second sort which was made on the tens position, the cards are in the pockets as follows:

9	8	7	6	5	4	3	2	1	0	11	12	R
								19				
			66					18				
			65			38		17				
			63		47	32	25	17				
91	83		63	59	47	31	22	14				
90	81	79	61	50	40	30	21	10	01			

These cards are removed so that the 0 cards are on the bottom, the 1 cards on top of the 0 cards, etc.

(c) Cards as removed from pockets after the second sort.

91, 90, 83, 81, 79, 66, 65, 63, 63, 61, 59, 50, 47, 47, 40, 38, 32, 31, 30, 25, 22, 21, 19, 18, 17, 17, 14, 10, 01

OBSERVE THE NUMERICAL SEQUENCE OF THE LEFT-HAND COLUMN!

Fig. 3-5. Sequencing (Courtesy of International Business Machines.)

MAJOR AND MINOR FIELDS

At times the desired order of cards may involve sorting more than one field. For instance, you may want to arrange the cards by city within state. You might want to have all the cities in Alabama in alphabetic order, then all the cities in Alaska, and so on. This allows ease in reading a report. Arranging the cards in this type of order is known as a ***major and minor sort.*** The category that is the subdivision is known as the minor field, while the other field is known as the major field. In the above example, the cities are the minor field, and the states are the major field.

Sometimes you may have to sort three fields to produce the desired sequence. You may want cities within county and counties within state. In this case, the city is the minor field, the county is the intermediate field, and the state is the major field.

The procedure for this type of sorting is to sort the lowest-level field first, starting with the units position and then the next highest-level field, again starting with the units position. In an application having only two fields you would first sort the minor field, then the major field. If there were three fields, you would first sort the minor, then the intermediate, and finally the major field. These fields may or may not be in adjacent card columns. In practice you can think of them as one field, since you always start sorting each field with the units position.

PROBLEM 3: Suppose you had to sort a deck that contained item number in card columns 15 to 20, customer number in card columns 31 to 36, and salesman number in card columns 76 and 77. The report you want to produce will show each salesman, his customers, and what items they have purchased. In what order would you sort these fields, and which card column of each field would you sort first?

TIMING FORMULA

This is a good place to explain how a sorting operation is timed. The formula for numerical sorts is:

$$\frac{\text{Number of cards x number of columns}}{\text{Rated speed of the sorter}}$$

Add 25 percent of the result for card-handling time. For example, if one wants to sort 13,000 cards on a five-digit field on an 82 Sorter with a rated speed of 650 cards per minute, the formula would look like this:

$$\frac{13{,}000 \text{ x } 5}{650} = 100 \text{ minutes}$$

plus 25 percent of 100 minutes = 25 minutes for a total of 125 minutes.

PROBLEM 4: How long will it take to sort 10,000 cards with a five-digit field (numeric) at 650 cards per minute?

BLOCK SORTING

When sorting, all of the cards must be sorted before the cards can be processed by the next machine in the system. When sorting large volumes of cards, ***block sorting*** will reduce the throughput time. Block sort by separating the file into logical blocks and then sorting each block separately. Suppose a concern had 20,000 employees, and you wanted to produce a list of employees in employee number order. If an employee's number was in a five-digit field in card columns 39 to 43, and you had an 82 Sorter whose speed was 650 cards per minute, with what you have already learned you would sort all 20,000 cards before they could be processed by the next machine. The formula would be:

$$\frac{20{,}000 \text{ x } 5}{650} = \text{approximately 154 minutes plus 39 minutes for card handling}$$

for a total of 193 minutes or three hours and 13 minutes before the first card would go into the next machine. If you were able to divide the 20,000 cards into some sort of logical blocks and then sort each block separately, you would then be able to overlap the sorting and printing time. You can accomplish this by block sorting. In the above example, you would first sort all 20,000 cards on the high-order digit in column 39.

The cards would then separate into a maximum of 10 blocks in the 0 to 9 pockets (excluding blanks). For simplicity, assume that we have an even distribution, so that we have 2,000 cards in each block as shown in Fig. 3-6. The next step would be to remove the 10 stacks, and then sort the remaining four columns in the normal manner, i.e., columns 43, 42, 41, and 40 of the 0 block. When this block is finished, it can be processed by the next machine while you follow the same procedure with blocks 1, 2, 3, 4, 5, 6, 7, 8, and 9.

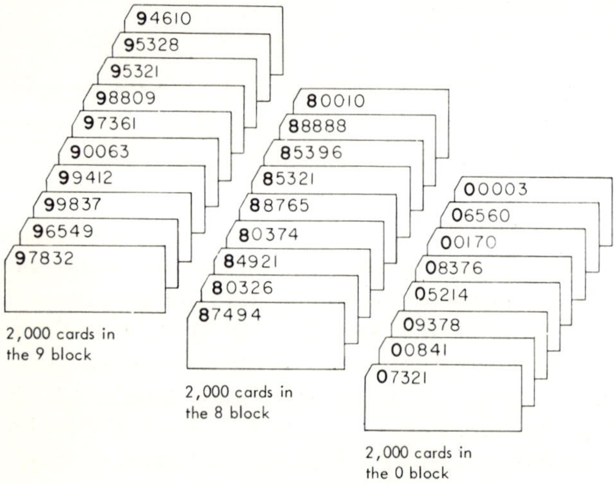

Fig. 3-6. Block sorting (Courtesy of International Business Machines.)

Block sorting by itself is not faster than normal sorting. This is shown by applying the formula:

$$\frac{20{,}000 \times 1}{650} = \text{approximately 30 minutes}$$

$$\frac{2{,}000 \times 4}{650} = \text{approximately 12.5 minutes} \times 10 \text{ blocks} = 125 \text{ minutes}$$

125 plus 30 = 155 minutes

See Fig. 3-7 to see how the total operation is shortened by doing a block sort.

If you have major and minor fields, you can first sort on the major field, then manually separate one major group at a time, and finally sort that group's minor field.

Another reason for block sorting is that when the installation has more than one sorter, you can use the other sorter or sorters at the same time as shown in Fig. 3-8. An added benefit of block sorting is that it is easier to trace and correct an error when you are working with smaller volumes of cards.

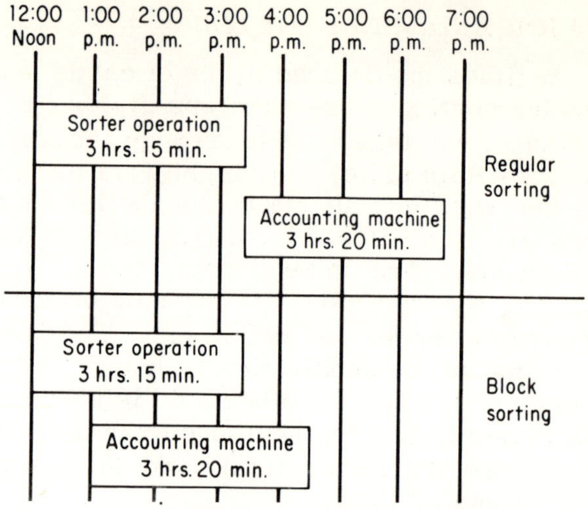

Fig. 3-7. Block sorting times (Courtesy of International Business Machines.)

ALPHABETIC SORTING

The final type of sort we will discuss is ***alphabetic sorting.*** There are times when one sorts on an alphabetic field, for example, name field, product description field, or location field.

If we had to sort once on each column during a numeric sort, how many times do we sort on a column in an alphabetic sort? Twice, because there are two punches per column to represent a letter.

The red sort switch, which is equivalent to the nine small prongs, is used primarily for alphabetic sorting. By moving the red switch toward the center you allow sorting of the zone punches only (12, 11, and 0), and all other cards fall into the reject pocket. You will see how this switch is used as we explain alphabetic sorting.

Sorting begins on the units position. Sort on the card column normally as in numeric sorting. Since the cards are fed 9 edge first, the card will be selected to a pocket corresponding to the digit punch of the letter. Then remove the cards, face down, going from right to left, stacking the cards progressively on top. Next you push the red sort switch toward the center. Remember,

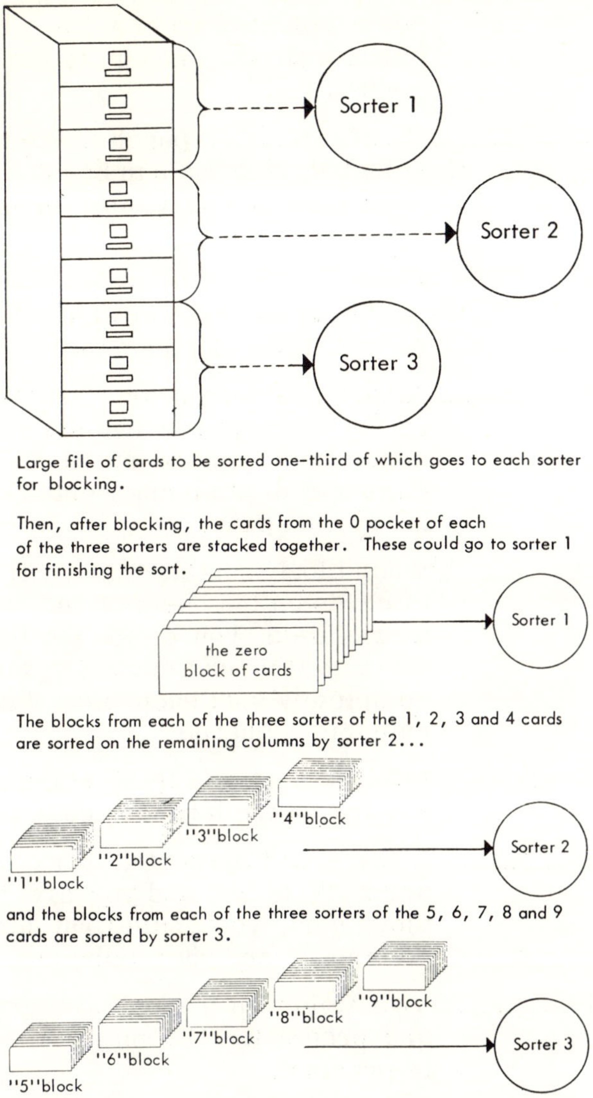

Fig. 3-8. Sorting large files of cards (Courtesy of International Business Machines.)

this has the effect of suppressing sorting of the 1 through 9 punches. As a result, on the second pass of the column you will sort only on the zone punches, 0, 11, or 12. Therefore, after the second pass on the column, the cards will be in the 0, 11, and 12 pockets in the following order: A through I in the 12 pocket, J through R in the 11 pocket, and S through Z in the 0 pocket. The cards in each pocket will be in alphabetic order. A card will fall into the R pocket if there are any blank card columns. Do not sort the cards in the R pocket on the second pass because they will only be selected to the R pocket again. After the second pass, place the blank cards at the front of the deck. Remember to reset the red sort switch before sorting the next card column.

The formula for timing alphabetic sorts is:

$$\frac{\text{Number of cards x number of columns x 2}}{\text{Rated speed of the sorter}}$$

plus 25 percent for card handling. For example, if we have 1,300 cards, a 650 cards per minute sorter, and we are going to alphabetically sort a five-position field, it would take:

$$\frac{1{,}300 \text{ x } 5 \text{ x } 2}{650} = \text{20 minutes plus five minutes for card handling}$$

for a total of 25 minutes.

PROBLEM 5: How long will it take to sort 10,000 cards on a five-column alphabetic field with a 650 cards per minute sorter?

The sorter is an important machine in an installation. It is a basic machine found not only in unit record installations but also in computer installations. Its function is to arrange the input cards for processing by other machines in the system.

It is important that the cards be grouped according to some definite sequence, since the end result of machine accounting is a printed report. The sorter is the machine which can arrange the cards in the desired sequence accurately, quickly, and economically.

Sorter Questions

Answer True or False

1. ________ To sort on a numeric field of more than one column, start sorting on the units (rightmost) column, then sort on the ten column, and so on, until the leftmost column of the field has been sorted.
2. ________ A card may fall into any one of 14 pockets.

3.________ Cards with no punch in the column being sorted fall into the R pocket.

4.________ Cards are placed into the hopper 9 edge first, face up.

5.________ There are the same number of pockets in the machine as there are rows on the card.

6.________ The general rule for sorting an alphabetic field is to sort on the leftmost column, then on the column to the right of that, and so forth, until the rightmost column of the field has been sorted.

7.________ Two passes are required when sorting one column numerically.

8.________ When sorting alphabetically, the alphabetic sort and the digit selection switches are set in the outer position for the first pass through the machine.

9.________ The only way the sort brush can be moved is by using the column selector handle.

10.________ During numeric sorting, all the selection switches must be in the outer position for the entire operation.

11.________ It is possible in a given pass to suppress the reading of one specified punch only.

12.________ When cards with a 5 punch are being selected from a file, the cards with a 5 punch go to the R pocket.

13.________ If cards with a 3 punch are to be selected, only the number 3 selection switch is placed in the outer position.

14.________ Cards are not selected to the R pocket in the order in which they were fed into the machine.

15.________ Alphabetic sorting on the IBM 82 Sorter requires two passes, zones being sorted on the first pass and digits being sorted on the second pass.

16.________ When block sorting a large file of cards on the basis of one numeric field, you divide the file into small blocks manually, and completely sort each block into numeric sequence.

17.________ In block sorting a field, start by sorting on the leftmost column.

18.________ If the field to be sorted is in columns 17 to 20, and you are to block sort, you would first sort column 17 and then column 18.

19.________ Two fields on a card are city and precinct. The major field is precinct.

20.________ To block sort on the basis of two numeric fields, sort first on the major field.

Section 4

BASIC PRINCIPLES OF WIRING

ELECTRICAL IMPULSES

It has been mentioned that the Hollerith Code enables the machines to read data. This is accomplished by electrical impulses. As you can see in Fig. 4-1, the card acts as an insulator as long as there is no hole. Once the 4 row with the punched hole (Fig. 4-1) passes beneath the reading brush, the insulation is broken, and the brush and the magnetized roller make contact. At that time, an electrical impulse travels through the brush. When the 5 row, which is not punched, feeds between the brush and roller, the insulation is restored (Fig. 4-1). Regardless of which row is punched, the electrical impulse is the same. The important difference is the time the contact was made. All of the unit record machines work on a timing cycle. Thus the electrical impulses do not run through the machines with numbered tags, saying, "I'm a 4 impulse," or "I'm an 11 timed impulse." The machine knows which row or rows were punched by the time the impulse passed from the roller to the brush. These impulses are available from the control-panel hubs.

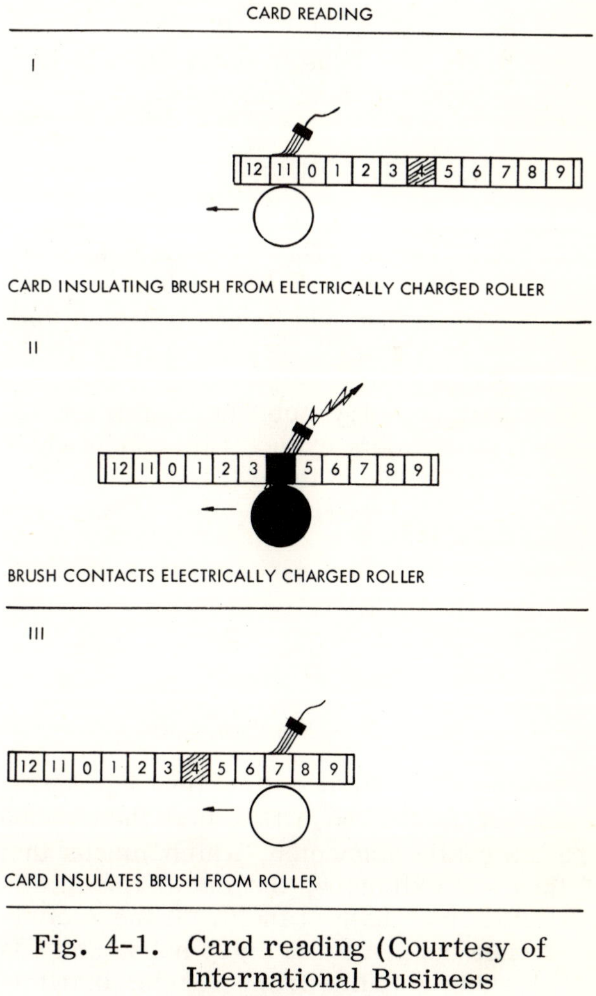

Fig. 4-1. Card reading (Courtesy of International Business Machines.)

CONTROL PANEL

Machine operations are controlled by external wiring in a ***control panel.*** The control panel is similar in principle to a telephone switchboard. An incoming call on a switchboard lights a signal light that tells the operator on which line the call is coming. After she answers the call, she plugs the cord into a hub on the board that is internally connected to the desired extension. Actually the operator has completed an electric circuit to give the correct result.

A control panel does exactly the same thing; it completes electric circuits through wires which are inserted into *hubs.*

WIRES

Electricity requires a path. This path on the control panel is provided by ***wires***, which are available in several colors. The only significance of the colors is to signify the lengths of the wires. Most wires allow current to pass in either direction, but there are ***one-way wires*** available that contain filters which allow the current to travel in only one direction. These wires have an arrow printed on them to show which way the current can travel. Wires carry impulses from exit hubs to entry hubs to perform specific machine functions.

CONTROL-PANEL HUBS

The wires are used to connect hubs on the control panel. There are basically two types of hubs - ***entry hubs*** which accept impulses from wires and ***exit hubs*** which emit impulses to wires (if there is a wire in the hub). Some hubs, as you will learn, are either exit or entry hubs depending on the time of the machine cycle. Other hubs which have a line between them (as shown in Fig. 4-2) are called ***common hubs.*** There may

Fig. 4-2. Common hubs

be two or more hubs with a line connecting them. This line signifies that these hubs are internally connected, which means that if they are exit hubs, the same impulse is available from both of them. If these common hubs happen to be entry hubs, and one receives an impulse from a wire, that impulse is available from the other hub. A similar type of hub is the ***bus hub*** as shown in Fig. 4-3. They are used when more than

Fig. 4-3. Bus Hubs

one of a certain impulse is needed.

The impulse from an exit hub is available from all the other bus hubs by connecting an exit hub and any one of the bus hubs with a wire. If bus hubs are not available, and it is necessary to connect one exit hub to more than one entry hub, it is accomplished though the use of a ***common connector*** (Fig. 4-4). An impulse to the connecting block is

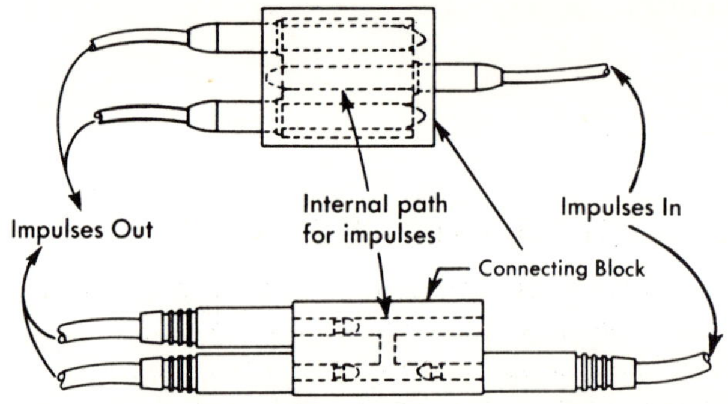

Fig. 4-4. Common connectors (Courtesy of International Business Machines.)

available from all the other terminals in the connector. This type of wiring is known as split wiring. ***Split wires*** are three or four wires connected at one point.

When two adjacent hubs are to be connected, you can use a ***jackplug*** (Fig. 4-5)

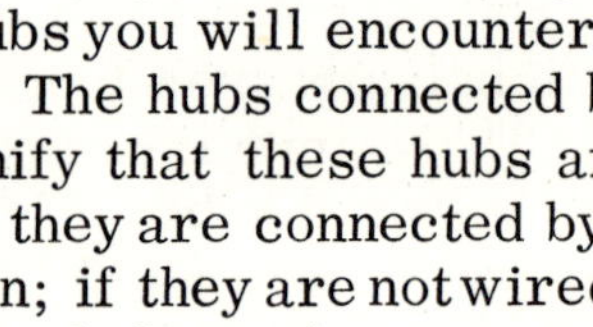

Fig. 4-5. Jackplug (Courtesy of International Business Machines.)

instead of a wire. Jackplugs are used simply because they are less bulky. Two other types of hubs you will encounter are seen in Fig. 4-6. The hubs connected by a straight arrow signify that these hubs are used as a switch. If they are connected by a wire, the switch is on; if they are not wired, the switch is off. The hubs with a curved arrow are

Fig. 4-6. Switches (Courtesy of International Business Machines.)

also switches, the difference being that a curved arrow signifies that the connecting wire may be wired via a selector. (Selectors will be discussed later.)

DIAGRAMMING CONVENTIONS

Throughout this book you will be referred to wiring diagrams of control panels and required to draw them. The following are wiring conventions:

1. When you draw a wire connecting two hubs, draw an arrow indicating in which direction the impulse is traveling (Fig. 4-7A).

2. If you are going to depict a field of consecutive columns being wired to a number of adjacent hubs, show this by drawing a horizontal line through the two sets of hubs and one line with an arrow connecting the two horizontal lines (Fig. 4-7B). On an actual panel there would be as many wires as there were hubs to be connected, but for ease of reading a diagram, the above convention is used.

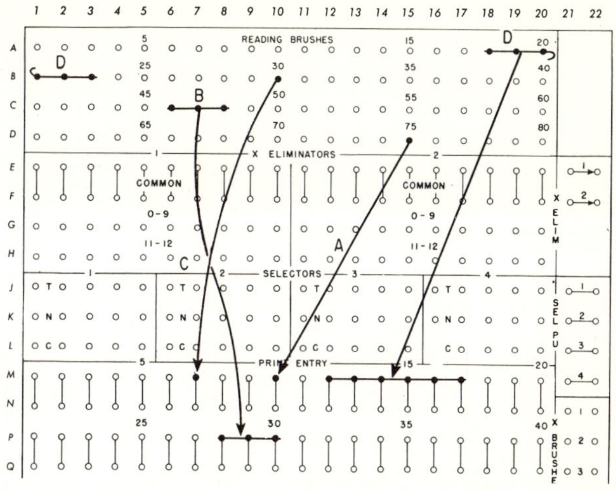

Fig. 4-7. Printing fields

3. Crossing of wires can be depicted as shown in Fig. 4-7C.

4. When using the above standards, and one of the hubs in the line happens to be at the end of the row, the continuation is shown by drawing a hook on the end of the line, as depicted in Fig. 4-7D.

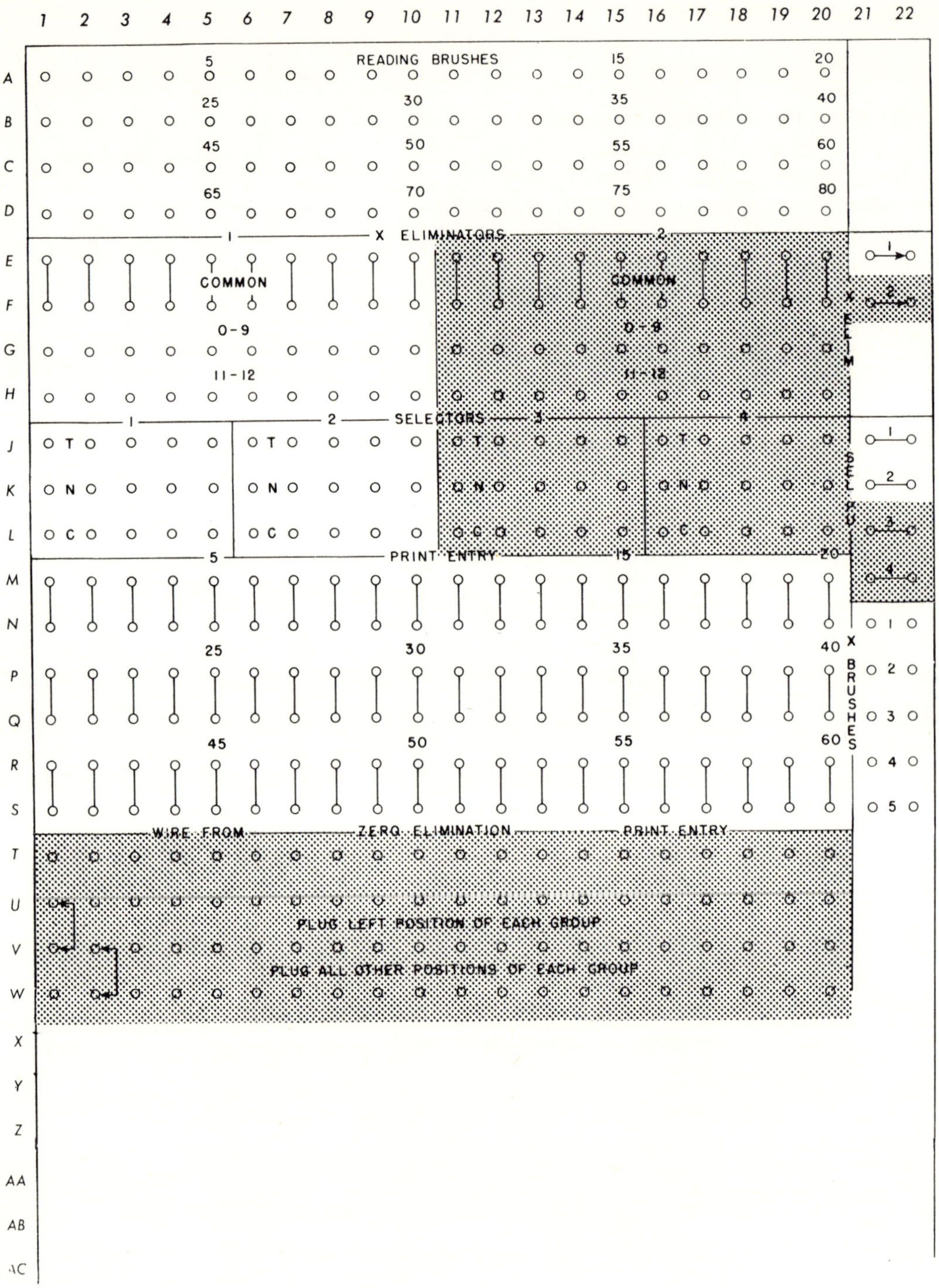

548 Control Panel. The shaded areas represent special features. (Courtesy of International Business Machines.)

Section 5

THE 548 INTERPRETER

The punched card frequently takes the form of a readable document (utility bills, checks, identification cards, etc.), and in the future, we will see even greater use of it. The ***interpreter*** (Fig. 5-1) makes this function of the punched card possible because of its ability to read the punched column and print its graphic representation on

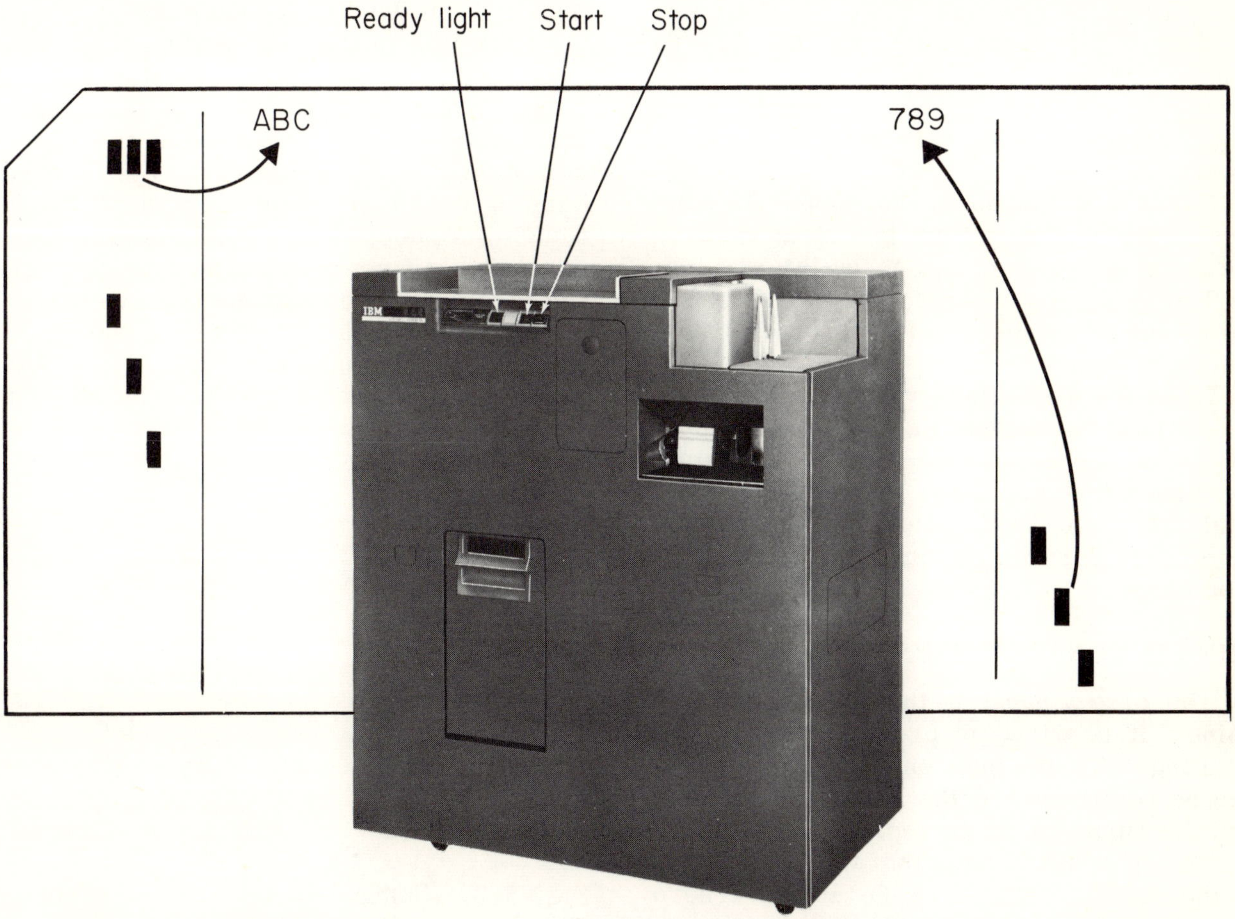

Fig. 5-1. IBM 548 Interpreter and interpreted card (Courtesy of International Business Machines.)

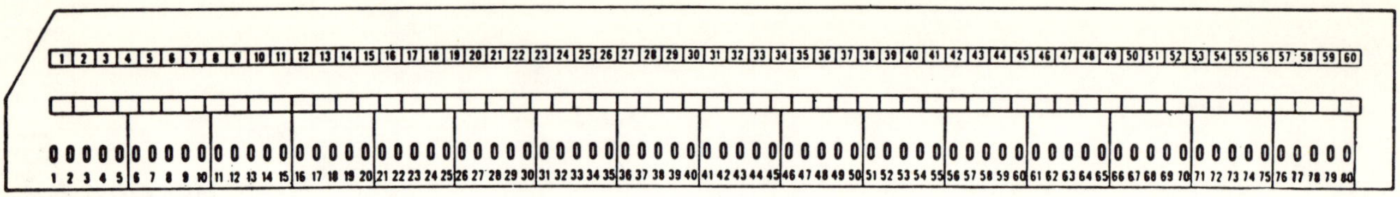

Fig. 5-2. Interpreter printing positions (Courtesy of International Business Machines.)

the face of the card, allowing visual reading of the data.

The 548 Interpreter can, through control-panel wiring, read up to 60 columns of punched data in any of the 80 card columns and print in any of the 60 print positions at the rate of 60 cards per minute (Fig. 5-2). To interpret all 80 card columns, two runs must be made on the machine, using two different control panels printing on two lines.

The interpreter can print on two lines - above the 12 row and between the 11 and 12 rows. Sixty characters can be printed on each of the two printing lines, which are selected by setting a two-position knob at the rear of the machine. The positions are marked U for upper and L for lower. To change positions, the knob is pulled out and turned (clockwise for above the 12 row, counterclockwise for between the 11 and 12 rows).

Cards are placed in the hopper 12 edge first, face up; therefore the front card in the deck is the last one to be interpreted.

The feed hopper holds approximately 700 cards and the stacker holds about 900 cards before stopping.

When the main-line switch is on, a green ready light indicates that the machine is ready for operation. To start the machine, the blue start key must be depressed and held for three feed cycles. The stop key stops the operation at any time during the feed cycle.

THE 548 CONTROL PANEL

The *control panel* is the brain of the machine. It is wired to produce the desired printing. All the hubs on the control panel can be referenced by the letters on the side and the numbers on the top.

The first set of hubs that we will discuss is the reading brushes (A-D, 1-20). There are 80 exit hubs from the 80 *reading brushes.* Figure 5-3 shows one of these brushes reading the card as it passes between the brushes and the roller. (There is a reading brush on each of the 80 columns.) A timed impulse is available from the corresponding hub each time a hole is encountered in the card column.

The ***print-entry hubs*** (M-S, 1-20) are the hubs that determine where on the card the character will print. There is one hub for each of the 60 typebars. Each of the typebars has 39 horizontal positions. They are 10 numerics, 0-9; 26 alphabetics, A-Z, and three special characters (Fig. 5-4).

The cards feed 12 edge first; therefore the typebar is positioned to one of four places - 12, 11, 0, or digits 1-9 by a zone punch or the lack of a zone punch.

After this initial positioning, the typebar continues to move in conjunction with the card. When the next punch is encountered, the typebar stops. Then when the card is completely read, a bar strikes the typebar, causing it to print. For example, if the letter C was punched in a card column, the 12 punch would first position the typebar. Then the typebar would continue to move until the 3 punch was read. At this time the typebar would stop. When the card was completely read, a bar would strike the typebar print-

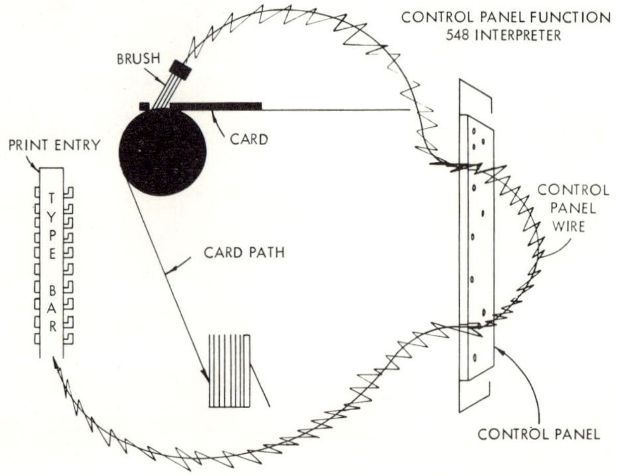

Fig. 5-3. Control-panel function (Courtesy of International Business Machines.)

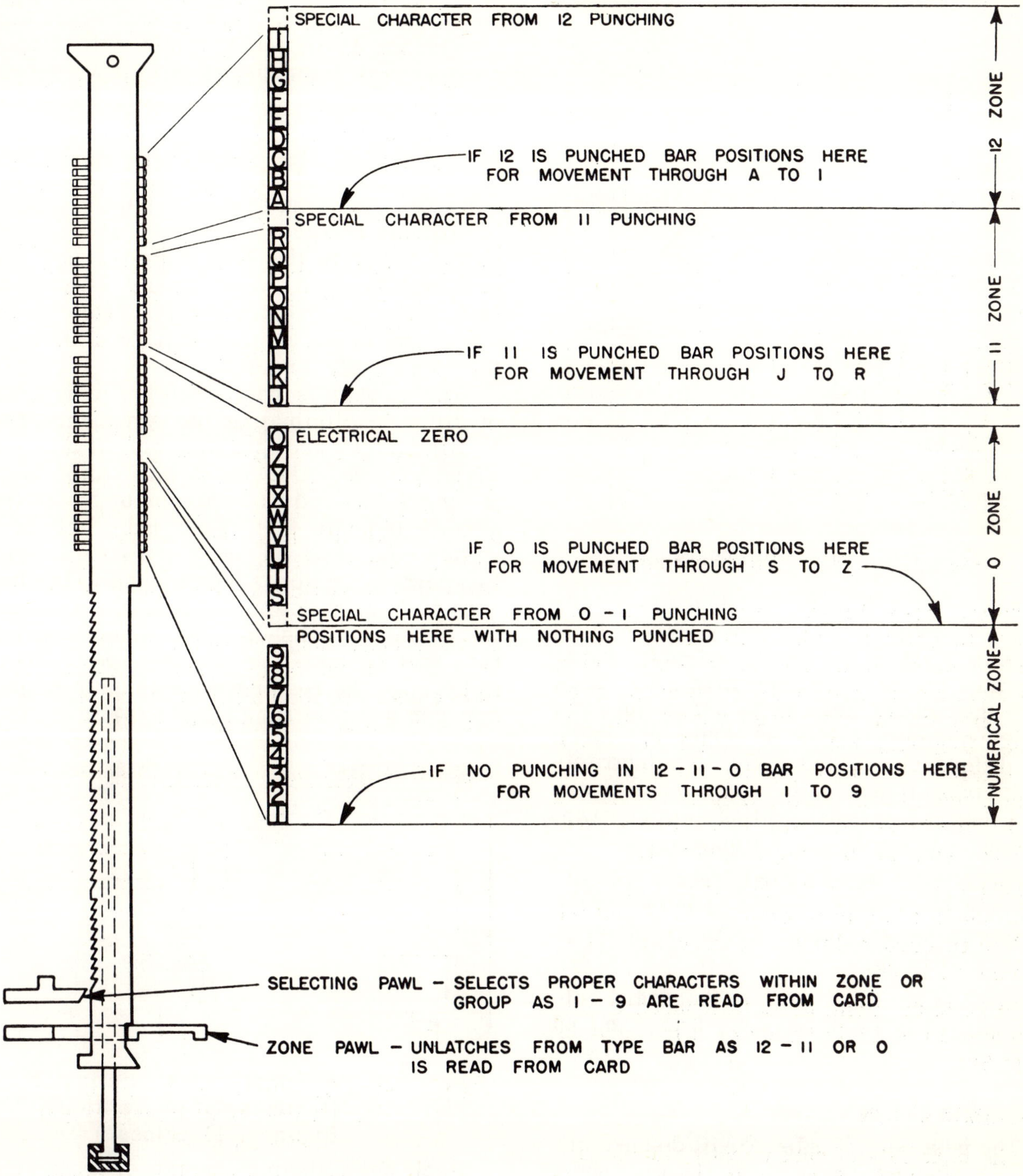

Fig. 5-4. Schematic of typebar (Courtesy of International Business Machines.)

ing the letter C. Look at Fig. 5-5; the data from card columns 3 to 7 is printed via entry typebars 1 to 5.

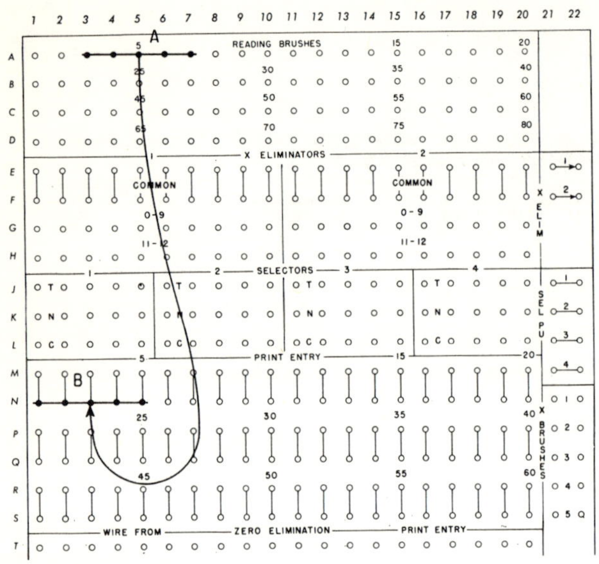

Fig. 5-5. Offset interpreting

Notice three things. First, it is not necessary to print in print-entry hubs 3 to 7. One can print in any five print-entry hubs; they need not be five consecutive hubs. Second, they could have been wired into the higher common hubs. It would not make any difference. Third, using the diagramming convention made the diagram easier to read than if five separate lines were drawn.

Now, you try drawing a diagram.

PROBLEM 1: Print the data from card columns 13 to 30 in typebars 1 to 18 and the data in card columns 63 to 68 in typebars 51 to 56.

PROBLEM 2: Print the data from card columns 10 to 13 in typebars 5 to 8 and 49 to 52.

X-ELIMINATION

The next sets of hubs we will discuss are the *X-eliminator hubs* (E-H, 1-20). Their purpose is to eliminate the printing of the X (11) and 12 punch. This is normally done for either of two conditions. One is if the X control punch is in the same card column as the data, and it becomes necessary to interpret the punch in that column. A letter J-R would print instead of the digit if the X punch in that column were not eliminated. It is doubtful that we would have another zone punch in the column, but in the event that we did, the X-eliminator would still be necessary. The other condition is if we have a negative number. In a previous section it was stated that a negative or minus field was recognized by an X punch in the units position. If we did not eliminate the X punch, the units position would print as a letter, making it difficult to read. You can, as you will learn, separate the X and digit punch and print the X punch, which prints as a dash, in a separate print position. This would enable one to see visually that the field contained a negative number.

The typebar is positioned to the no-zone position by eliminating the X punch. The X-eliminators are operative only if they are wired on connecting the X-eliminator hubs (E and F, 21 and 22). Remember that the arrows indicate that these hubs act as a switch - on if wired, off if not wired. The two pairs of switches correspond to the two sets of X-eliminators. You will encounter X-eliminator hubs on other machines, but they will be known as *column splits.* This is because the reading of the column is split between 0 and 11 time (Fig. 5-6).

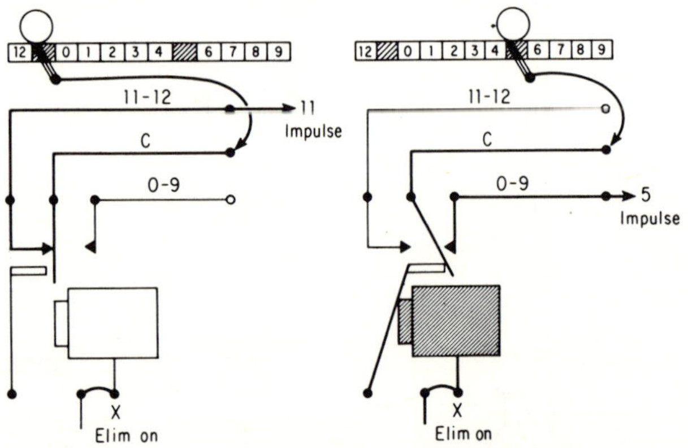

Fig. 5-6. Schematic of X-eliminator (Courtesy of International Business Machines.)

Each X-eliminator consists of three sets of hubs - the common hubs, the 0-9 hub, and the 11 and 12 hub. At 12 and 11 time an impulse into the common hub is available from the 11 and 12 hub. By 0 time, the armature connecting the common and 11 and 12 hubs is broken and connected to the 0-9 hub. Electricity needs a path to travel on; consequently, the impulse into common will be available out of the hub which is connected by the armature to the common hub. The inverse is also true, in that an impulse wired into the 11 and 12 hub and/or the 0-9 hub would be available from the common hub.

An analogous situation would be that of a railroad. Suppose there was a single track leaving the station, and a mechanical device enabled this single track to combine with one of two possible tracks. Now suppose there were local trains that ran only between 11:00 A.M. and 1:00 P.M. The mechanical device would connect the single outgoing track with the local line track at 11:00 A.M., and then at 1:00 P.M. it would break this connection and attach the outgoing track to the express track for the balance of the time. Remember that the opposite is also true, in that trains returning to the station on the local line could only proceed past the fork between 11:00 A.M. and 1:00 P.M.

Getting back to X-eliminators, bear in mind that if there is no wire in the 11 and 12 or 0-9 hubs, the impulse entering the common hub will be lost at the hub without a wire. Now look at Fig. 5-7 and notice that X-eliminator group 1 is operative because its switch is wired on. Reading-

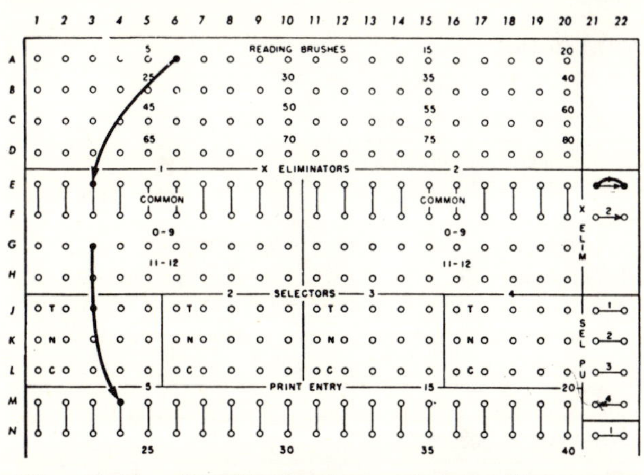

Fig. 5-7. X-eliminator wiring (Courtesy of International Business Machines.)

brush 6 is wired into common of X-eliminator 3. The 0-9 hub of the same X-eliminator is wired to print entry 4. If column 6 of any of the cards being read contained an 11 or 12 punch they would not be printed. Only a digit punch in column 6 would be printed.

PROBLEM 3: Eliminate X punches in card columns 5 and 10. Print the digits in print entry hubs 21 and 31. Wire from reading brush hub 5 into common of an X-eliminator, from reading brush hub 10 into 0-9 hub of an X-eliminator. Wire reading brush hub 15 via an X-eliminator to print the digit punch in print entry 39 and the 11 punch of column 15 to print entry 40.

PROBLEM 4: What would be printed by typebars 21, 31, 39, and 40 if card column 5 contained a C, column 10 an S, and column 15 an M?

SELECTORS: J-L, 1-20

Selectors, two of which are standard and two optional on the 548, are encountered on every unit record machine. Selectors are similar to X-eliminators in that each selector has three sets of hubs - common, normal, and transfer - and only two of these three hubs can be connected internally at any time. There is an internal connection between the C (common) and N (normal) hubs, unless the selector is activated. When activated, the connection between C and N is broken and an internal connection between C and T (transfer) is made. There can never be a connection between N and T. Imagine a railroad that normally runs a train between the station and North city, but will send a train to South city when enough passengers accumulated (Fig. 5-8). When the dispatcher sees that the number of passengers warrants dispatching a train to South city, he telephones the lineman to throw the lever that switches the main or common track from the normal track going to North city. The connection is made between the main track, which is now transferred, and the track to South city. Selectors operate in the same manner. The machine must have some way of determining when an X card is going to be read by the reading brushes as the dispatcher determined when to send a train to South city, and then notifying the control panel. The control panel will then cause some change in the panel wiring.

Fig. 5-8. Railroad depot

When a selector is normal (not transferred) the impulse will travel from common to normal or from normal to common (Fig. 5-9). When the selector pickup is impulsed, the electromagnet causes the armature to leave the normal hub and align with the transferred hub (Fig. 5-10).

The selector pickup hubs (J-M, 21 and 22) are normally wired from the ***X-brush*** hubs (N-S, 21 and 22). There are four common SEL PU hubs numbered from 1 to 4, each one associated with the respectively numbered selectors.

Figure 5-11 shows the five X-brushes that are positioned in front of the reading brushes. As a result, the cards are read by the X-brushes one cycle before they are read by the reading brushes. The X-brushes are timed to read only X punches in the card.

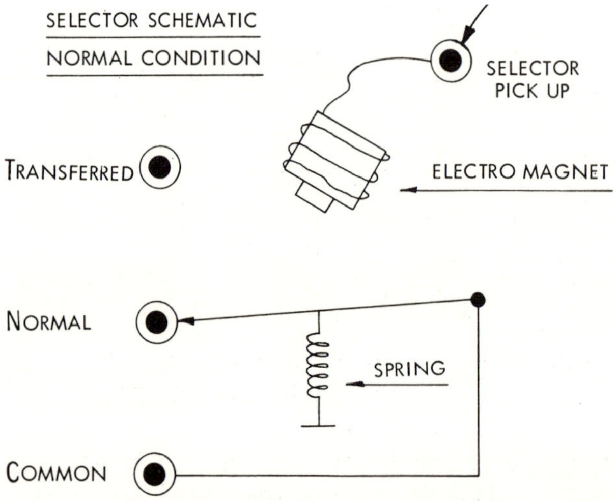

Fig. 5-9. Schematic of Selector (normal condition) (Courtesy of International Business Machines.)

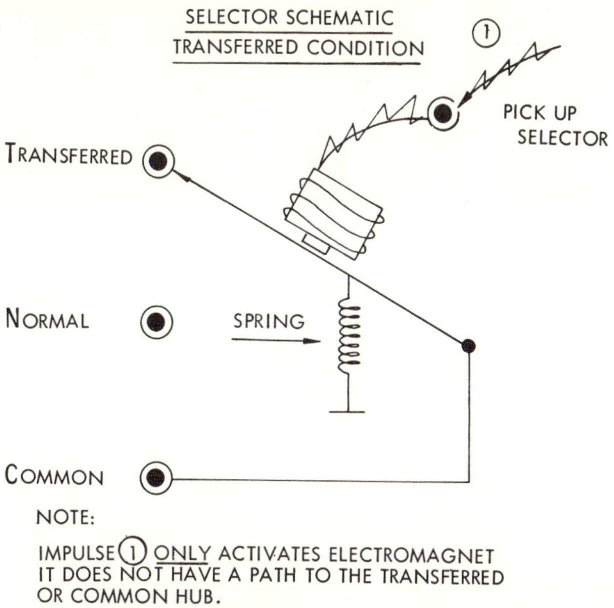

Fig. 5-10. Schematic of Selector (transferred condition) (Courtesy of International Business Machines.)

Any of the five X-brushes may be positioned to read any card column. At least two columns must separate adjacent brushes. These brushes have their own five-hub X-panel (Fig. 5-11). The five hubs are numbered 1, 2, 3, 4, and 5. Any of the five X-brushes are wired to any one of the five hubs. These hubs are internally connected to the corresponding five X-brush hubs on the control panel, N-S, 21 and 22. As a result, if there is an X punch in the card column being read by one of these brushes, an impulse will be available from each of the two X-brush hubs on the control panel that corresponds to that particular X-panel hub. These hubs are normally wired to transfer selectors.

The purpose of these X-brushes is to enable the control panel to distinguish between X and no-X cards before the card passes beneath the 80 reading brushes. This is necessary if you intend to perform functions for X cards different from no-X cards

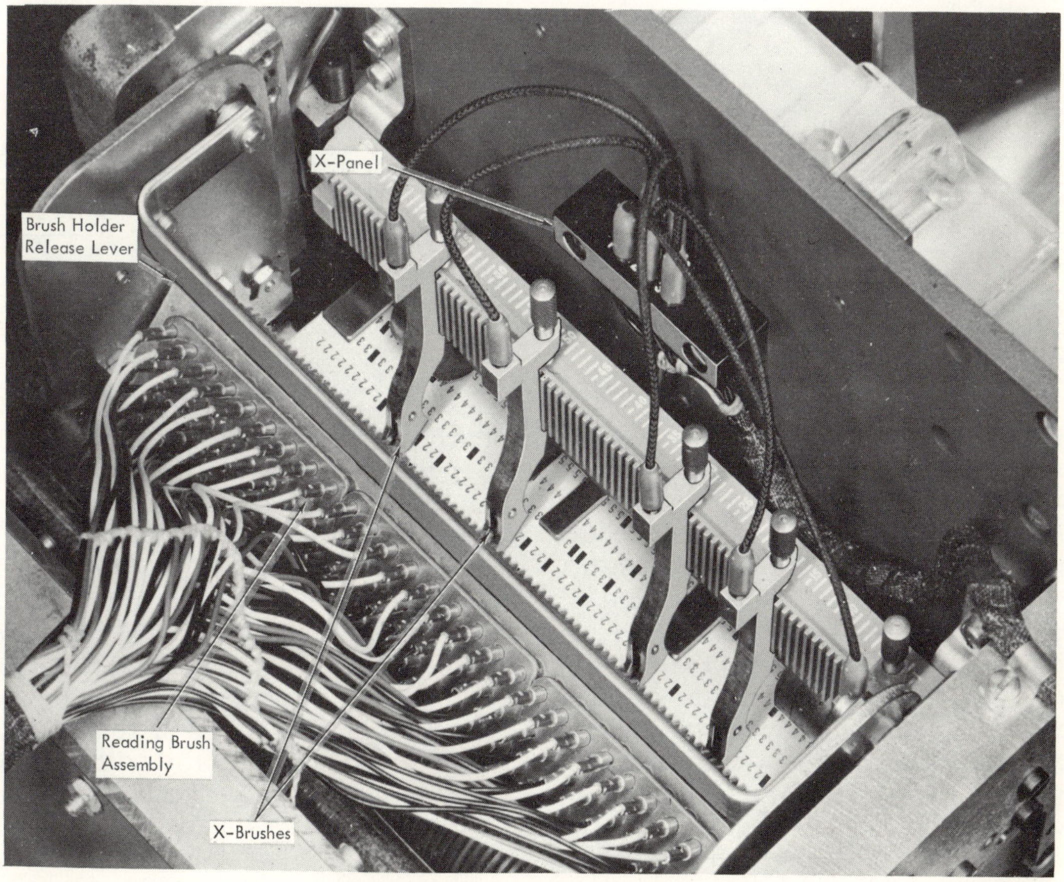

Fig. 5-11. X-brushes, X-panel (Courtesy of International Business Machines.)

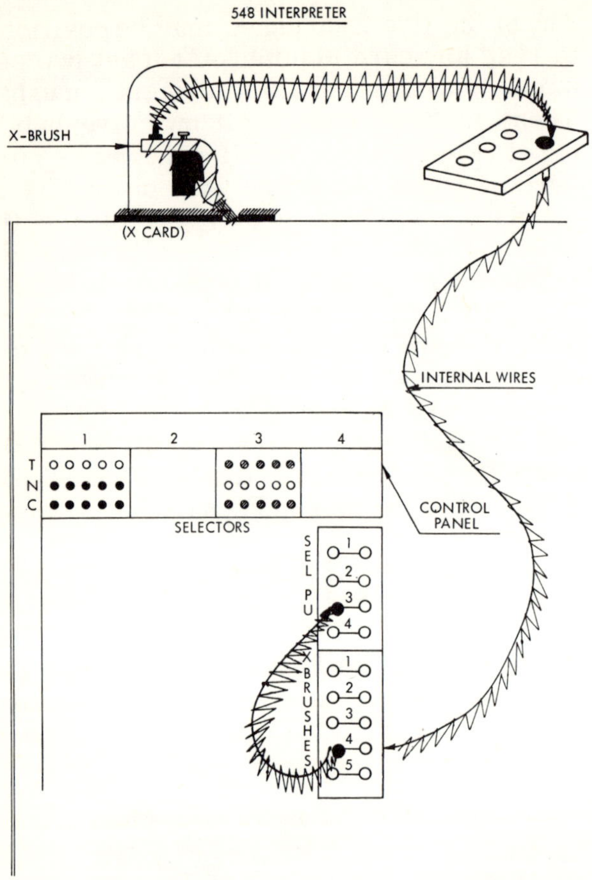

Fig. 5-12. Schematic of X-brushes, X-panel (Courtesy of International Business Machines.)

(Fig. 5-12). (From now on no-X cards will be referred to as NX cards.)

There are two types of selection, class or field (Fig. 5-13). Now we will see how these selectors are used.

CLASS SELECTION

In *class selection* there are two types of cards, and both have fields in the same card columns. One of the cards must have an X punch in order to distinguish it from the NX card. This is necessary when you want to print in one of two possible places, the X cards in one and the NX cards in the other. In the following example, there are gas and electric cards, and the amount field is in card columns 16 to 20 in both cards (Fig. 5-14). In this example we want to print the gas amounts in print positions 31 to 35 and the electricity amounts in print positions 56 to 60. There is an X punch in the electric card in order to distinguish between the two cards. Assume that an X-brush is positioned over card column 80 which contains the X punch in the electricity cards, and the brush is wired to hub 2 of the five-hub panel. The solution is shown in Fig. 5-15. In class selection the impulses come from one field and are selected to print into one of two possible places; therefore, one wires from field A into C of a selector which can make contact internally with either N or T (field B or C). X-brush 2 is wired to selector pickup 2, not because they are both numbered 2, but because selector 2 was used.

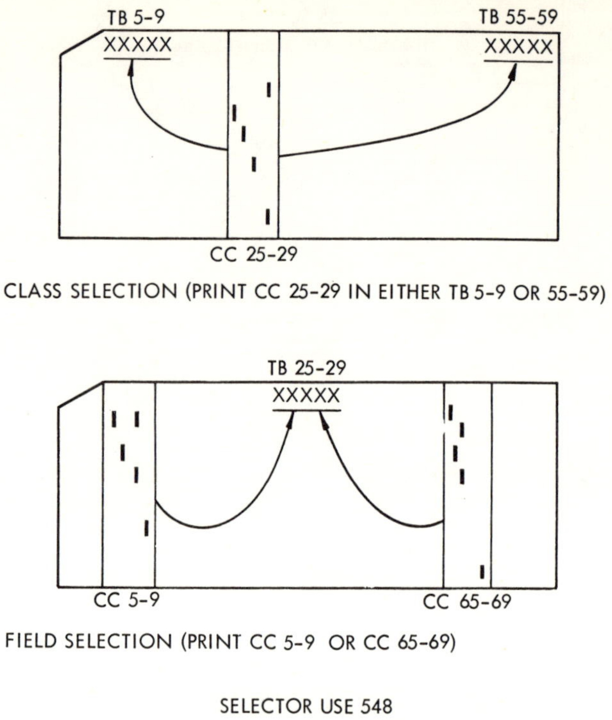

Fig. 5-13. Schematic of class and field selection (Courtesy of International Business Machines.)

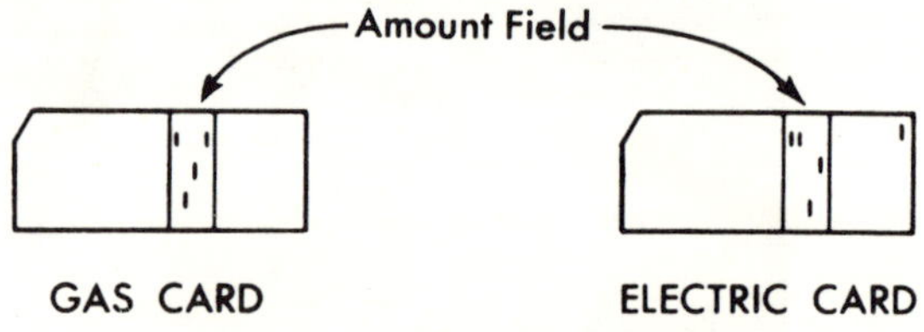

Fig. 5-14. Amount punched in the same field (Courtesy of International Business Machines.)

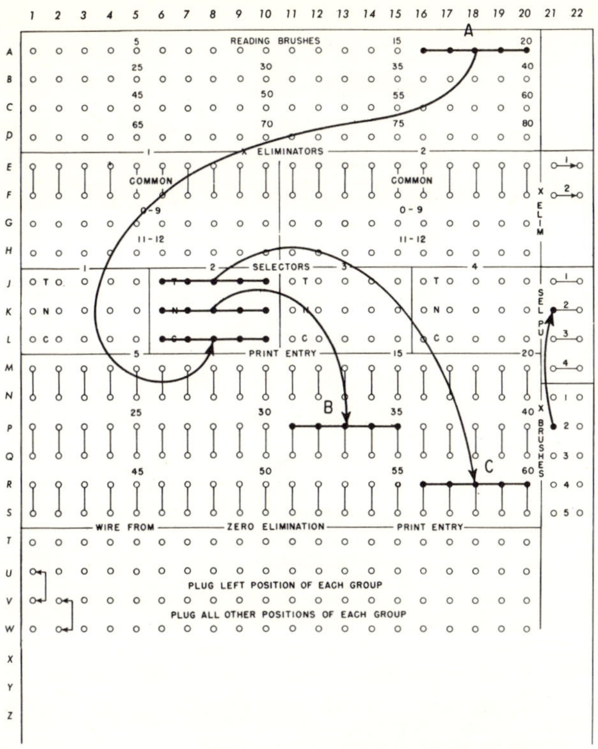

Fig. 5-15. Class selection (Courtesy of International Business Machines.)

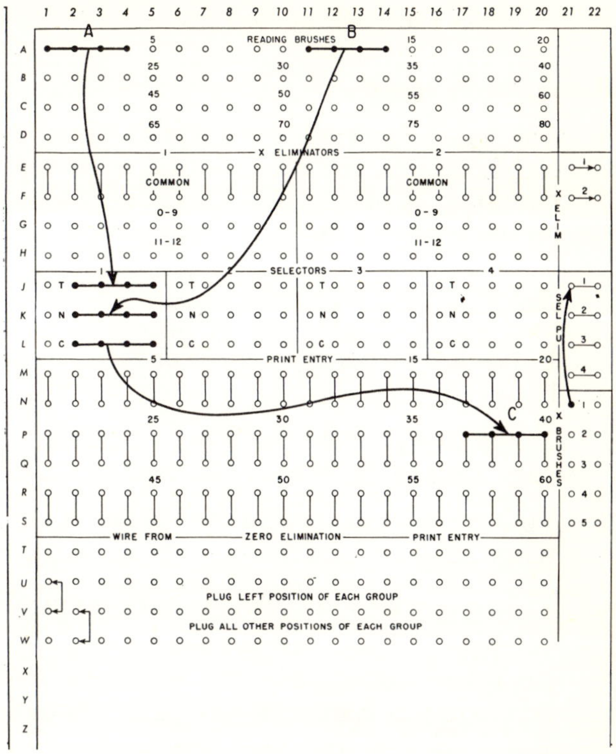

Fig. 5-16. Field selection

FIELD SELECTION

Field selection is the opposite of class selection. There are two fields in the cards, but we want to print only one. The presence or absence of an X in the card determines which of the two fields is selected to print. To illustrate the use of field selection, let us modify the previous example of class selection. In this example, the electricity cards, which have the X punch, contain the amount in columns 1 to 4. The NX cards have the gas amount in columns 11 to 14. In this example we want to print the electricity and gas amounts in print positions 37 to 40. Assume that an X-brush is positioned over the column containing the X punch, and there is a wire from this brush to hub 1 of the five-hub panel (Fig. 5-16). Notice that there is a wire from X-brush hub 1 to selector pickup 1, not because they are both numbered 1, but simply because selector 1 was used.

In field selection you come from two fields but go to only one field; therefore, you wire the field from the X card to transfer and the field from the NX card to normal. Both transfer and normal can connect to common, which in turn is wired to one destination.

PROBLEM 5: Bank transactions (deposits and withdrawals) are punched in card columns 30 to 35. Withdrawals have an X punch in card column 35. Print withdrawals in typebars 25 to 30. Print deposits in typebars 45 to 50. Assume there is an X-brush reading card column 35. Use X-brush hub 4 and selectors 1 and 2.

PROBLEM 6: Bank transaction cards have deposits punched in card columns 21 to 26 and withdrawals in card columns 11 to 16. The withdrawals are X punched in card column 16. Account balance cards contain the customer's balance in card columns 21 to 26 and are X punched in card column 80. Assume there is an X-brush reading card column 80. Print the withdrawal and balance fields in print entry 10 to 14 of their respective cards. Print a minus sign in print entry 16 on the withdrawal cards. Use X-brush hub 4 and selectors 1 and 2.

548 Interpreter Questions

Fill in blank spaces

1. The basic function of the 548 is to read ________ data in a card and translate it into ________ data on the same card.
2. ________ characters can be printed on one line of a card.
3. Printing can be performed on ________ lines.
4. Cards are put into the hopper ________ edge toward the throat and face ________.
5. To wire an interpreter to print, wire from ________ to ________.
6. The X-eliminator on the interpreter transfers between ______ and ______ time.
7. Forty-two hundred cards could be interpreted in approximately ______ hours and ______ minutes, machine time.

Answer True or False

8. ________ All 80 columns of a card can be interpreted on one pass through the machine.
9. ________ The line on which printing is performed is controlled by the control-panel wiring.
10. ________ The output sample is used to check that interpretation has been performed correctly according to the interpreter instructions.
11. ________ Cards feeding out of the hopper first pass the X-brushes.
12. ________ The printed character must be in the same column as the punches for that character.
13. ________ In field selection, the field to be interpreted is common to both X and NX cards.
14. ________ The control punch used in class selection is read by an X-brush.
15. ________ An X-brush may be set to read any one of the 80 card columns.

Answer briefly

16. To make the typebar print an alphabetic character, will the zone or the numeric impulse be received first?
17. When must a selector be used?
18. What is the purpose of an X-eliminator?
19. If a card is punched JONES and interprets as JNOES, what do you think the trouble is?
20. What control-panel hubs are used to eliminate an X punch and retain the digit punches?

Multiple choice

21. Which of the following hubs are exit hubs? Entry hubs? Either?

    a. Reading brushes
    b. Typebars
    c. X-eliminator (common)
    d. X-brush hubs 1 to 5
    e. Selector pickup
    f. N hub of selector

22. In Fig. P5-1,

    X-brush 1 on card column 30
    X-brush 2 on card column 1
    X-brush 3 on card column 45
    X-brush 4 on card column 80

    a. When will field A print?
    b. When will field B print?
    c. When will field C print?
    d. When will field D print?
    e. When will field E print?

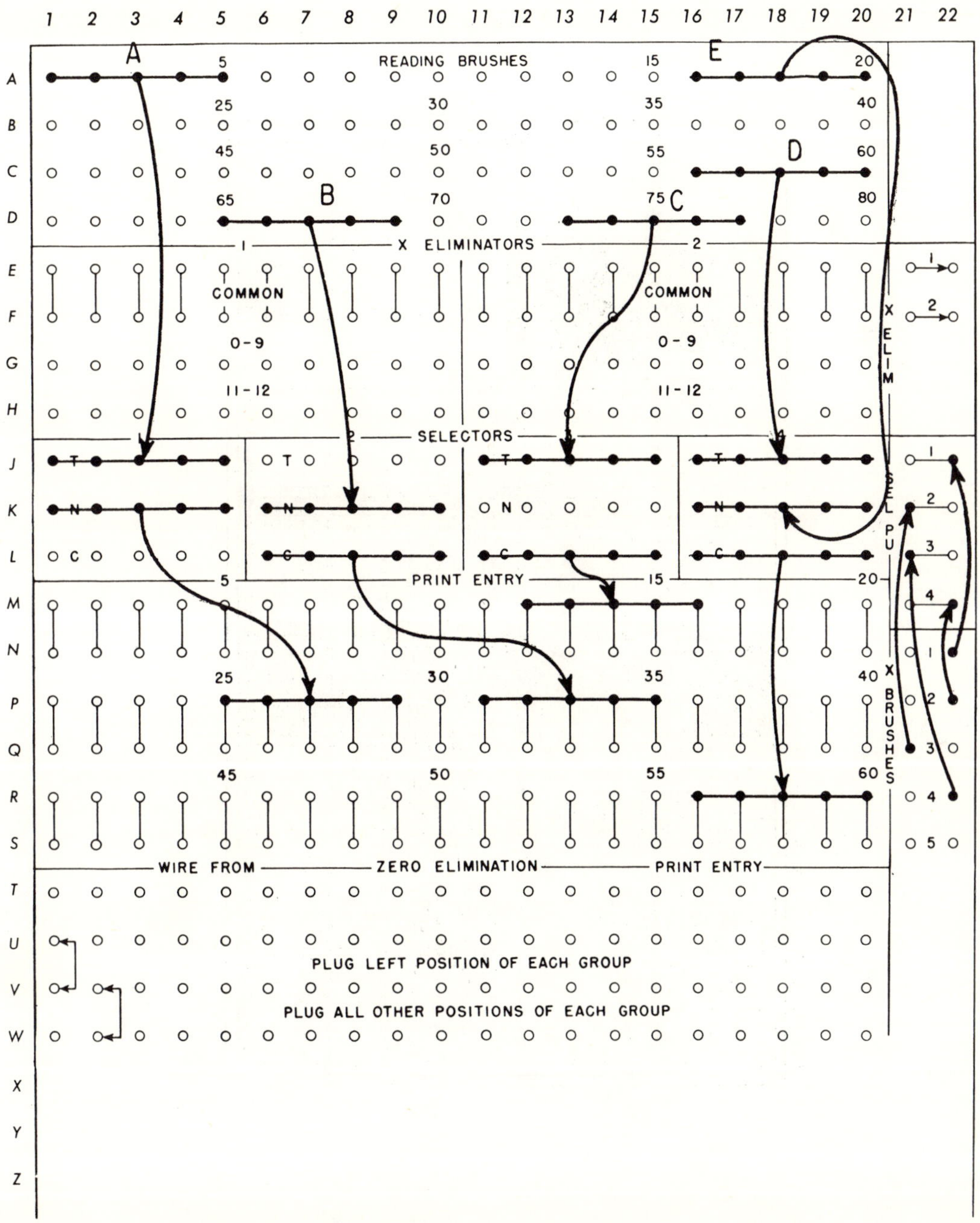

Fig. p5-1. (Courtesy of International Business Machines.)

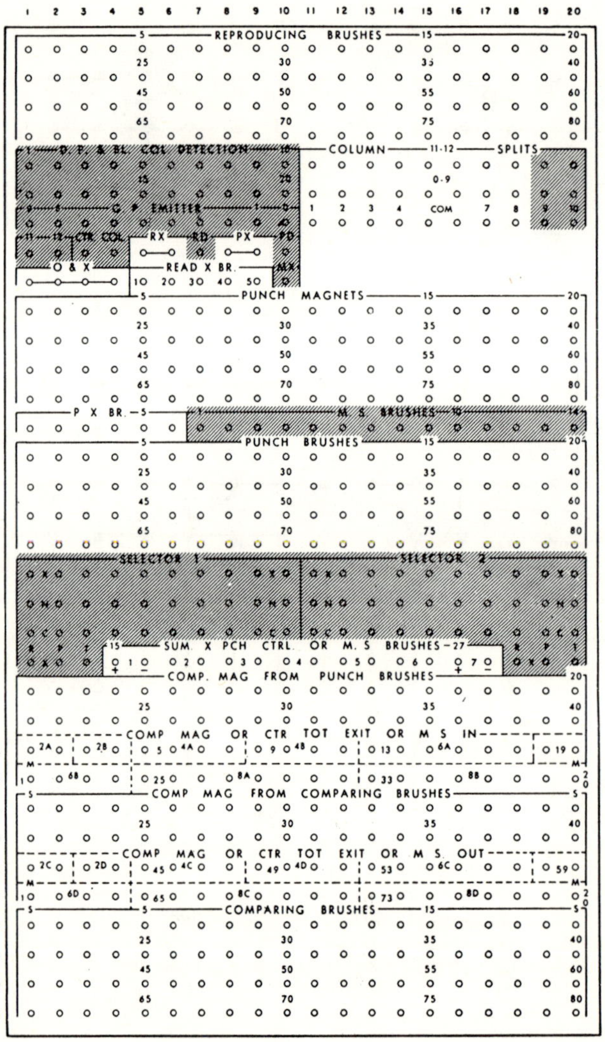

514 Control Panel. The shaded areas represent special features. (Courtesy of International Business Machines.)

Section 6

THE 514 REPRODUCING PUNCH

The primary function of the reproducer is to sense the punched holes and repeat these punches in other cards. The machine can punch any or all of the 80 columns from a card or cards into a blank card or cards.

Repetition is a characteristic of the keeping of manual records. These operations can be performed automatically by the IBM 514 Reproducer (Fig. 6-1). The reproducer has two card-feed hoppers - a read-unit

Fig. 6-1. IBM 514 Reproducing Punch (Courtesy of International Business Machines.)

hopper on the left, and a punch unit hopper on the right. In a reproducing operation, one unit of the machine reads previously punched cards, while the other unit punches blank cards that are to become copies of the original.

Because the card files (original and copy) are to remain separate, the machine also has two stackers that receive the processed cards - one for the cards fed through the read unit and the other for the cards fed through the punch unit.

The standard IBM 514 operates at a rated speed of 100 cards per minute. The 514 series 50 is rated at 50 cards per minute. These speeds are constant whether reproducing a card with one column or 80 columns of punched data.

Other functions of the 514 are verifying, gangpunching, and summary punching.

OPERATING FEATURES

Control panel - determines functions that the machine is to perform

Start and stop keys - control the card feeding

Reset key - reset double punch and blank column detection circuits

DP (double punch) and BC (blank column) light (optional) - are extinguished by pushing the reset key.

Compare light - indicates an error in verifying and stopping of card feeding. Extinguished by pushing reset lever.

Unlabeled light - indicates no cards are being fed

Two hoppers - each hold 800 cards which are fed 12 edge, face down

Stackers - two stackers hold 1,000 cards each. Card feeding stops automatically when either stacker is filled.

SCHEMATIC

In order to comprehend fully how any of the unit record machines function, one must understand the machine's *schematic* and be able to relate the schematic to the hubs on the control panel. Figure 6-2 shows the schematic of the 514 Reproducing Punch, the read, and the punch units.

We will now discuss the card paths. The card from the read feed hopper passes beneath the 5 read X-brushes which perform the same function as the X-brushes of the 548 Interpreter. They can be positioned over any column. The card is then read by the 80 reproducing brushes which are similar to the reading brushes of the 548 Interpreter. The card passes these two stations on one card cycle. The next cycle in the card path is the 80 comparing brushes. Therefore when the 5 row of the first card in the reading unit is being read by the comparing brushes, the 5 row of the next card is being read by the reproducing brushes. The card is then moved into the stacker.

The card from the punch feed hopper first passes beneath the 6 punch X-brushes, which are similar to the X-brushes of the 548 Interpreter and can be positioned over any column. Next the card passes above the *mark - sensing* brushes (if the machine contains this special feature). The card then proceeds to the punching dies, which do the actual punching. This movement is the first card cycle. During the next cycle, the card passes under the 80 punch brushes and then into the stacker.

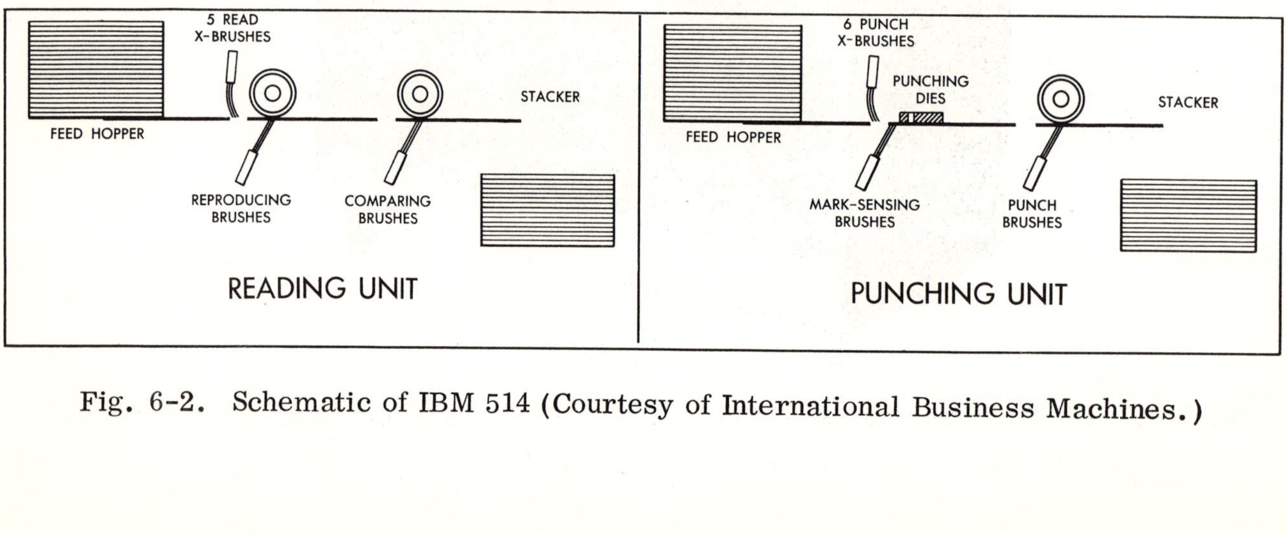

Fig. 6-2. Schematic of IBM 514 (Courtesy of International Business Machines.)

Both units are used together during many operations. At that time, due to the fact that the two units are synchronized, the cards are fed simultaneously through both units. Therefore when the X row of a card in the reading unit is being read by the read X-brushes, the X row of the card in the punching unit is being read by the punch X-brushes. At the time the 4 row of a card is being read in the reading unit by the reproducing brushes, the 4 row of a card in the punching unit is at the punch position. As the card in the reading unit passes to the comparing brushes, the card in the punch unit passes on to the punch brushes. At the same time the 4 row in the card in the reading unit is being read by the comparing brushes, the 4 row of the card in the punching unit is being read by the punch brushes.

In summary, when using both feeds in a reproducing operation, the same row is being read or punched by the reproducing brushes, comparing brushes, punch magnets, and punch brushes. Therefore, one should be aware that the card is being punched in *parallel* (Fig. 6-3) and not *serially* as the key punch. That is why the number of punched columns does not affect the reproducing time.

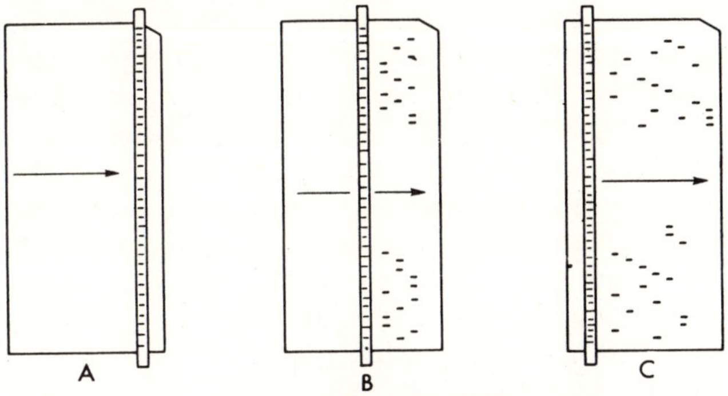

Fig. 6-3. Parallel punching (Courtesy of International Business Machines.)

REPRODUCING

In reproducing operations the reading and punching units are synchronized. The original (source) cards are placed in the reading unit. The cards to be punched (the reproduced cards) are placed in the punching unit. The entire card need not be blank; only the columns to be punched should be blank. As the card feeds in the reading unit, a card feeds in the punching unit. As the card in the reading unit passes under the reproducing brushes, the punched information is sensed and transmitted to the punch magnets. The card under the punch magnets is then punched.

Reproducing enables you to have any data in a card automatically punched into another card, thereby avoiding additional keypunching.

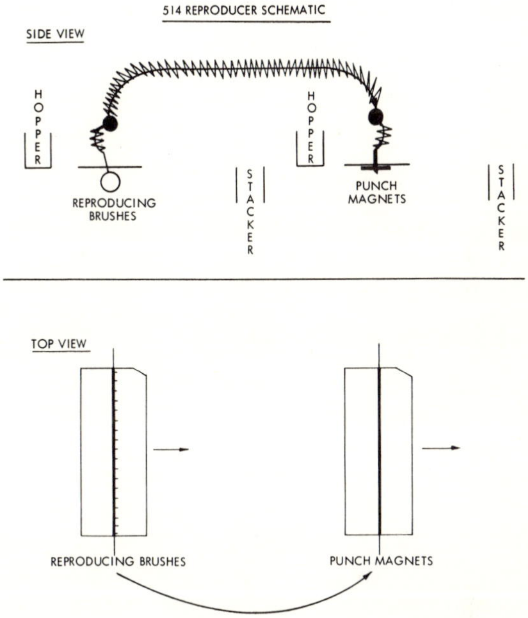

Fig. 6-4. Schematic of reproducing (Courtesy of International Business Machines.)

There are four types of reproducing: *Straight reproducing, offset reproducing, selection*, and *selective reproducing*, all of which will be discussed later.

The schematic for straight, offset, selection, and *selective* reproducing is the same (Fig. 6-4). The reproducing brushes are wired to the *punch dies.* The card we take information from must pass under a set of reproducing brushes at the same time the card we want to punch passes under the punch magnets. The proper card columns to be read and punched must be connected by wires.

STRAIGHT REPRODUCING

Straight reproducing is the punching of data into the same card columns as those from which it is read; field A into field B of Fig. 6-5.

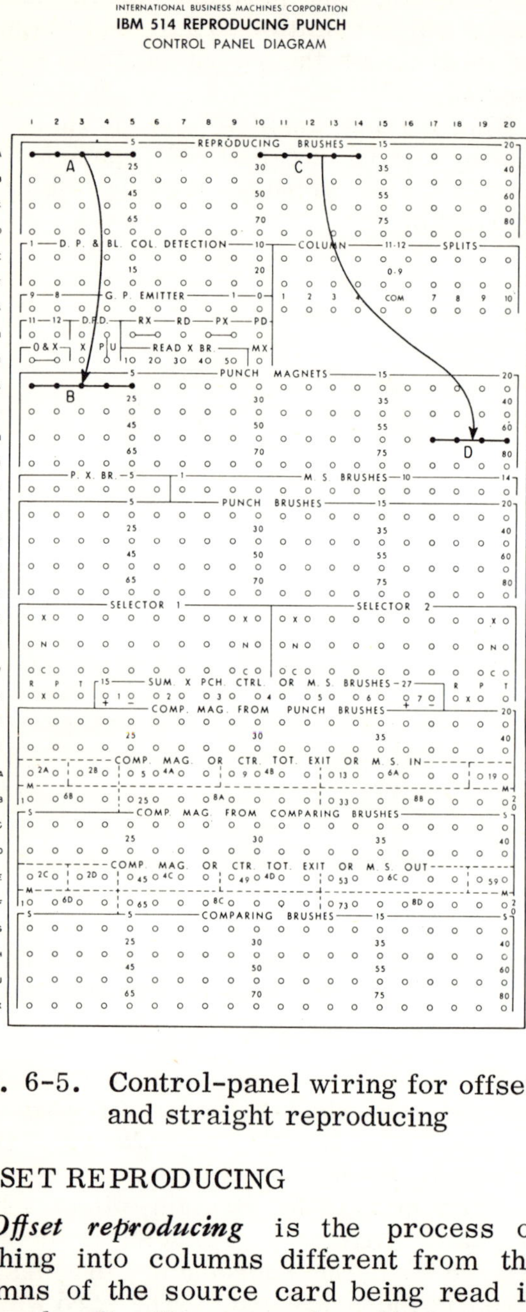

Fig. 6-5. Control-panel wiring for offset and straight reproducing

OFFSET REPRODUCING

Offset reproducing is the process of punching into columns different from the columns of the source card being read in the read unit. For example, offset reproducing would be performed if one wanted to produce an employee's weekly attendance card from the employee's master card, and the information had to be reproduced into different card columns. Figure 6-5 field C into field D shows an example of offset reproducing wiring.

When doing any type of reproducing, the ***reproduce switch*** (Fig. 6-6) must be on in order to synchronize the reading and punching feeds. When a card is fed in the reading unit, one is fed in the punching unit. If either hopper empties, the machine automatically stops. The reproducing switch must be on when the two feeds are used to perform a single operation. It is turned off when the two feeds operate independently to perform separate operations or when only one feed is used.

PROBLEM 1: Reproduce card columns 30 to 36 into card columns 30 to 36 and card columns 75 to 80 into card columns 75 to 80.

PROBLEM 2: Reproduce columns 22 to 25 into columns 8 to 11.

VERIFICATION

The reproduced data can be verified one card cycle later, during the same operation. As the source card passes the comparing brushes in the read feed, the corresponding reproduced card passes the punch brushes in the punch feed. If the holes sensed by the two sets of brushes are in the same position, the machine continues. If there is any discrepancy the comparing light goes on, and the machine stops. At the same time the comparing indicator (Fig. 6-1) shows which comparing positions recognized the discrepancy.

A comparing check is advisable since it does not involve any additional machine time. Verification by comparing is available in two capacities - 45 or 80 columns of comparing positions. The standard machine contains 45 comparing magnets.

Fig. 6-6. IBM 514 switches (Courtesy of International Business Machines.)

If card feeding stops for a comparing error, remove the cards from both hoppers and stackers. Note the comparing indicator for the comparing magnet which found the error. Push the *restoring lever* (Fig. 6-1) and press the start key to run-out the cards in the machine. The discrepancy is in one of the two first cards in the stacker.

45 or 80 COMPARING MAGNETS: Y-AB, 1-20, AC-AF, 1-20

The comparing magnets are comprised of two sets of opposing hubs. Normally, one set is wired from the punch brushes, and the other set is wired from the comparing brushes. These same hubs are used for mark sensing and summary punching.

A comparing magnet is formed by two opposing magnets with an armature between them (Fig. 6-7). The magnets are wired

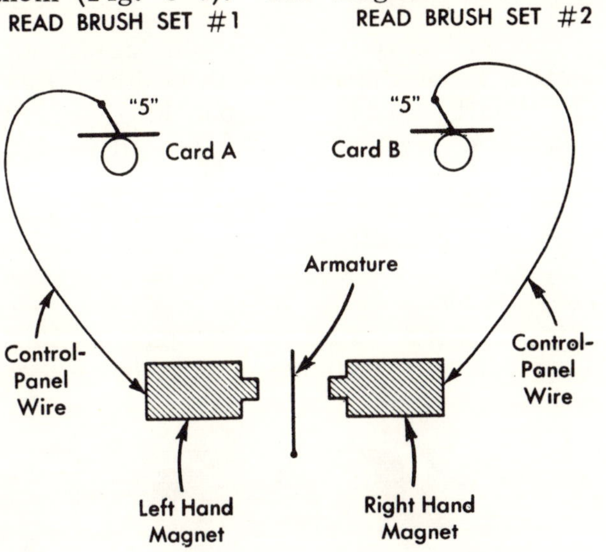

Fig. 6-7. Comparing (equal condition) (Courtesy of International Business Machines.)

from two sets of reading brushes, each hub of the reading brushes being wired to a comparing magnet hub. If the same row is punched in the same column, an impulse will travel to the magnets at the same time. If the magnets are impulsed at the same time, their attracting power is balanced. When this happens, the armature remains centered. The armature will be attracted to one of the magnets if the magnet is impulsed before the opposing magnet is impulsed. In Fig. 6-7, cards A and B both contain a 5 punch in the same column; therefore, the armature remains stationary. In Fig. 6-8, card A contains a 5 punch and card B contains a 9 punch. Since the cards

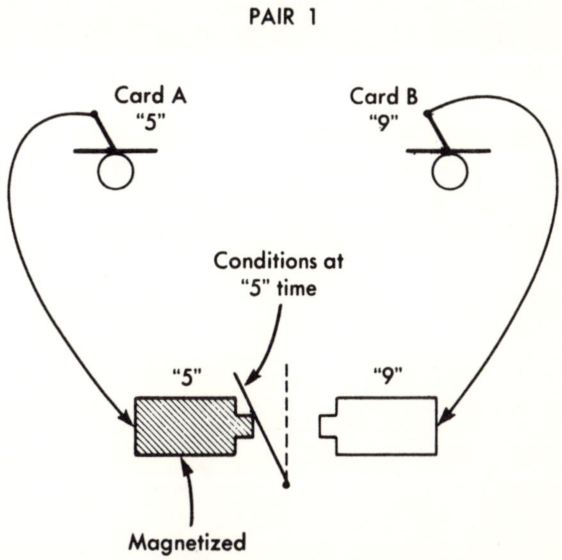

Fig. 6-8. Comparing (unequal condition), 5 and 9 impulses (Courtesy of International Business Machines.)

are fed 12 edge first, the impulse from the 5 row is available first. When this impulse arrives at the magnet, it attracts the armature to leave its center position and to make contact with the magnet. The schematic of this operation can be seen in Fig. 6-9. An example of wiring for straight reproducing

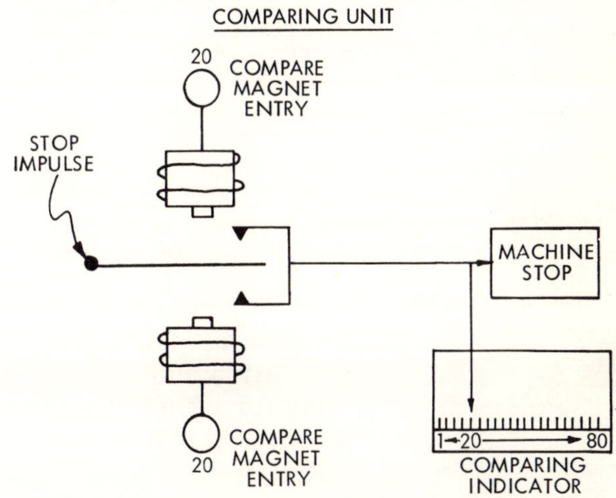

Fig. 6-9. Schematic of comparing unit (Courtesy of International Business Machines.)

and verification and offset reproducing and verification is shown in Fig. 6-10. Notice that in the wiring of offset reproducing the comparing brushes and reproducing brushes use the same columns. This is because the columns that were reproduced are next read by the comparing brushes. The wires from the punch magnets and the punch brushes use the same columns. This is because the columns punched by the punch dies must next be read by the punch brushes. Any comparing-magnet hubs can be used as long as opposing magnets are wired.

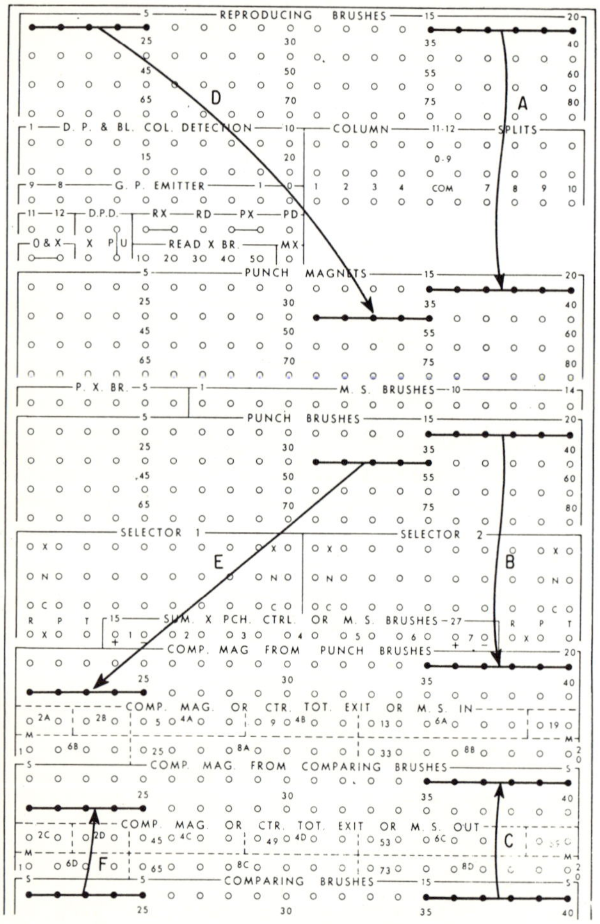

Fig. 6-10. Wiring for straight reproducing and verification and wiring for offset reproducing and verification

PROBLEM 3: Add the wiring for verification to your diagram for PROBLEM 1. Use comparing magnets 25 to 30 and 32 to 37.

PROBLEM 4: Add the wiring for verification to your diagram for PROBLEM 2. Use comparing magnets 1 to 4.

COLUMN SPLITS: E-G, 11-20

Column splits were called X-eliminators on the 548 Interpreter. The only difference is that, on the 514 Reproducer, a switch does not have to be wired to make the column splits operative.

PROBLEM 5: Reproduce from card columns 31 to 35 into card columns 41 to 45. Use comparing magnets 11 to 15 for verification. Eliminate any X punch that may be punched in column 35. Punch the X in column 46. Remember also to verify the X punch.

GANGPUNCHING

Gangpunching is the reproducing of information from a master card into the following detail cards. Gangpunching permits automatic reproducing of repetitive data. Information can be keypunched into a master card. This data can then be gangpunched back into the following cards. An application would be to gangpunch the date into cash receipts cards (Fig. 6-11). Only the punch unit is used to perform gangpunching. Therefore all switches are in the off position.

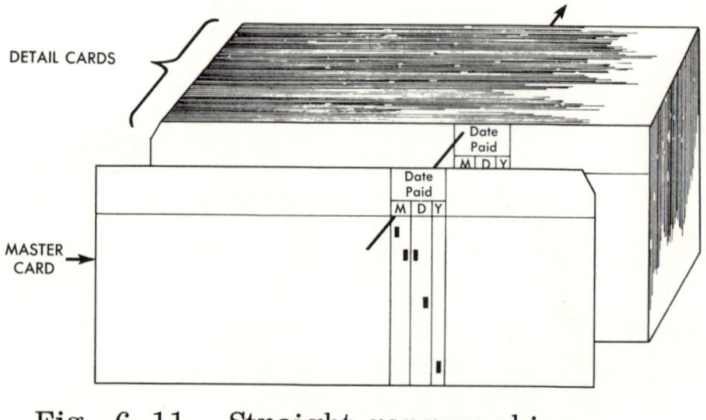

Fig. 6-11. Straight gangpunching (Courtesy of International Business Machines.)

As in reproducing, there are several types of gangpunching - ***straight, offset,*** and ***interspersed master*** gangpunching. The schematic is the same for all three types (Fig. 6-12). As the master card is read by the punch brushes, the information is punched into the card at the punch station. On the next card cycle, this card is at the punch brushes, and the process is repeated.

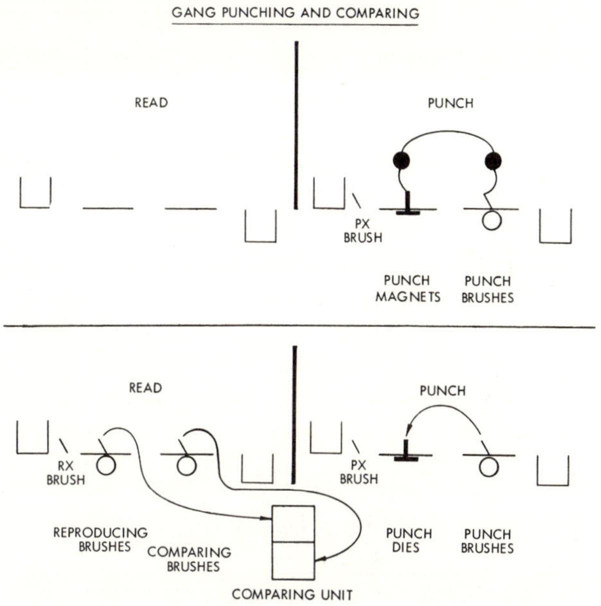

Fig. 6-12. Schematic of gangpunching and comparing (Courtesy of International Business Machines.)

STRAIGHT GANGPUNCHING

Gangpunching, as shown in the schematic, involves having the punch brushes being wired to the punch magnets. In straight gangpunching, the data from the master card is gangpunched into the following cards in the same card columns as shown in Fig. 6-13. Straight gangpunching is column for column gangpunching from one card to another. Only one master card is required.

Before we consider interspersed master gangpunching or offset gangpunching, we will explore the verification of gangpunched cards.

GANGPUNCH VERIFICATION

One can sight check by looking through the holes of the punched columns or visually comparing the master card with the last detail card (Fig. 6-14). This is because if there were an error, the error would be perpetuated to the last detail card.

Another method of gangpunch verification is using the comparing feature of the read

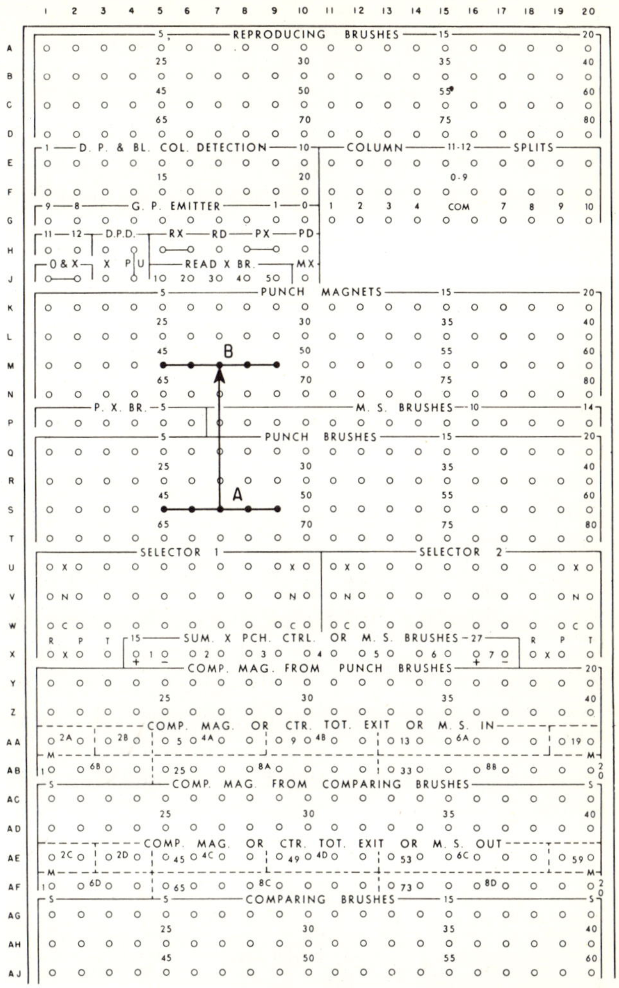

Fig. 6-13. Wiring for gangpunching (Courtesy of International Business Machines.)

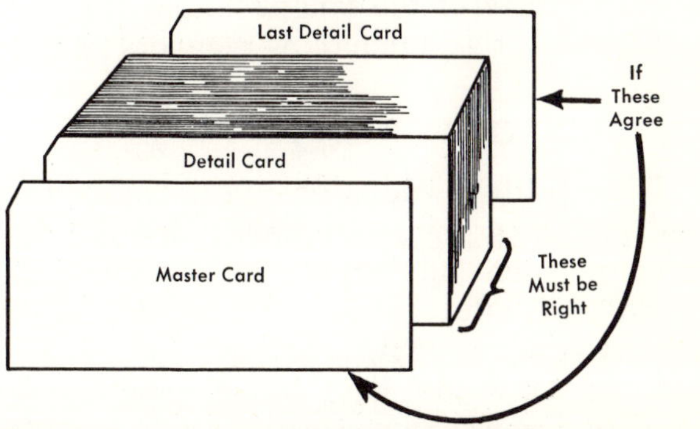

Fig. 6-14. Verification of gangpunching (Courtesy of International Business Machines.)

unit. In fact, one can verify while still gangpunching, since the read unit is not used to gangpunch. This can be accomplished by removing cards from the punch stacker and placing them into the read feed hopper. The schematic for the gangpunching and verification operation is shown in Fig. 6-12. The wiring for verification of straight gangpunching is carried out by having the card at the comparing brushes compared to the card at the reproducing brushes. On the following card cycle, the cards will move up. Then the card that was at the comparing brushes will feed into the stacker, and the card at the reproducing brushes will move to the comparing brushes where it will be compared with the card that just fed from the hopper to the reproducing brushes.

As long as the cards agree, the operation continues. If they disagree the machine stops, and a light signals an error. The comparing magnet in error is indicated in the comparing indicator unit. Remember, the column in error is not indicated unless the same numbered comparing magnets as the card columns being compared are used. The wiring to perform verification and gangpunching simultaneously is shown in Fig. 6-15.

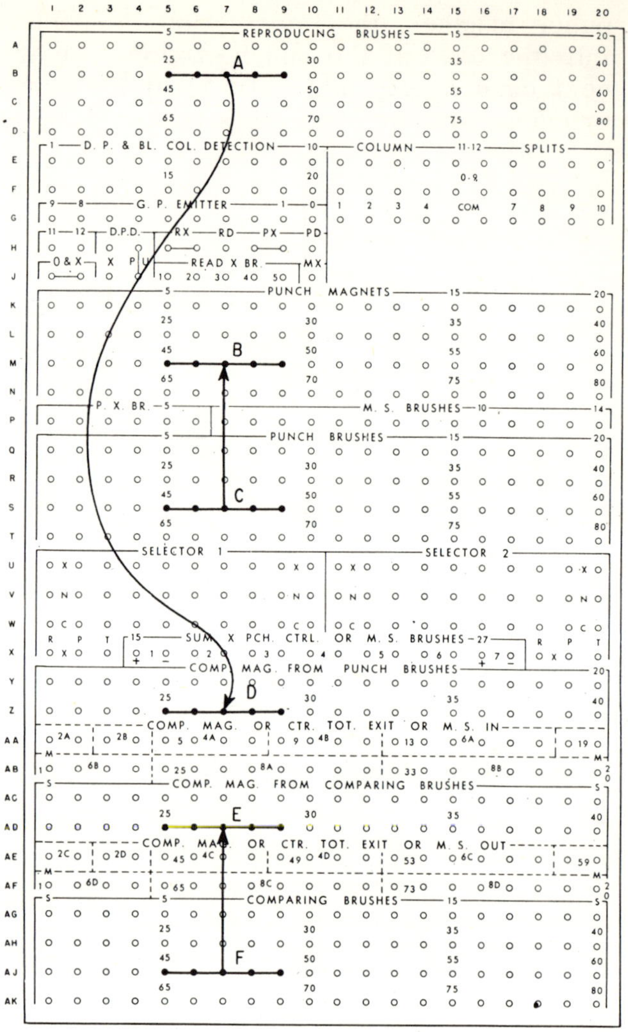

Fig. 6-15. Wiring for gangpunching and verification

PROBLEM 6: Gangpunch data into card columns 17 to 21 and card columns 30 to 34, from a master card containing these two fields in the same card columns.

PROBLEM 7: Add the wiring necessary for verification of the gangpunching in PROBLEM 6. Use comparing magnets 26 to 35.

EMITTER: G, 1-10 and H, 1-2

The Emitter, which has 12 hubs, one for each punching row, is a useful special feature for such operations as gangpunching without a master card. The emitter is capable of generating its own impulses. Figure 6-16 shows some data being gangpunched from a master card while other data is being emitted. Notice that the letter A is being emitted into column 55.

PROBLEM 8: Gangpunch columns 60 to 63 into 60 to 63. Reproduce columns 64 to 68 into 64 to 68 and verify. Eliminate the X punch in column 68. Remember also to eliminate the X punch when verifying. Use comparing magnets 64 to 68.

READ X-BRUSHES (Fig. 6-2)

There are five read X-brushes on the read unit. There is also a five-hub X-panel to accept wired impulses from these brushes. The impulse is then available from the read X BR hubs (J, 5-9) on the control panel. The five numbered hubs correspond to the five hubs on the X-panel. The read X-brush hubs on the control panel are usually wired to the two common RX hubs (H, 5 and 6) or the RX pickup hubs of the selectors (X, 18 or X, 1).

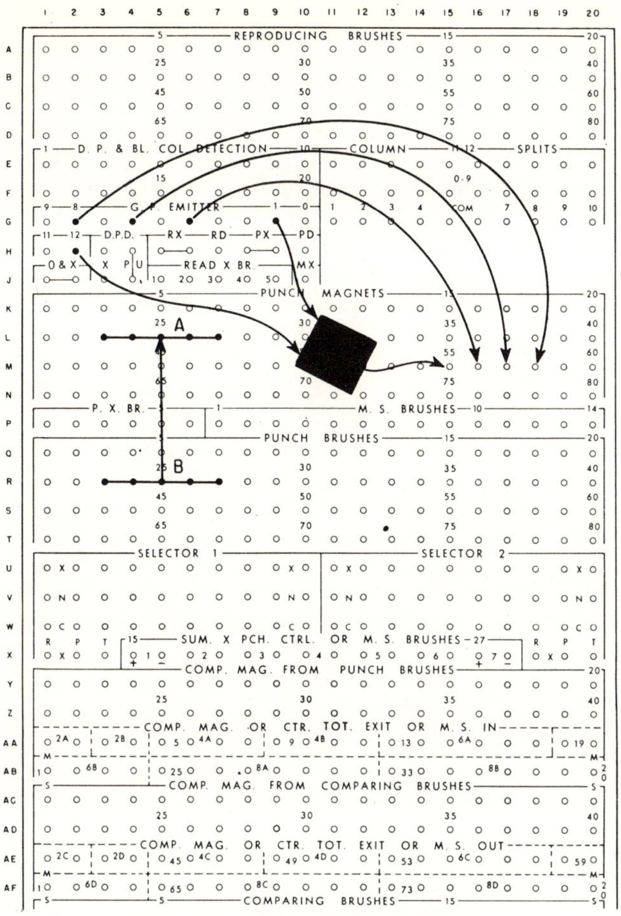

Fig. 6-16. Gangpunching emitter wiring

PUNCH X-BRUSHES (Fig. 6-2)

The six punch X-brushes function the same way as the read X-brushes, except that they are located in the punch unit. The X impulses that they read are available from the six PX BR hubs (P, 1-6) on the control panel. These hubs are normally wired to PX hubs (H, 8 and 9) or the selector P pick-up hubs (X, 2 or X, 19).

PX AND PD HUBS: H, 8-10

The common PX hubs accept impulses from the PX brushes. The PX hubs will be effective either from X master cards or NX master cards depending on the setting of the detail master switch (Fig. 6-6). If the switch is set to master, the PX hubs will be effective for X master cards. If the switch is set to detail, the PX hubs will be effective for NX masters. The schematic of the PX function is depicted in Fig. 6-17. The impulse to the PX hub is available one cycle later from the PD hub. If the PX is effective, the functions of the machine will be affected in three ways, for either X or NX master, depending upon the setting of the master-detail switch.

The three functions that can be made inoperative by impulsing the PX hub are:

1. Punch magnets
2. Read unit card feed
3. Comparing magnets

Certain functions must be inoperative for one card cycle in order to perform the following:

1. Interspersed master gangpunching
2. Selective reproducing
3. Reproducing and interspersed master gangpunching.

Most of the above operations will be explained, and you will see why certain functions of the machine must be crippled for one card cycle.

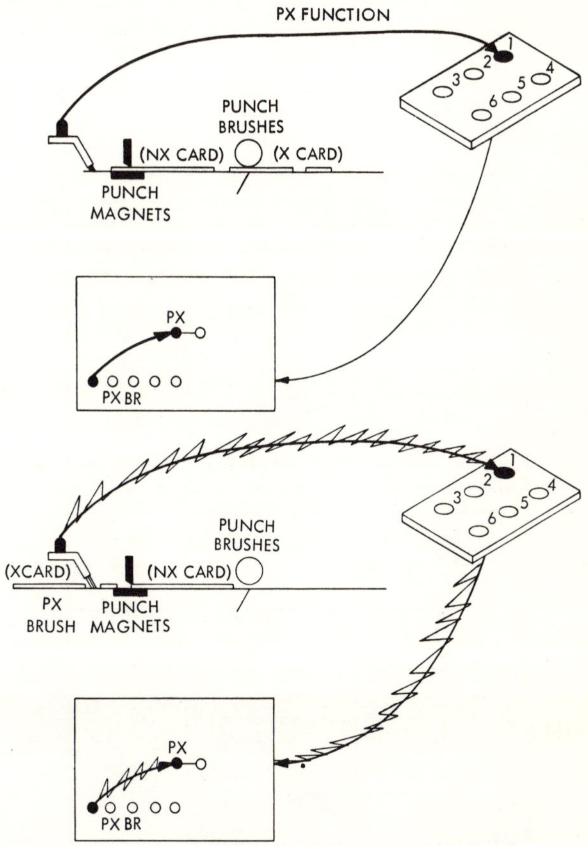

Fig. 6-17. PX function (Courtesy of International Business Machines.)

INTERSPERSED MASTER GANGPUNCHING

Interspersed gangpunching occurs when many groups of detail cards are each preceded by an individual master card from which data must be punched. Instead of processing each group separately (straight gangpunching), the groups are processed together, as one complete file, because of the great reduction in card-handling time. This results in a much faster operation, especially when some of the groups contain only a few cards.

A typical interspersed gangpunching operation can be found in a payroll application where employee master cards are used to gangpunch hourly rates into individual job tickets (Fig. 6-18).

Each employee may receive a pay rate

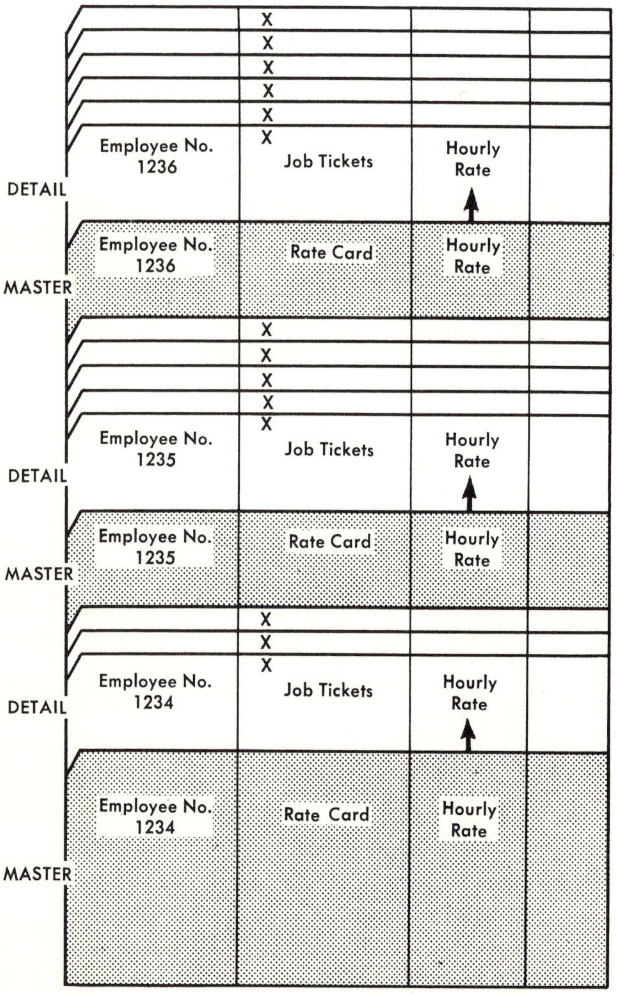

Fig. 6-18. Interspersed gangpunching (Courtesy of International Business Machines.)

different from the one preceding or following him. We want to pick up new gangpunching data as each new master card is fed into the machine. In addition, we must suspend gangpunching when the last detail card of each group passes the punch brushes, or the rate for that employee will be overpunched in the following employee's master card and, from there, into the detail cards. This is called *lacing*.

Suspending punching from group to group is controlled by the X punches. The X may be placed in either the master card or the detail cards. The punching of master cards is suspended by the presence or absence of the X punch which is detected by the punch X-brushes. Figure 6-19 shows the schematic for interspersed master gangpunching.

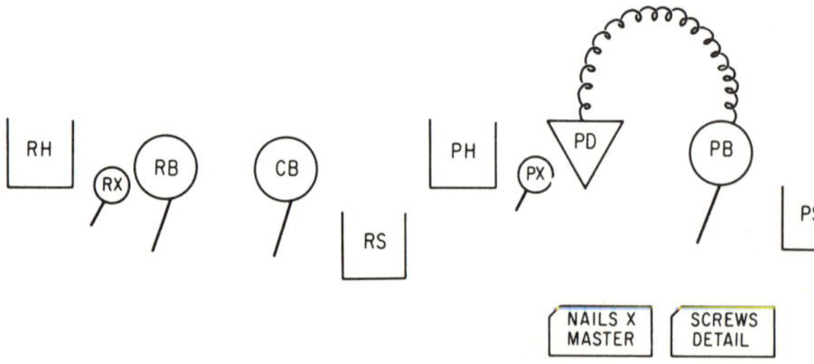

Fig. 6-19. Schematic of interspersed master gangpunching

In this illustration, the last detail card of the previous group is under the punch brushes and the X master card of the next group is under the punching dies. If the punching dies were not made inoperative at this time, the item description "screws" would be punched back into the field containing the item description "nails" and laced cards would result in all of the following cards. Figure 6-20 illustrates the wiring for an interspersed master gangpunching operation.

The master-detail switch must be set to the proper position, depending on whether the X punch is in the master or detail cards. A punch X-brush must be positioned and wired to the six-hub panel, and all of the switches must be off.

Verification of interspersed master gangpunching is accomplished by the use of the RX and RD hubs (H, 5 to 6), which are wired from the read X-brush hubs (Fig. 6-21). Like the PX hub, the RX hub is effective for

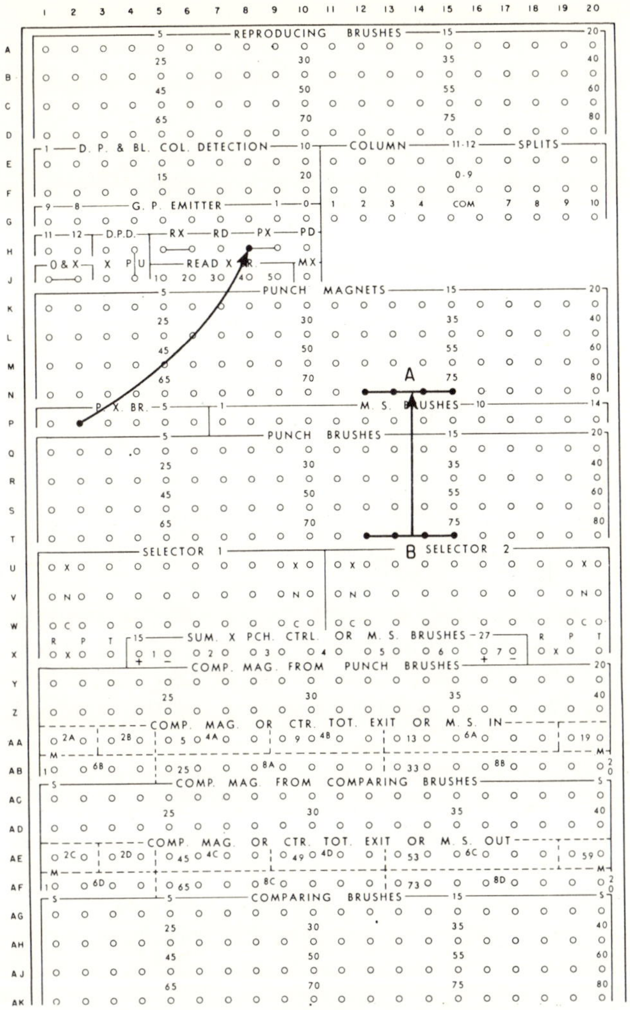

Fig. 6-20. Wiring for interspersed master gangpunching

either an X or NX master, depending on the setting of the master-detail switch. When the RX is effective, and the X or NX master

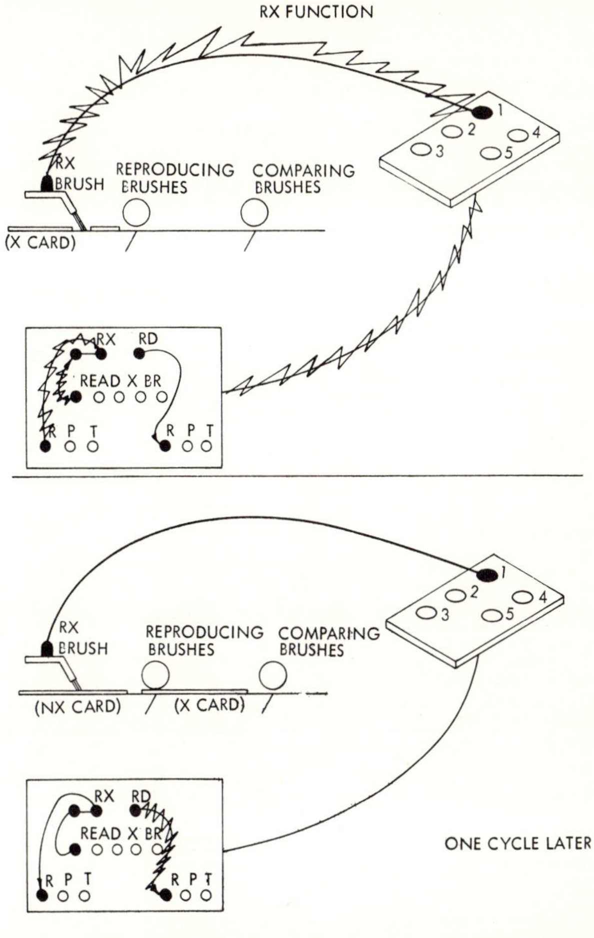

Fig. 6-21. RX function (Courtesy of International Business Machines.)

card is at the reproducing brushes and the preceding card is at the comparing brushes, comparing is inoperative for one cycle (Fig. 6-22). If the comparing was not inoperative at this time, the last detail card of the preceding group would be compared with the master card of the next group. The impulse

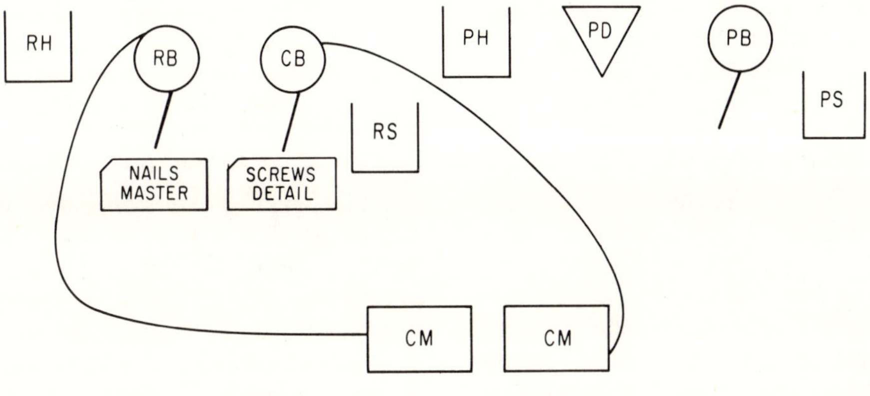

Fig. 6-22. Schematic of verification of interspersed master gangpunching

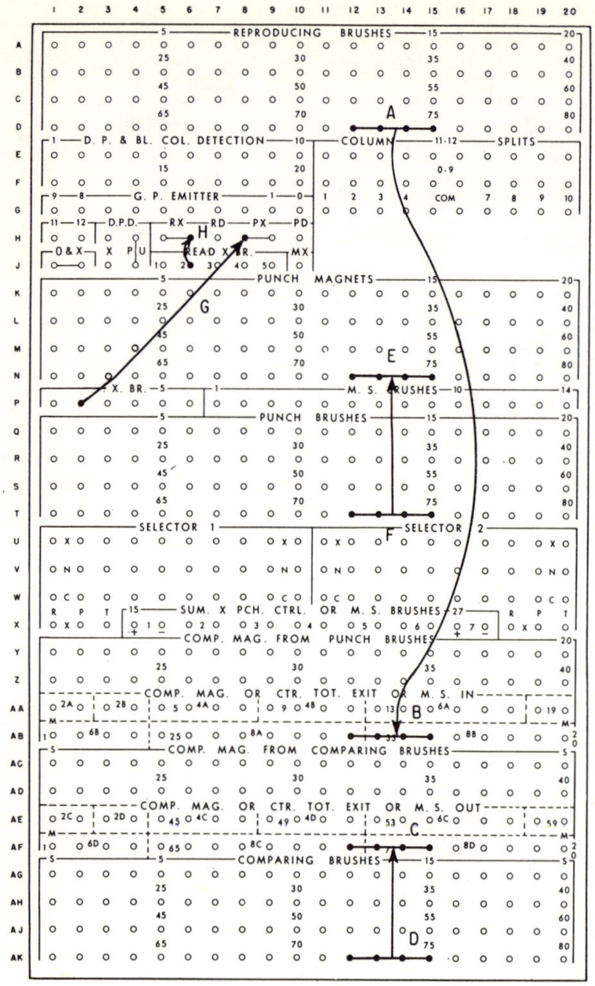

Fig. 6-23. Wiring for interspersed master gangpunching and verification

to the RX hub is available from the RD hub one cycle later. If you are performing interspersed master gangpunching and verification at the same time, the SEL REPD and GP compare switch must be on and the reproduce switch off. The RX hub is used for verification of offset and interspersed-master gangpunching.

When on, the SEL REPD compare switch allows continuous feeding in the reading unit. The switch should be on only when a selective reproducing or a gangpunch and comparing operation is being run. If the switch is off, an impulse to the PX hub causes the feeding in the reading unit to stop for the following card cycle, while a card is fed in the punching unit. The verification wiring for the previous example is illustrated in Fig. 6-23.

PROBLEM 9: Wire a diagram for an interspersed master gangpunching and verification. Gangpunch into card columns 67 to 72. Use PX Brush 6, RX Brush 1, and comparing magnets 35-40.

SELECTIVE REPRODUCING

We know that the read X-brushes at the control station can recognize distinctive X punches in cards and signal various machine operations. In this way, it is possible to pass a master file of cards through the read side of an automatic punch and reproduce only those cards with a control X or only those without the control X. This is called *selective reproducing.*

An example of this might be the reproducing of all the cards in a certain product category from a file of perpetual inventory cards. The inventory cards in the special category have a distinctive X punch.

By selective reproducing, only the cards with Xs are reproduced (Fig. 6-24). A blank card passes through the punch feed for every card not reproduced. Then the reproduced set is sorted to remove the blank cards so that only the special-category cards remain.

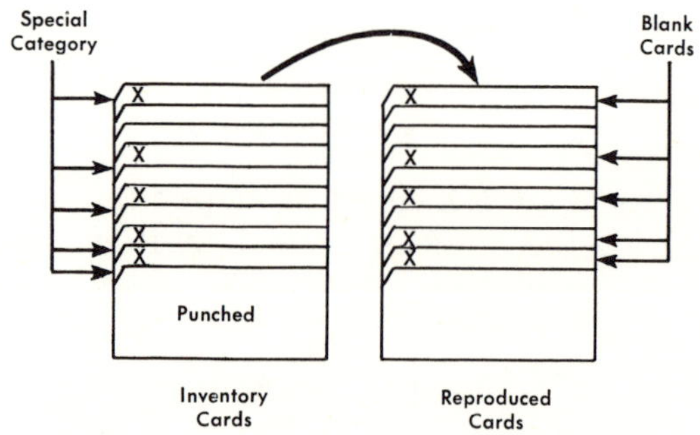

Fig. 6-24. Selective reproducing (Courtesy of International Business Machines.)

The wiring for selective reproducing is illustrated in Fig. 6-25. The reproduce switch must be on and all other switches must be off. A read X-brush must be positioned over the card column containing the X control punch. In Fig. 6-25, the read X control brush is wired to hub 2 of the five-hub panel.

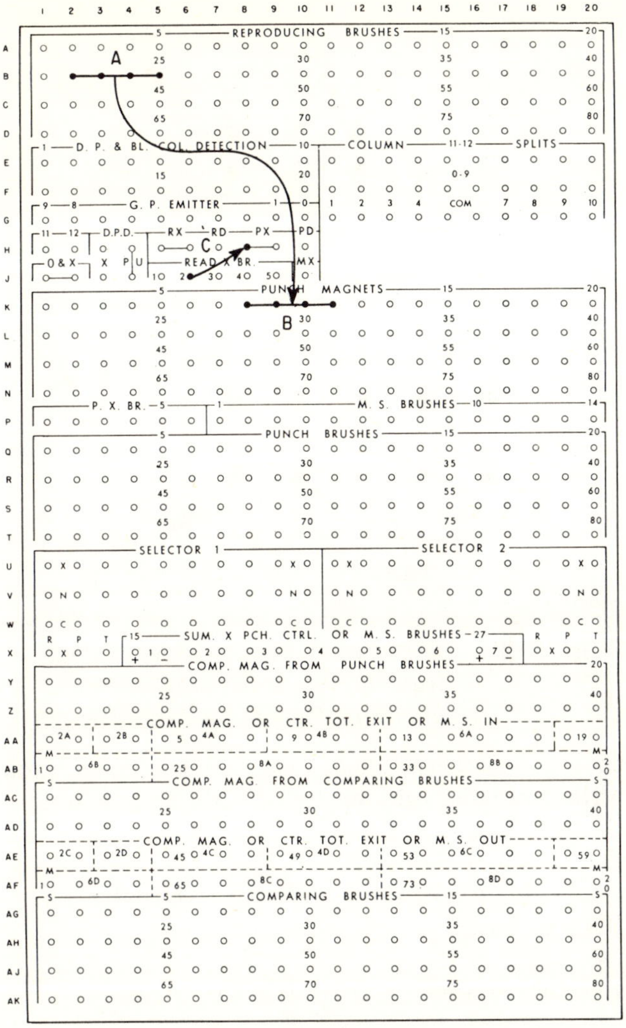

Fig. 6-25. Wiring for selective reproducing

SELECTIVE REPRODUCING AND VERIFICATION

Selective reproducing and verification can take place on the same pass (Fig. 6-26). The comparing magnets are inoperative on the following cycle when the blank card is under the punch brushes and the nonreproduced cards are under the comparing brushes. The reproduce switch and the selective reproduce and gangpunch compare switch must be on. All other switches must be off.

If the reproduce switch is on and the PX hub receives an impulse, comparing will be inoperative during the following cycle. If the switch is off and the RX hubs receive an impulse, comparing is inoperative during the same cycle. Figure 6-27 illustrates the wiring necessary for selective reproducing and verification.

PROBLEM 10: Draw a diagram to reproduce cards selectively and verify. Reproduce columns 45 to 49 into columns 45 to 49. Use PX brush hub 1 and comparing magnets 30-34.

SELECTORS

The two special-feature selectors can be found on the control panel at U-X, 1-10 and at U-X, 11-20. Each selector can be picked up (transferred) by one of three hubs. These three hubs are labeled R, X P, and T and are located on the control panel at X,

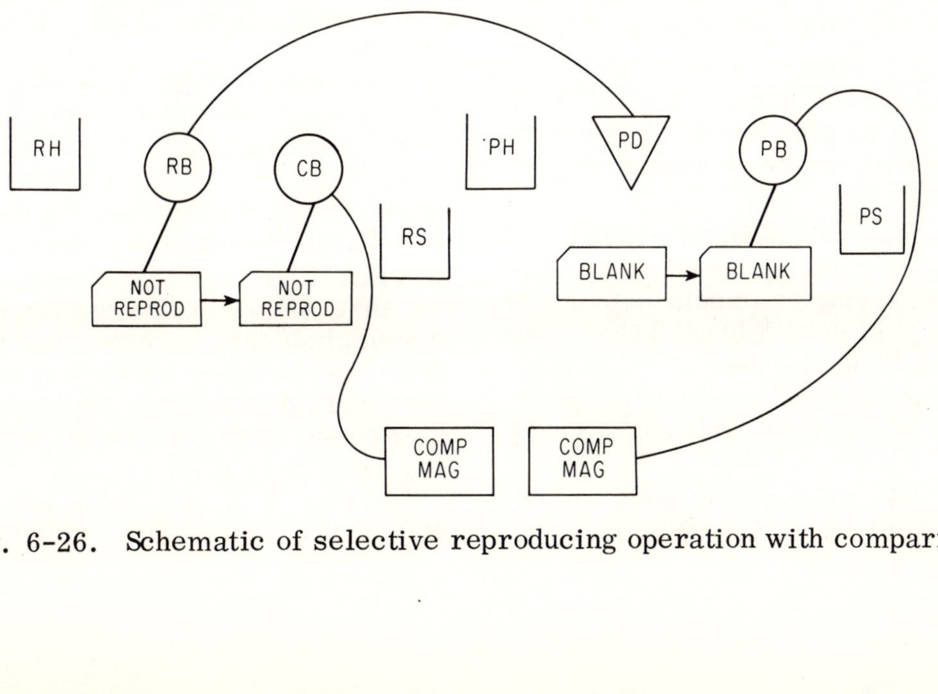

Fig. 6-26. Schematic of selective reproducing operation with comparing

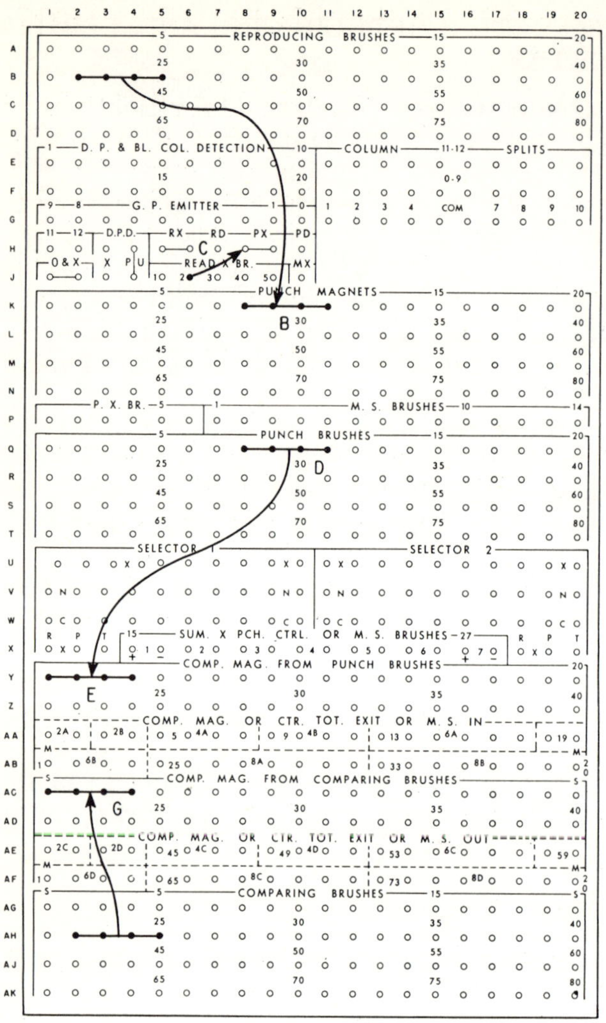

Fig. 6-27. Wiring for selective reproducing operation with comparing

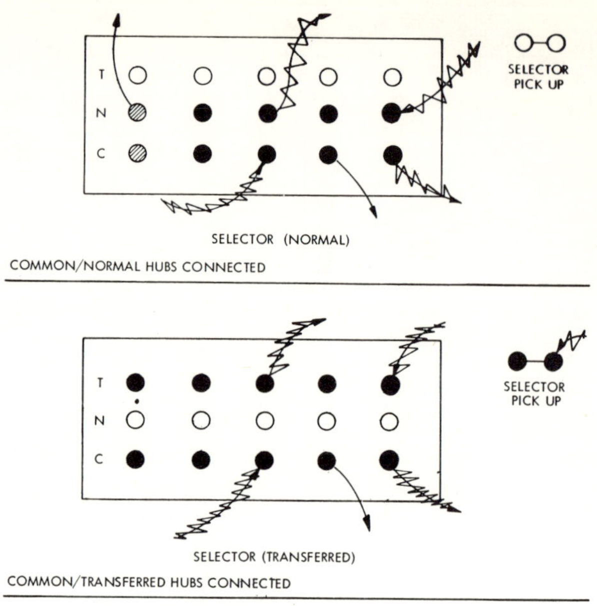

Fig. 6-28. Selectors (normal and transferred) (Courtesy of International Business Machines.)

1-3 and X, 18-20. When one of these hubs is impulsed, the entire corresponding selector is transferred (Fig. 6-28). The T hub is used in conjunction with summary punching and will not be discussed in this section.

The PX pickup hub should be used if the selector must hold for a punching-unit card cycle. This hub may be impulsed from the PX, PD, or one of the PX brush hubs. The RX pickup hub should be used if the selector must hold for a reading-unit card cycle. This hub may be impulsed from the RX, RD, or one of the RX brush hubs.

As on the 548 Interpreter, we are concerned with field and class selection. On the 548 Interpreter, we were concerned with printing one of two fields in one place or printing one field in one of two places. On the 514 Reproducer we have the same problem, except now we want to punch rather than print.

FIELD-SELECTED REPRODUCING

It is sometimes necessary to select information from one of two punched fields in source cards and reproduce the selected field into a single field in the reproduced cards. This operation is called *field-selected reproducing.*

An example of this operation can be found in payroll, where it is necessary to reproduce attendance cards from the master payroll file. Two hourly rates are punched in the employee master card - a first-shift rate and a second-shift rate. Second-shift cards are identified by an X-punch code (Fig. 6-29).

An example of the wiring necessary to accomplish the above is illustrated in Fig. 6-30. This figure illustrates straight, offset, and field-selected reproducing.

Now we shall see how we would verify on the same pass (Fig. 6-31).

In Fig. 6-30 you could also wire from Read X Brush 3 directly to R PU.

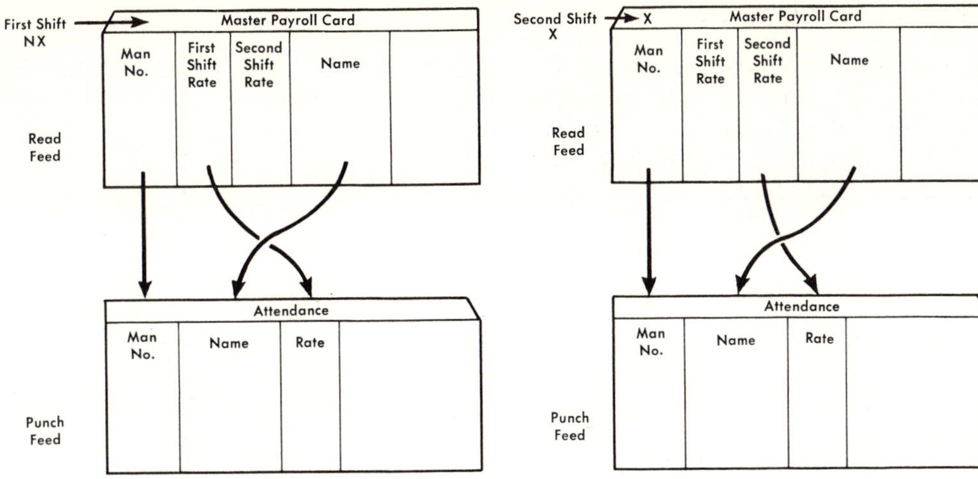

Fig. 6-29. Field-selected reproducing (Courtesy of International Business Machines.)

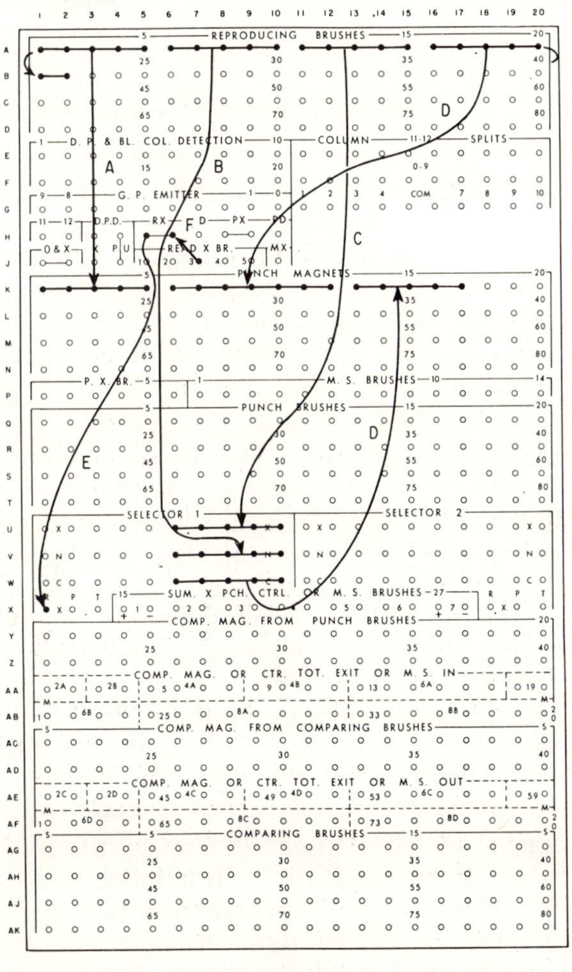

Fig. 6-30. Wiring for field-selected reproducing

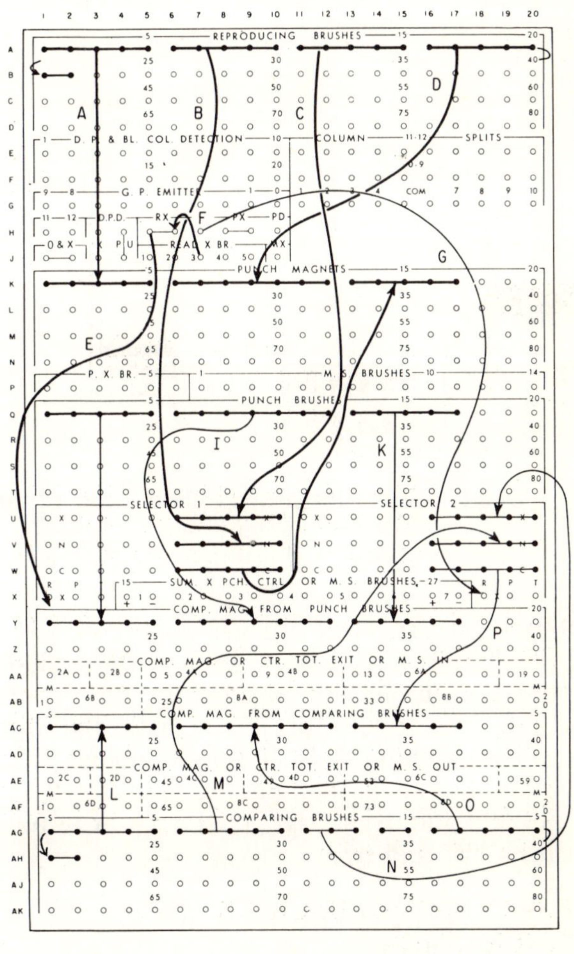

Fig. 6-31. Wiring for field-selected reproducing and verification

CLASS SELECTED REPRODUCING

In class selection we always read one field and punch into one of two possible fields, depending on whether the source card is an X or NX card (Fig. 6-32). We have the same considerations in verifying class selection as in field selection (Fig. 6-33). The reproduce switch is on for selected reproducing.

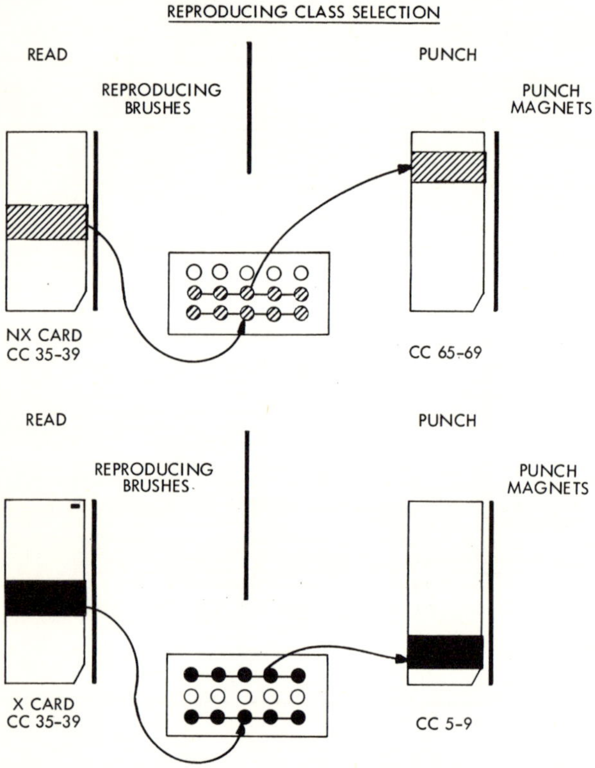

Fig. 6-32. Schematic of reproducing class selection (Courtesy of International Business Machines.)

PROBLEM 11: Wire for class selected reproducing and verification. Reproduce card columns 35 to 39 into card columns 65 to 69 for NX cards and into card columns 5 to 9 for X cards. Use read X hub 5, comparing magnets 21 to 25 and the first five positions of selectors one and two.

OFFSET GANGPUNCHING AND VERIFICATION

Offset gangpunching and verification are the last functions of the 514 to be explained.

In our discussions of straight gangpunching and interspersed gangpunching, the information read from the master card was located in the same card columns as the gangpunched information in the detail cards. We called this ***column - for - column gangpunching.*** Most jobs using gangpunching (straight or interspersed) are done this way. Whenever it is possible, cards are designed so that common information falls in the same fields in all of the cards involved. This is not only to make gangpunching more convenient, but also to make card handling, in general, more efficient.

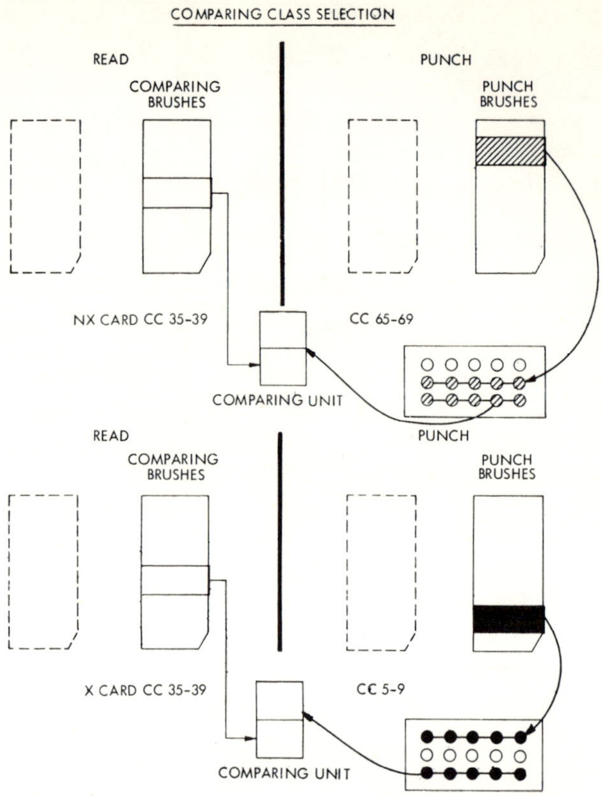

Fig. 6-33. Schematic of comparing class selection (Courtesy of International Business Machines.)

Offset gangpunching accommodates gangpunching common information in which the card fields are not the same in the detail cards as in the masters (Fig. 6-34).

In the production cards shown, the master job cards contain the job number and the order number. This information is common to all the job tickets used as the production pieces move through the plant. But in some instances, problems of card design make it impossible to use the same card fields for the order number. Therefore, when job number and order number are gangpunched from the master cards into the job tickets, order number must be offset from columns 61 to 70 in the masters to columns 71 to 80 in the detail cards.

The master card feeds in first. No punching takes place. Then the punch brushes read columns 1 to 10 (job number) and punch into columns 1 to 10 in the next card which is a detail card. Simultaneously, the punch brushes read columns 61 to 70 (order number) in the master card and punch into columns 71 to 80 of the detail card.

The cards move one station, and the first detail card is now at the punch-brush station; the second detail card is at the punch station. The punch brushes can read columns 1 to 10 just as they did with the first card, but there is no punching in columns 61 to 70 as there was before. Now the information is in columns 71 to 80. This is the problem of offset gangpunching, and it requires the use of selectors to handle it. A selector group must be used to pick up the proper field. A second selector group must be used to check the gangpunching. The wiring to accomplish the above example can be seen in Fig. 6-35.

When just offset gangpunching, all switches are off; but if we are verifying at the same time, the SEL REPD and GP comp switch is on.

PROBLEM 12: Wire the diagram to accomplish the following offset gangpunching and verification. The master gangpunch card had the data that is to be gangpunched in columns 45 to 48. It is to be gangpunched back into columns 52 to 55. Use the last four positions of selector one for the gangpunching and the last four positions of selector two for the verification. Use PX brush hub 2 and RX brush hub 2. Use comparing magnets 1 to 4.

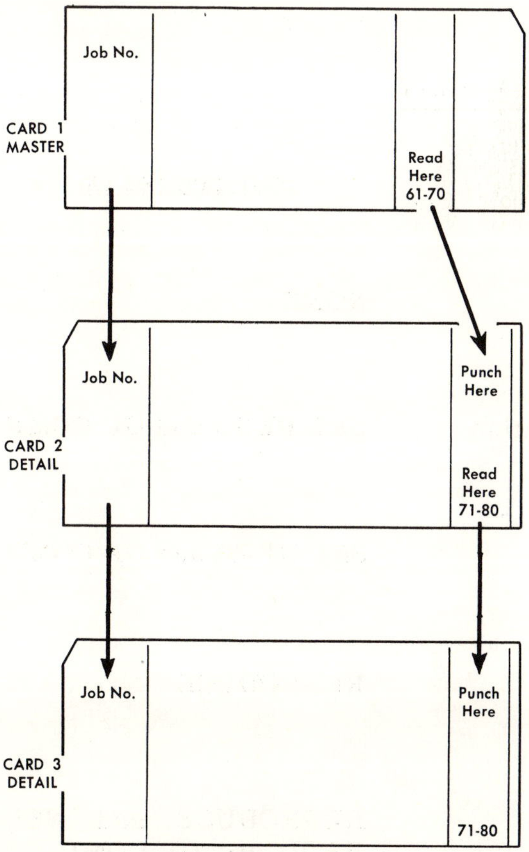

Fig. 6-34. Offset gangpunching (Courtesy of International Business Machines.)

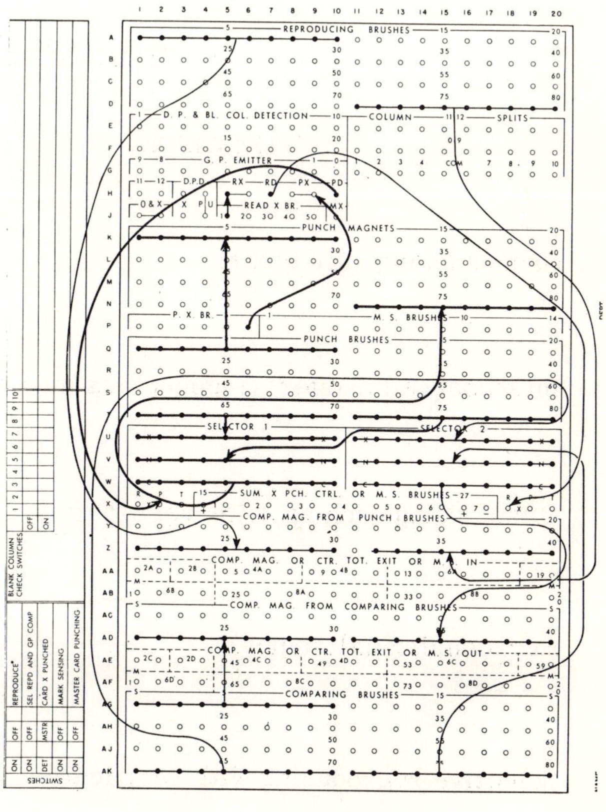

Fig. 6-35. Wiring for offset gangpunching and verification

SUMMARY OF PX HUB FUNCTIONS

Depending on the setting of the detail master switch, the PX Hub is effected for NX or X cards in the following ways:

Inoperative	When	Operation Being Performed	Prevents
Punch magnets	X or NX master gang-punch cards are under the punch dies	Interspersed master gang-punching	Punching into the master gangpunch cards
Read unit card feed	X or NX master gang-punch cards are under the punch dies	Combined reproducing and gangpunching	Punching into the master gangpunch cards
Comparing circuitry	One cycle later when the X or NX card is under the comparing brushes	Selective reproducing and verification	Comparing the blank card at the punch brushes with the non-reproduced card at the comparing brushes

SWITCH SETTING SUMMARY

Operation	Switches Set On
Gangpunching (all types)	NONE
Interspersed master gangpunching with verification	SEL REPD and GP COMP
Offset gangpunching with verification	SEL REPD and GP COMP
Reproducing (all types)	REPRODUCE
Selective reproducing with verification	REPRODUCE and SEL REPD and GP COMP
Combined reproducing and gangpunching	REPRODUCE

SUMMARY OF REPRODUCE AND SEL REPD AND GP COMP SWITCHES

SWITCH	CONDITION	HUB IMPULSED	EFFECT
REPRODUCE	ON	PX	No comparing on the following cycle. Synchronizes the reading and punching feeds.
	OFF	RX	No comparing on the same cycle. Two feeds operated independently to perform separate operations or when only one feed is used.
SEL REPD AND GP COMP	ON	NONE	Allows continuous feeding in the reading unit.
	OFF	PX	The feeding in the reading unit will stop on the same card cycle, while a card is fed in the punching unit.

SUMMARY OF MASTER-DETAIL SWITCH

SWITCH	PX HUB	FUNCTION INOPERATIVE	WHEN THE
MASTER	Impulsed by X	Punching in the same cycle	X card is under the punch dies or the reproducing brushes.
		Comparing on the following cycle	X card is under the comparing brushes or under the punch brushes.
		Read unit for the same cycle	X card is under the punch dies or under the reproducing brushes.
DETAIL	Not impulsed by X	Punching on the same cycle	NX card is under the punch dies or under the reproducing brushes.
		Comparing on the following cycle	NX card is under the comparing brushes or under the punch brushes.
		Read unit for the same cycle	NX card is under the punch dies or under the reproducing brushes.

SUMMARY OF THE RX AND PX HUB FUNCTIONS

Depending on the setting of the detail master switch, the PX and the RX hubs are effected for NX or X cards in the following ways:

Hub	Inoperative	When	Operation Being Performed	Prevents
PX	Punch magnets on the same cycle	X or NX master gangpunch cards are under the punch dies	Interspersed master gangpunching or selective reproducing	Punching into the master gangpunch cards
	Read unit card feed if the SEL REPD GP COMP switch is off[1]	X or NX master gangpunch cards are under the punch dies	Combined reproducing and interspersed master gangpunching	The source card from being fed and therefore ***not*** being reproduced
	Comparing circuitry on the following cycle if the reproduce switch is on[2]	One cycle later when the X or NX card is under the comparing brushes	Selective reproducing	Comparing the blank card at the punch brushes with the nonreproduced card at the comparing brushes
RX[3]	Comparing circuitry on the same cycle if the reproduce switch is off and the SEL REPD GP COMP switch is on[4]	X or NX master card is under the reproducing brushes and the preceding card is under the comparing brushes	Verification of offset or interspersed master gangpunching	Comparing the card at the comparing brushes with the card at the reproducing brushes

1 The feeds would operate independently if the SEL REPD GP COMP switch was on.

2 If the Reproduce Switch was off, the feeds would not operate together and comparing would be inoperative on the same cycle.

3 The RX hub is impulsed in order to obtain an impulse from the RD hub on the following cycle for field or class selection.

4 If the SEL REPD GP COMP switch was off during verification, the read unit would be stopped for one cycle.

514 Reproducer Questions

Fill in blank spaces

1. The X reading brushes on the 514 are used to read X cards in the __________ unit.
2. Excluding X-brushes, there are ______ (give the number) reading stations on the 514.
3. The 514 and 402 are connected by cable for the operation known as __________.
4. Cards can be reproduced in four ways - straight reproducing, __________ reproducing, __________ reproducing, and ________ reproducing.
5. Assume card columns 50 to 56 are to be reproduced in card columns 70 to 76, and comparing magnets 30 to 36 are to be used. What card columns would be wired to compare magnets from punch brushes?
6. On a 514 Reproducer column splits are frequently used in an operation known as __________.
7. In a gangpunching operation wires must connect the __________ with the __________ (name of the stations connected).
8. In interspersed master gangpunching you want to prevent gangpunching from the last __________ card into the __________ card.
9. The comparing indicator denotes the __________ in which the error was detected.
10. Cards are fed ____ edge, face ______.
11. If it takes 10 minutes to reproduce 1,000 cards that have 80 columns of punched data, it takes ____ minutes to reproduce 1,000 cards that have 40 columns of punched data.
12. The selectors on a 514 are internally wired so that normal and common are connected when __________.
13. The selectors on a 514 are internally wired so that normal and transferred are connected when __________.
14. If the PX hub is impulsed, the impulse is available one cycle later from the __________ hub.
15. Draw a schematic diagram of the 514 Reproducer (label all stations).

Multiple choice

16. In Fig. P6-1 RX brush 1 is over card column 80. Card columns 41 to 45 will be punched in
    a. card columns 67 to 71 for all X80 cards, card columns 44 to 48 for all NX cards.
    b. card columns 44 to 48 for all X80 cards, card columns 67 to 71 for all NX80 cards.
    c. card columns 67 to 71 for all cards.
    d. card columns 44 to 48 for all cards.
17. What will punch in card column 17?
18. In Fig. P6-2, RX brush 1 is on card column 75. Card columns 50 to 53 will be reproduced in card columns 55 to 58 for
    a. all cards.
    b. all X75 cards.
    c. the card following an X75 card.
    d. all NX75 cards.
19. In Fig. P6-3 operation is to reproduce card columns 30 to 34 into card columns 35 to 39. Which numbered wire is incorrect?
    a. 1
    b. 2
    c. 3
    d. 4
20. What will punch in card column 25?

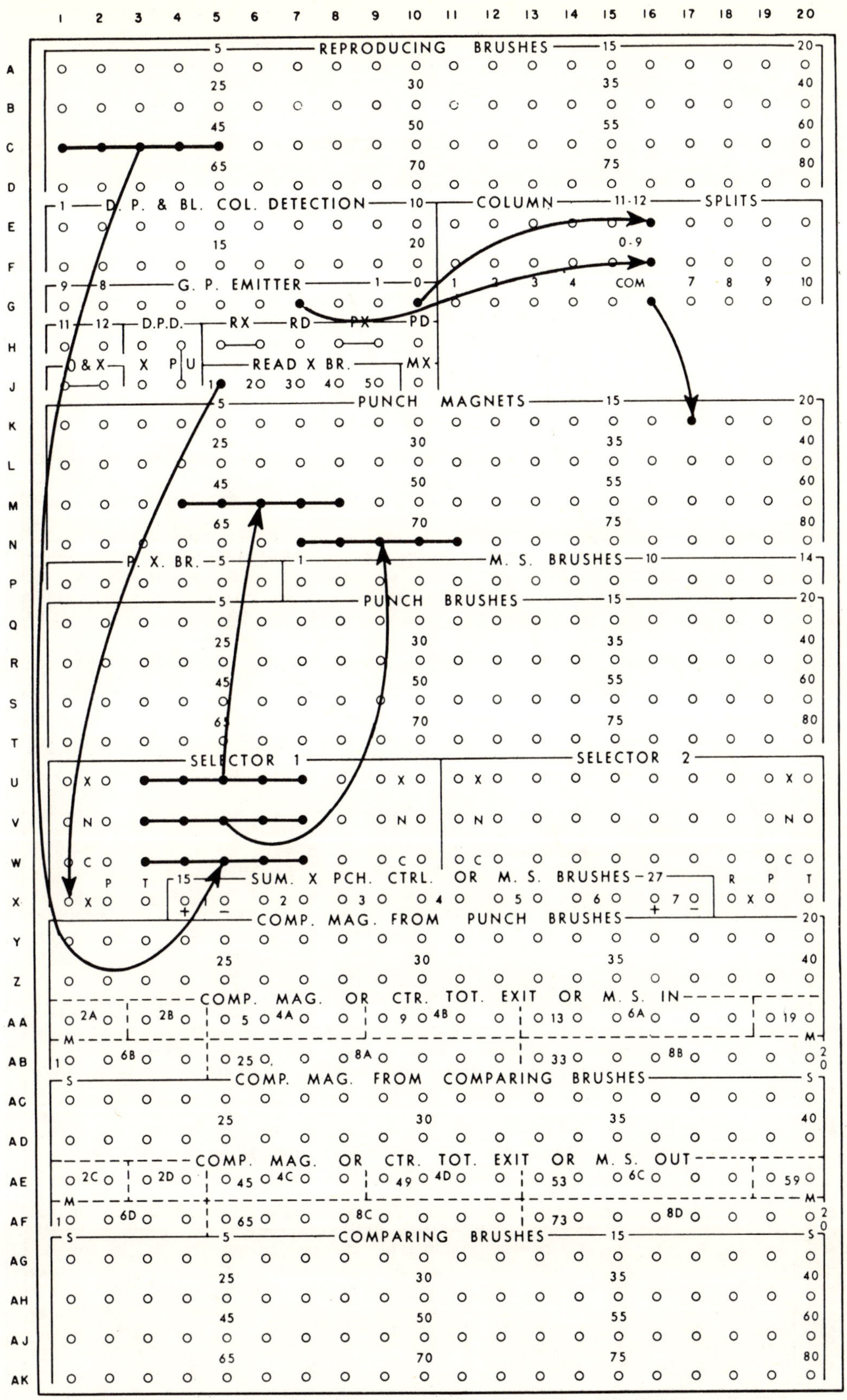

Fig. p6-1 (Courtesy of International Business Machines.)

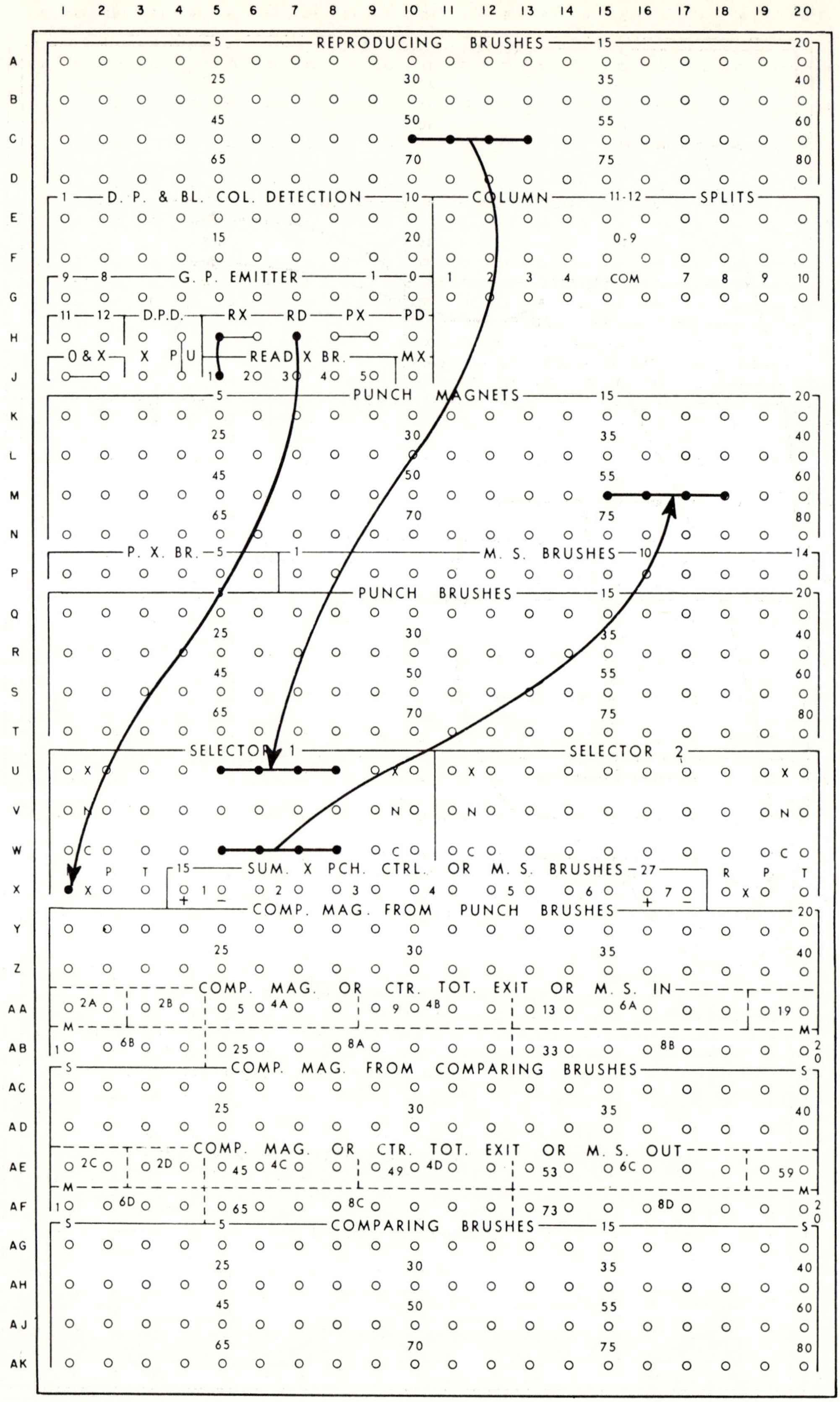

Fig. p6-2 (Courtesy of International Business Machines.)

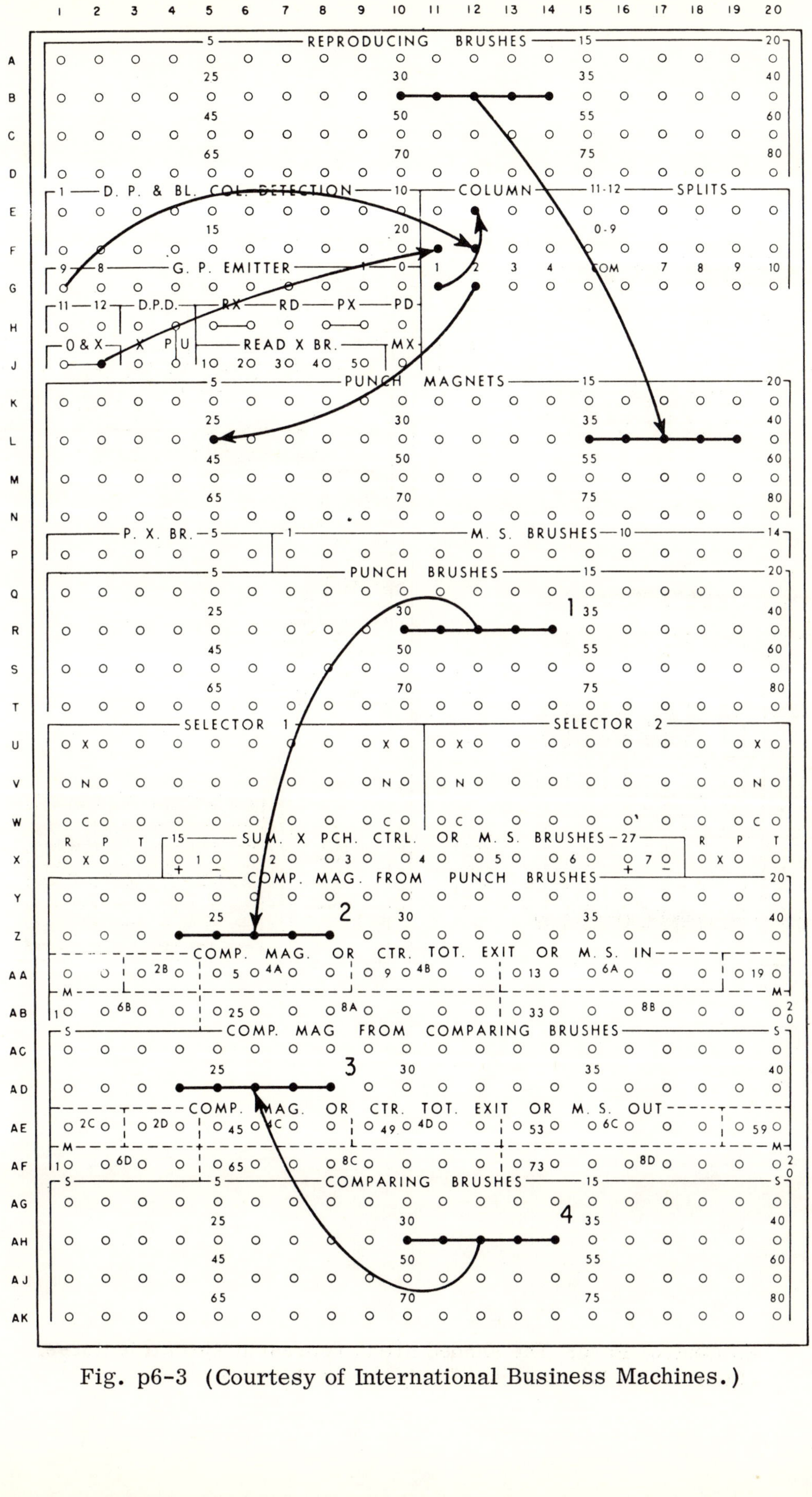

Fig. p6-3 (Courtesy of International Business Machines.)

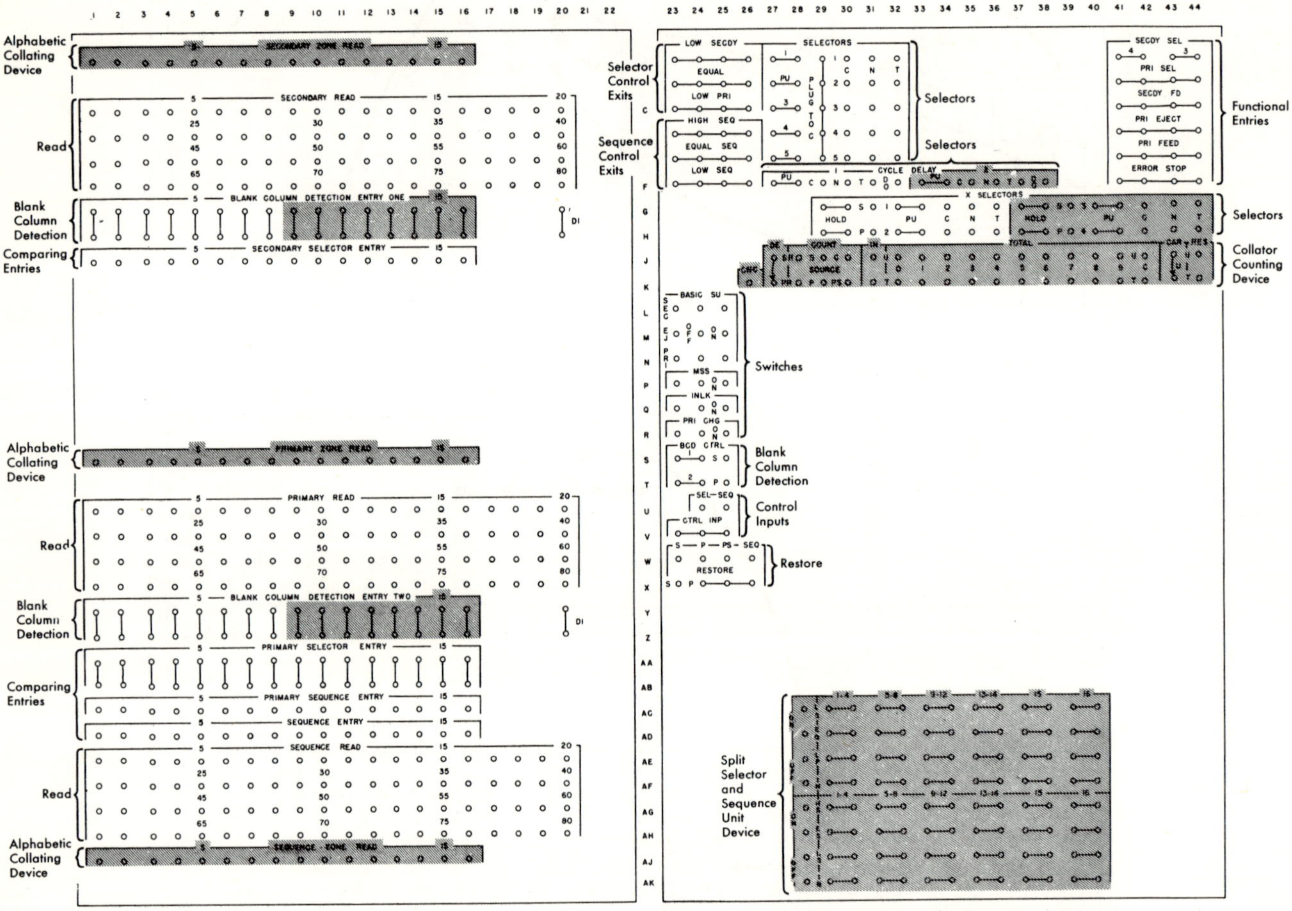

85 Control Panel. The shaded areas represent special features. (Courtesy of International Business Machines.)

Section 7

THE 85 COLLATOR

The IBM 85 Collator is a filing machine that arranges cards into a predetermined pattern for subsequent processing (Fig. 7-1). The function of the collator is to feed and

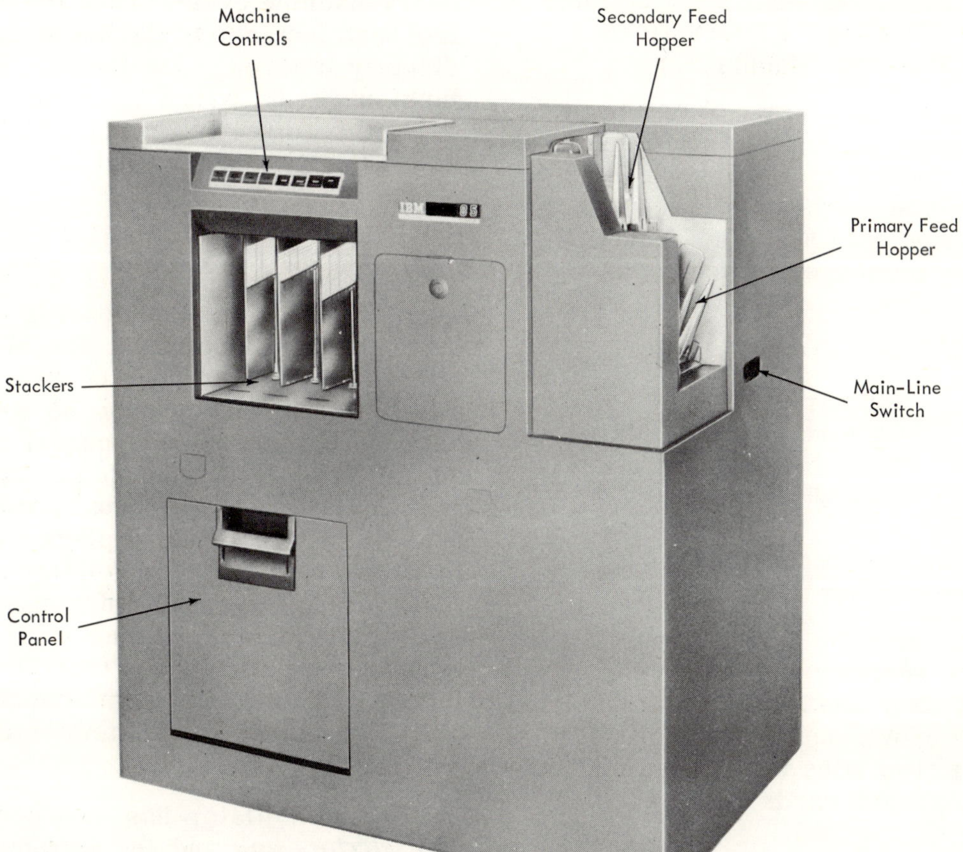

Fig. 7-1. IBM 85 Collator (Courtesy of International Business Machines.)

compare two files of punched cards simultaneously and match and combine them into one file.

The two card-feed hoppers, which hold about 800 cards each, are called the ***primary-*** and ***secondary - feed hoppers.*** Unlike the previous machines we have covered, the feed hoppers of the collator must be impulsed by control-panel wiring to cause card feeding. Cards are fed 9-edge first, face down, at a maximum rate of 240 cpm per feed. The cards from the two feeds, the primary and secondary (Fig. 7-2), feed

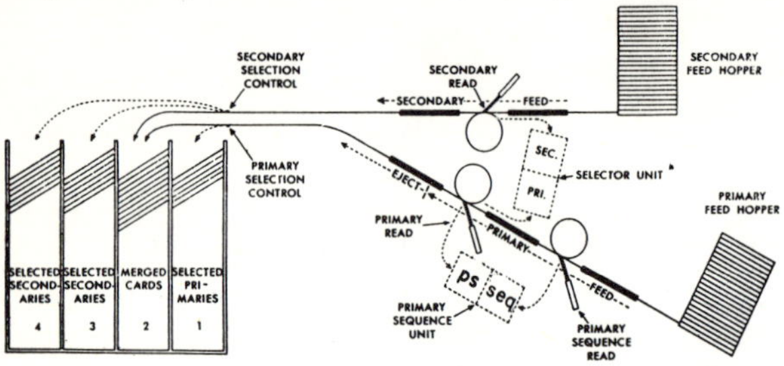

Fig. 7-2. Schematic of IBM 85 Collator (Courtesy of International Business Machines.)

into four stacker pockets. These pockets are numbered 1, 2, 3, and 4 from right to left. Each stacker is capable of holding about a thousand cards before causing the machine to stop feeding. The pockets can receive cards from specific feeds only:

Pocket	Feed
1	Primary
2	Primary and Secondary
3	Secondary
4	Secondary

The four basic operations that can be performed on the collator are:

1. ***selecting*** specific cards from a file
2. ***sequence checking*** the cards in a file
3. ***merging*** two files into one complete file with or without selection
4. ***matching*** two files while selecting out any unmatched cards from each file.

OPERATING FEATURES

The main-line switch controls the machine's power and must be turned on before operating.

When the stop key is pressed, card feeding is stopped. When the last card is fed from either hopper, the machine stops. Then the run-out key must be pressed until the feed is emptied of cards. The red error light goes on whenever control-panel wiring recognizes an error; then the error reset key must be pressed before card reading can be restarted. A green running indicator light goes on whenever the main-line switch is on and cards are not passing through the machine. The start key starts card feeding and must be held down for three cycles before automatic operation begins.

There are several sets of hubs that need explanation before we can pursue the functions of the collator.

PLUG TO C: A-E, 29

The first of these sets of hubs are the five common hubs which emit an impulse on every machine cycle. They are used to control card feeding and stacker selection either directly or through a selector. PLUG TO C must never be wired to error stop (F, 41-44) either directly or via a selector, because it will cause a card jam.

COMPARING

The comparing units of the 85 follow a logic similar to the comparing magnets on the 514 Reproducer. On the 514 we were interested only in one of two conditions equal or unequal. On the 85 we are concerned with equal and unequal conditions, and additionally with which comparing unit is high or low on an unequal condition. Because of this, comparing plays a major part in the operations of the collator.

In filing operations, information is compared with other information to determine its proper relationship. Therefore in a collating machine, the first requisite is the ability to compare one item of information with another.

The 85 Collator has two control units, the ***selector unit*** and the ***primary - sequence unit*** (Fig. 7-2). Although they are alike in function, each is named according to its primary operation - primary-sequence unit for comparing card sequence in the primary

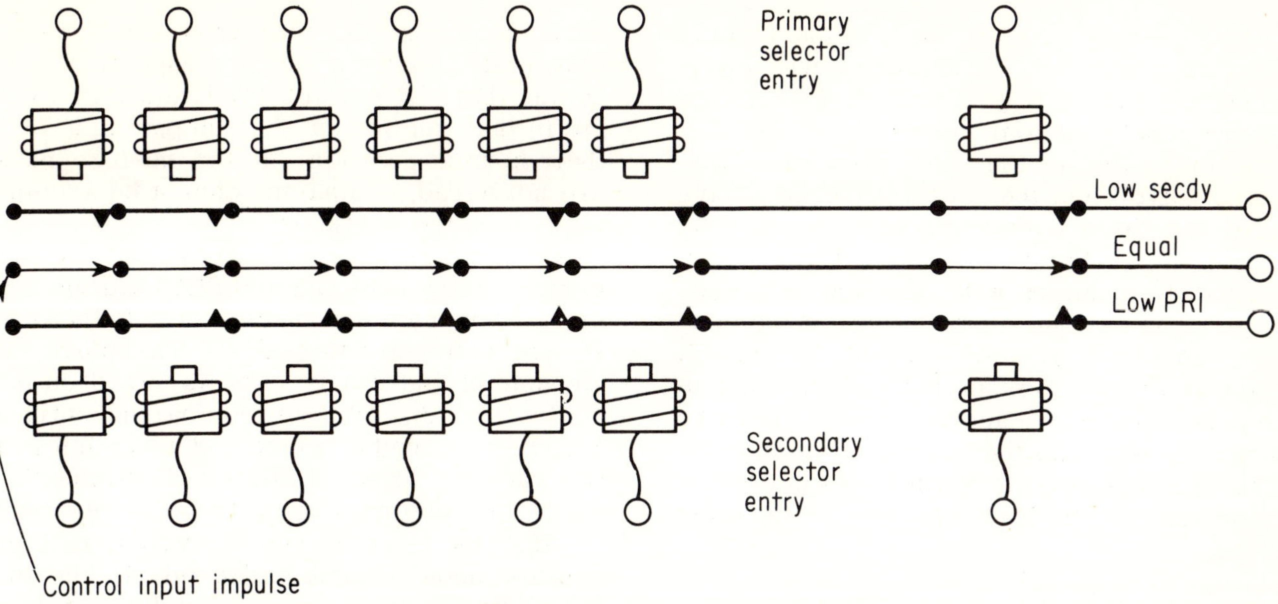

Fig. 7-3. Schematic of Selector Comparing Unit
(Courtesy of International Business Machines.)

feed and the selector unit for comparing cards between the feeds. Each control unit has two sections, which records one piece of numeric data and compares it with numeric information in the other section. The Selector Comparing Unit (Fig. 7-3) consists of the Primary Selector Entry (AA-AB, 1-16) and the Secondary Selector Entry (J, 1-16). The Sequence Comparing Unit (Fig. 7-4) consists of the primary-sequence entry (AC, 1-16) and the sequence entry (AD, 1-16).

CONTROL EXIT HUBS

The comparing units of the collator are capable of determining three types of conditions - equal, low, or high. This is ac-

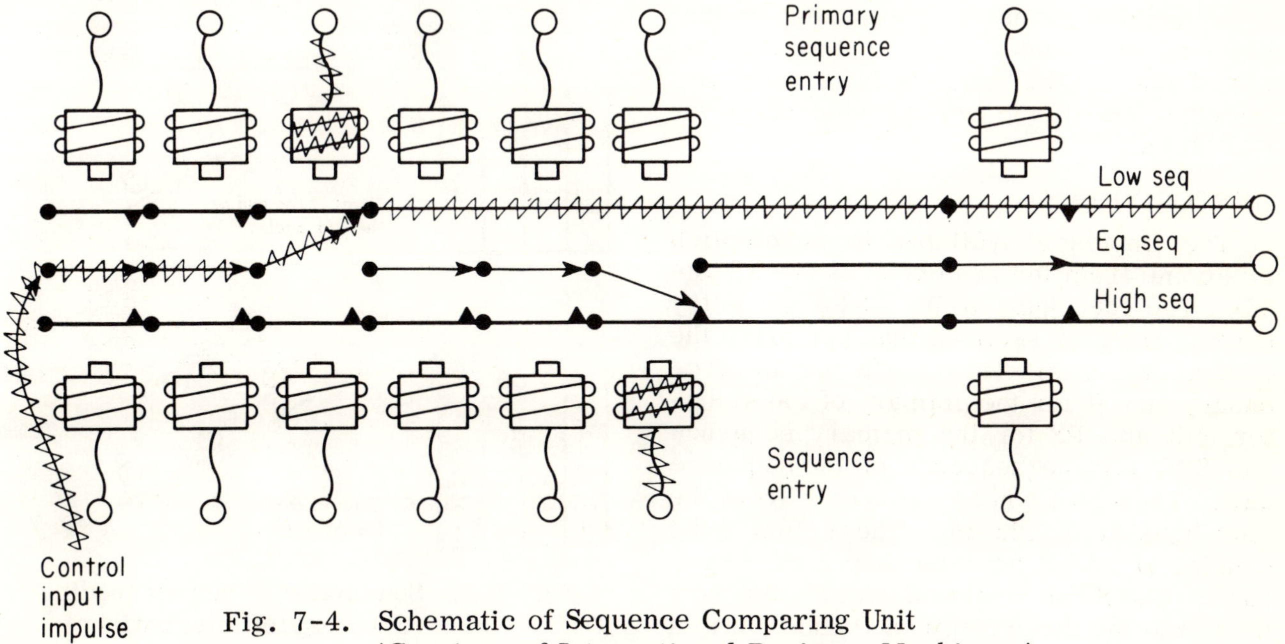

Fig. 7-4. Schematic of Sequence Comparing Unit
(Courtesy of International Business Machines.)

complished by sending an impulse through the comparing unit. This impulse will travel along any available path until it gets to one of the functional exit hubs (Fig. 7-4). You will notice that in Fig. 7-4, the control impulse travels via the equal-sequence relays until the third comparing position. At the third comparing position, the relay is transferred to connect with the low-sequence path. The exit hubs which emit these control impulses are situated at V, 23-25. They are three common hubs which emit an impulse on every machine cycle. They are normally wired to the hubs at U, 24 and 25. The SEL and SEQ entry hubs accept control impulses to their respective comparing units.

CONTROL EXITS

The control exits depicted in Figs. 7-3 and 7-4 are found on the control panel at A-F, 23-26. The first three sets of common hubs are control exit hubs for the three possible resulting conditions from the selector unit. The next three sets of common hubs (D-F, 23-26) are control exit hubs for the three possible resulting conditions from the sequence unit.

The control exit impulses are wired to the functional entries (A-F, 41-44) to perform functions such as card feeding, stacker selecting, and error stopping.

An impulse is necessary to restore the relays to their center position after the relays of one of the magnets have been attracted to one of the two opposing magnets (Fig. 7-4).

RESTORE HUBS

The impulses available to accomplish this come from the restore hubs (W-X, 23-26). The four hubs at W, 23-26 are entry hubs to the four sections that comprise the comparing units. They are S for the secondary and P for the primary of the selector unit and PS for the primary sequence and SEQ for the sequence of the sequence unit. These four hubs are wired from the four hubs at X, 23-26. These four hubs consist of one S hub and three common P hubs. The S hub emits on every secondary feed, and the three common P hubs emit on every primary feed. When these hubs are wired to any of the four hubs above them, they emit impulses on the respective feed cycles that will restore any transferred relay in that section of the comparing unit to their normal position. If the restore hubs are not wired, comparing cannot be accomplished on the next card.

On the first two ***run-in*** cycles, the two restore entry hubs (PS and SEQ) and the restore entry hubs for the selector unit (S and P) are common internally. Therefore, if any one of these four hubs is wired on the control panel, all four comparing entries will be restored (cleared and read-into) on the run-in. This initializes all comparing units for the operation to be performed.

After the first two run-in cycles, all four restore hubs become independent, and the comparing entries are restored separately according to the control-panel wiring.

In Fig. 7-5 on the first cycle (A), one card is fed from the primary feed hopper

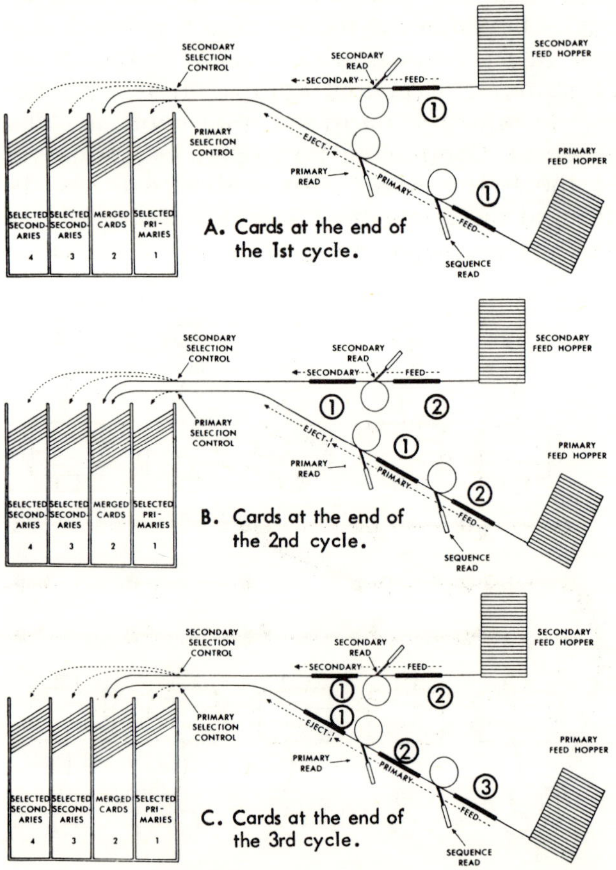

Fig. 7-5. Schematic of run-in feeding (Courtesy of International Buriness Machines.)

and one from the secondary feed hopper; on the second cycle (B), a second card is fed from each hopper; and on the third cycle (C), a third card is fed from the primary feed hopper. The secondary feeding is normally inoperative, but can be made operative by control panel wiring.

BLANK-COLUMN DETECTION

Next are the blank-column-detection hubs (G-H, 1-8 and Y-Z, 1-8). The machine comes equipped with two eight-position groups, but you can add two more groups of eight positions each. These hubs are used to check cards in either feed for blank columns. Card feeding stops and a blank-column-detection light (BCD 1 or BCD 2) turns on, if a blank column is detected. The BCD light can be turned off and card feeding resumed by first pressing the reset key and then the start key. The error card will then be the next card stacked from the feed containing the blank column. This operation can be performed separately but is normally performed in combination with other operations.

BLANK-COLUMN-DETECTION CONTROL

The blank-column-detection hubs are not operative unless their corresponding blank-column-detection-control hubs (S-T, 23-25) are wired (Fig. 7-6, wire 5). The control-

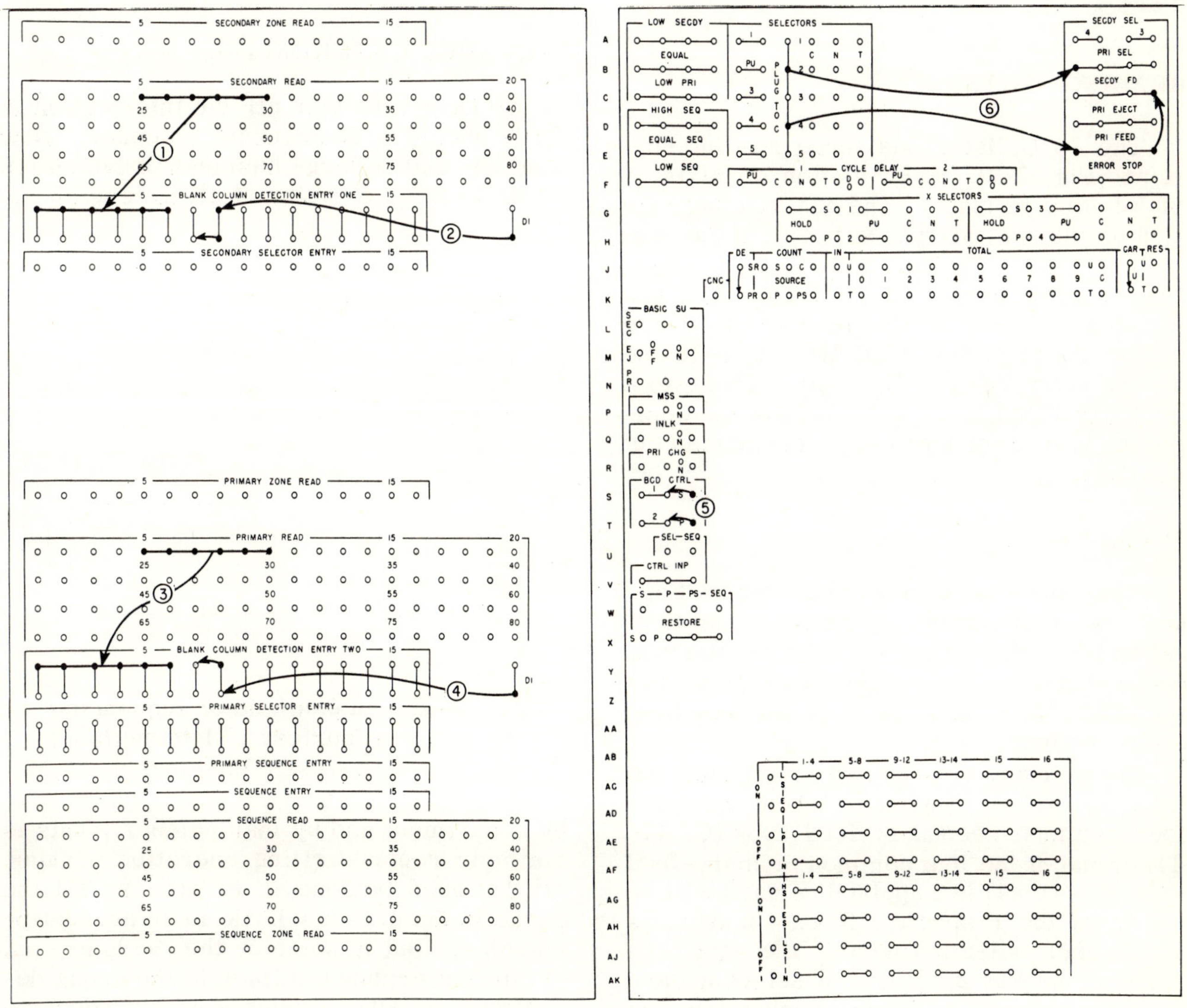

Fig. 7-6. Blank-column detection (both feeds)
(Courtesy of International Business Machines.)

entry hubs are normally wired from either the S or P hubs. The S hub emits an impulse to hold a unit between secondary feed cycles, and the P hub emits an impulse to hold a unit between primary feed cycles. The S and P hubs are both wired to control blank-column-detection-entry 1 and/or 2 to check 16 columns.

DIRECT IMPULSE

The DI hubs (G-H, 20; Y-Z, 20) provide an impulse to unused blank-column-detection entry hubs, thereby preventing the machine from stopping because of a false blank-column indication as shown in Fig. 7-6 by wires 2 and 4.

READING STATIONS

The 85 Collator has three reading stations (Fig. 7-2). Each station consists of 80 reading brushes. The one reading station on the secondary feed is called the secondary read. The exit hubs of these reading brushes are at B-F, 1-20. The two reading stations on the primary feed are called the sequence read AD-AH, 1-20 and the primary read U-X, 1-20. These exit hubs are wired to the entry hubs of the comparing unit, in order to make comparison of the data.

POCKETS

It has been pointed out that the 85 Collator has four pockets or stackers and that cards from the primary feed can stack in pockets one or two, while cards from the secondary feed can stack in pockets two, three, or four.

The primary or secondary feed must be impulsed to feed by wiring. When one of the four common secondary-feed hubs (C, 41-44) or one of the four common primary-feed hubs (E, 41-44) is impulsed, a card will be fed from the respective feeds. If there is no stacker selection wired, the card will stack in pocket 2. You can select a card from the secondary feed into pocket 4 by impulsing one of the two common secondary select 4 hubs (A, 41-42); or you can select a card from the secondary feed into pocket 3 by impulsing one of the two common secondary select 3 hubs (A, 43-44). You can select a card from the primary feed into pocket 1 by impulsing one of the four common primary select hubs (B, 41-44).

SELECTORS: A-E, 27-32

These five horizontal selectors consist of PU, C, N, and T hubs. They function exactly like the vertical selectors encountered on the 548 and 514. When the PU hub is impulsed, the internal connection between C and N is broken and an internal connection between C and T is established.

SEQUENCE CHECKING (Fig. 7-7)

We have said that all the information in a file should be in accurate sequence. Now suppose that a large business organization wants to print a roster of all its employees

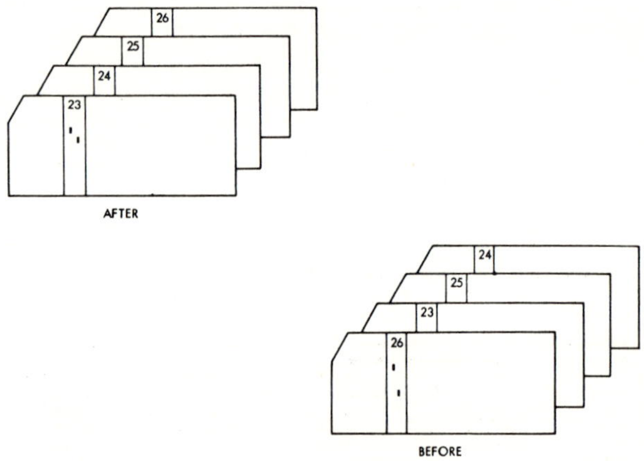

Fig. 7-7. An example of sequencing (Courtesy of International Business Machines.)

by department and by man number. This is a simple report-writing operation because all that need be done is to process all the cards in the personnel file in an accounting machine. But if some of the cards are out of correct sequence (either in the wrong department or out of sequence within a department), it might be necessary to rewrite the entire roster report. It is economically justifiable to check the accuracy of the sequence in the file.

THE PRINCIPLE

As cards pass through the machine, the collator compares each card with the previous one. Since checking sequence is normally done for ascending order, an error in sequence is defined as a step-down condition in which a card is recognized as lower in number than the preceding card. An impulse, through control-panel wiring, normally stops card feeding and turns on the error light.

Obviously, there should be no equals or an employee number is duplicated. If the machine recognizes a low situation, a card is out of sequence, and it should be brought to the attention of the operator in some way. If the machine recognizes a high situation, it is perfectly all right, and the operation should proceed.

The employee cards feed from the primary hopper into the machine. When the first employee card reaches the primary read station, the second employee card is at the primary sequence station (Fig. 7-8). The collator compares the two cards. The second employee number (for example, 10468) is higher than the first employee number (09363). The collator recognizes this and proceeds. The first employee card goes into a stacker pocket; the next employee card moves to the primary-read station; and a third employee card in the hopper moves to the primary-sequence station.

Now the situation is different. The third employee number (10112) is lower than the previous employee number (10468). Obviously, it is out of numerical sequence. But the operator instructed the machine (by control-panel wiring) to stop and flash a red signal whenever comparison showed anything other than a high situation; so the machine stops and an error light goes on. Now the account clerk can remove the cards from the machine, locate the error, and place the misfiled card in its proper position.

When cards are run out for a sequence-error condition, the step-down card is the second one run out. However, this card

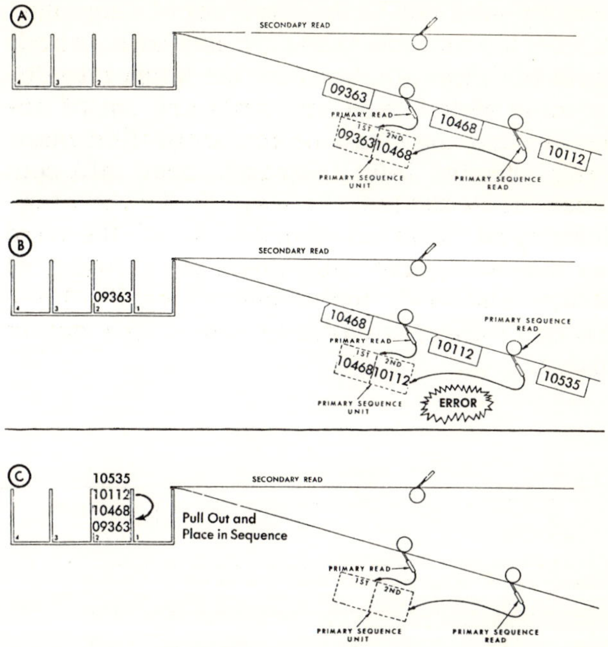

Fig. 7-8. Schematic of sequence checking (Courtesy of International Business Machines.)

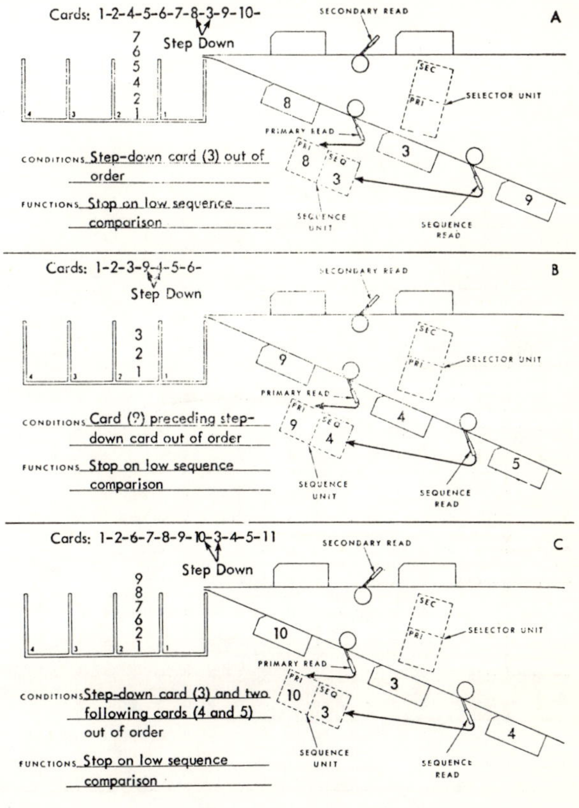

Fig. 7-9. Types of sequence errors (Courtesy of International Business Machines.)

may or may not be the card out of sequence. A check must be made of several cards from both the stacker and the hopper to determine which card or cards are out of order so that they can be properly filed manually. Figure 7-9 illustrates three different types of sequence errors: In A, the step-down card (3) is out of order; in B, the card (9) preceding the step-down card is out of order; and in C, the step-down card (3) and the two following cards (4 and 5) are out of order.

Now let's see how you would wire a panel to sequence check a file on card columns 41 to 45 (Fig. 7-10) and to error stop on low sequence. Notice several things. Only BCD CTRL 2 is wired from the P hub because we are using only the primary feed. The control impulse is wired to the sequence unit only, since the selector unit is not used for sequence checking. For the same reason, the restore hubs to the primary sequence entries and the sequence entries are wired from the P common hubs. The DI hub for

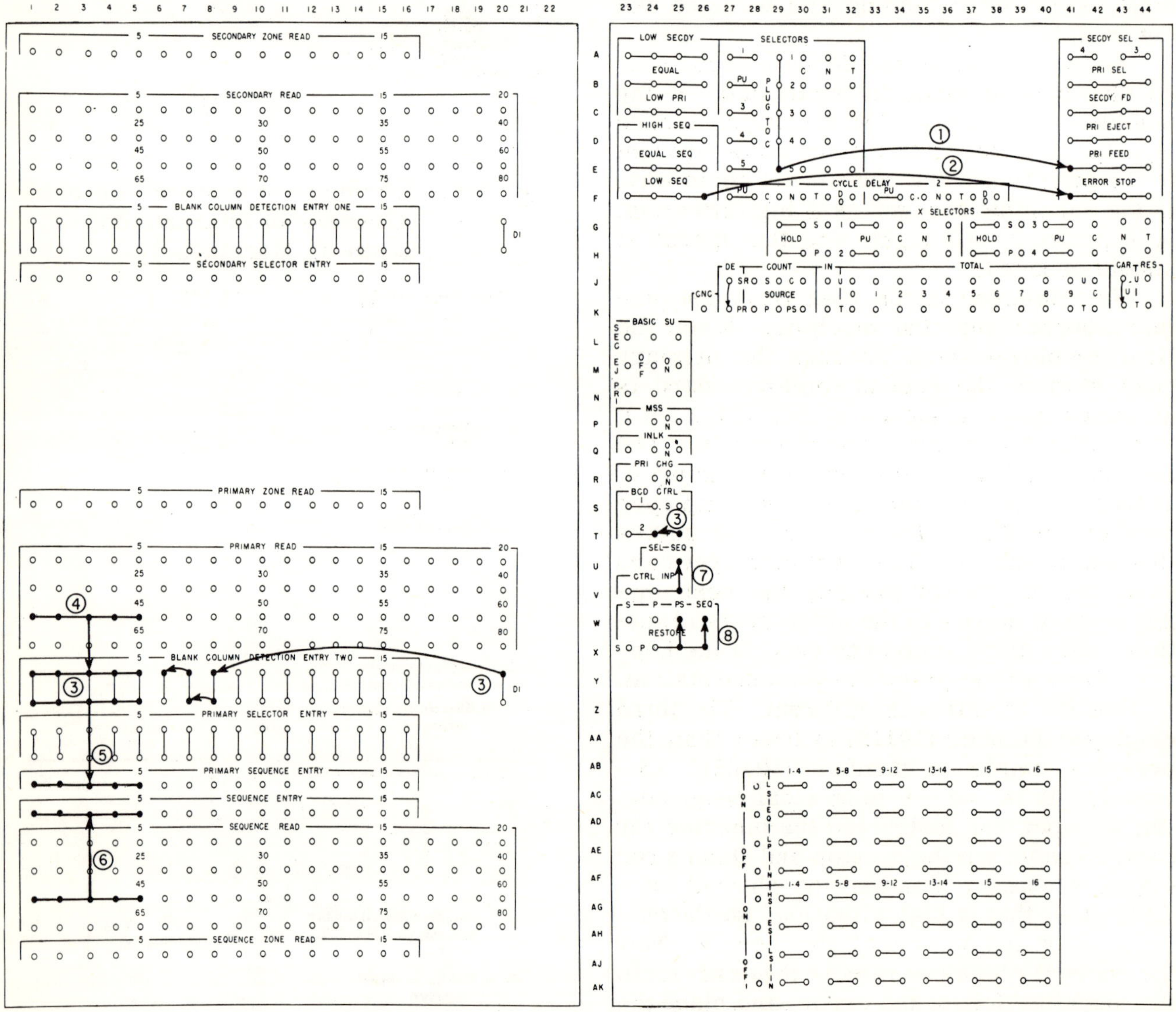

Fig. 7-10. Wiring for sequence checking (Courtesy of International Business Machines.)

blank column detection is necessary because not all eight positions are being used. The primary feed will feed a card on every machine cycle because it is being impulsed by Plug to C. The equal and high sequence cards will stack in pocket 2 because primary select is not wired. Low-sequence cards will cause an error stop.

ERROR INSTRUCTIONS

This, then, is sequence checking. The collator verifies the desired sequence of a file of cards. Whenever it encounters an out-of-sequence condition, the machine follows the instructions set up by control-panel wiring.

1. It can stop the machine and flash an error light. The operator can then rearrange the sequence properly.
2. It can insert a signal card at the place where the out-of-sequence condition occurred and continue sequence checking (Fig. 7-11). This is a faster method because the machine does not stop. The operator can correct the out-of-sequence condition while the machine continues to run. The signal card can have a distinctive color or a corner cut different from the corner cut on the file cards.

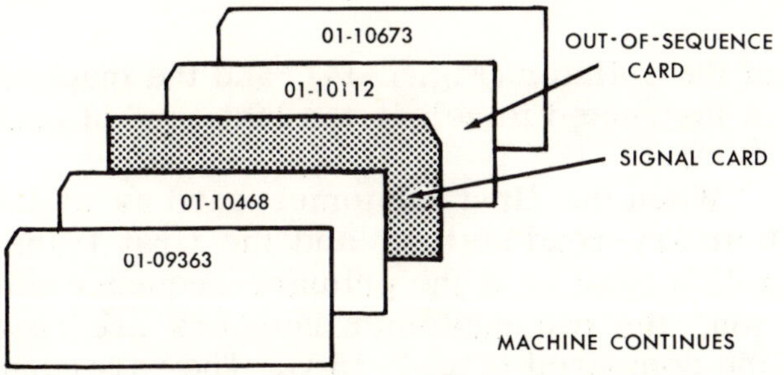

Fig. 7-11. Inserting signal card for sequence error (Courtesy of International Businesss Machines.)

3. The machine can select out-of-position cards and feed them into another pocket. The machine continues to run, and cards that have been selected into pocket 1 (Fig. 7-12) can be placed in the proper position later.

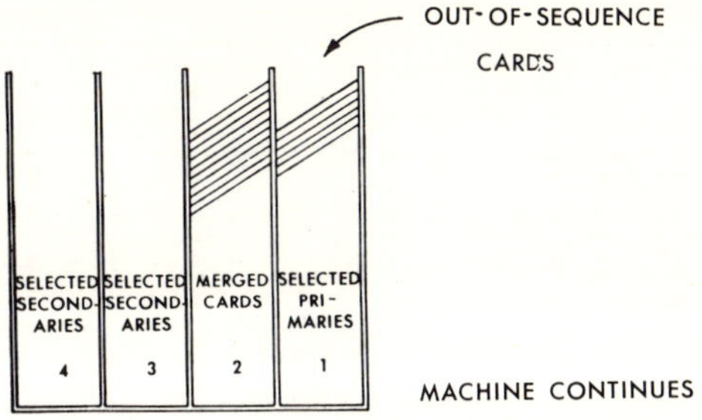

Fig. 7-12. Selecting out-of-sequence cards (Courtesy of International Business Machines.)

PROBLEM 1: Draw a wiring diagram to sequence check an employee number in columns 14 to 21. Check for blank columns. Wire for error stop on low sequence.

PROBLEM 2: Perform the same operation as PROBLEM 1, except select duplicate cards to pocket 1, and insert a signal card for a sequence error.

In the problem depicted in Fig. 7-11 there were two fields, major and minor. The major field was department number, and the minor field was employee number. As in sorting, we can treat them as one field. Since the major field is more significant than the minor field, it is wired into the high-order position during comparing. By comparing within the high-order positions you will have an ascending sequence. The 04 month will be behind the 01, 02, and 03 months. Within the months, the days will also be in ascending order. If the two columns containing the month were in the units position, you would have all the days in ascending order, but the months would be intermixed. Figure 7-13 shows the wiring to sequence check a major and minor field.

PROBLEM 3: Draw the necessary wiring if the fields mentioned in Fig. 7-11 were punched with department in columns 34 and 35 and employee number in columns 30 to 33. Check for blank columns and a high sequence. This means we want the file in descending order. On high sequence feed a signal card from second feed.

We will now examine a second function of the collator.

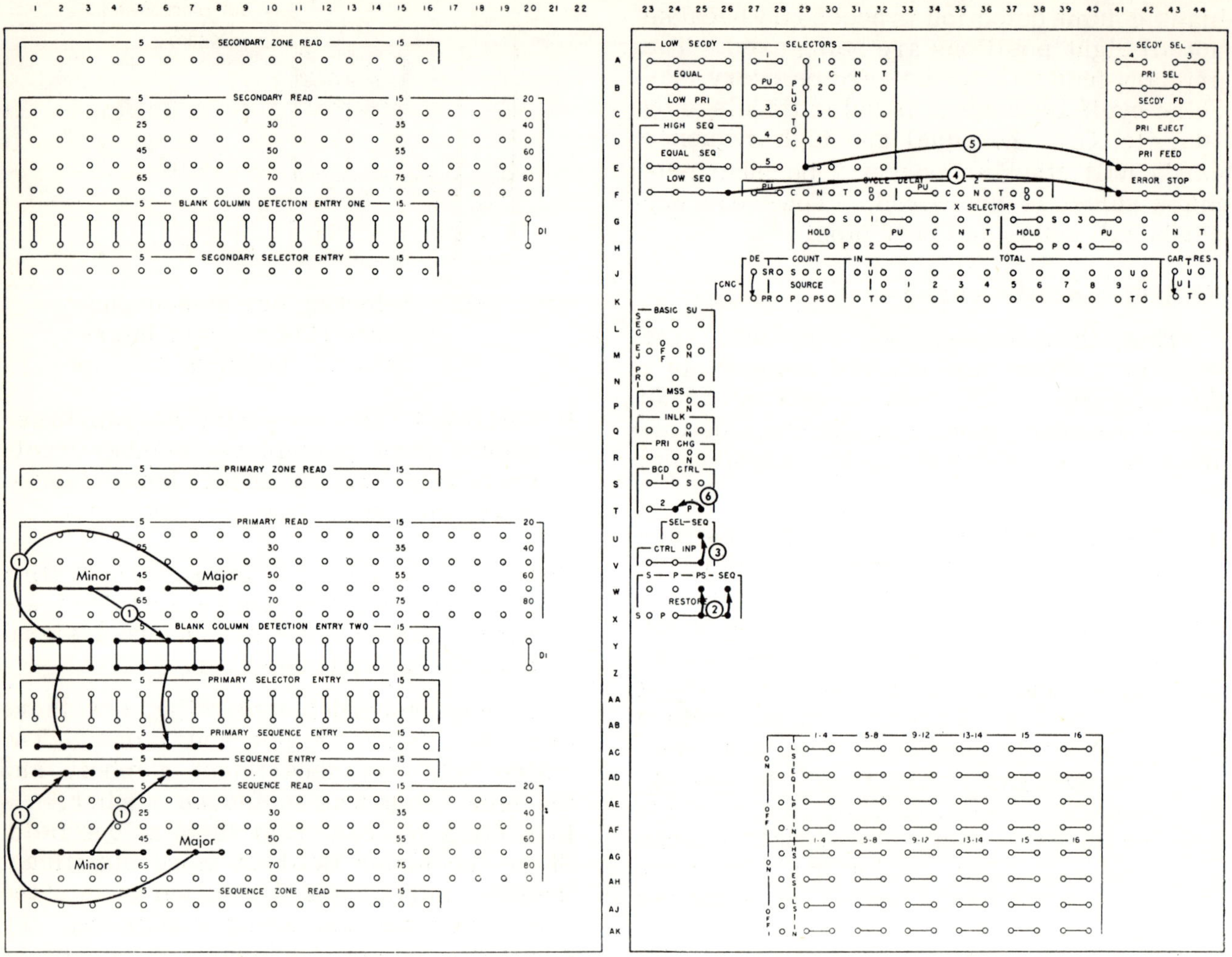

Fig. 7-13. Checking sequence (major and minor) (Courtesy of International Business Machines.)

SELECTING

Information must be accessible. It should be possible to locate a given piece of information and remove it from the files quickly. Obviously, if it is necessary to refer to a card in the files, a clerk can locate the card manually, remove it, and replace it when it is no longer needed.

As cards pass through the feeds of a collator, they are normally directed in the primary feed to pocket 2. It is possible to divert primary cards into pocket 1. The operation is similar in the secondary feeds except cards can be directed into pockets 3 and 4.

Now look at an example of card selection.

SELECTING THE LAST CARD OF EACH GROUP

The cards are placed in the primary feed of the collator (Fig. 7-14), and the machine is instructed to select the last card of each group.

When the first customer card is at the primary-read station, and the first transaction card is at the primary-sequence station, the two customer numbers are read and compared (Fig. 7-15A). They are equal because they belong in the same group, and they continue to advance.

All the transaction cards in this customer number show equal readings (Fig. 7-15B) until the master card of the next group reaches the primary sequence station (Fig. 7-15C). At the same time, the last card of the previous group is read at the primary-read station.

Now there is a change in customer number. The file is arranged in ascending se-

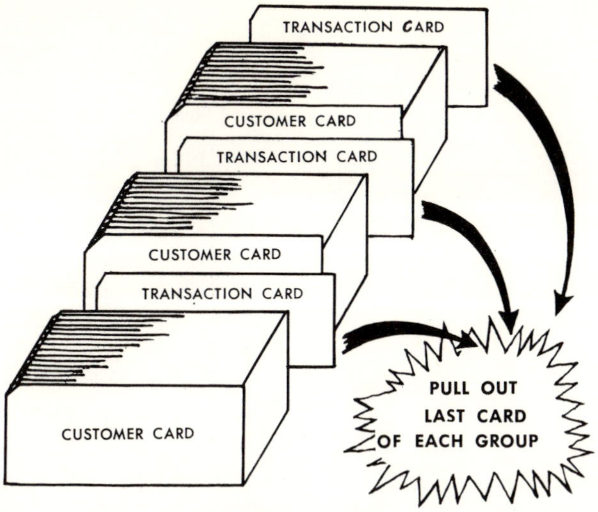

Fig. 7-14. Selection of last card of each group (Courtesy of International Business Machines.)

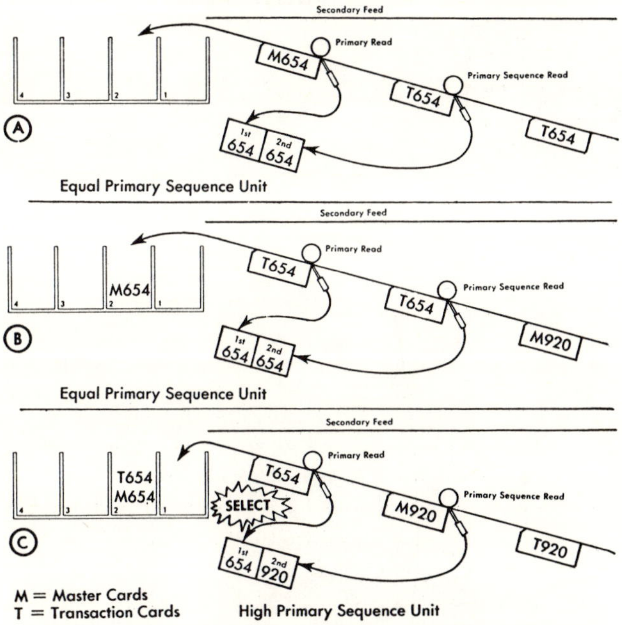

Fig. 7-15. Schematic of card selection (last card of each group) (Courtesy of International Business Machines.)

quence; the low customer numbers are followed by higher customer numbers. Therefore, the comparing unit recognizes a change from equal readings to a high reading. The collator flashes a signal to the primary-select magnet, and the last card of the group is diverted into pocket 1. During this entire operation of feeding, reading, comparing, and selecting, the feeds do not stop. Maximum speed is achieved.

Figure 7-16 shows the wiring to pull out the last card of each group if the customer transaction cards in Fig. 7-15 had the customer number punched in card columns 25 to 30. The schematic in Fig. 7-15 shows that the last card of the group was recognized in the sequence unit by a high sequence. At this time, besides knowing that the last card of a group was just read by the primary read, we also know that the first card of a group just passed the sequence read and will be available for selection on the next cycle.

SELECTING THE FIRST CARD OF EACH GROUP

A use for this type of section might be the selection of a master card from a merged file of master and detail cards. Another application might be to place the open accounts receivable file in the primary feed and to select the first (oldest) open receivable for each customer. This type of selection follows the same logic as selecting the last card of each group, in that this condition is also recognized by a high sequence in the sequence unit. To retain this knowledge until the next cycle so that the card can be selected, use the cycle-delay selectors F, 27-39.

CYCLE-DELAY SELECTORS

The cycle-delay selectors consist of a two-hub common pickup; a common, normal, and transfer hub; and a drop-out hub. The cycle-delay selector (only one is standard on the machine) is a selector which, when picked up, transfers on the following cycle rather than immediately. Another difference is that, unlike the previous selectors discussed, the cycle-delay selector will remain transferred until it is impulsed to return to normal (dropped out). An impulse to the DO Hub (drop-out) will cause the selector to return to normal. An example of this wiring can be seen in Fig. 7-17.

PROBLEM 4: Select the first card of each group to pocket one. The identifying number is punched in columns 21 to 25. If cards are out of sequence, select an indicator (signal) card. In addition, check for blank columns.

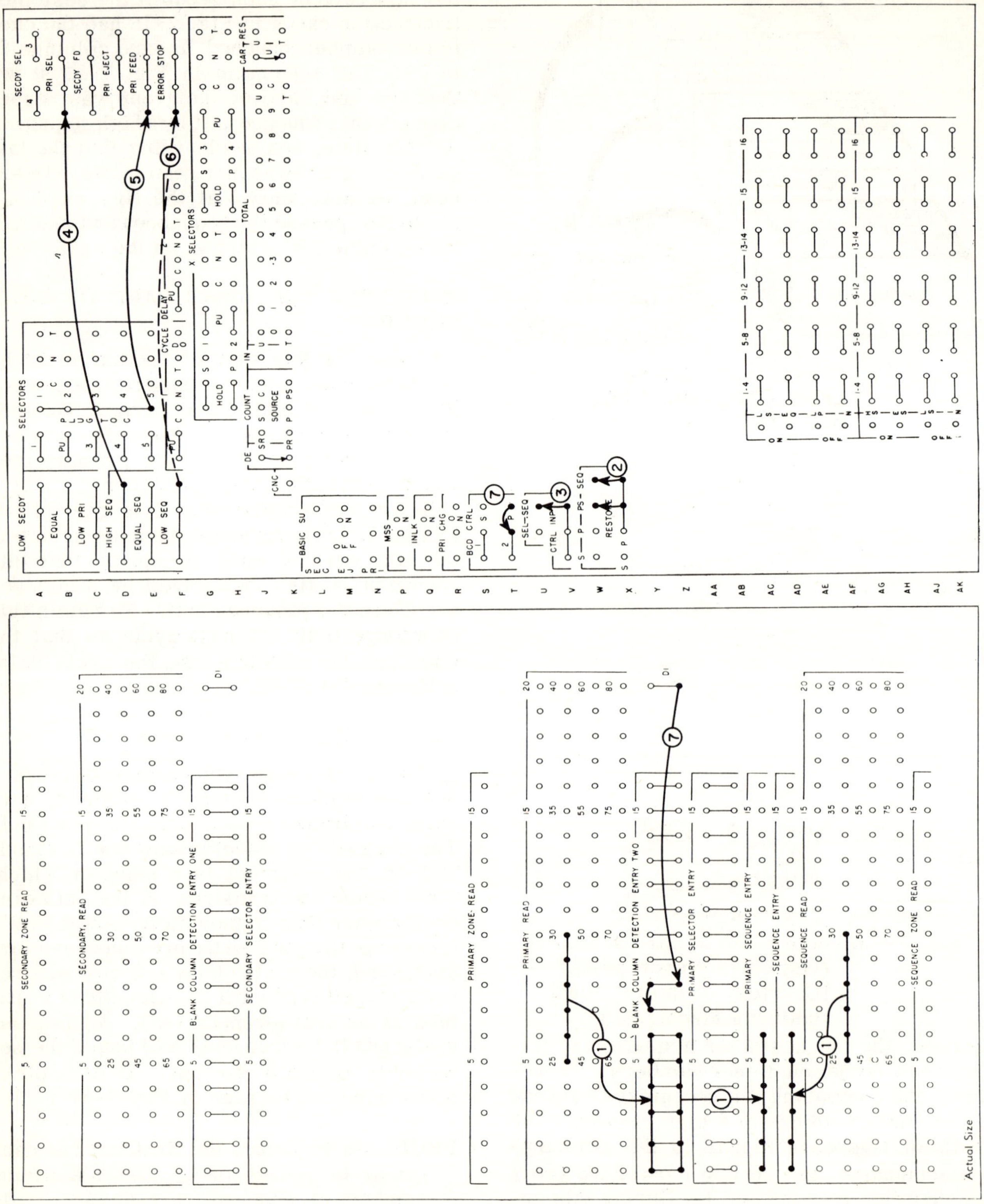

Fig. 7-16. Wiring for selecting the last card of a group (Courtesy of International Business Machines.)

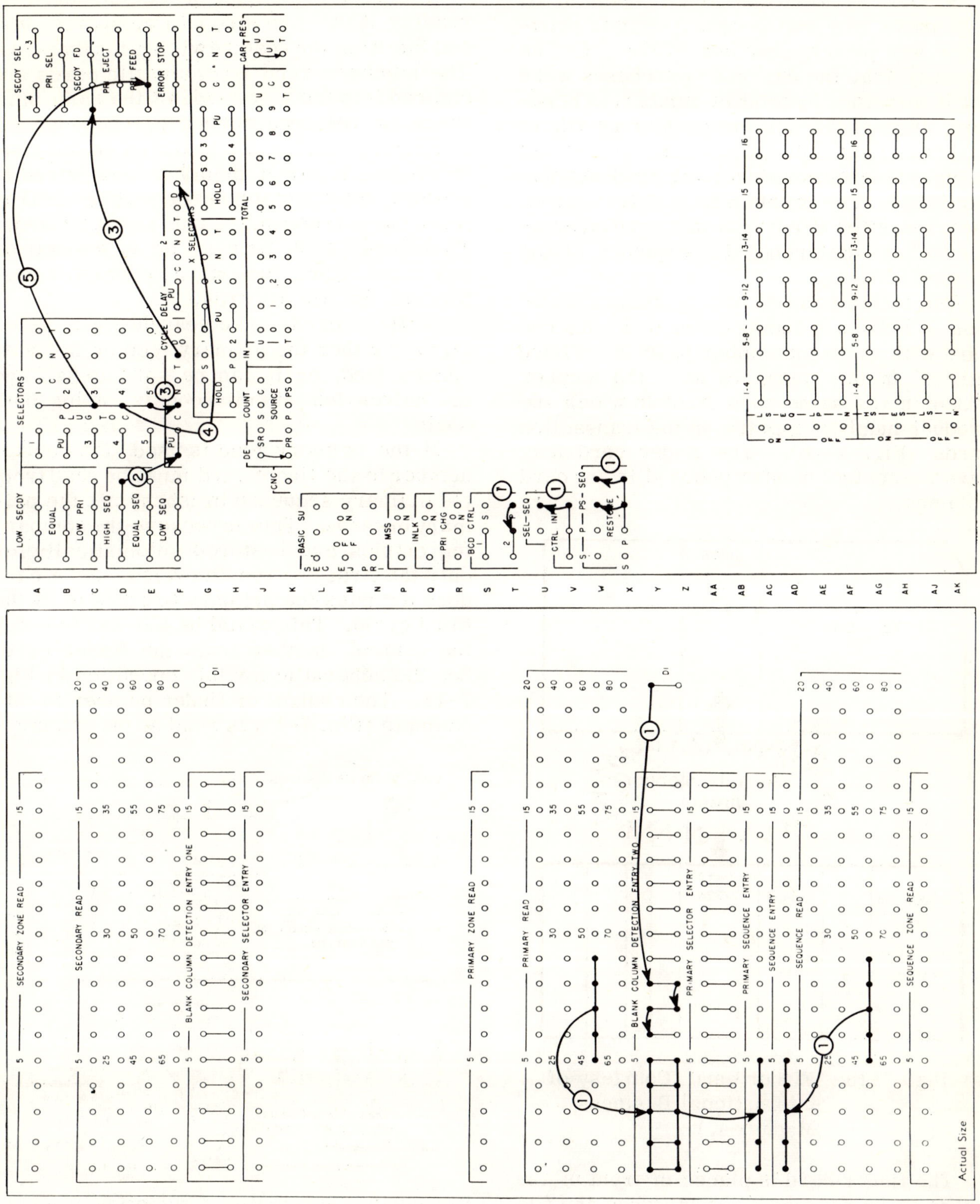

Fig. 7-17. Wiring for selecting the first card of a group

FILE SEARCH

Suppose we wanted to run a report of all customers who had bought a certain product - say product number 37326. Let us also say that the customer purchases were not in sequence by product number. Therefore, throughout this entire history file of customers and their purchases, there would be many transactions involving product number 37326. The problem is to select out all the transaction cards with that product number without disturbing the sequence of the master file.

The collator can do this by using a ***finder card.*** This is a name given to a punched card with a control number to locate related cards. In this case, we have the number 37326 in the same card field in which the product number appears in the transaction cards (Fig. 7-18). The finder card may have the control number punched in any card columns.

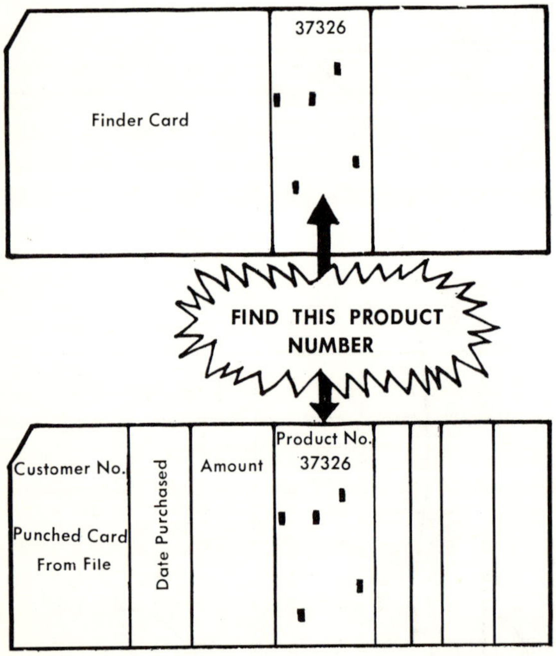

Fig. 7-18. Finder card (Courtesy of International Business Machines.)

The finder card is placed in front of the cards to be searched. Then, when the file is run through the machine, the control number from the finder card is read and remembered. It is then compared with the following cards.

The control number is remembered by reading it into one side of a comparing unit and omitting the restore wiring for that side. The numbers read from the file cards are entered into the other side of the same unit, which is restored normally. Because all comparing entries are restored on the run-in cycles, if any of them has been wired to restore, the control number will be cleared from the corresponding unit on each run-in. Therefore, each time a run is started or restarted after a run-out, a finder card must precede the file of cards.

A file of cards to be searched can be fed through either the primary feed or the secondary feed, or it can be split in half and the halves fed simultaneously, using both feeds.

If the primary feed is used, the control number in the finder card must be read from the primary sequence brushes, not the primary brushes. This is because the comparing entries are restored automatically for only the first two run-in cycles, and a card does not pass the primary brushes until the third cycle. This would be too late to enter the control number from the finder card. See the schematic for this operation in Fig. 7-19. The control or finder number in this example (Fig. 7-18) is read at the primary-

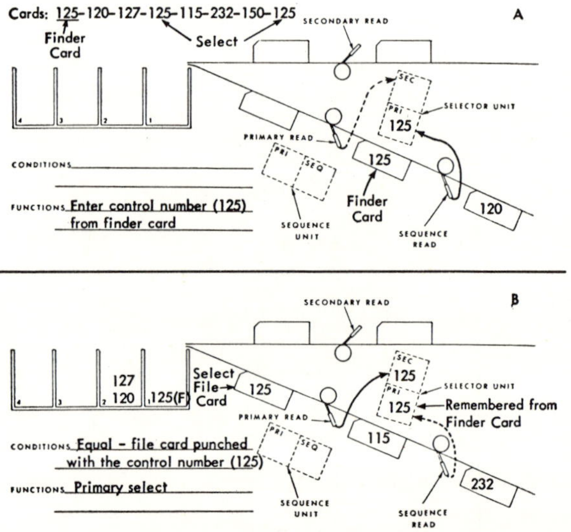

Fig. 7-19. Schematic of selection of cards by a control number (Courtesy of International Business Machines.)

sequence station and held in one-half of the control unit. No other information is read from the primary-sequence station during the entire process; therefore, this number remains in half of the comparing unit until the operation is completed.

The collator is instructed to select any cards passing the primary-read station with a product number equal to that in the control card.

The control card is the first one to reach the primary-read station. The number is compared with the control number. It is equal to the control number, and the collator emits an impulse to the select magnet to select this card. Therefore, the finder card is selected into pocket 1 (Fig. 7-20).

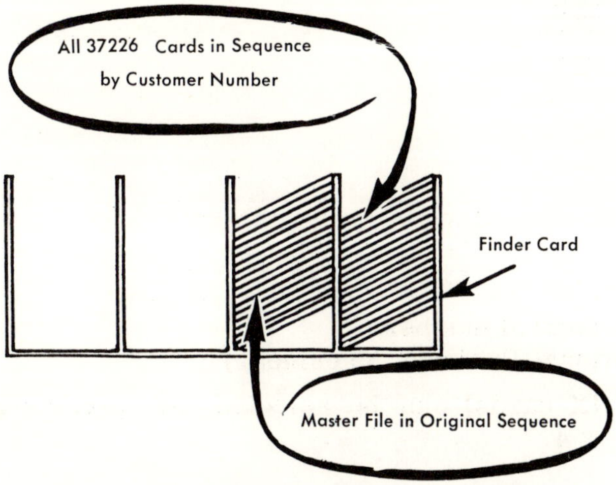

Fig. 7-20. Final grouping (Courtesy of International Business Machines.)

The cards advance. The next card does not have the same product number. It may be a customer master with nothing punched in the product field. This card is allowed to feed directly into pocket 2. Each card passing the primary-read station is examined the same way. The number in the product field is compared with the control number punched in the finder card. Whenever the comparison results in an equal reading, the card is diverted into pocket 1. In all other cases the card proceeds directly to pocket 2.

When the entire file has been processed by the collator in this way, we have two groups of cards (Fig. 7-20). Figure 7-21 depicts the necessary wiring.

PROBLEM 5: Draw a diagram to select cards with an equal control number using the primary feed. The control number is in columns 1 to 8. Check for blank columns using BCD entry one and insert a signal card for every equal control number card selected to pocket 1.

PROBLEM 6: Draw the same diagram as in PROBLEM 5, except select out cards with a number less than the control number in the finder card.

PROBLEM 7: Using the secondary feed only, select all cards equal to the finder card to pocket 4. Select out less than the control number cards to pocket 3. Read the finder control number into the PRI section of the Selector Unit. Use BCD Entry two for blank-column detection. Both the finder card and the file contain the control number in columns 1 to 8.

INTERSPERSED X-FINDER CARDS

There are many times in business when you might want to search on several control numbers. The numbers you are searching for must be grouped in some order; otherwise you will not get an accurate search. If finder cards are interspersed throughout a file, they must be identified by X punching. The X is normally punched in the finder cards, and the cards are fed through the primary feed. The X is read when the X-finder card passes the sequence brushes. It is used to control the restoring of the comparing entry in which the finder-card control number is held. Then when the X-finder card passes the primary brushes, the new control number is read in. Because two reading stations are required (one to identify the X-finder card and the following to read-in the control number from the X-finder card), the operation can be performed only in the primary feed. As in the preceding example, cards punched with numbers equal to, higher than, or lower than the control number can be selected.

X-SELECTORS

To perform this operation, you must use the selectors G-H, 28-44. The selectors consist of the familiar pickup, common,

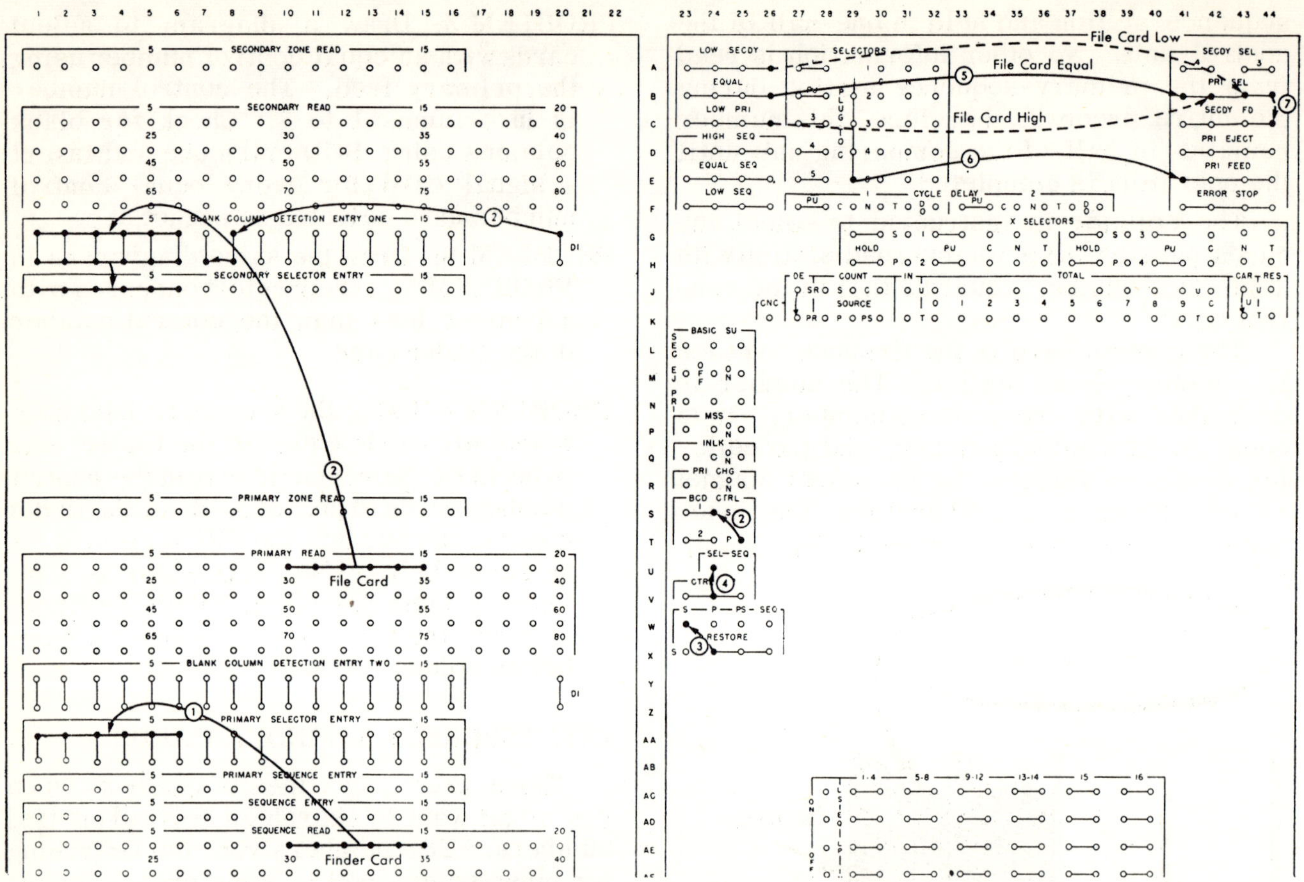

Fig. 7-21. Selecting cards by a control number (Courtesy of International Business Machines.)

normal, and transfer hubs. These selectors have additional hold P and S hubs.

Each X-selector is controlled to operate with either the primary or secondary feed by wiring its hold hubs from the P (primary) or S (secondary) hub. P emits an impulse to hold a selector between primary-feed cycles, and S emits an impulse to hold a selector between secondary-feed cycles.

When hold is wired and the pickup is impulsed, the selector transfers immediately and remains transferred until the X card moves to the next station. If hold is wired from the P hub and PU is wired from the primary read, the selector will be transferred when the X card is in the eject position and, therefore, the selection of X cards (or NX cards) into pocket 1 can be controlled. If PU is wired from sequence read, selection of the card preceding the X card can be controlled.

If hold is wired from the S hub and PU is wired from secondary-read, X cards (or NX cards) can be selected into pockets 3 or 4.

If hold is wired from	PU impulsed from	Selector transferred for	Pocket selected
P hub	Primary read	X card at eject	1
P hub	Sequence read	Card preceding X	1
S hub	Secondary read	X or NX cards	3 or 4

In the illustration (Fig. 7-22), both the control number in the finder card and the numbers in the file cards are punched in the same card field, and the selector unit is to compare the numbers. Finder cards are X punched in column 75. Selection can be performed by itself or in combination with the other operations of the collator.

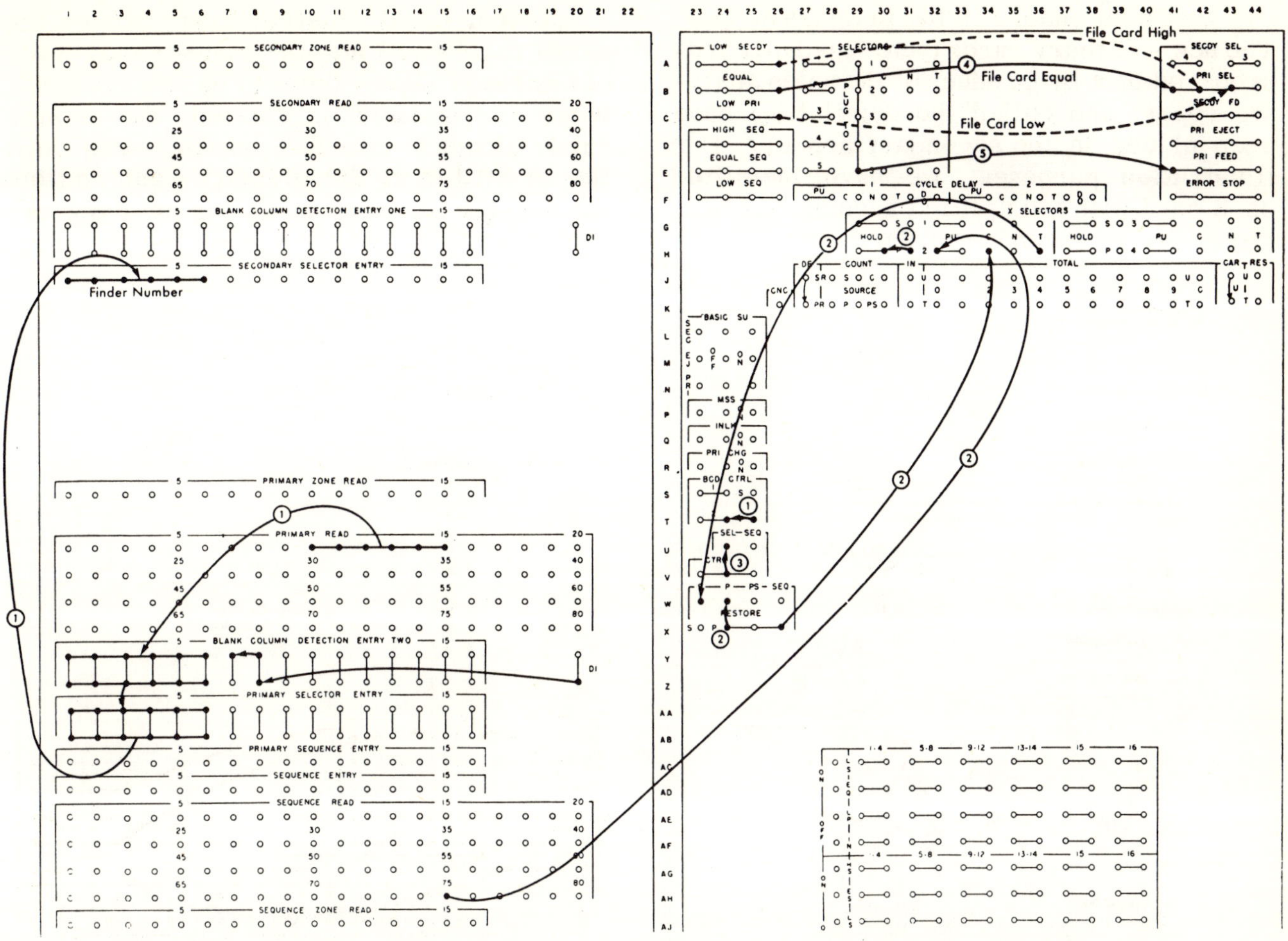

Fig. 7-22. Selecting cards by a control number; interspersed X-finder cards (primary feed) (Courtesy of International Business Machines.)

MERGING

It must be possible to get data into the file easily. If a file is kept up to date, information is constantly added to it. This added information must be placed in its proper location in the files.

As we saw in the discussion of card selection, information is often removed from the files. After it has been used, it must be returned to the files easily and quickly. This is interfiling, or merging. When merging, the collator combines two files of cards already in sequence to produce one complete file, also in the proper sequence (Fig. 7-23). This is one of the most important and useful features of the collator.

Now look at the schematic drawing of merging two files and the collator feeds (Fig. 7-24). The cards from the master

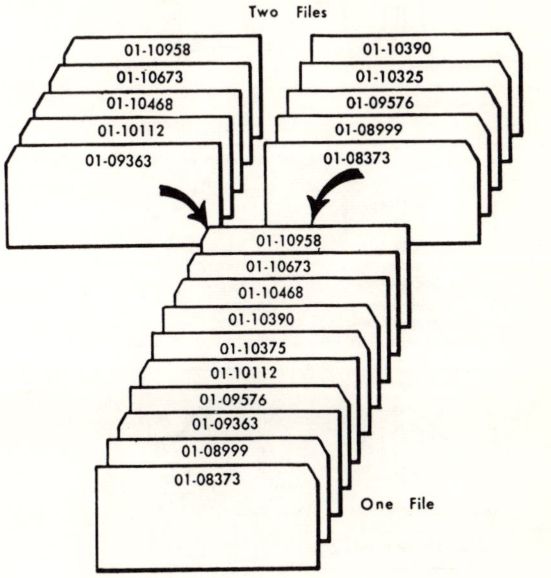

Fig. 7-23. Merging two files (Courtesy of International Business Machines.)

file have been placed in the primary hopper. The new summary cards (year-to-date cards prepared as a by-product of the sales analysis report and called the detail file) have been placed in the secondary hopper. For illustration purposes, we have identified each card with a simplified account number. Cards are in ascending order.

Control-panel instructions allow the cards to proceed into the stacker only when comparison shows them to be low or equal. When the machine is started, the master cards advance into the primary feed until the 10 card is at the primary-read station; the master 12 card is at the primary-sequence station. At the same time the sum-

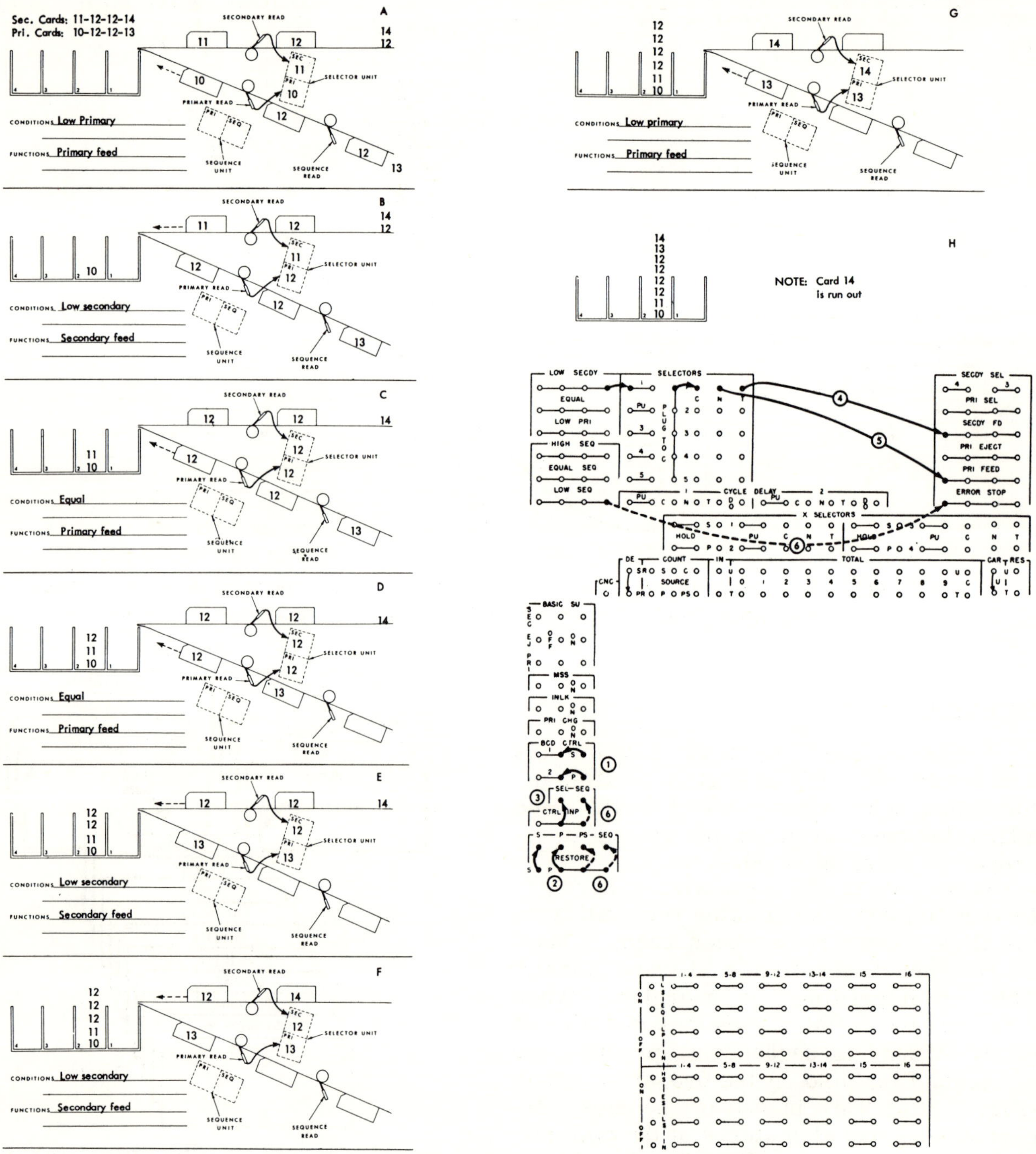

Fig. 7-24. Merging (feeding from one feed at a time)
(Courtesy of International Business Machines.)

mary 11 card has reached the secondary-read station. The brushes read the account number information to the control unit.

In this operation, the control unit compares the master card at the primary-read station with the summary card at the secondary-read station. The comparison shows that the master card is low (Fig. 7-24A). The machine is instructed to advance all primary cards one position: The 10 card goes into the merge pocket 2. The 12 card moves to the primary read station. The 13 card moves to the primary sequence station. The summary 11 card remains at the secondary read station. Since the secondary feed did not operate, the half of the comparing unit that is reading account numbers from the summary card does not change. It retains the 11 reading. But when the primary feed advances the master cards, the reading for the 10 card is restored to 0, and the unit then reads master 12 card.

Now the control unit compares the summary 11 card with the master 12 card in the primary (Fig. 7-24B). The account number of the summary card is lower, and this card obviously belongs in the file behind the master 10 card. The machine instructs the secondary feed to advance one card while the primary remains stationary. The 11 card goes into the stacker pocket directly behind the 10 card, and the summary 12 card is advanced to the secondary-read station. The primary half of the control unit retained its 12 reading; the secondary half of the unit restored to 0 and then accepted the reading 12.

Now the control unit compares the master 12 card in the primary with the summary 12 card in the secondary (Fig. 7-24C). The account numbers are equal. Both cards belong behind the 11 card. Normally, however, we want the master card ahead of detail cards in a file.

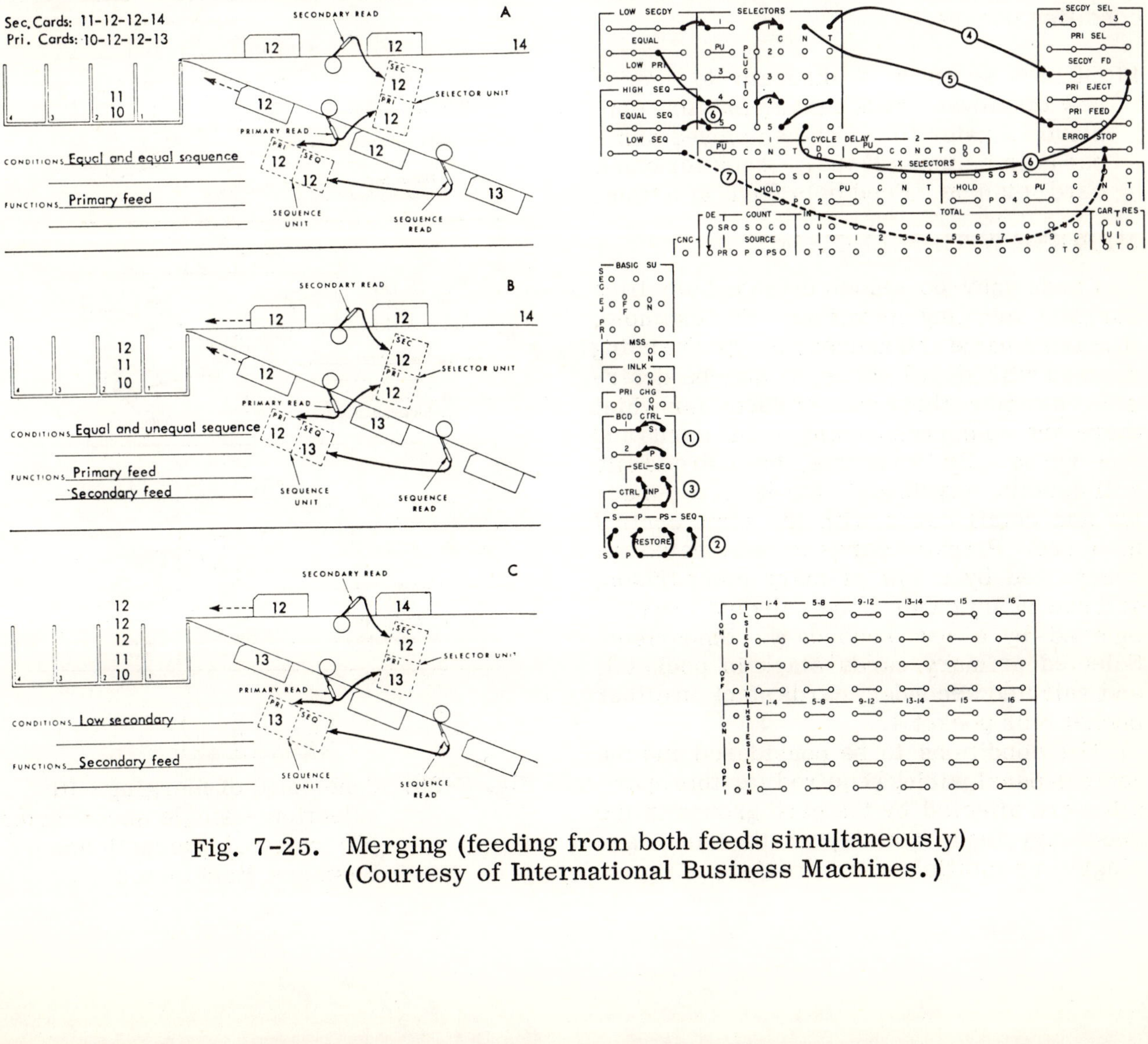

Fig. 7-25. Merging (feeding from both feeds simultaneously) (Courtesy of International Business Machines.)

The machine instructs both primary and secondary feeds to advance one card. Because of the design of the collator, the master 12 card falls into pocket 2 ahead of the summary 12 card. Both halves of the control unit then restore to 0 and accept the next reading.

When several cards with the same number occur in both files, the machine normally feeds all those from the primary (master file) ahead of those from the secondary. The last of the master file and the first of the detail file then are fed as equals (Fig. 7-24D).

There are two types of merging-feeding from one feed at a time (Fig. 7-24) and feeding from both feeds simultaneously (Fig. 7-25). When you have the condition depicted in Fig. 7-25B you know that you only have one more card to feed from the primary feed before feeding from the secondary feed. By feeding from both feeds simultaneously, you can cause both feeds to feed whenever this condition occurs.

PROBLEM 8: Draw a diagram to merge new employee cards into an existing employee master file. The employee number is in columns 27-31. Check for blank card columns. Feed both feeds at a time.

MERGING WITH SELECTION

Cards may be selected from both files during a merging operation. For example, if master name and address cards are being merged with detail cards, it may be desirable to remove those master cards for which there are no corresponding detail cards and vice versa. By doing this, the merged file will contain only "equal" cards, i.e., master and detail cards with the same control numbers. Primary cards to be selected are recognized by a low primary comparison, and secondary cards to be selected are recognized by a low secondary comparison. Selected primary cards stack in pocket 1, and selected secondary cards stack in either pocket 3 or pocket 4.

The conditions to be considered and the control-panel wiring required for this operation are affected by the card groups in the secondary feed, that is, whether they are single- or multiple-card groups.

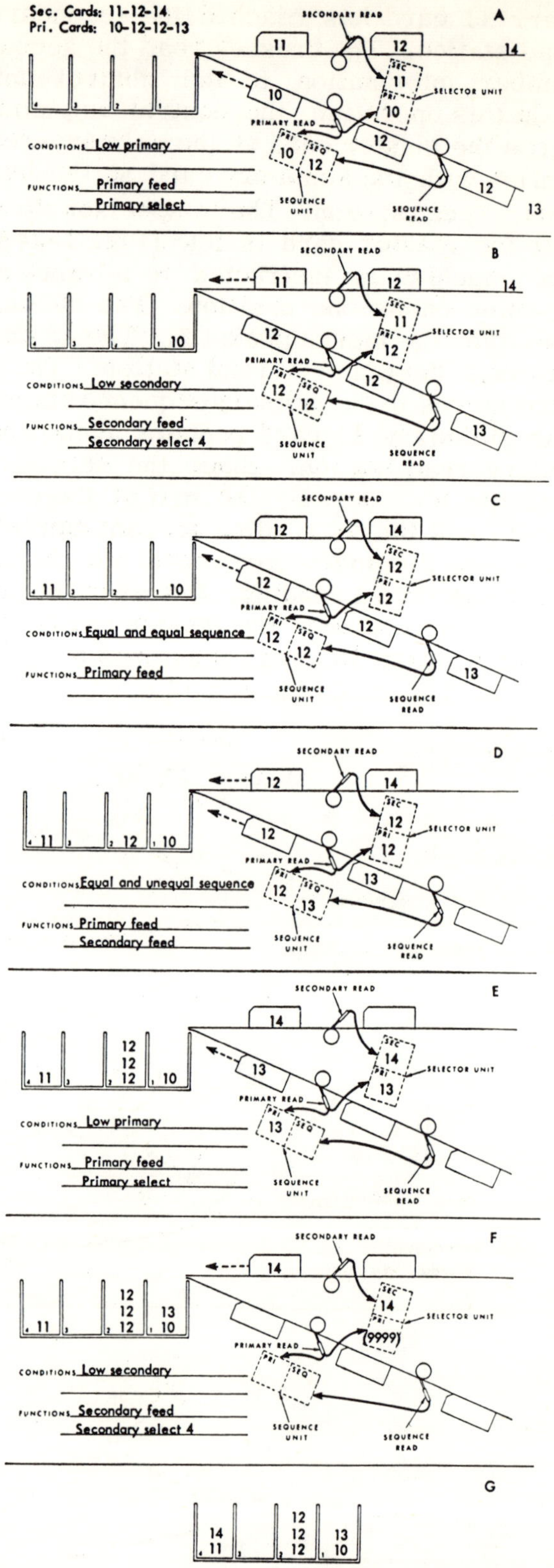

Fig. 7-26. Schematic of merging with selection - single secondaries (Courtesy of International Business Machines.)

SINGLE SECONDARIES

When the file in the secondary feed contains only single-card groups, cards can be selected by adding the wiring for selection to that for straight merging.

There is a new hub that must be used. The INLK *(interlock)* hubs (Q, 23-25) must be wired on if cards are to be selected in a merging or matching operation to ensure proper selection on the run-out. It may be wired off or disregarded at all other times.

This switch is necessary because when the run-out key is depressed, automatic 9s are emitted into the comparing entries whose feed has run out of cards. This causes the cards in the other feed to be forced out. But a problem arises if one of these cards happens to have a control field of all 9s. This will cause improper selection if INLK were not wired on.

Fig. 7-26 illustrates schematically the feeding and selection of cards, with single-card groups in the secondary feed. Steps A and E show the selection of low primary cards; steps B and F show the selection of low secondary cards; step C shows equal selector and equal sequence, while step D shows an equal selector but an unequal sequence and step G shows how the cards are stacked after all have been fed.

PROBLEM 9: Draw a diagram to merge a miscellaneous instructions card behind name and address cards on customer number, columns 34 to 38. Select out to pocket 3 any miscellaneous cards which do have name and address cards. Check for blank card columns. Feeding from both feeds simultaneously, there will be only one miscellaneous card per name and address card.

MULTIPLE SECONDARIES

In a straight merging operation without selection, multiple secondary cards are fed as illustrated in Fig. 7-25. The first secondary card of an equal group is fed on an equal and unequal sequence condition (step B), and additional secondary cards in the same group are fed on a low secondary (step C). However, when secondary cards are to be selected during a merging operation, they are selected on a low secondary. Thus all secondary cards after the first in an equal group would be selected erroneously if the plan used for selection with single-card secondaries were used with multiple-card secondary groups.

To correct this condition, feeding must be controlled so that all cards in an equal secondary group are fed as equals. This can be done by eliminating a primary feed and causing only a primary ejection when the last card of the primary group is detected. A ***primary ejection*** moves the card that has been read by the primary brushes to the stacker without causing a primary feed cycle. No other cards in the primary feed are moved, and the restore exit hubs are inactive. Therefore the number read from the last primary card is held in the comparing units, and all multiple secondary cards are compared, as equal, with the last primary card of the corresponding group.

PRIMARY EJECT (M, 23-25)

Impulsing one of the four common primary eject hubs (D, 41-44) will cause a card to go from the primary feed eject position (Fig. 7-2) to a pocket. All other cards in the primary feed will remain stationary. The primary eject hubs become exit hubs when there is a primary feed.

Figure 7-27 illustrates schematically the feeding of cards when there are multiple-card groups in the secondary feed and selection is required. In step B, the last primary card of a group (12) is ejected (stacked), but another primary card is not fed, and the first equal secondary card (12) is fed. In step C, the additional secondary card (12) in the equal group is compared to the number held from the last primary card (12) and therefore fed on an equal and unequal sequence condition. In step D, a low primary causes a primary feed, thus moving card 13 past primary read.

The comparisons and feeding required to merge cards, when there are multiple-card groups in the secondary feed and selection is required, can be summarized as follows:

Low secondary - secondary feed

Low primary - primary feed

Equal and unequal sequence - secondary feed (same as straight merging without selection)

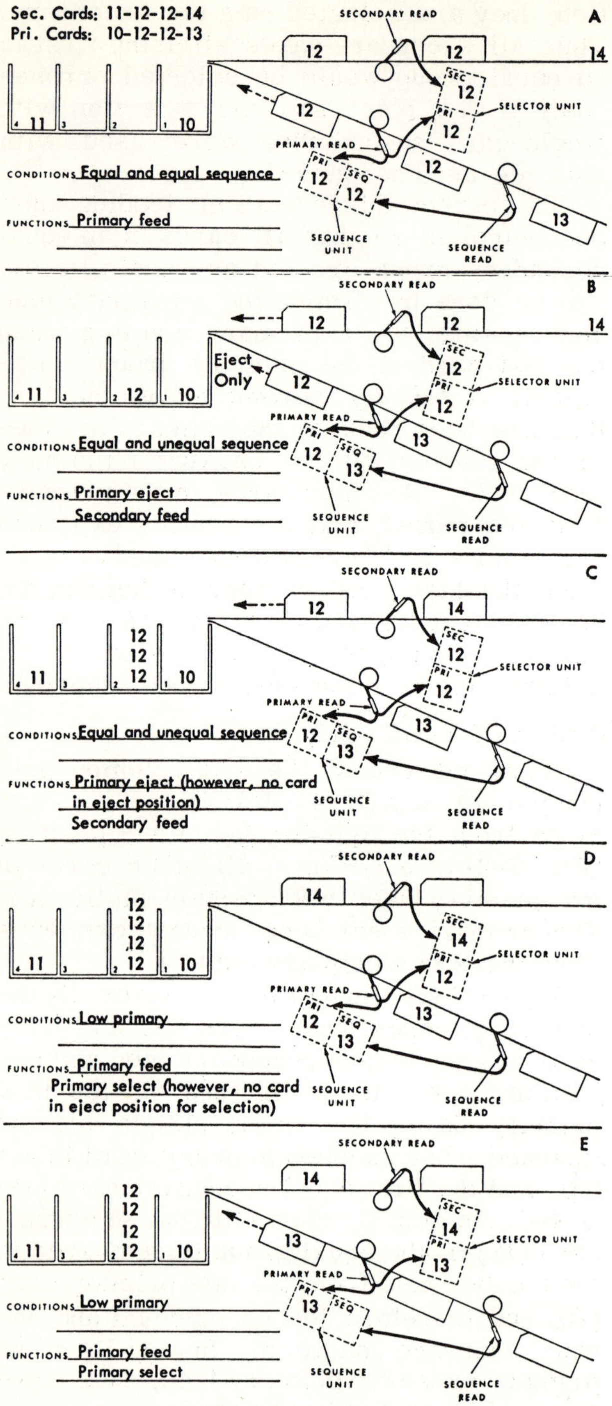

Fig. 7-27. Schematic of merging with selection - multiple secondaries (Courtesy of International Business Machines.)

Equal and unequal sequence - primary eject

Equal and equal sequence - primary feed

Thus, primary cards are fed on a low primary or on an equal and equal sequence condition; primary cards are ejected on an equal and unequal sequence condition. Secondary cards are fed on a low secondary or on an equal and unequal sequence condition. Primary cards are selected on a low primary and secondary cards on a low secondary.

This operation is diagrammed in Fig. 7-28 in the following manner:

1. The card fields are wired for blank-column detection and comparison in the normal manner for a merging operation.
2. S, P, PS, and SEQ RESTORE are wired normally.
3. SEL and SEQ CONTROL INPUT are wired normally.
4. The secondary is wired to the pickup of selector 1, and plug to C is wired through the transferred side of the selector to secondary feed. This causes the secondary card to be fed when it is lower than the primary card.
5. Equal is wired to the pickup of selector 2, and plug to C is wired through the transferred side of the selector to Primary Eject. This causes the primary card to be stacked whenever it is equal to the secondary card. The purpose of this wire is to stack the last card of an equal primary group (equal and unequal sequence condition) without feeding another primary card.
6. Low primary is wired to the pickup of selector 3, and plug to C is wired through the transferred side of the selector to Primary Feed. This causes a primary feed when the primary card is lower than the secondary card.
7. Equal is wired to the pickup of selector 4, and equal sequence is wired to the pickup of selector 5. Plug to C is wired through the transferred side of selector 4 and the normal side of selector 5 to Secondary Feed. This causes the secondary card to be fed when it is equal to the last primary card of a group.

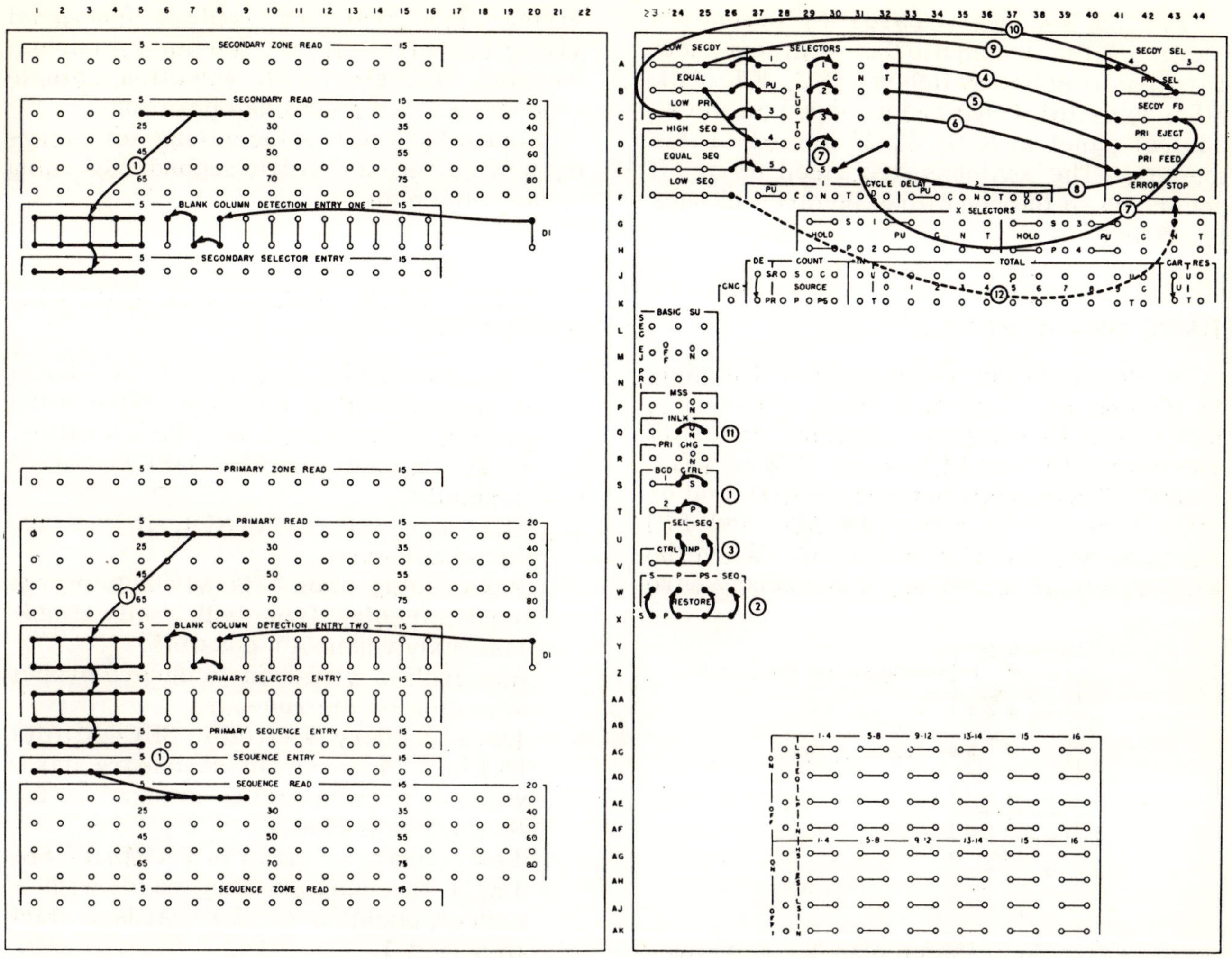

Fig. 7-28. Merging with selection - multiple secondaries
(Courtesy of International Business Machines.)

8. Plug to C is wired through the transferred side of both selectors 4 and 5 to Primary Feed. This causes a primary-feed cycle when the primary card is equal to the secondary card and is not the last card of a group. A primary feed must not occur when the equal primary card is the last card of a group. This is prevented by selector 5.
9. Low secondary is wired to Secondary Select 4 to cause secondary cards without corresponding primary cards to stack in pocket 4.
10. Low primary is wired to Primary Select to cause primary cards without corresponding secondary cards to stack in pocket 1.
11. Interlock is wired on to ensure proper selection on the run-out.
12. Low sequence can be wired to Error Stop to stop card feeding for an error in primary-card sequence (dotted wiring).

BASIC-SETUP SWITCHES

There are three basic-setup plans that can replace functional wiring to control all card feeding for normal merging, merging with selection, and matching operations. Normal operations assume that cards are arranged in ascending sequence and that all primary cards will be fed ahead of all secondary cards with the same control number.

The basic consideration in any of these operations is to control the feeding of primary and secondary cards to produce a merged (or matched) file that is in sequence. Five basic-setup switches (SEC, EJ, PRI, MSS, and PRI CHG) are provided on the 85 control panel at K-R, 23-25 to control this feeding. The switches are wired on or off according to the conditions involved in each operation.

BASIC-SETUP PLAN 1

In Fig. 7-24 the wiring to control feeding by feeding one feed at a time, wires 4, 5, and 6, can be replaced by wiring basic SU switches, SEC and PRI on and MSS off (Fig. 7-29). These switches can be wired on or off. Figure 7-29 shows the SEC and PRI wired on and the MSS wired off. When the SEC switch is wired on, a secondary card

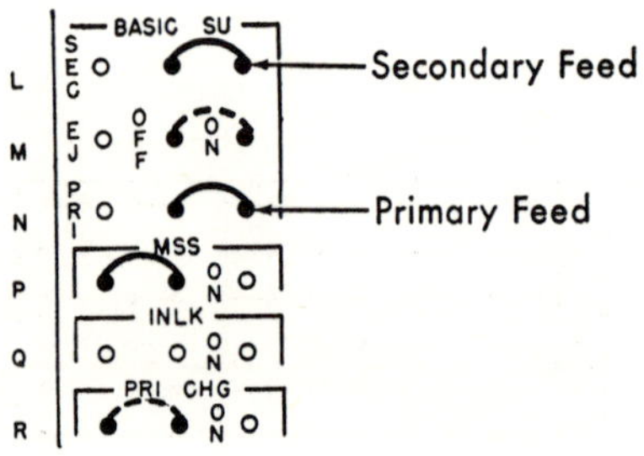

Fig. 7-29. Basic-setup plan 1 - merging feeding from one feed at a time (Courtesy of International Business Machines.)

is fed whenever a low secondary comparison is detected. When the PRI switch is wired on, a primary card is fed whenever a low primary comparison is detected.

In addition, when this switch is wired on, and the MSS switch is wired off, a primary card is fed whenever an equal comparison is detected.

BASIC-SETUP PLAN 2

The wiring to control primary and secondary feeding in Fig. 7-25 (wiring 4, 5, and 6) can be replaced by wiring basic-setup switches (SEC, PRI, and PRI CHG) on the 85 control panel as shown in Fig. 7-30. This is the second of the three basic-setup wiring plans that can replace functional wiring to control all card feeding for normal merging, merging with selection, single secondaries and matching operations.

Figure 7-30 shows the wiring for merging with selection - single secondaries using basic-setup plan 2.

MERGING WITH SELECTION - SINGLE SECONDARY

1. The card fields are wired for blank-column detection and comparison in the normal manner for a merging operation.
2. S, P, PS, and SEQ RESTORE are wired normally.
3. SEL and SEQ CONTROL INPUT are wired normally.
4. Basic-setup plan 2 is wired to merge cards, feeding from both feeds simultaneously whenever possible.
5. Interlock is wired on to ensure proper selection on the run-out.
6. Low secondary is wired to SECONDARY SELECT 4 to cause secondary cards without corresponding primary cards to stack in pocket 4.
7. Low primary is wired to PRIMARY SELECT to cause primary cards without corresponding secondary cards to stack in pocket 1.
8. Low sequence can be wired to ERROR STOP to stop card feeding for an error in sequence in the primary feed (dotted wiring).

Feeding simultaneously from both feeds differs in only one respect from feeding from one feed at a time. That is, a secondary card is to be fed when both an equal (selector) comparison and an unequal sequence comparison occur. All other control of feeding is the same as in the preceding operation. To recognize the change in control between the cards in the primary feed, the PRI CHG switch is wired on; the PRI CHG (Primary Change) switch (R, 23-25) is wired on whenever a control change in the primary cards is to affect card feeding during a merging operation. When on, it conditions the function of the secondary feed (SEC) switch. That is, if the SEC switch is on, a secondary card is fed whenever both

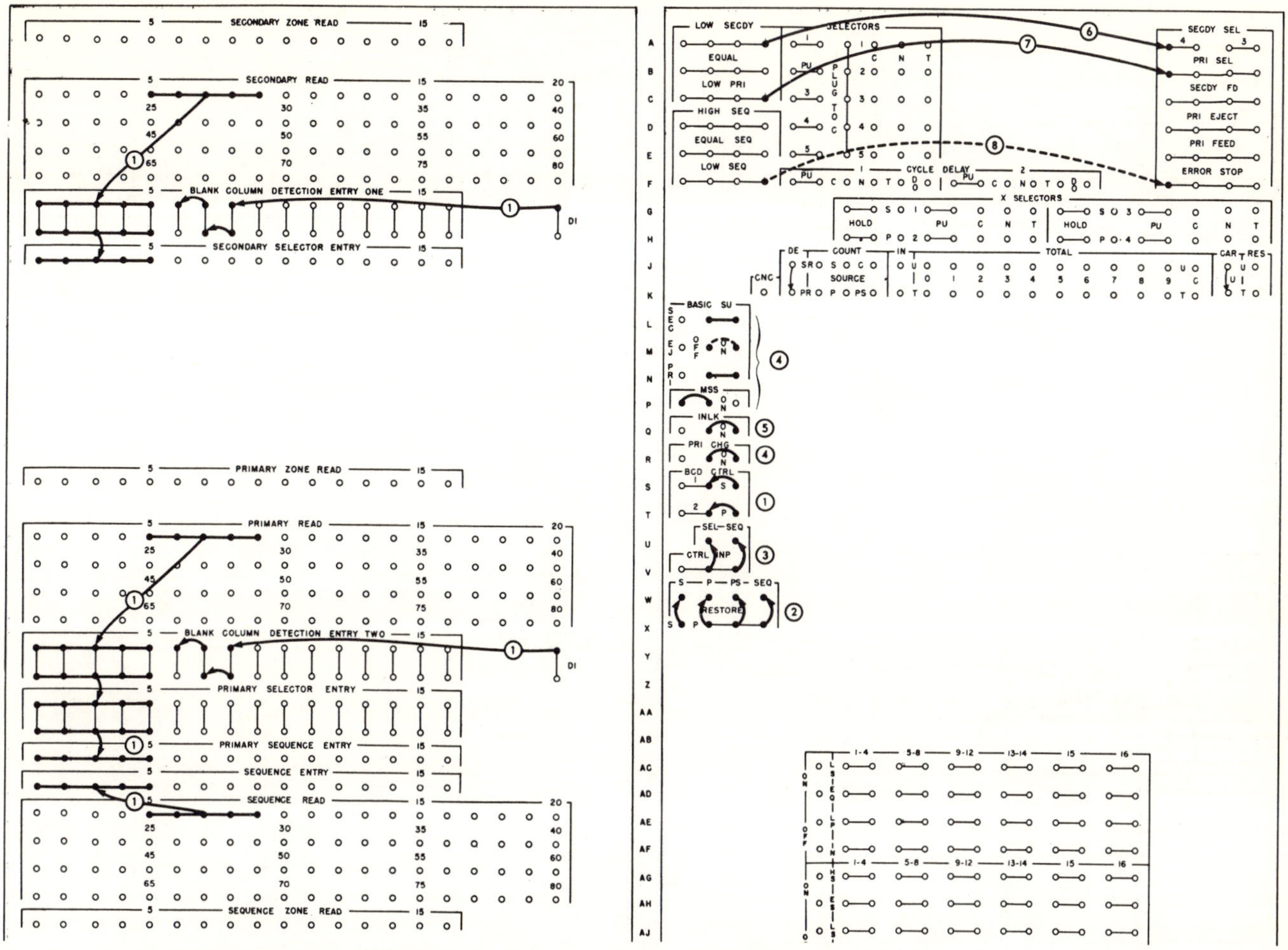

Fig. 7-30. Basic-setup plan 2 - merging with selection (single secondaries) (Courtesy of International Business Machines.)

an equal (selector) comparison and an unequal sequence comparison are detected. This is in addition to the normal function of the SEC switch which is feeding low secondaries.

BASIC-SETUP PLAN 3

The wiring to control primary and secondary feeding in Fig. 7-28 can be replaced by wiring all five basic-setup switches.

Merging with multiple secondaries and selection differs from the operation of straight merging without selection (Basic-setup plan 2) only in the feeding of primary cards on an equal (selector) condition. If an equal primary card is the last card of a group, it must be ejected, but another primary card must not be fed; if the equal primary card is not the last card of a group, it must be ejected and another primary card must be fed. The EJ, MSS, and PRI CHG switches are wired on to control this operation.

The MSS switch is used for multiple secondaries and selection. This switch must be wired on in a merging or matching operation whenever there are two or more secondary cards with the same control number, and selection is required. For all other operations this switch is wired off. When the EJ switch is wired on, a primary card is ejected whenever a low primary or equal comparison is detected. However, an impulse to primary feed on a low primary or on an equal and unequal sequence condition will also cause a primary ejection. Therefore, the main purpose on this switch is to cause only a primary ejection on an equal and unequal sequence condition.

Figure 7-31 shows the complete diagram

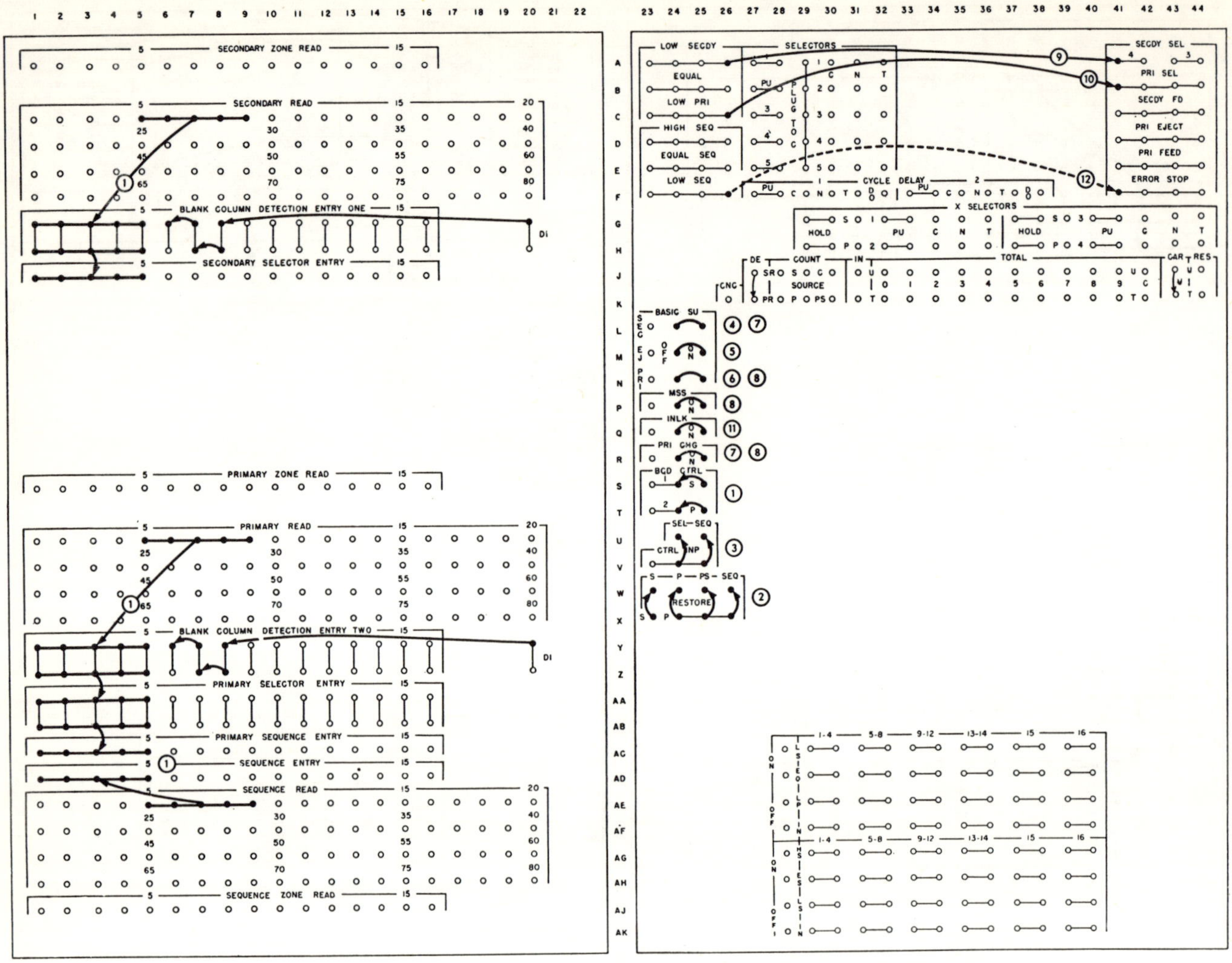

Fig. 7-31. Basic-setup plan 3 - merging with selection (multiple secondaries) (Courtesy of International Business Machines.)

for merging with selection-multiple secondaries using the basic-setup switches. This control-panel wiring performs exactly the same operation as that in Fig. 7-28. Wiring 1, 2, 3, 9, 10, 11, and 12 is identical to that in Fig. 7-31 and the basic-setup switches replace wires 4, 5, 6, 7, and 8.

PROBLEM 10: Use basic-setup plan 3 to merge two files whose control number is located in columns 34 to 38. Check for blank columns and error stop on low sequence. Select unmatched cards to pockets 1 and 3.

Plan	Hubs wired on	Function performed
1	PRI, SEC	Feeding one feed at a time
2	PRI, SEC, PRI CHG	Feeding both feeds simultaneously with or without selection of single secondaries
3	PRI, SEC, PRI CHG, EJ, MSS	Feeding both feeds simultaneously with or without selection of multiple secondaries

MATCHING

It must be possible to check a file for all data fitting master patterns. Any data that does not correspond should be removed from the files without disturbing the sequence of the remaining data. This is a *matching* operation.

Matching involves two files of cards (Fig. 7-32). One file (the master file) is searched

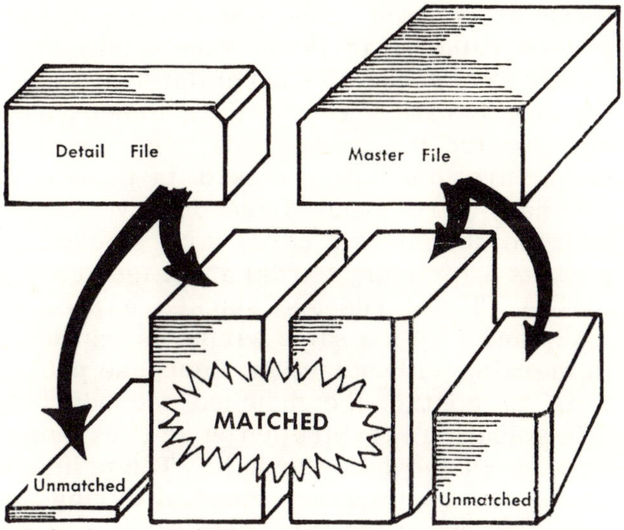

Fig. 7-32. Matching function (Courtesy of (International Business Machines.)

for any cards corresponding to the cards in the second, or detail file. Unmatched cards are separated from either file.

This is very much like selection, except that the finder information changes as soon as it has been matched. Instead of trying to find all cards in the master file that agree with a finder card, we are looking for the one card (or group of cards) that agrees with the first detail card to be matched, then the one card (or group) agreeing with the next detail card, and so on. Very frequently, check reconciliation uses the collator's ability to match cards. For instance, the paymaster of a corporation may issue 10,000 paychecks. At the end of a week, he can reasonably assume that most of these checks have been cashed or deposited and have been returned from the banks. He should have received a cancelled check for each employee who had been paid on the previous payday. Therefore, there should be one

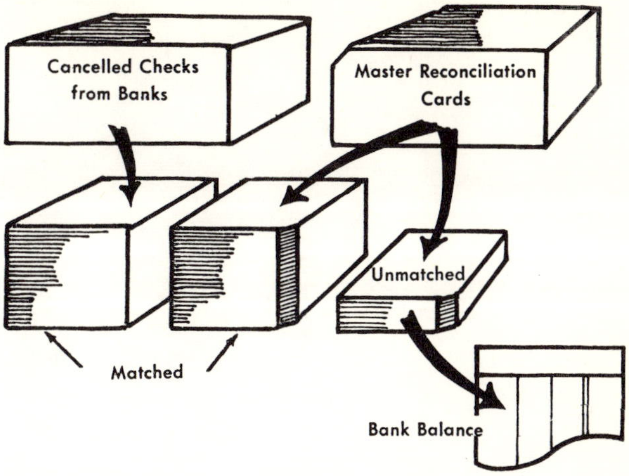

Fig. 7-33. Check reconciliation (Courtesy of International Business Machines.)

cancelled check in the file for each check written the previous week (Fig. 7-33).

By matching the current file of cancelled checks against the reconciliation file, the payroll department can determine which checks have not cleared the bank. There should be one cancelled check for each reconciliation card.

The active reconciliation file is placed in the primary feed of the collator, and the cancelled checks in the secondary feed (Fig. 7-34). Control-panel wiring instructs the collator to match these cards against each other.

As the cards pass through the two feeds, comparisons are made between the reconciliation cards and cancelled checks (Fig. 7-34A). Whenever the check number is the same as the number punched in the reconciliation card, the machine is instructed to divert the check into pocket 3. Simultaneously, the reconciliation card with the matching check number is fed into pocket 2 (Fig. 7-34B).

When the check number in the reconciliation card is lower than the number of the cancelled check at the secondary read station, it means that the check has not cleared the bank. Therefore, the unmatched reconciliation card in the primary feed is diverted into pocket 1 (Fig. 7-34C).

There should be no unmatched checks in the secondary. Obviously, there should be no check issued without a corresponding

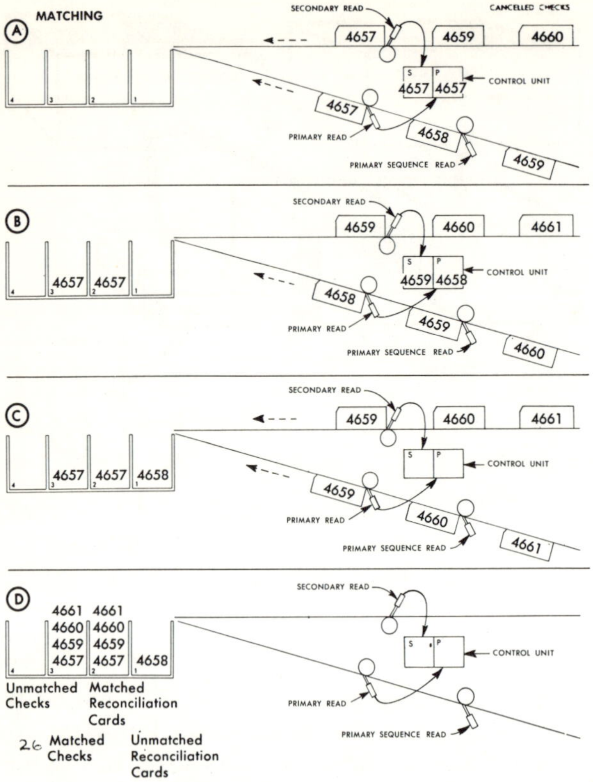

Fig. 7-34. Schematic of matching for check reconciliation on collators (Courtesy of International Business Machines.)

card in the reconciliation file. This is a good control check on the procedure because it tells us that no checks were issued without reconciliation cards and that no reconciliation cards have been removed.

The collator processes both files this way (Fig. 7-34D):

1. Matched primary cards (reconciliation cards) are in pocket 2.
2. Matched secondaries (cancelled checks) are in pocket 3.
3. Unmatched reconciliation cards fall into pocket 1. The payroll department uses these unmatched reconciliation cards to verify the balance on the bank statement.
4. Unmatched cancelled checks (if there are any) are diverted into pocket 4. These unmatched cancelled checks are given special handling to determine why no reconciliation cards are in the file.

This is the basic matching operation. It illustrates only the principle of matching and the way the IBM collator does it. There are many variations of the matching operation.

The two original files of cards are arranged in sequence, and each of the four groups is also in sequence when the operation is completed.

This matching differs in only one respect from merging with selection. The matched cards from both files are stacked in two groups rather than in one combined group.

All four pockets in the collator are used for this operation, two for the matched cards and two for the unmatched. The matched cards are normally stacked in pockets 2 (primary cards) and 3 (secondary cards), and the unmatched cards are stacked in pockets 1 (primary cards) and 4 (secondary cards). The cards are stacked in pockets 1, 2, and 4 by the same wiring as that used in merging with selection. Because pocket 3 is to contain the matched secondaries, this selection is controlled on an equal comparison in the selector unit. The primary cards can be sequence checked during the matching operation (Fig. 7-35).

COMBINED COLLATOR OPERATIONS

The IBM collator has been built for versatility; although each of the functions that has been described so far - sequence checking, card selecting, merging, and matching - is individually valuable in handling problems of filing and file maintenance, most applications combine two or more of the basic functions of the collator. Filing problems are so correlated in the IBM data processing method that a single collator procedure can serve several purposes at one time. Each combination of operations reduces record-keeping costs.

IBM 85 Collator Questions

Answer briefly

1. Name four functions which can be performed on the 85 Collator.

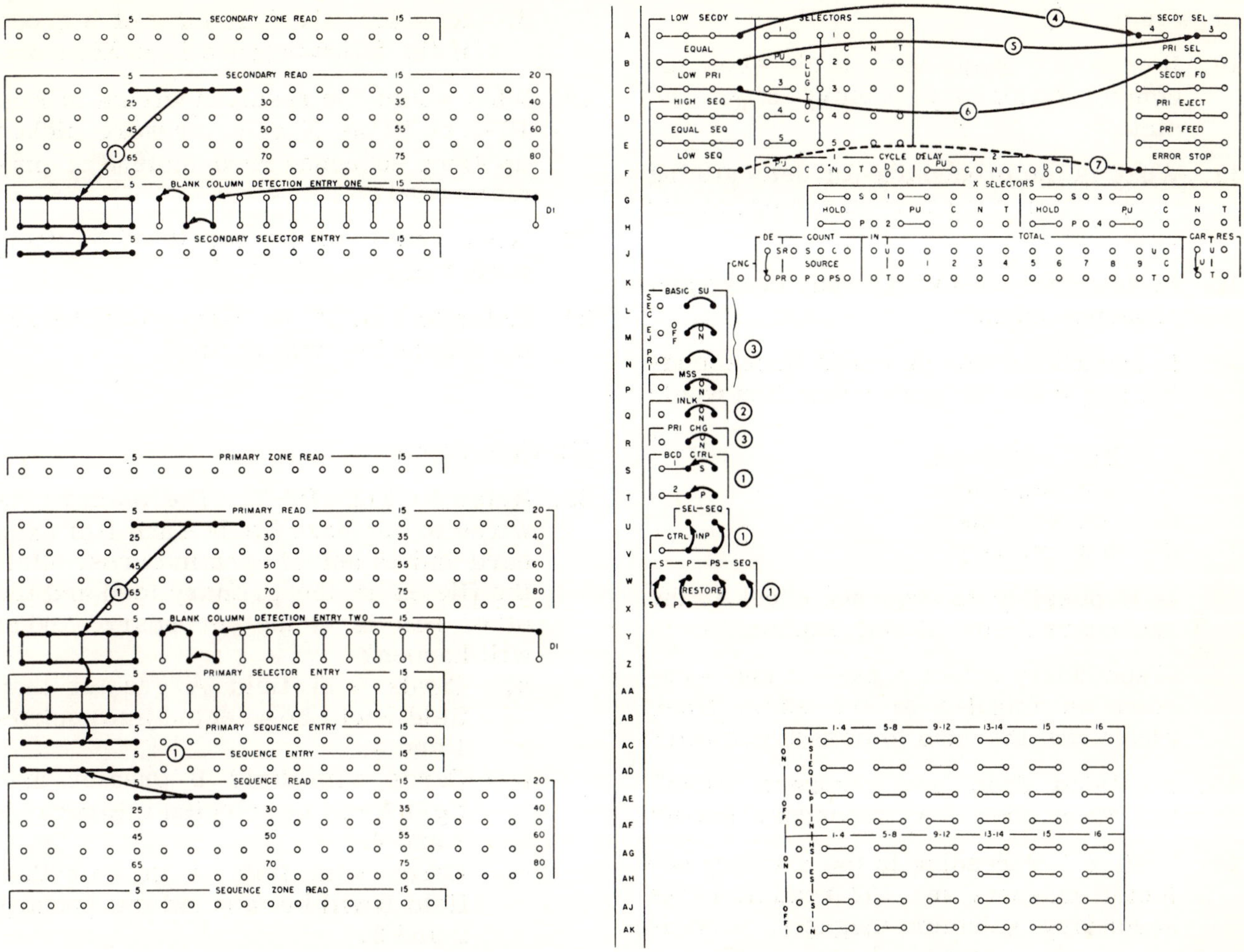

Fig. 7-35. Matching (Courtesy of International Business Machines.)

2. Discuss the functions of
   a. the run-out key
   b. the error light
   c. the reset key

3. How are the cards placed in the hoppers?

4. What is the speed of the collator?

5. How many reading stations are there in the primary feed? What are their names?

6. a. Cards from the primary feed can fall into which pockets?
   b. Cards from the secondary feed can fall into which pockets?

7. Which feed must be used when using Interspersed X-finder cards?

8. When is a control input impulse available?

Multiple choice

9. Refer to Fig. P7-1. What will be the result of the wiring?
   a. X80 cards will be selected into pockets 2 and 3.
   b. NX80 cards will be selected into pockets 1 and 3.
   c. X80 cards will be selected into pockets 1 and 3.
   d. The card following an X80 in either feed will be selected into pockets 1 and 3.

Answer briefly

10. How do we sequence check when the control fields are county, city, and state?

11. What is the procedure for determining what error condition has stopped the collator?

12. In sequence checking, what does equal sequence mean?

13. In sequence checking cards in descending sequence, an error condition would be a
    a. high sequence
    b. low sequence
    c. low secondary
    d. low primary

14. Is it possible to sequence check in the secondary feed? If not, explain.

15. If secondary select pockets 3 and 4 receive an impulse at the same time, where will the card to be selected fall?

16. a. What does low sequence mean?
    b. What does low secondary mean?

17. With a 100 reading in the primary selector magnets and 102 reading in the secondary selector magnets, what is the condition of the selector unit?

18. Refer to Fig. P7-2. The result of the wiring would be
    a. to select the first card of a group if it is an X65.
    b. to select the last card of a group if it is an X65.
    c. to select the last card of a group if the preceding card was an X65 card.
    d. to select the last card of a group if the following card is an X65 card.

19. What would the result of wiring in Fig. P7-2 be if the X selector were picked up from sequence read instead of primary read?

20. What would be the result of omitting wire 1 in Fig. P7-3?

21. Refer to Fig. P7-4. What would be accomplished by this wiring?

Multiple choice

22. Refer to Fig. P7-5. The diagram is wired to compare fields A and B of each card and to select certain cards. Half the file is in the primary feed and the other half is in the secondary. What will happen?
    a. Cards with field A greater than field B will be selected into pockets 1 and 4.
    b. Cards with field B greater than field A will be selected into pockets 2 and 4.
    c. Cards with field A greater than field B will be selected into pockets 2 and 3.
    d. Cards with field B greater than field A will be selected into pockets 1 and 4.

23. If wire 1 was omitted from Fig. P7-5
    a. cards with B greater than A would stack in pocket 1.
    b. cards with field A greater than field B would stack in pocket 1.
    c. no cards will stack in pocket 1.
    d. all cards will stack in pocket 1.

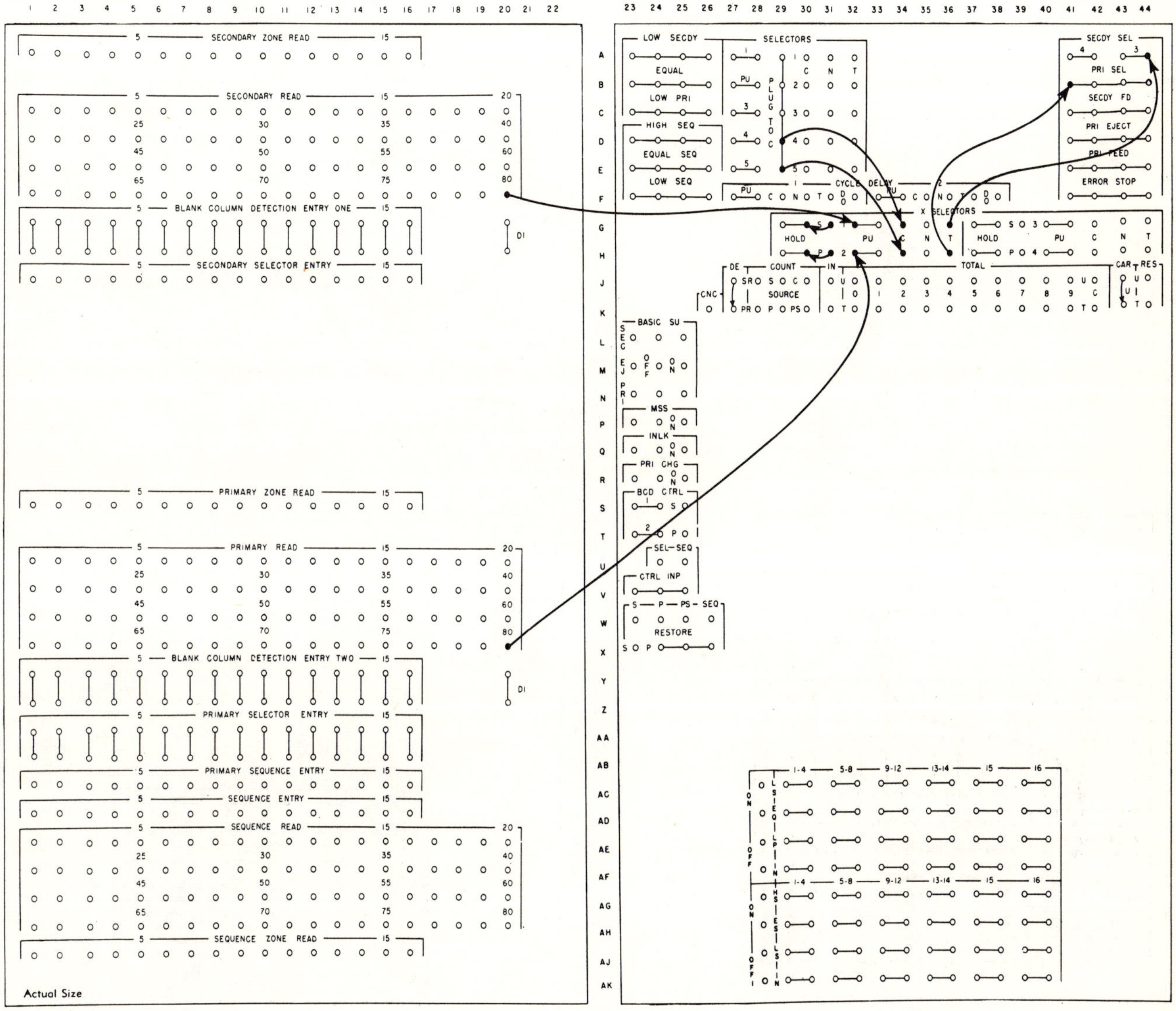

Fig. p7-1 (Courtesy of International Business Machines.)

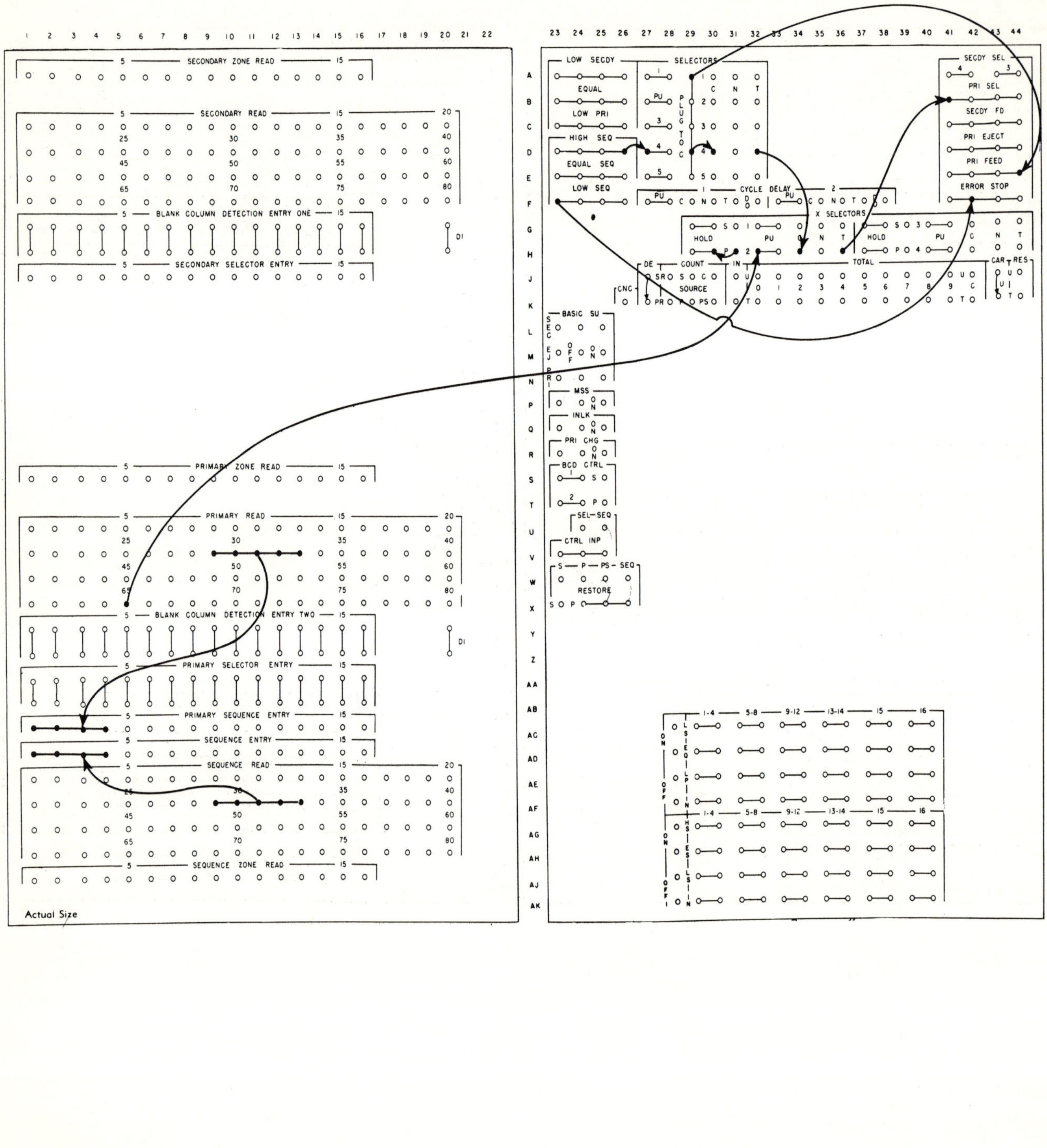

Fig. p7-2 (Courtesy of International Business Machines.)

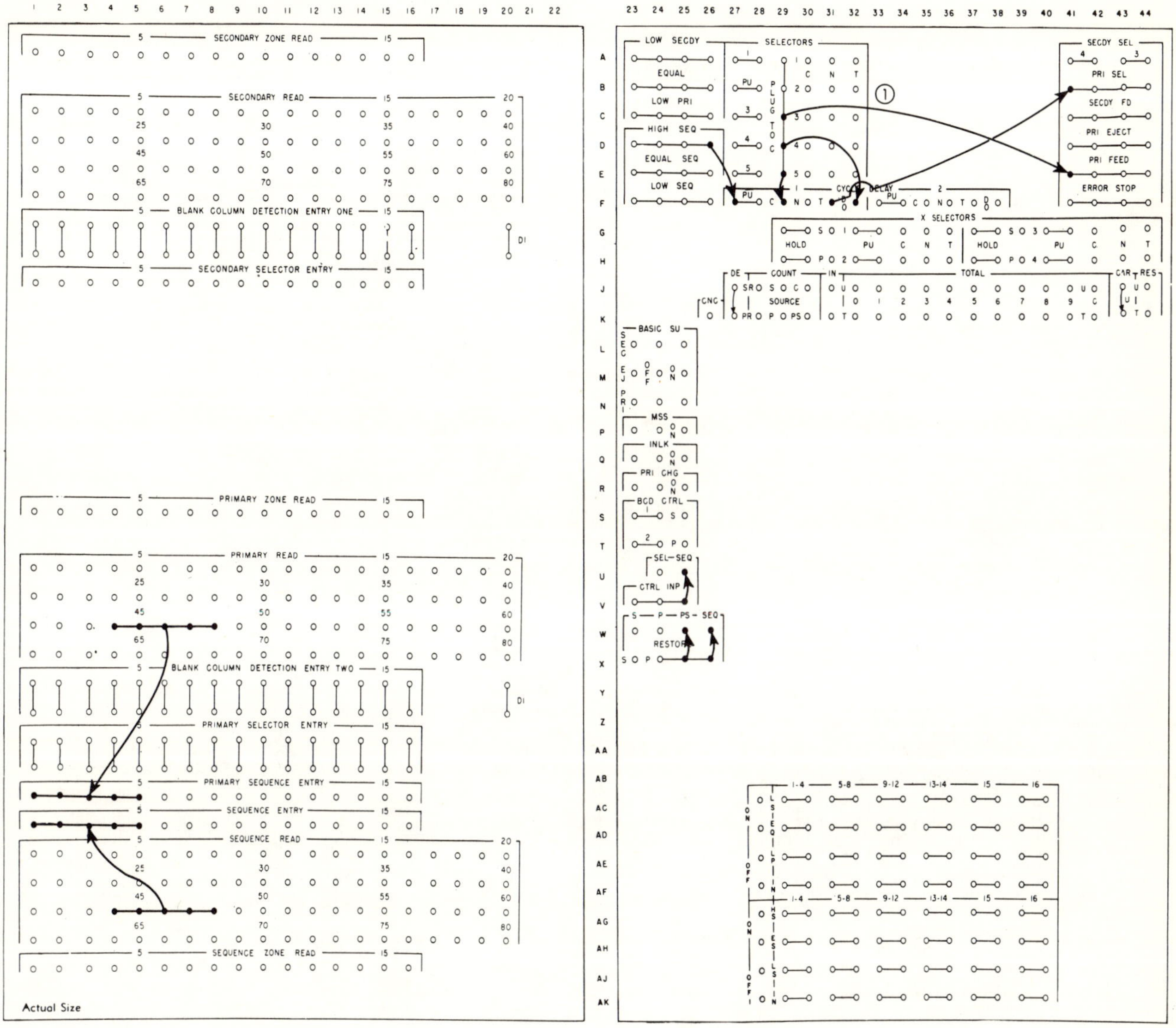

Fig. p7-3 (Courtesy of International Business Machines.)

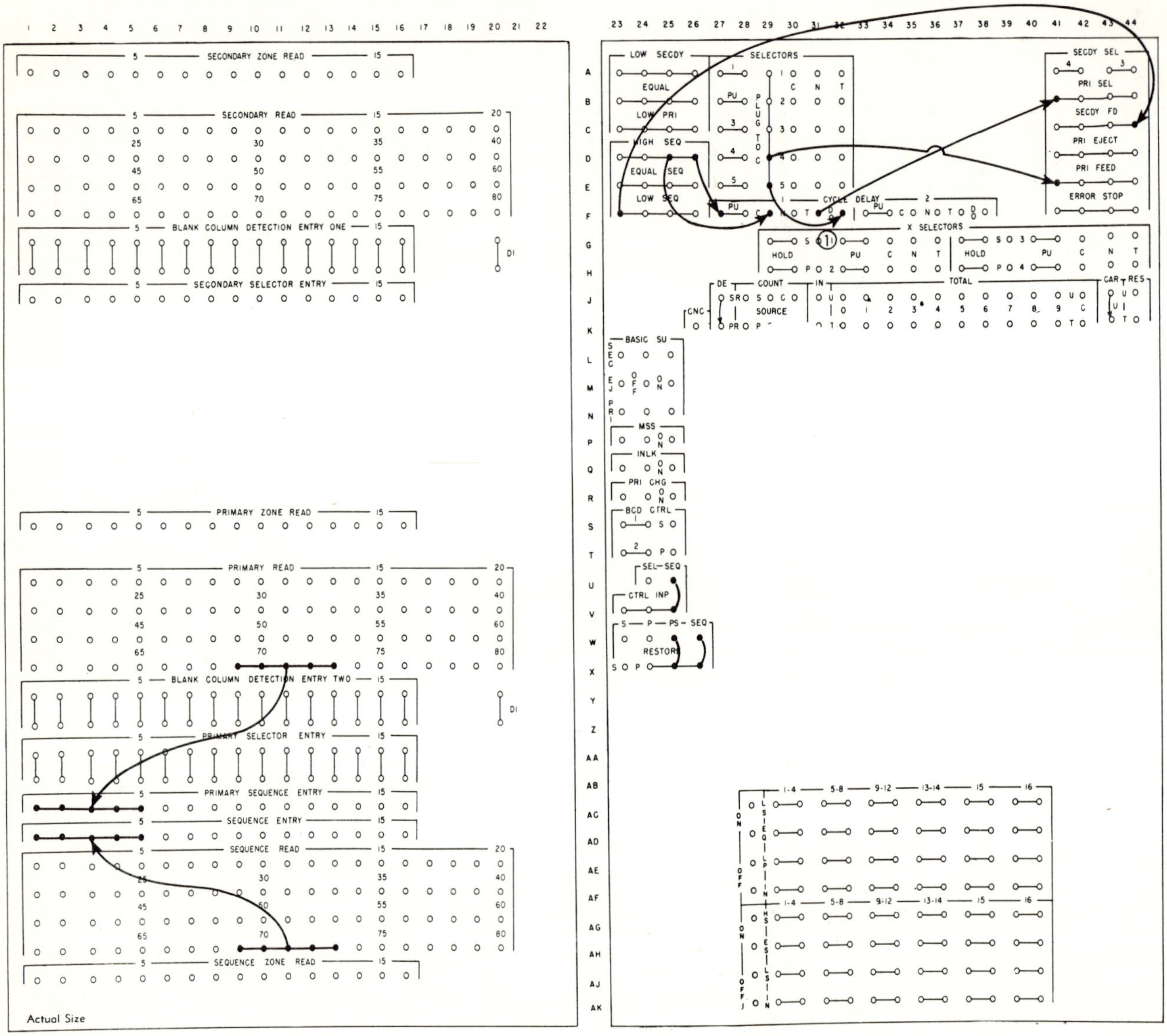

Fig. p7-4 (Courtesy of Internationel Business Machines.)

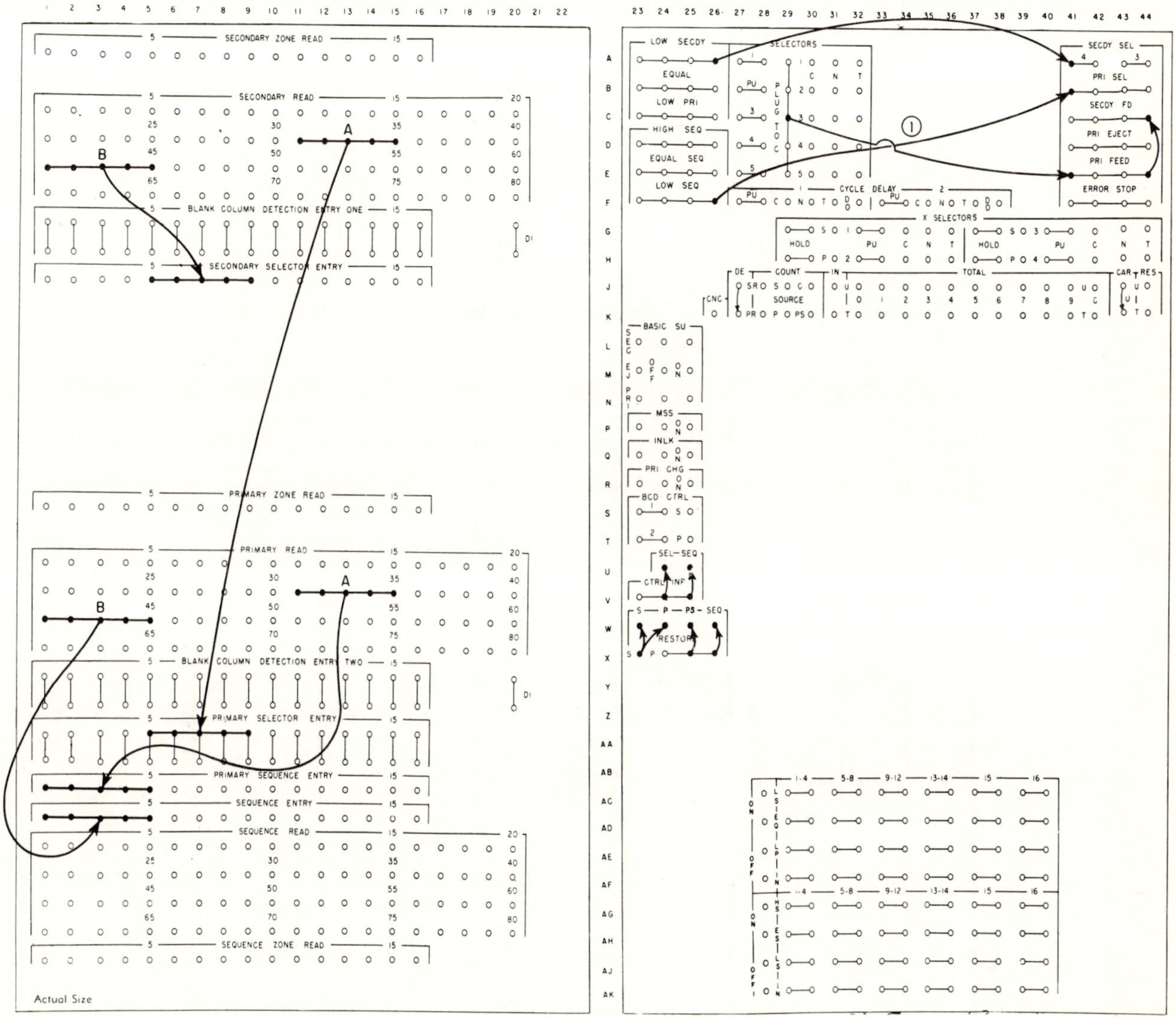

Fig. p7-5 (Courtesy of International Business Machines.)

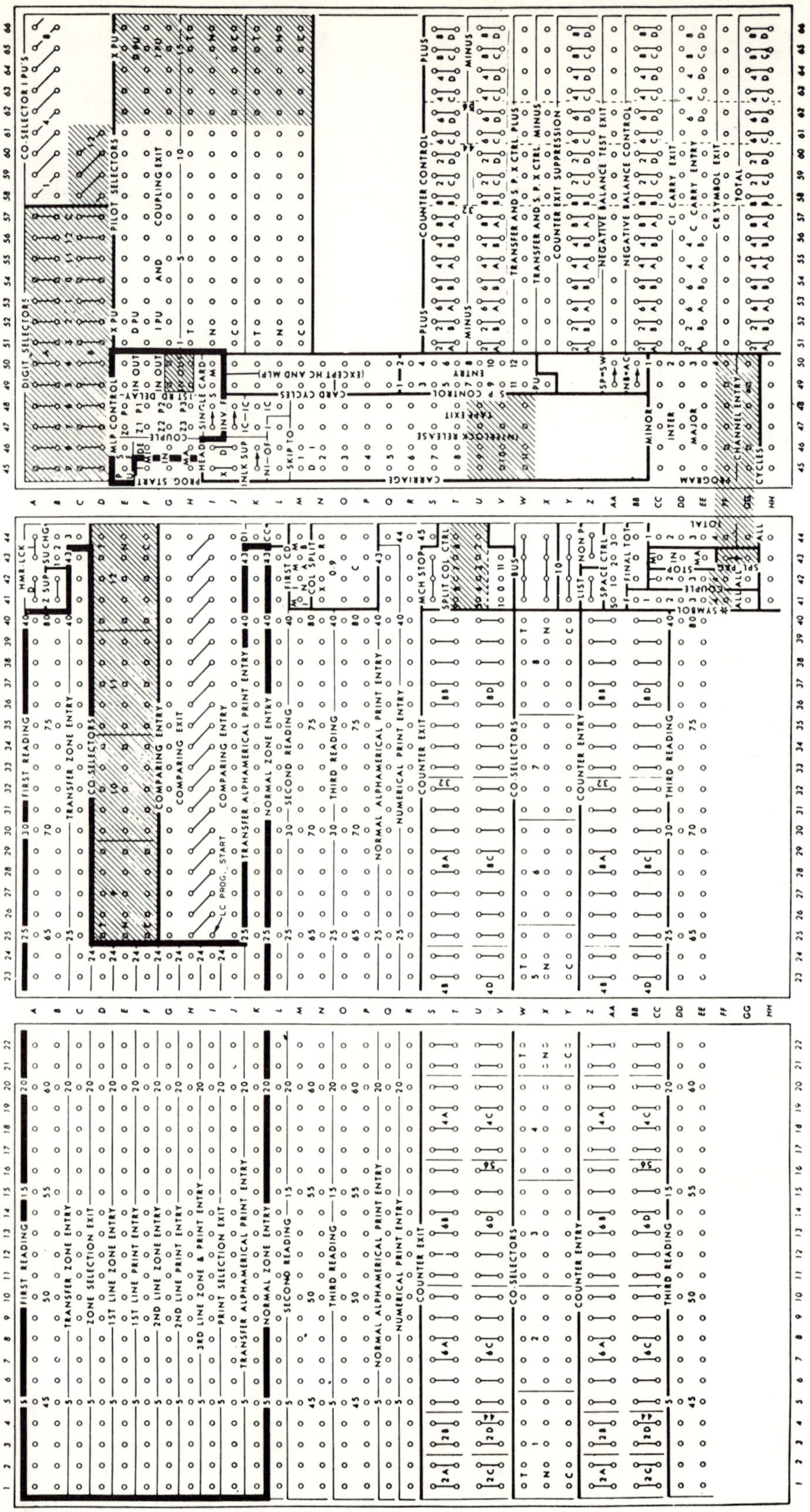

402 Control Panel. The shaded areas represent special features. (Courtesy of International Business Machines.)

Section 8

THE 402 ACCOUNTING MACHINE

The function of the 402 Accounting Machine (Fig. 8-1) is to produce printed reports automatically while selectively adding and/or subtracting (multiplying and dividing with a special feature). The 402 operates automatically in both the feeding of cards and the printing of results. The information punched in the card is read and printed at a maximum speed of 50 to 150 cards per minute (depending on machine model); at the

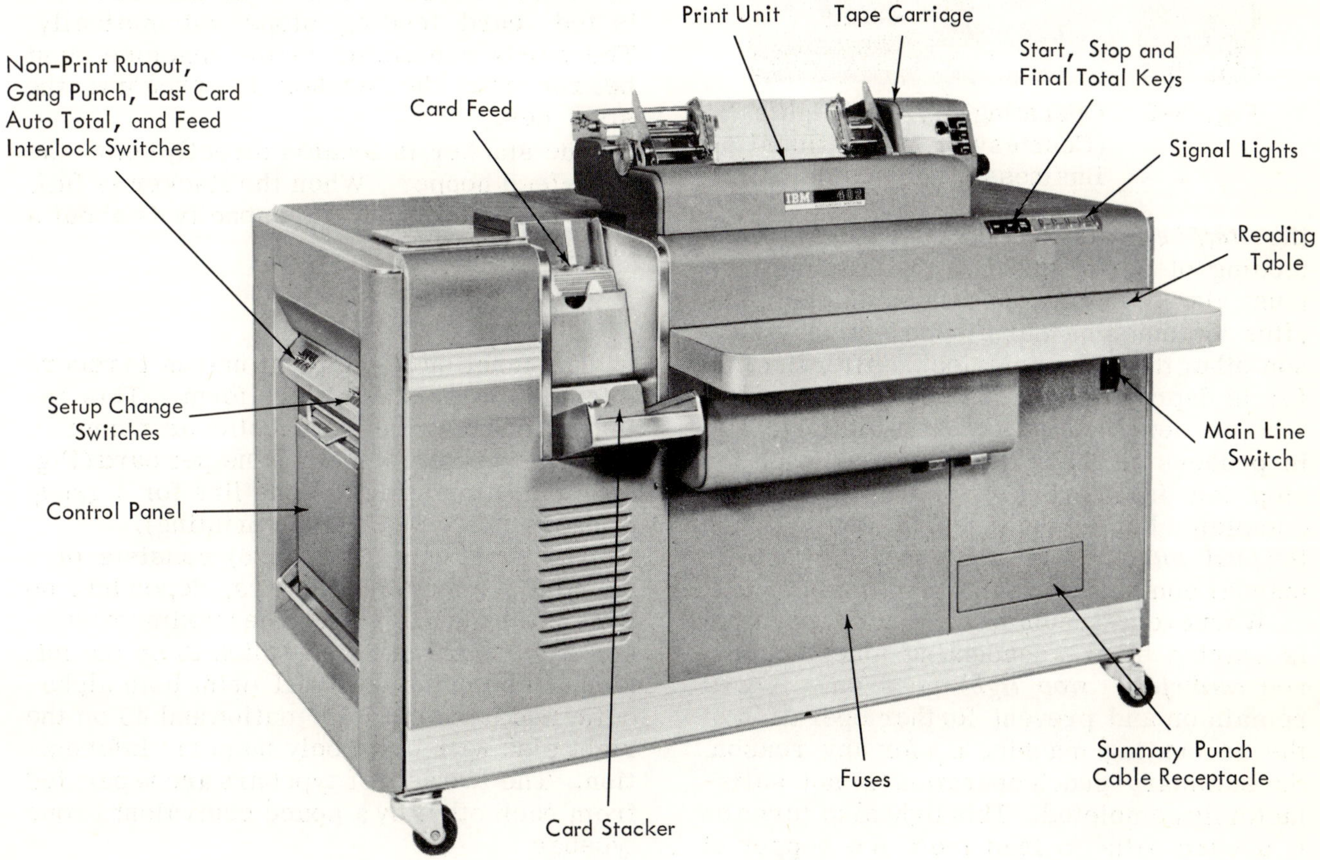

Fig. 8-1. IBM 402 Accounting Machine (Courtesy of International Business Machines.)

same time, it may be added, subtracted, compared, or selected, according to the requirements of the report. Complete flexibility is provided in the arrangement of the printed data on the report form, and summary cards can be punched simultaneously with the preparation of reports. The 402 normally prints one line from a card.

The tape-controlled carriage, a feature of the 402, controls the feeding and spacing of report forms which are prepared by the accounting machine.

OPERATING KEYS AND LIGHTS (Fig. 8-2)

To operate the machine, the ***main-line switch,*** located below the right end of the reading table, must be turned on. Next,

Fig. 8-2. Operating keys and lights (Courtesy of International Business Machines.)

the ***start key*** must be depressed to start the feeding of cards through the machine. It must also be depressed to resume operation after the machine has stopped for any reason other than feed interlock. After the ***stop key*** is depressed, the machine will stop before the next card is fed. If a total cycle is in process or about to be started when the stop key is depressed, the cycle will be completed before the machine stops. When the ***final-total key*** is depressed, it permits manual control over total printing.

Whenever a summary-punch operation is started by the accounting machine, the red ***card-feed stop light*** goes on. It will remain on and prevent further operation of the accounting machine if, for any reason, the summary punch operation is not satisfactorily completed. This light also turns on if a card fails to feed from the hopper of either the accounting machine or the summary punch or if the summary punch hopper runs out of cards.

The red ***unlabeled light*** will go on when the main-line switch is turned on and the machine is idling. This light also turns on when the hopper runs out of cards. The red ***stop light*** will go on whenever the machine stops, because of an impulse received by a machine-stop hub on the control panel. While the stop light is on, the machine cannot be restarted. To turn it off, the final-total key must be depressed. Whenever a fuse burns out, the red ***fuse light*** goes on and the machine stops. The fuses are located toward the bottom of the machine, below the reading table. The red ***form light*** goes on and the machine stops whenever the last form is within 10 in. of the platen.

HOPPER AND STACKER

The card-feed hopper is located at the left end of the machine. Cards are placed in the hopper face down, with the 9 edge toward the throat. The hopper holds from 800 to 900 cards. As soon as the last card is fed, card feeding stops automatically. The cards remaining in the machine must be run into the stacker by pressing the start key.

The stacker is located directly below the card-feed hopper. When the stacker is full, card feeding stops. Its capacity is about a thousand cards.

THE PRINT UNIT

The function of the print unit is to record information on the report form. This information may be alphabetic or numeric, and it may be printed one line per card (Fig. 8-3, detail printing) or one line for a group of cards (Fig. 8-4, group printing).

The print unit (Fig. 8-5) consists of a variable number of typebars, depending on the size of the machine. The maximum number of typebars is 88, of which 43 on the left side of the print unit will print both alphabetic and numeric information and 45 on the right side will print only numeric information. The two sets of typebars are separated from each other by a space equivalent to one typebar.

Each alphameric typebar consists of 26 alphabetic characters, the numbers 0 through 9, and the ampersand (&). Each numeric

UNITS: EA = EACH, C = HUNDRED, DZ = DOZEN, GR = GROSS, M = THOUSAND

INVENTORY TRANSACTION LISTING

TRANSACTION CODES: 1. BALANCE FORWARD 2. RECEIPTS FROM VENDORS 3. RETURNS TO VENDORS 4. ISSUES FROM STOCK 5. RETURNS TO STOCK 6. DEBIT ADJUSTMENT 7. CREDIT ADJUSTMENT

DATE: 3/ 31 /

PART NUMBER	PART NAME	UNIT	UNIT COST	TRANSACTION REFERENCE NUMBER	TRANSACTION DATE	TRANS CODE	OPENING BALANCE	TRANSACTIONS RECEIPTS	TRANSACTIONS ISSUES	ON HAND
171203	WATER PAIL 1 G	EA	1.89		2/28	1	68			
171203	WATER PAIL 1 G	EA	1.89	16129	3/03	4			36	
171203	WATER PAIL 1 G	EA	1.89	16431	3/07	4			18	
171203	WATER PAIL 1 G	EA	1.89	A0649	3/10	2		144		
171203	WATER PAIL 1 G	EA	1.89	16842	3/14	4			40	
171203	WATER PAIL 1 G	EA	1.89	17361	3/21	4			12	
171203	WATER PAIL 1 G	EA	1.89	C0036	3/22	5		1		
171203	WATER PAIL 1 G	EA	1.89	D0567	3/22	3			1	
171203	WATER PAIL 1 G	EA	1.89	18902	3/30	4			24	
171203						1				82 *
171364	FRYING PAN 4 IN	EA	.94		2/28	1	84			
171364	FRYING PAN 4 IN	EA	.94	15937	3/01	4			6	
171364	FRYING PAN 4 IN	EA	.94	16389	3/04	4			15	
171364	FRYING PAN 4 IN	EA	.94	B1089	3/07	6			1	
171364	FRYING PAN 4 IN	EA	.94	17361	3/21	4			36	
171364	FRYING PAN 4 IN	EA	.94	18437	3/25	4			6	
171364	FRYING PAN 4 IN	EA	.94	18866	3/29	4			18	
171364	FRYING PAN 4 IN	EA	1.04	A0676	3/30	2		156		
171364						1				158 *
171366	FRYING PAN 6 IN	EA	1.25			1	148			
171366	FRYING PAN 6 IN	EA	1.25	16150	3/03	4			24	
171366	FRYING PAN 6 IN	EA	1.25	A0640	3/08	2		180	36	
171366	FRYING PAN 6 IN	EA	1.25	16820	3/14	4			12	

Fig. 8-3. Inventory transaction listing
(Courtesy of International Business Machines.)

STOCK STATUS SUMMARY

DATE: 3/ 31 /

PART NUMBER	PART NAME	UNIT	UNIT COST	OPENING BALANCE	TRANSACTIONS RECEIPTS	TRANSACTIONS ISSUES	ON HAND
171203	WATER PAIL 1 G	EA	1.89	68	145	131	82 *
171364	FRYING PAN 4 IN	EA	1.04	84	156	82	158 *
171366	FRYING PAN 6 IN	EA	1.25	148	180	175	153 *
171368	FRYING PAN 8 IN	EA	1.38	75	288	184	179 *
171370	FRYING PAN 10	EA	1.54	64	72	56	80 *

Fig. 8-4. Stock status summary
(Courtesy of International Business Machines.)

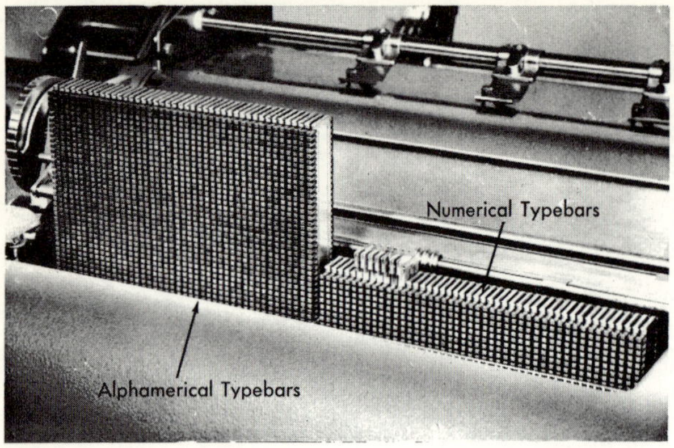

Fig. 8-5. Print unit (Courtesy of International Business Machines.)

typebar consists of 10 numerals and one symbol. In odd-numbered typebars the symbol is an asterisk (*), and in the even-numbered typebars it is a credit symbol (CR).

The character in the typebar which will be positioned for printing is determined by the holes punched in the card or by the totals which the machine has accumulated.

The 402 has two sets of 80 reading brushes, labeled second and third reading (Fig. 8-6). On the 402 the card is read at the third-reading station for printing. The cards pass the second- and third-reading stations in synchronization, meaning that as the 5 row is being read at second read, the 5 row is being read at third read.

Now let us explain some of the control-panel hubs.

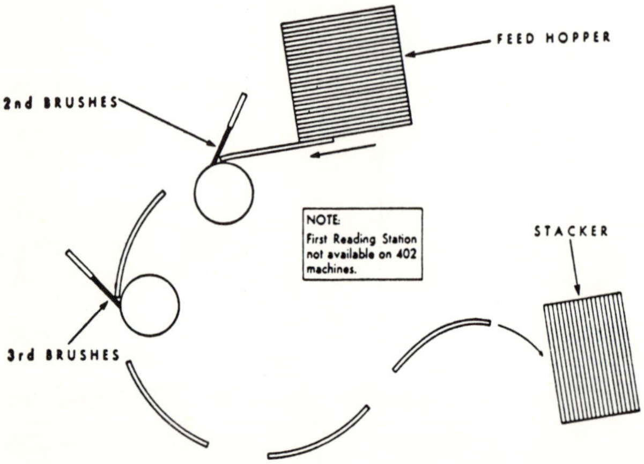

Fig. 8-6. Path of the card through the 402 feed (Courtesy of International Business Machines.)

The second-reading hubs (M and N, 1-40) are used primarily for reading control punches, zone punches, and comparing with the card at third read. The third-reading hubs (O and P, 1-40, DD and EE, 1-40) are used for normal reading operations and are wired to counters and print-entry hubs. The third-read hubs are also used for comparing with the card at second read.

The ***normal alphameric print entry hubs*** (Q, 1-43) contain an alphameric typebar for each entry hub. They are wired to print the numeric information punched in the corresponding card columns.

The ***numeric print-entry hubs*** (R, 1-44 and S, 44) contain an entry for each numeric typebar. They are used to print the numeric fields punched in the card.

To print an alphabetic character, the typebar must receive a zone impulse on one cycle and a digit impulse on the next cycle. The zone impulse is read in the normal zone-entry hubs (L, 1-43) from second read, and the digit impulse is read in the normal alphameric print entry from third read.

Before we can cover the actual printing, we must explain several other hubs which are:

ALL CYCLES

The all-cycles hubs (HH, 41-50) are available on every machine cycle. They are used to control many functions in the machine.

LIST

The list hubs (Z, 41-42) are two common hubs which, when impulsed, cause all 88 typebars to rise every time a card passes the third-reading station. If there are holes in the card and the control panel is properly wired, the typebars will print each time they rise. This operation is called ***detail printing*** and is done at the rate of 50 to 150 cards per minute (depending upon machine model). Single spacing is automatic before each line prints.

DETAIL PRINTING - NUMERIC INFORMATION

In the report shown in Fig. 8-7, the fields

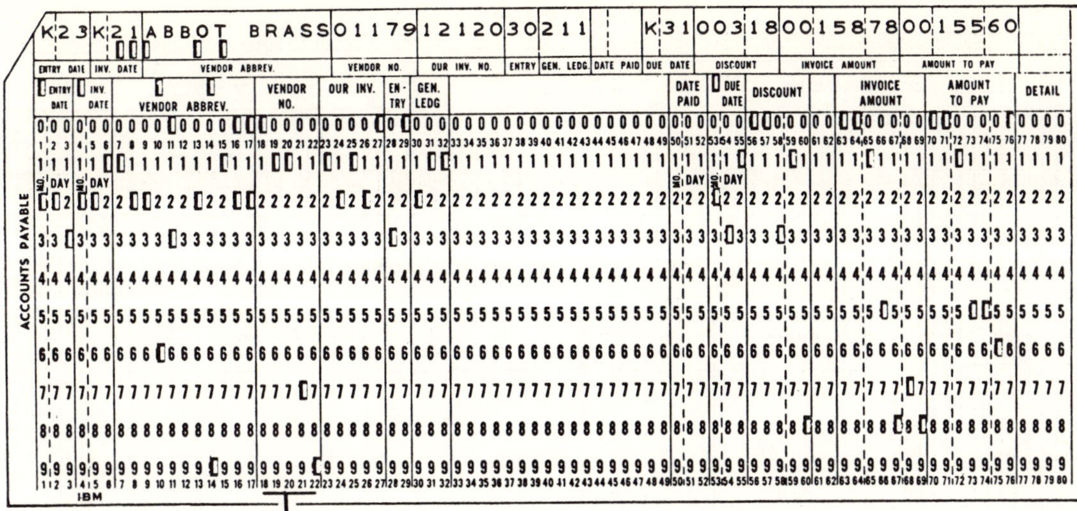

CASH REQUIREMENTS STATEMENT

VENDOR ABBREVIATION	VENDOR NUMBER	DUE DATE MO.	DUE DATE DAY	DISCOUNT	INVOICE AMOUNT	AMOUNT TO PAY	TOTAL BY DATE
ABBOT BRASS	1179	12	31	318	15878	15560	
ABBOT BRASS	1179	12	31	196	9813	9617	
ABRAMS COAL	1180	12	31	831	27735	26904	
ABRAMS COAL	1180	12	31	1050	30000	28950	
BARR MACH	3076	12	31	15077	301527	286450	
EL TRUST CO	29521	12	31		5125	5125	
KARTAGE INC	44860	12	31		21875	21875	
LEHIGH COAL	48678	12	31	1384	69178	67794	
MAIZE REF	58091	12	31		11823	11823	
N MILT SUPP	60035	12	31		21415	21415	
N Y GAS EL	61221	12	31		67595	67595	
STATE N Y	74213	12	31		179286	179286	
W COR TEL	81469	12	31		23729	23729	
WICKWIRE BR	86341	12	31		36043	36043	
WISELO INC	88213	12	31		19518	19518	

Fig. 8-7. Cash requirements statement and accounts payable card (Courtesy of International Business Machines.)

in the card must be printed below the corresponding headings of the report. This is accomplished by using a spacing chart (Fig. 8-8). You will notice that when the cash requirements statement report is aligned, the vendor number positions are within alphameric typebars 35 to 39. Now look at Fig. 8-7. The vendor number is punched in columns 18 to 22. Figure 8-9 depicts the wiring for listing the vendor number for the report in Fig. 8-7. You will notice that wire 2 is an all-cycles impulse to list. This will cause the printing of each card as it passes third read. Wire 1 transmits the punched

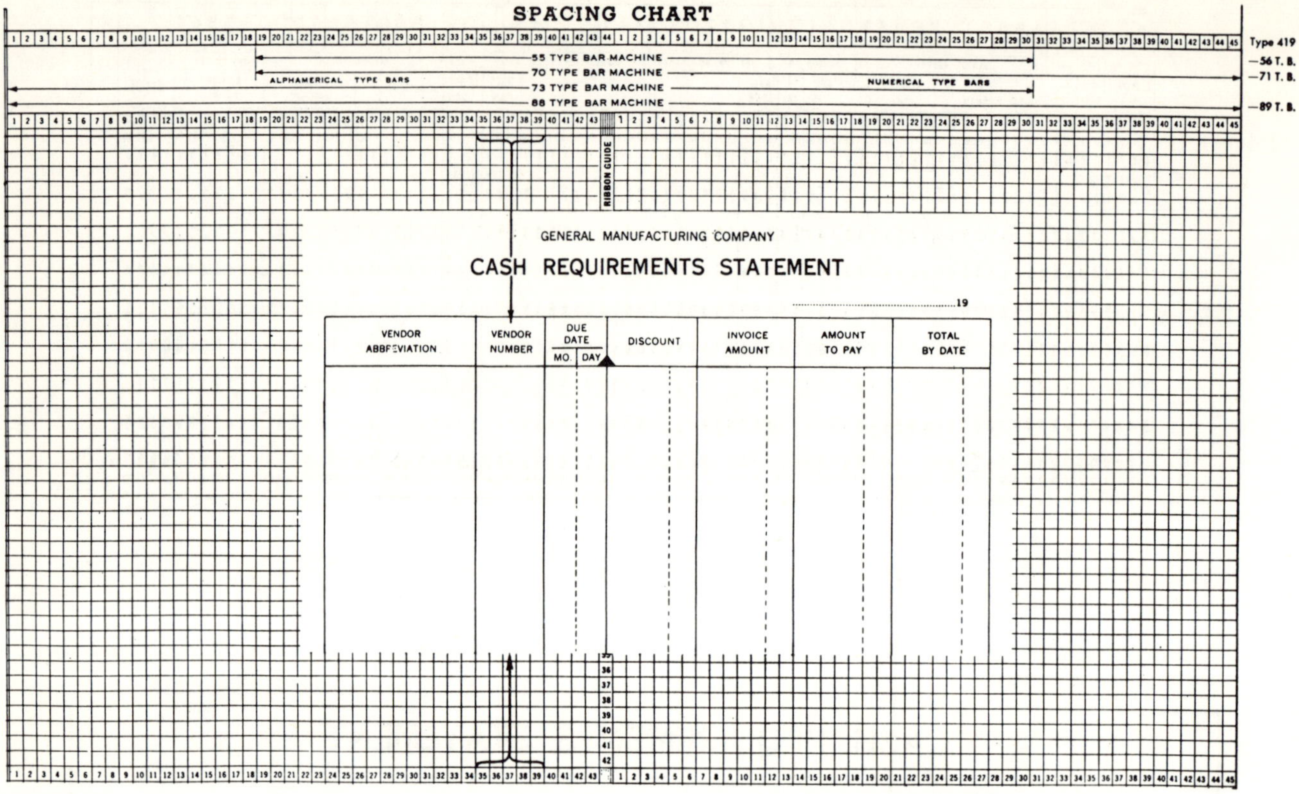

NOTE: On the 402, 403 Alphabetic Accounting Machines, the alphameric type bars (1-43) are separated from the numeric type bars (1-45) by a ribbon guide position. On the 419 Numerical Accounting Machine the ribbon guide is removed and an additional type bar (44) is inserted in its place. Thus, the numerical type bars on the 419 are numbered 1-44 on the left and 1-45 on the right.

Fig. 8-8. Report and spacing chart (Courtesy of International Business Machines.)

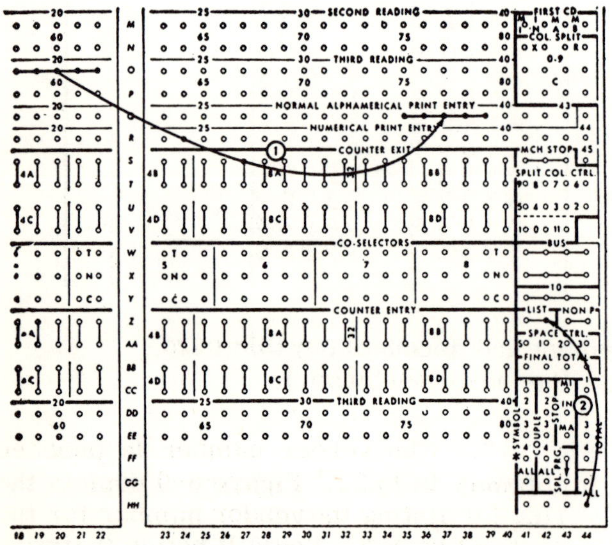

Fig. 8-9. Wiring for numeric detail printing (Courtesy of International Business Machines.)

data from third read hubs 18-22 into normal alphameric print-entry hubs 35-39.

DETAIL PRINTING - ALPHABETIC INFORMATION

Letters as well as numbers may be printed from the 43 alphameric typebars located on the left side of the print unit. To print letters, a typebar must be impulsed from two holes in the same column - a zone punch and a digit punch.

NORMAL-ZONE ENTRY

To print an alphabetic character, the typebar must receive a zone impulse (0, 11, or 12) on one cycle. Zone punches are read from the second-reading brushes and are accepted by any of the 43 normal-zone entry hubs at L, 1-43 to zone the typebars so

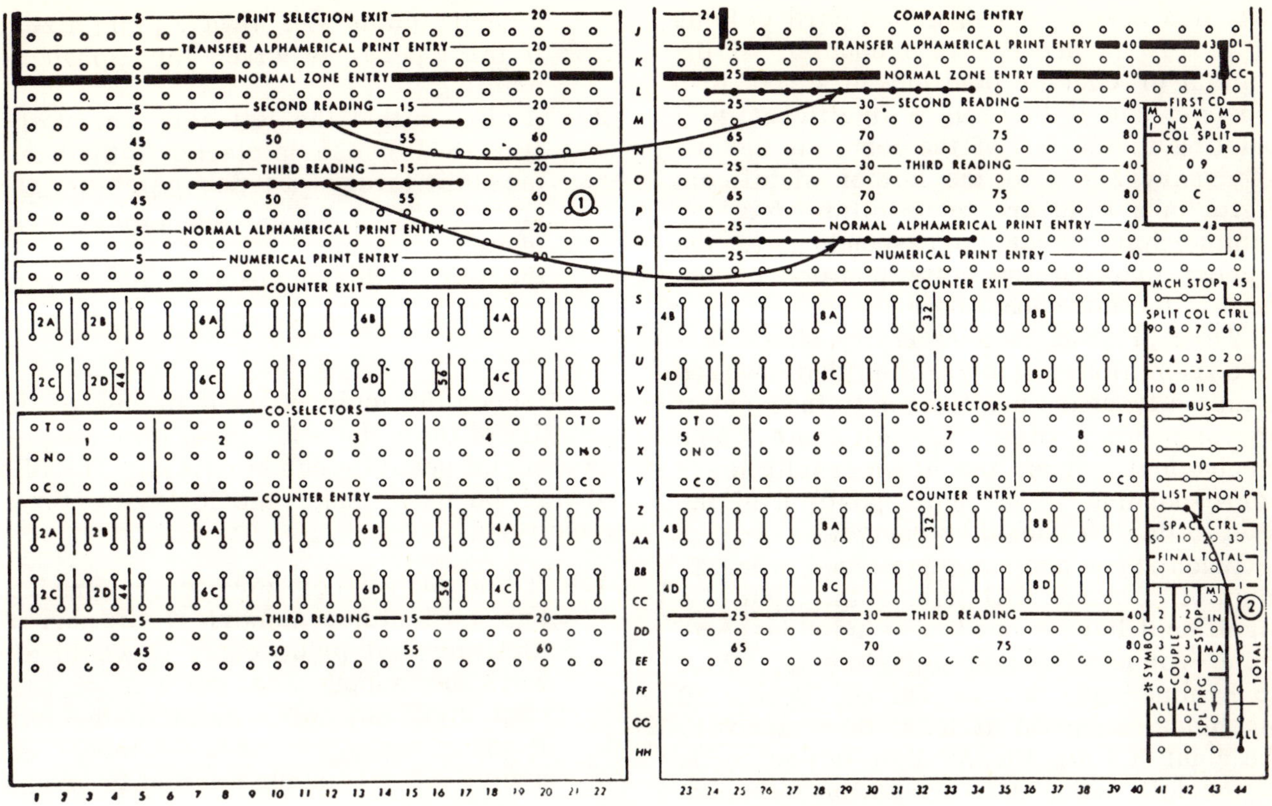

Fig. 8-10. Wiring for alphabetic detail printing (Courtesy of International Business Machines.)

that the proper letter will print on the following cycle when the digit punch is read. Normal-zone entry hubs will accept only zone impulses. Figure 8-10 illustrates the wiring for the alphabetic printing of vendor abbreviation from columns 7 to 17 into normal alphameric print entry 24 to 34. Notice that the same card columns are wired from both the second- and third-reading stations, the difference being that second read is wired to normal zone entry. (Note that the same numbered entry hubs are used.)

PROBLEM 1: Draw a diagram to detail print the numeric data (vendor number, discount, invoice amount, amount to pay) in Fig. 8-7 in the print-entry positions shown in Fig. 8-8. (Due date is three columns and prints in four positions.)

PROBLEM 2: Add to the diagram of PROBLEM 1, the printing of alphabetic data (vendor) in Fig. 8-7 in the print-entry positions as shown in Fig. 8-8.

ZERO PRINTING

Printing of zeros from both alphameric and numeric typebars is controlled by the ***hammersplit levers,*** also referred to as the ***zero-suppression levers*** (Fig. 8-11). There are 88 of these levers, one for each typebar. When any hammersplit lever is raised, zeros and special character positions to the right of it, up to the next significant digit (other than zero), are suppressed.

The alphameric typebars print zeros,

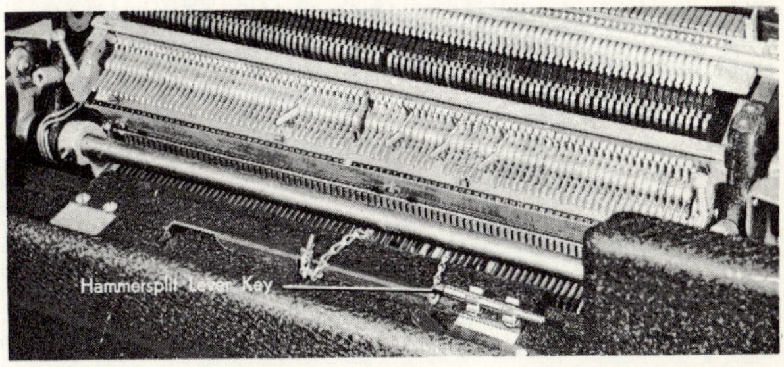

Fig. 8-11. Hammersplit levers (Courtesy of International Business Machines.)

only if a zero is punched in a card column or a zero is present in a counter, if the column or counter position is wired to a typebar, and if there is a significant digit printing to the left of the zero. If the unnecessary zeros to the left of significant digits in a field are to be eliminated, the hammersplit lever corresponding to the typebar printing the units position of the field to the left should be raised.

Zero printing in numeric typebars differs from alphameric zeros in that unwired numeric typebars print zeros to the right of any significant digit. To eliminate these mechanical zeros, the hammersplit lever corresponding to the units position of the field to the left should be raised.

When zeros are not suppressed, a maximum of 10 zeros will print to the right of a significant digit, depending on individual machine components and adjustments. With no hammersplit levers raised, Series 50 machines can print at least three zeros to the right of a significant digit or five zeros to the left, using a five-position ***left- zero carry clip***. Where fields are separated at intervals by raised hammersplit levers, one operated typebar prints up to 10 zeros to the right within a field (Fig. 8-12).

A special character (located in the special-character position) can be printed on the alphameric typebars by a single 12 punch. The printing of this character is under the control of the hammersplit levers in the same way as is the zero position.

It is possible to print a zero from any typebar, without a significant digit to the left, in one of the following ways:

1. The combination of a 1 and a 0 punch in a card column will always print a zero if the typebar is wired for alphabetic printing.
2. A clip, called the left-zero carry clip (Fig. 8-13), can be placed on the hammersplit lever of a typebar printing the units position and on the hammersplit levers of as many as six typebars to the left of this position to cause zero printing.

A zero clip would be used to ensure the printing of the high-order zero, for example, in a social security number field. The clip should be used under the following three conditions:

1. If the high-order zero were wired to hub 1 of either numerical or normal alphamerical print entry it would always be suppressed since a significant digit can never print to the left.
2. If any of the typebars to the left of the social security number failed to print a significant digit the high-order zero would be suppressed when printing in the normal alphamerical typebars.
3. If printing in the numerical typebars and the hammersplit lever in the units position of the field to the immediate left was not raised (in order to print the high-order zero of the social security number) but the hammersplit lever in the units position in the field to its left was raised. The problem arises when the middle field fails to print a significant digit. The result would be suppression of the high-order zero of the social security number.

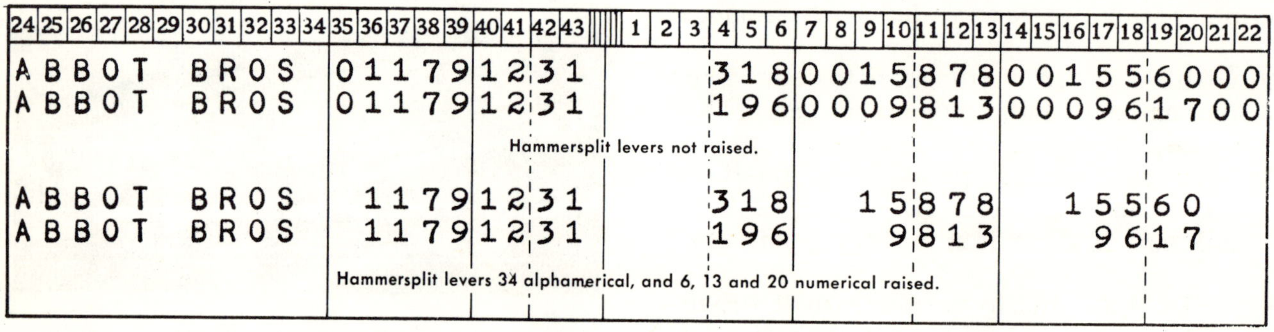

Fig. 8-12. Zero printing
(Courtesy of International Business Machines.)

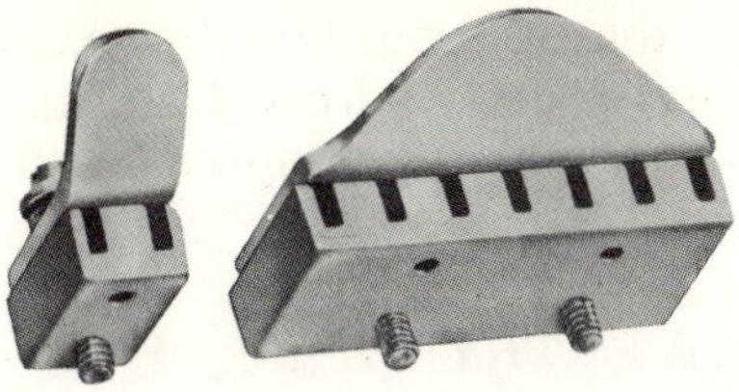

Fig. 8-13. Zero carry clip (Courtesy of International Business Machines.)

ADDITION

One of the functions of the 402 is that of accumulation, which is performed by a series of single one-position accumulators, each capable of adding up to 9. These single-position accumulators or counter wheels are grouped into units called counters, which vary in size from a two-position counter to an eight-position counter. Within each counter a single position will add up to 9 and then carry over to the next position to its left. These two counter positions in turn add up to 99 and then carry over into the third position, and so on. The carry over within each counter is automatic.

Each counter is identified by a number and a letter, the number indicating how many positions the counter contains and the letter identifying the counter. (The counters entries are located on the control panel at Z-CC, 1-40.) For example, 2A is the first two-position counter and 8D is the fourth eight-position counter. (The number of counters depends upon the particular machine. Ask your instructor which counters are available on your particular machine.) An 80 counter machine consists of the following groupings:

2A	4A	6A	8A
2B	4B	6B	8B
2C	4C	6C	8C
2D	4D	6D	8D

Now let us see how the counters actually add. When we impulse the counter-control-plus hub of the particular counter, we allow the digits punched in the card to reach the counter wheels. When the first card starts through the 402 Accounting Machine, 9 edge first, the wheels of all the counters stand at 0. When impulses from the card reach the counter, the counter wheels start turning.

In Fig. 8-14, the counter is standing at 0 and the impulse from the hole in the card has just reached the counter wheel. The wheel now starts to move past the reading brushes in time with the movement of the card. From the time the wheel starts to move, until it stops at 0 time, four positions of the card move past the third-reading brushes. As the four punching positions of the card pass the reading brushes, the counter wheel advances four numbers and stops at 0 time. The digit 4 has been added into the counter wheel as shown.

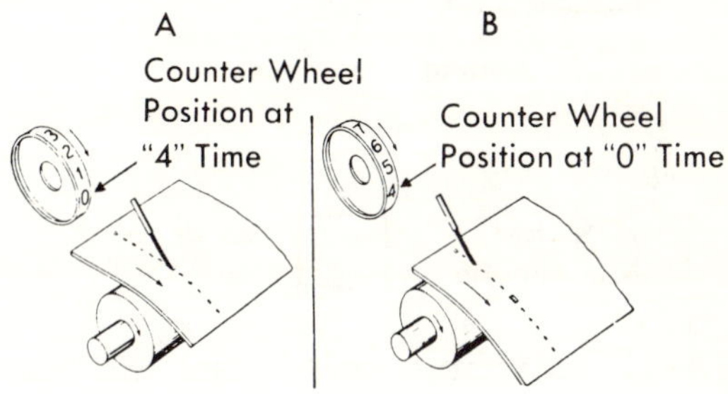

Fig. 8-14. Movement of counterwheel in addition (Courtesy of International Business Machines.)

When adding in a counter, it is only necessary to start the adding wheel in motion electrically. The wheel is stopped mechanically and automatically at 0 time of the machine cycle.

Figure 8-15 shows this on a counter chart. Assume that we have zeros in the counter wheels and that we are using a two-position counter. The units-position wheel does not move until the 4-hole in the card is read by the brush. At that time the impulse to the start magnet starts the wheel moving. The adding wheel continues to turn until it is stopped mechanically at 0 time of the machine cycle. The tens-position adding wheel did not turn because the card was not punched in the tens column. At the completion of the card-feed cycle we have 04 standing in the counter wheels.

Counters may be *coupled* with one another in any desired arrangement. For

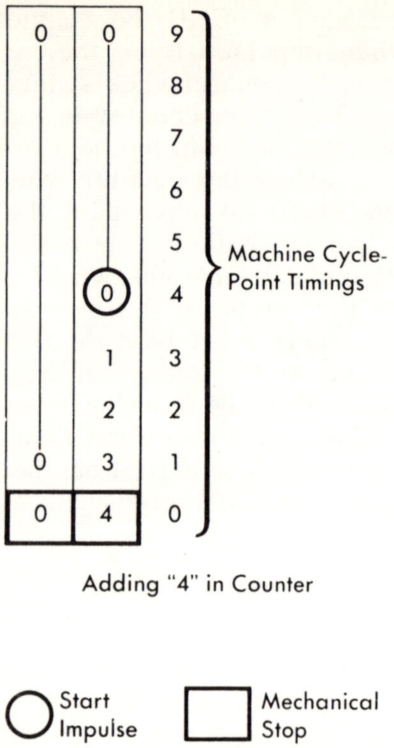

Fig. 8-15. Machine-cycle point timings in addition (Courtesy of International Business Machines.)

example an eight-position counter may be coupled with a two-position counter to form a ten-position counter.

For best operation, no more than 16-counter positions should be coupled. Coupling of counters will be covered in detail later.

The four basic steps in wiring for addition are:

1. What information is to be accumulated? (counter entry)
2. Which cards are to be added? (counter control)
3. When should the total be printed? (counter read-out and reset)
4. Where should the total be printed? (counter exit to typebars)

CARD CYCLES: J-Q, 49-50

The upper five-hubs in the left column are active on every card-feed cycle including *heading* cards. (Heading cards are the name card, the street card, and the city and state card.) The other 11 hubs are active for cards that are not heading cards. They are normally used, directly or through selectors, to control counters to add or subtract.

COUNTER ENTRY: Z-CC, 1-40

The counter entry hubs accept information to be added or subtracted in a counter. They are normally wired from third reading for addition or subtraction. Each counter is identified with a number representing its size and a letter identifying its location.

COUNTER CONTROL PLUS: S-T, 51-66

Each counter has a corresponding plus entry, which must be impulsed to cause the counter to add as the card passes the third-reading station. If a counter is to add a field from every card, a card-cycles impulse is wired directly to the plus hubs of that counter.

COUNTER TOTAL: GG-HH, 51-66

Each counter has a pair of common total-entry hubs. When they are impulsed, the counter will ***read-out*** (print the accumulated total) and ***clear*** (reset to zero). When the total will print depends on the type of impulse wired to the total entry hubs.

FINAL TOTAL: BB, 42-44

There are three final-total exit hubs, each independent of the other. They are tied in directly with a final-total key located to the right of the stop key, on the front of the machine. They emit impulses only when the machine is idling, the hopper is empty, the last card is in the stacker, and the start key is depressed with the final total key held down. They are normally wired to counter total hubs to print final totals after the conditions already mentioned have been satisfied, thus preventing accidental clearing. All normal spacing is suppressed during the final-total cycle.

COUNTER EXIT: S-V, 1-40

Each counter entry has a corresponding counter exit from which all counter detail printing and total printing is obtained. These hubs are normally wired to the alphameric or numeric print entry for counter detail printing and total printing or to the exits of other counters for total transfer or cross-footing operations (to be described later).

The use of all the hubs just described is illustrated in Fig. 8-16. Wire 1 reads the amounts into counter 8D and wire 2 impulses counter 8D to add on every card cycle. The amounts will be printed in the numeric type-bars by the wires shown in 3. Wire 4 will cause the final total in counter 8D to be printed under the control of the final-total key, while wire 5 will cause the amounts to be printed from each card.

PROBLEM 3: Add the wiring to the diagram from PROBLEM 2 to total the discount, invoice amount, and amount to pay in counters 6A, 8A, and 8B. Detail print these amounts, and print the accumulated totals from the respective counters.

PROGRAM CONTROL

Program control is the function by means of which the machine can distinguish the cards of one classification from those of another. The cards in a single classification are referred to as a ***program group;*** for example, after payables distribution cards have been sorted by department number, the cards for one particular department are referred to as a single-program group.

The machine, by the use of the second and third sets of reading brushes, can read simultaneously the holes punched in two successive cards. Each card, when it is at the second station, is compared with the preceding card, which is at the third station. When a card passes the third station, it is compared with the succeeding card, which is at the second station. Thus, each card passing through the machine is compared twice, once with the card ahead of it and once with the card following it. If the fields are punched the same, indicating that the cards are of the same program group, the machine will continue to feed cards. When the punching in the field of one card does not compare with the punching in the field of the card preceding it and the panel is properly wired, the machine will automatically start a total-program cycle.

Three types of totals are possible on the 402 - minor, intermediate, and major. They are also known as program levels 1, 2, and 3. A minor program is used for the classification representing the smallest grouping, intermediate program for the next larger

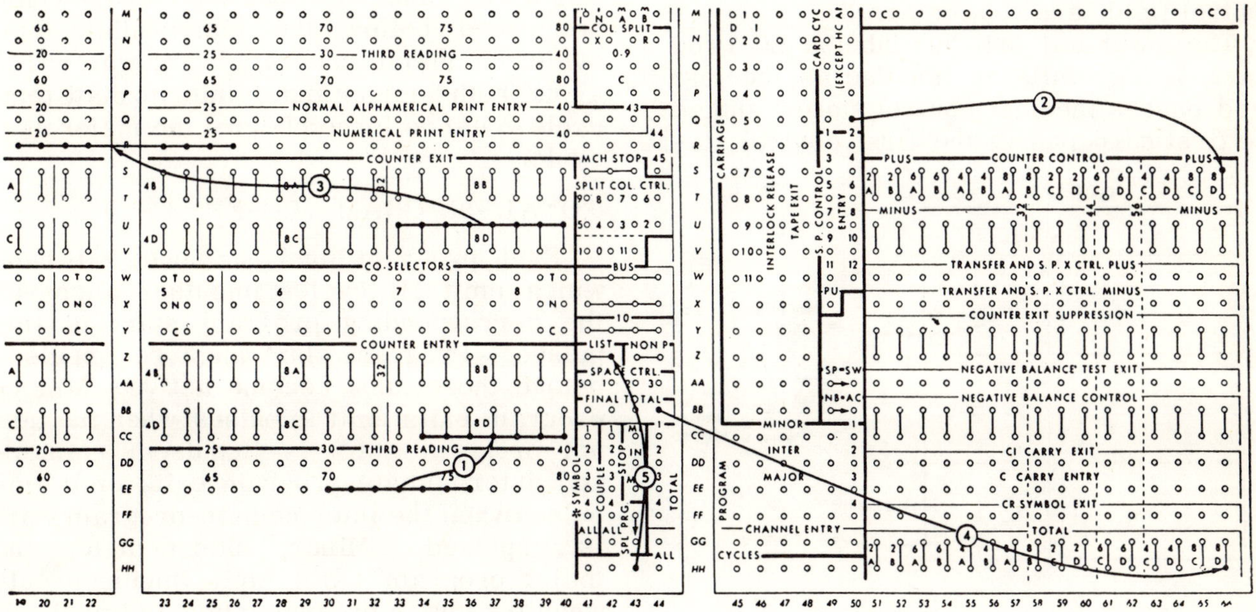

Fig. 8-16. Wiring for addition (Courtesy of International Business Machines.)

grouping, and major program for the largest group. If totals of sales amount were to be printed by state, by city, and by customer number, customer number would be considered a minor group, city an intermediate group, and state a major group.

COMPARING UNIT: G-J, 25-44

The number of comparing positions depends upon the model of the machine. Each position consists of two comparing entry hubs and two comparing exit hubs. The two common comparing exit hubs are diagonally arranged to facilitate wiring.

Comparison is accomplished by wiring the fields to be compared from the second reading hubs to one row of comparing entries and from the third reading hubs to the other row of comparing entries (Fig. 8-17). Either row of comparing entries may be wired from either set of brushes. Although any hubs within a comparing entry row may be used, the corresponding hubs in the other comparing entry row must be wired.

During each card cycle, 1-9 and 11-12 readings to both sides of the comparing entries are compared. If the readings entered into the comparing unit are not identical, impulses are available at the two common comparing exit hubs. Zeros, whether used in a numeric or alphabetic control field, are not compared.

The lower left exit hub labeled LC Prog Start, I, 25, emits an impulse as the last card passes the last control station and as the first card passes the first control station, and may be used to initiate programs on the run-in and on the run-out. It is wired to Program Start Immediate on the 402. The LC hub must never be connected to comparing exit hubs. The comparing exit hubs are jacked together in order to allow all unequal impulses to be available from one of the exit hubs. The number of exit hubs jacked is always one less than the number of entry hubs used (see Fig. 8-19).

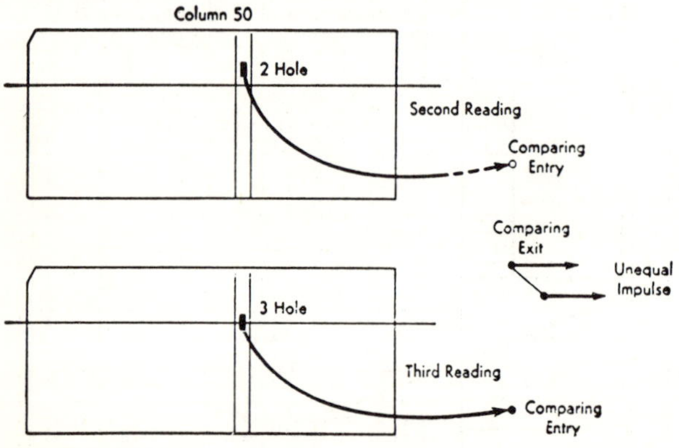

Fig. 8-17. Comparing (Courtesy of International Business Machines.)

The two cards shown in Fig. 8-17 pass their respective reading stations at the same time. Because the cards are fed into the machine face down, 9 edge first, the 3 hole at the third-reading station is read before the 2 hole at the second-reading station. Therefore, the 3 impulse reaches the comparing unit before the 2 impulse, setting up an unequal condition in the unit and making impulses available at the comparing exit hubs. The impulses can be used to stop the feeding of cards and start total programs.

PROGRAM START

The three I (immediate) hubs, labeled minor, intermediate, and major (F-H, 45), receive comparing exit impulses from comparing exit hubs to stop card feeding and start total programming, one program for minor, two for intermediate, and three for major. If intermediate program start was wired alone, a minor total cycle would be forced before the intermediate-total cycle. If major program start was wired alone, both a minor and an intermediate total cycle would be forced before the major total cycle.

TOTAL PROGRAM: CC-FF, 45-50

Each program level has seven exit hubs which emit all cycles impulses whenever the corresponding program start is impulsed. Program start must be impulsed before these hubs become active. Minor-program exits emit impulses when the minor-program start is impulsed. Minor- and intermediate-program exits emit impulses when the intermediate-program start is impulsed. Minor, intermediate, and major program exits emit impulses only when the major program start is impulsed.

Each row of hubs is completely independent of the other row of hubs and only one row is active at a time. Counters read-out and reset automatically when a total program is wired to a counter total entry. After total printing, the machine restarts automatically for the following group. The fourth level shown on the diagram is a special feature.

ASTERISK (*) SYMBOL: CC-GG, 41

An asterisk may be printed from all odd-numbered numeric typebars by wiring one of the asterisk symbol hubs to numeric print entry - hub F to print an asterisk for final totals, hub 1 for minor totals, hub 2 for intermediate totals, and hub 3 for major totals. Hub 4 is used with the special program. The hub labeled ALL will emit a 10 impulse to print an asterisk for all total programs.

DETAIL PRINTING - MINOR, INTERMEDIATE, AND MAJOR PROGRAM

The expense distribution form shown in Fig. 8-18 is a detail-printed report. The smallest group on this report is subledger number and is therefore referred to as the minor group. The largest group is department and is referred to as the major group. The group between the minor and major is general ledger and is referred to as the intermediate group.

For each of the three groups mentioned, there is a corresponding total. The first minor total, $1,409.42, was printed from one counter when the machine recognized a change from 660 to 700 in the subledger number. The first intermediate total, $2;085.37, was printed from another counter when the machine recognized a change from 913 to 915 in the general ledger number. The first major total, $4,204.87, was printed from a third counter when the machine recognized a change from 41 to 43 in department number.

Just as the three groups are known as the minor, intermediate, and major groups, the totals are known as minor, intermediate, and major totals.

Wiring for programming (Fig. 8-19) is illustrated by the following:

1. Subledger is wired from columns 33 to 35 of both second and third reading to comparing entry. Two jackplugs in the corresponding comparing exits make all three comparing positions common, so that if there is an unequal condition in any one of the three, a comparing exit impulse will be available either from the fourth hub in the top row or the seventh hub in the second row. This impulse is directed to program-start minor and causes the machine to initiate a program cycle for every change in subledger group.
2. General ledger is wired from columns 30 to 32 of both second and third reading to comparing entry. The comparing exit is wired to program-start intermediate to initiate a second program cycle for every change in general ledger group.
3. Department is wired from columns 36 to 38 of both second and third reading to comparing entry. The comparing exit is wired to program-start major to initiate a third program cycle for every change in department group.
4. Counter 8A is wired to read-out and reset on a minor program, counter 8B on an intermediate program, and counter 8C on a major program. The counter entry and exit wiring is not shown on the diagram.
5. Subledger, general ledger, and department are printed for each card by wiring each of the three fields from third reading directly to alphameric print entry.
6. An asterisk is printed to the right of every minor total by wiring asterisk symbol hub 1 to numeric print entry 9.
7. The machine is wired to detail print every card.

PROBLEM 4: Prepare a diagram to show comparing, addition, detail printing, and counter total read-out and reset. The minor control field is in columns 11 to 13; the intermediate control field is in columns 21 to 23; and the major control field is in columns 31 to 33. Add the minor, intermediate, and major amounts in card columns 14 to 16, 24 to 26, and 34 to 38 into counters 4A, 4B, and 6C.

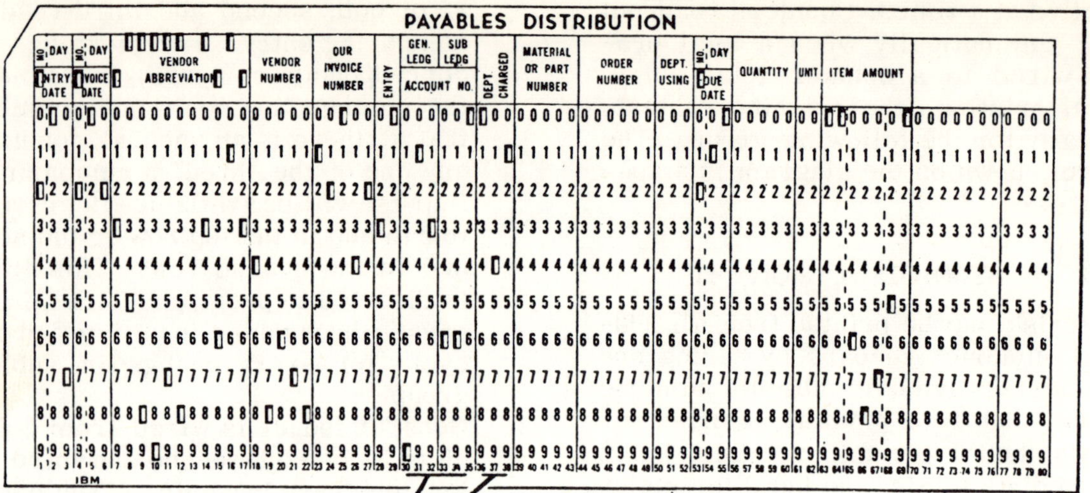

EXPENSE DISTRIBUTION
BY DEPARTMENT OR BRANCH

DEPT. OR BRANCH	ACCOUNT No. GEN. LEDG.	ACCOUNT No. SUB. LEDG.	OUR INVOICE NUMBER	DATE MO.	DATE DAY	AMOUNT	AMOUNT BY ACCOUNT	AMOUNT BY DEPT. OR BRANCH
41	913	660	12042	12	07	68750		
41	913	660	12084	12	14	72192		
						140942 *		
41	913	700	12125	12	23	67595		
						67595 *		
							208537	
41	915	760	12086	12	15	211950		
						211950 *		
							211950	
								420487
43	913	730	12171	12	31	4740		
						4740 *		
43	913	740	12164	12	31	61193		
						61193 *		
43	913	750	12089	12	15	20000		
						20000 *		

Fig. 8-18. Expense distribution statement and payables distribution card (Courtesy of International Business Machines.)

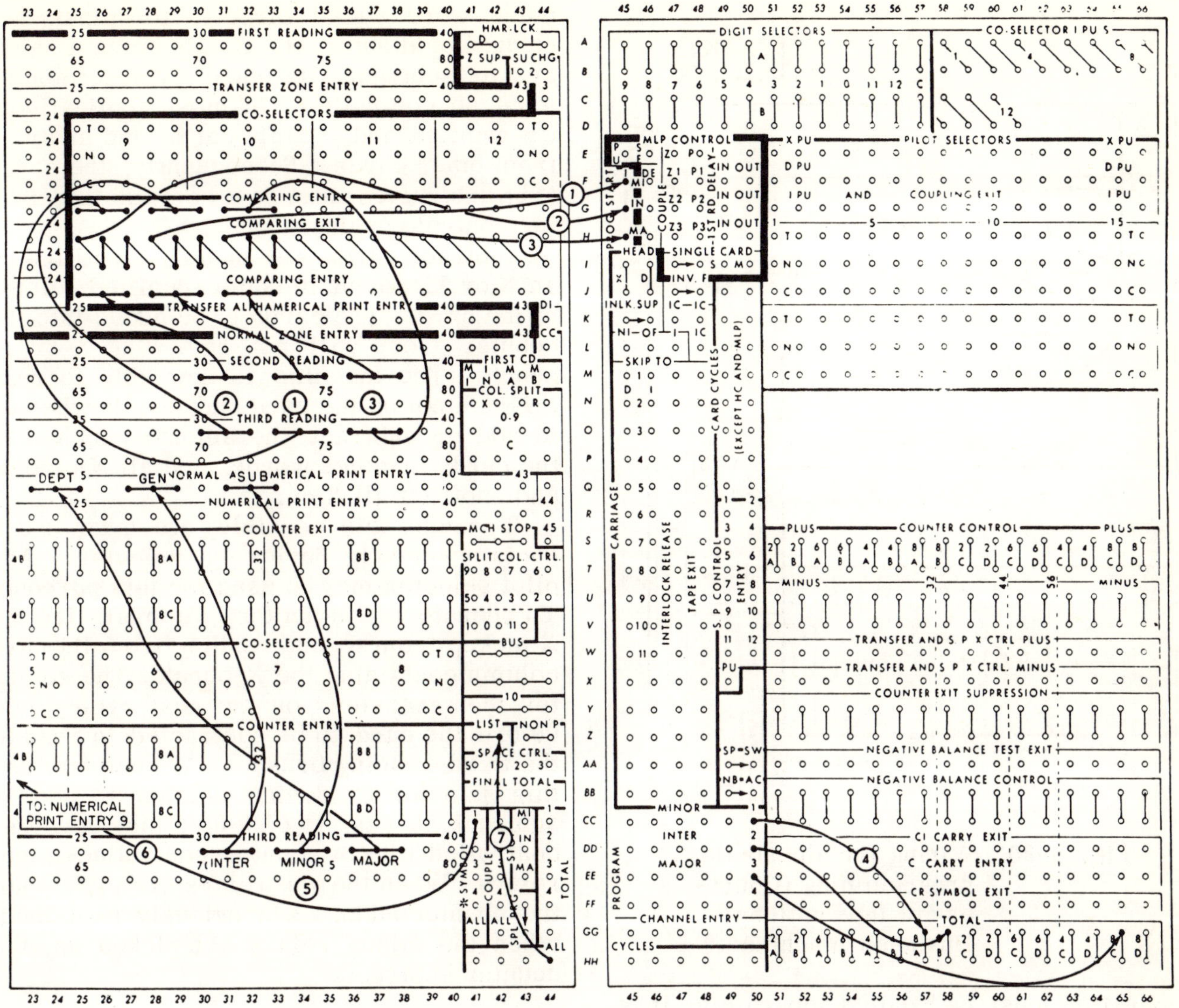

Fig. 8-19. Wiring for numeric programming (Courtesy of International Business Machines.)

Print the totals in numeric print entry typebars 21 to 24, 26 to 29, and 9 to 14. Print asterisks for each level of totals in numeric print entry types 25 for minor, 31 for intermediate, and 15 for major totals. (Indicate necessary hammer-splits.)

PROGRAM CONTROL ON ALPHABETIC FIELDS

Alphabetic as well as numeric information may be compared and printed. As shown in Fig. 8-20, the wiring to the comparing unit is the same.

In order to print as well as compare alphabetic information, two uses must be made of the second reading station - one to zone and one to compare. Therefore, split wires are necessary.

SUBTRACTION IN THE IBM 402 ACCOUNTING MACHINES

We often find it necessary to subtract as well as add amounts in a counter. An example of this is subtracting income tax deductions when preparing payroll checks. It is possible to both add and subtract in a counter of an accounting machine. Each

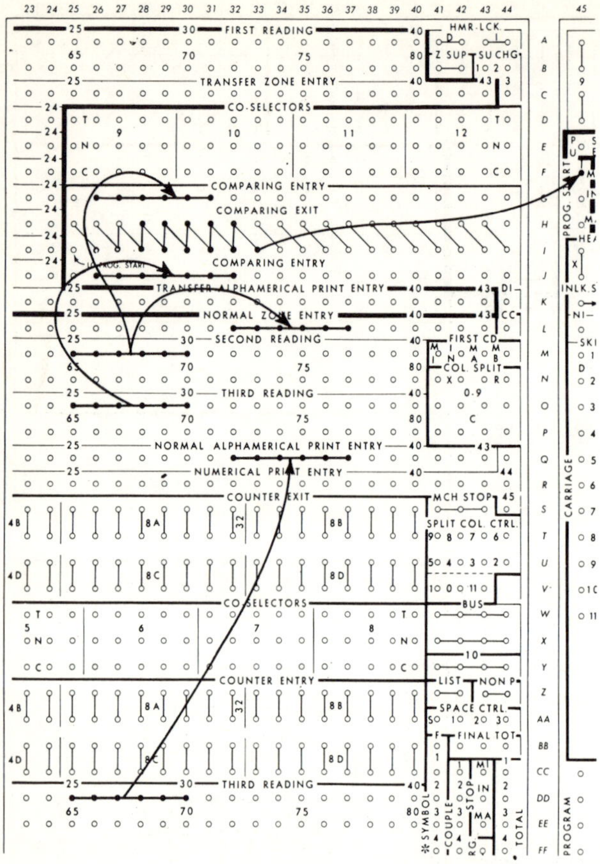

Fig. 8-20. Wiring for alphabetic programming (Courtesy of International Business Machines.)

operation must be handled separately; it is impossible to add and subtract in one counter group during the same machine cycle.

When adding, we instructed the counter to add the contents of a field from a card at third read by impulsing the counter control plus. When subtracting, the field to be subtracted must be wired from third reading to counter control entry, but instead of impulsing counter control plus, the counter control minus hub must be impulsed.

COUNTER CONTROL MINUS: U-V, 51-66

Each counter has two common minus hubs which, when wired from a card cycles impulse, cause the counter to subtract. Subtraction on the 402 is accomplished by a system of complementary arithmetic where, in order to subtract, the 9s complement of the number is added. If a card cycles impulse were wired directly to minus, all cards would subtract. If only certain cards are to subtract, the card cycles impulse must be controlled. In most applications, we want to add certain cards and subtract from other cards. Subsequently, the cards to be subtracted must have some distinguishing control punch.

Subtract cards are usually identified by an X or 11 punch in some specified column of the card. The cards to be added into the counter group will not have the X or 11 punch. The machine is now able to read this column of the card and decide whether to add or subtract the amount punched in the card; in other words, add all NX cards and subtract all X cards.

To make this possible, we must use a decision-making device - a selector. Any pilot selector may be used for this purpose. To operate this selector, we must wire the X pickup from second reading from the card column containing the X-punch. The selector then transfers on the next cycle, just before the card to be subtracted is read at the third-reading brushes. We can now use this selector to decide whether to add or subtract, that is, to pick up either counter-controlled-plus or counter-controlled-minus relays. When the plus relays are picked up, the counter adds, as previously explained. When the minus relays are picked up, the counter subtracts.

PILOT SELECTORS: E-M, 51-66

The number of two-position pilot selectors depends upon the model of the machine. They can be used independently, or in conjunction with other selectors (coselectors: W-Y, 1-40, D-F, 25-44) on the control panel. The guiding function they perform when used with coselectors gives them the name ***pilot selectors.***

The two positions in each selector are vertically arranged. Each position has a C (common), an N (normal), and a T (transferred) hub and three pickup hubs (X, D for digit, and I for immediate). These pickup hubs are used to control the selectors, which, in turn, are used to control various machine functions, such as to add amounts from certain cards and to subtract amounts from other cards.

One of the most common methods of distinguishing one card from another is by an X punch in some column of the card.

A digit may also be used as a distinguishing punch to pick up a pilot selector. The column in which it is punched is wired to the digit-pickup hub. If more than one digit is punched in the column wired to the D pickup, the distinguishing digit must be selected. Once the digit impulse has reached the pilot-selector pickup, the action of the selector is identical to that of one picked up by an X punch. The difference between the two pickups is that a D pickup will accept any digit impulse from 9 through 12, while an X pickup will accept only X or 12 impulses.

The immediate-pickup hubs for each selector will accept any impulse and transfer the selector immediately, instead of one cycle later. When the X or D hubs are impulsed, the I hub will emit an impulse as the selector transfers for the following cycle and will emit this impulse once each cycle thereafter, if the selector remains transferred. This impulse is a short-pickup impulse which can be used as a means of expanding the pilot selector beyond two positions by picking up coselectors (A and B, 58-66; C and D, 58-61). When an I pickup hub is used in this manner, it is called a *coupling exit*. Thus, any coselector to which it is wired functions exactly like the pilot selector.

Whenever the X or D hub of a selector is impulsed, the selector transfers on the following cycle and remains transferred until the controlling card has been read at third reading. Thus, if card feeding is interrupted for any reason, such as for total printing, the selector would be transferred during the printing cycle and the following card cycle.

Whenever the I hub of the selector is impulsed, the selector transfers during the same cycle and remains transferred for that cycle only.

The following summarizes the action of selectors:

Coselectors - transfer immediately and return to normal at the end of the cycle on which they were picked up. I Pickup - transfers immediately and returns to normal at the end of that cycle. D and X Pickup - transfers on the following machine cycle and returns to normal at the end of the following card-feed cycle.

INTERNAL SCHEMATIC SUBTRACTION

When adding into a counter, it was necessary only to start the adding wheel in motion electrically. It was stopped mechanically at 0 time. However, when subtracting, it is necessary to start and stop movement of the adding wheel electrically.

When the minus relays are picked up, we complete an internal electric circuit to start advancing all the wheels in the counter group at 9 time. The wheels continue to advance until stopped by an impulse to the stop magnets. These impulses are received from the third-reading brushes reading the holes punched in the card. Let us assume that we already have 06 accumulated in counter group 2A (Fig. 8-21). The next card

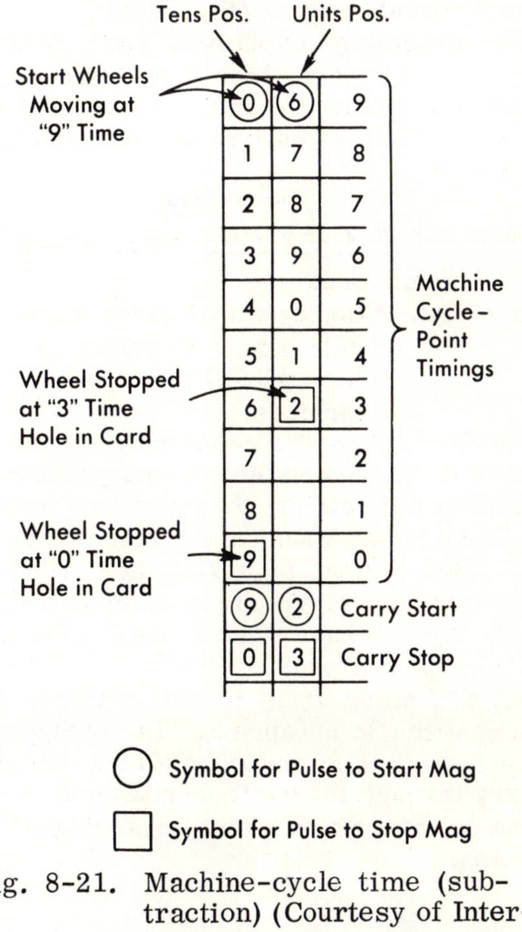

Fig. 8-21. Machine-cycle time (subtraction) (Courtesy of International Business Machines.)

to pass the third-reading brushes is a subtract card with 03 punched in the amount field. Because the minus relays are picked up, we start advancing both counter wheels at 9 time. The units-position wheel does not stop until the 3 hole in the card is read by the brush. Don't overlook the fact that we are starting out with a 6 already in the counter wheel.

Looking at the illustration, we find that 6 cycle points have passed before the 3 hole was read by the brush (9 to 3); this means that the adding wheel was advanced 6 cycle points before being stopped. That is, the wheel advanced from 6 to 7 to 8 to 9 to 0 to 1 to 2 (Fig. 8-22).

The 10s-position counter wheel was treated in the same manner, only in this position we have a 0 punched in the card and we started with a 0 standing in the counter wheel.

The wheel was advanced 9 cycle points before being stopped and the counter wheels are now standing at 92 (Fig. 8-21).

As previously explained, each time a counter wheel moves from 9 to 0, the wheel to its left within the same counter group automatically rotates one position more at carry time.

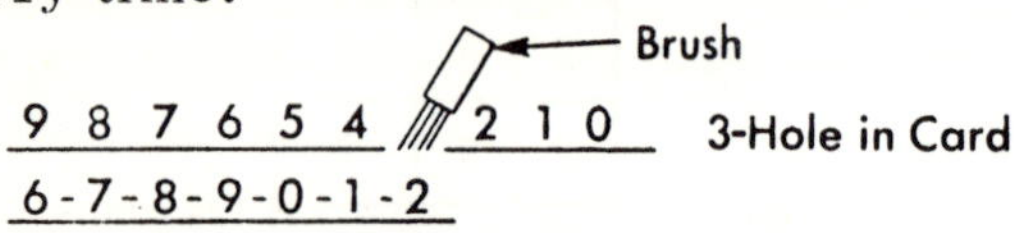

Fig. 8-22. Counter wheel advanced six cycle points (Courtesy of International Business Machines.)

As the high-order counter wheel moves from 9 to 0, we complete a circuit through control-panel wiring to cause the units-position counter wheel to advance one position. This is done by wiring the carry impulse exit hub to the carry entry hub (Fig. 8-23). We now have 92 standing in the counter wheels. However, the units-position wheel did move from 9 to 0, causing the tens position to advance 1. The tens-position wheel then moved from 9 to 0, causing a carry through the control-panel wire back to the units-position wheel advancing it one position.

06 In counter
96 Nines complement of 03 added in counter

92 In counter before CARRY time
1 Carry impulse held until CARRY time

(1) 02 In counter due to carry in tens position as during CARRY time (internal circuits)
1 Carry impulse transferred from high to units position during CARRY time by CI to C wiring

03 Standing in counter at end of card cycle

So we complete this card cycle with 03 standing in the counter wheels. This is the correct total for our problem of 06 minus 03.

CARRY EXIT, CARRY ENTRY: DD and EE, 51-66

These hubs have two functions, counter coupling and carry-back in subtraction. Two or more counters, up to a maximum of 16 positions, may be coupled together by wiring the CI of the counter containing the units position to the C of the coupled counter.

The CI and C hubs are also used for carry back from the left position of a counter to the units position of the same counter or from CI to C. This is necessary when subtracting, to compensate for the shortages that

Positive Result		**Negative Result**	
Problem	**Counter Action**	**Problem**	**Counter Action**
	(6 position)		(6 position)
+175	000175	- 175	999824
- 96	999903	+ 96	000096
	(1)000078 → 1		999920
	000079		
- 102	999897	+102	000102
	999976		(1)000022 → 1
			000023
+ 75	000075	- 75	999924
	(1)000051 → 1		999947
+ 52	000052	- 52	(9's complement of 52)

Fig. 8-23. Positive and negative results (Courtesy of International Business Machines.)

would result because of the use of the 9s complement method. The carry over is added back into the units position when the high order position goes from 9 to 0, by wiring CI to C of the same counter. If the carry back is omitted, every positive total would be short, and every negative total would be over after being converted (Fig. 8-23).

Now you might ask, "Suppose the amount being subtracted in a counter group is larger than the positive amount we already have accumulated in the counter?" The answer is, the counter then turns negative. For example, let's use a four-position counter group and assume we already have 0745 accumulated in the counter. From this amount we subtract 0856:

Manual Computation:	-0856	
	+0745	
	-0111	
Machine Computation:	0745	Standing in counter
	9143	Add nines complement of 0856
	9888	Total

We now have 9888 accumulated in the counter at the end of our computation. The 9 standing in the high-order position of the counter indicates to the machine that this is a negative or credit amount. When subtracting into a counter in the 402 it is imperative that the high-order position always be left available for this purpose.

NEGATIVE-BALANCE-TEST EXIT: AA, 51-66

Each counter has a negative-text exit hub which emits an impulse when the counter is negative on a program cycle. Negative-balance-test exit is normally wired to negative-balance control to convert complements to true figures or to a pilot-selector pickup.

A negative-balance-test exit also emits an impulse for a zero balance in the counter when zero balances are indicated by nines.

NEGATIVE-BALANCE CONTROL. BB and CC, 51-66

Each counter has a pair of common negative-balance-control entry hubs which, when impulsed from negative-balance-test exit, cause a complement figure to be converted to a true figure before it is printed. When counters to be converted are coupled, the negative-balance-control hubs for those counters must also be coupled. The negative-balance-test exit of the high-order counter only must be wired to negative-balance-control.

Our counter is now standing at 9888 or 0111 negative. If the next card to be accumulated is a positive or an add card, and the amount is greater than 0111, the counter will then turn positive again and a 0 should appear in the high-order position. Assume the next card is positive and the amount is 0245:

Manual computation	Machine computation	
+0245	9888	Amount in wheels
-0111	+0245	+ amount in card
+0134	9023	
0 indicates positive amount	1111	Carry
	0134	Total

To have a conversion take place, we must wire the control panel as shown in Fig. 8-25, wire 9.

The fact that we have the negative-balance-test exit hub wired to the negative-balance control hub allows the machine to test the high-order position of the counter group. If there is a 9 present, the machine knows that the amount is negative and should be converted before printing takes place. The total cycle is then held up, and the machine takes a conversion cycle. During a conversion cycle, the machine adds 1, 3, 5, 7, or 9 to the amount already standing in the wheels. All carry operations are suspended during a conversion cycle. Let us see how we convert 9888 to 0111 before printing:

9888
1333 added during conversion cycle
―――
0111

The 1333 added came from internal circuits established when the machine decided conversion was necessary for this counter. The high-order position of a counter group is tested for the presence of a 9 only when the counter is impulsed to total.

CONVERSION - 402

When subtracting, we found that a counter may turn negative, such as the 9888 we had previously. If the machine at this particular time had sensed a control change and signaled for this counter to print a total, the total printed would have been 9888. The operator might believe this to be a positive total of $98.88, which is not so. Actually, the total is $1.11 negative or credit. So, a conversion of the complement to a true negative figure should take place prior to printing the total.

How do we wire the 402 control panel if two counter groups are coupled together to form a larger counter group? Assume we are coupling counter groups 8A and 8B together to form one 16-position counter group.

First, we must consider carrying from one group to the other. We must wire the CI hub of counter group 8B to the C hub of counter group 8A. This will enable us to carry from the eighth-position counter wheel into the ninth-position counter wheel. If the sixteenth-position counter wheel advances from 9 to 0, we must also be able to carry back into the units-position wheel in counter group 8B. This is accomplished by wiring the CI of counter 8A to the C of counter 8B.

What control-panel wiring is necessary to convert 8A and 8B? With the two counter groups coupled together, the high-order position of counter 8B has now lost its identity. The high-order position of the two combined counter groups is the high-order position of counter 8A. Now this is the position the machine must test for a 9 indicating a negative amount. Therefore, the negative-balance test exit for counter group 8A must be wired to 8A negative-balance control. We must also wire the negative-balance control hub of counter 8B; otherwise only 8A is converted.

COUNTER EXIT SUPPRESSION: Y and Z, 51-66

Each counter also has a pair of counter exit suppression hubs. They are entries to suppress printing amounts from the counters. They can be impulsed by the following impulses:

When impulsed by	Printing is suppressed for
Negative-balance-test exit	Total printing when the counter is negative
Card cycles	Detail printing from a counter
First card minor, intermediate, or major	First card printing in a group printing operation
Total program (minor, major, intermediate, and final)	Total printing

When counter exits are suppressed, CR symbols exits are also suppressed.

CR SYMBOL EXIT: FF, 51-66

Each counter has a credit-symbol exit hub which emits an impulse which can be used to print a CR symbol either for a subtracted item or for a negative total. Credit symbols print from all even-numbered numeric typebars. If the CR hub is wired to such a typebar, it will print a CR symbol whenever the minus hub of the counter is impulsed on a card cycle and whenever the counter prints a converted negative total. Therefore a CR symbol would print for zero balances. Whenever counter exits are suppressed, the CR symbol exit is also suppressed.

The following is an example of subtraction:

The X punch in one of the sales accounting cards shown in Fig. 8-24 identifies it as a charge back to the salesman's commission account. The NX card is a debit card and is punched with the commission amount. Whenever the X card is read, the amount

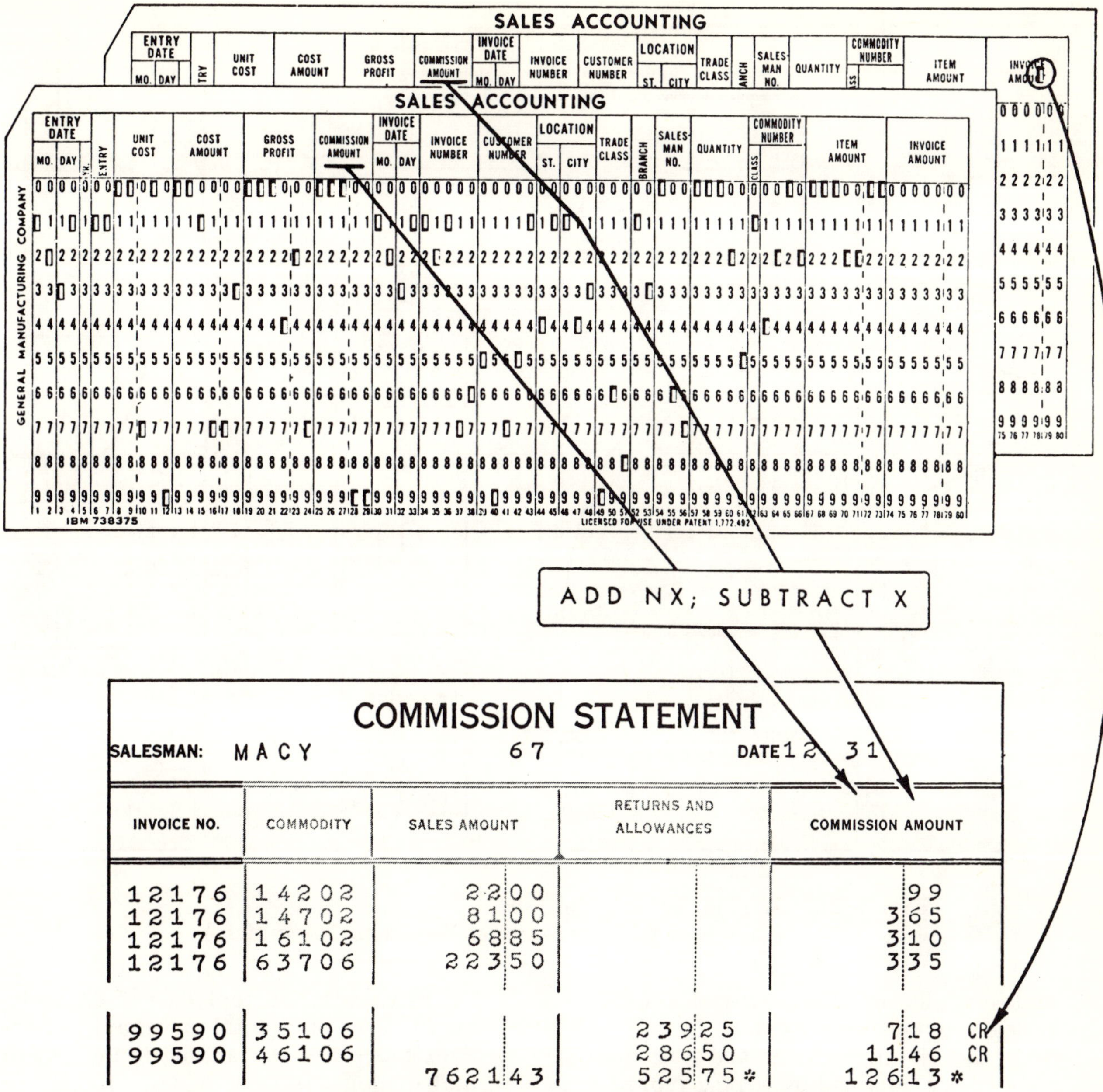

Fig. 8-24. Commission statement and sales accounting card (Courtesy of International Business Machines.)

punched in the commission field is subtracted in counter 8A; whenever an NX card is read, the amount punched in the commission field is added in counter 8A.

The following wiring for subtraction is depicted in Fig. 8-25.

1. The commission amount is wired from third reading to counter 8A entry.
2. The X in column 78, identifying credit cards, is wired from the second-reading station to the X pickup of pilot-selector 1. The X must be read from the second-reading station so that the pilot selector will be transferred by the time the card reaches the third-reading station.
3. A card-cycles impulse is wired to the common of the pilot selector. An X in the card transfers the selector, and the card cycles impulse controls counter 8A to subtract. An NX card does not transfer the selector, and the card cycles impulse controls counter 8A to add.

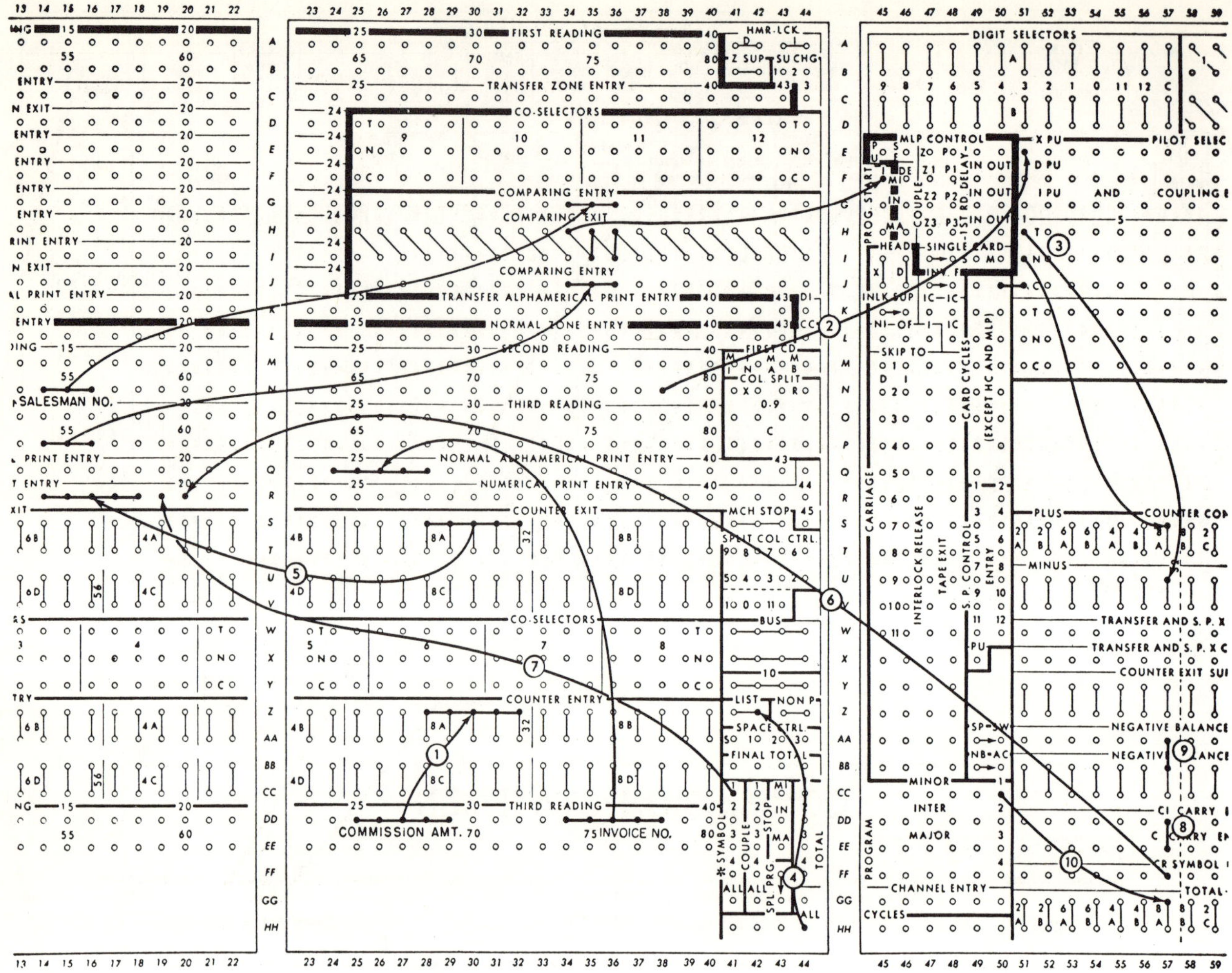

Fig. 8-25. Wiring for subtraction (Courtesy of International Business Machines.)

4. An all-cycles impulse is wired to LIST, to detail print every card.
5. Both the detail amount and the total amount are obtained by wiring from 8A exit to numeric print entry 14-18.
6. Credit listings and credit totals are identified by wiring the credit symbol exit of 8A to numeric print entry 20.
7. Minor totals are identified by wiring the * symbol hub (minor) to print entry 19.
8. Whenever amounts are to be subtracted in a counter, the CI and C of that counter must be wired.
9. A complement amount standing in counter 8A is converted to a true figure by wiring the negative-balance-test exit of 8A to the negative-balance control of 8A. Negative-balance-test exit of 8A emits an impulse on a total program, whenever there is a 9 standing in the left or high-order position of 8A. Negative-balance control receives an impulse from negative-balance-test exit on a total program to cause conversion factors to be added to the complement figure.
10. Counter 8A is cleared for total printing on a minor-total program. The program is initiated by an impulse from the comparing exit resulting from a change in salesman number.

PROBLEM 5: Draw a diagram to show the wiring for the following: Compare on card columns 1 and 2, on a change of group take a minor total. Add columns 6 to 12 into counter 2C and 8C, unless it is an X80 card, then subtract columns 6 to 12 from counter 2C and 8C. Detail print the amounts in numeric print entry typebars 17 to 26. When printing a negative amount print a CR symbol in numeric typebar 28. Print an asterisk on every minor total in number typebar 27.

X-SELECTION

Selectors play a more important part on the accounting machine than on any of the other unit record machines. You have just seen how they were used to determine whether to add or subtract in a counter. You should bear in mind that even though the selectors that have been discussed in this text vary in some aspects, their main function is the same. That function is to allow an impulse to pass through the transfer hubs under specific conditions; otherwise the impulse is available from the normal hub.

In the following illustration the selectors are used to allow amounts for different types of transactions to be added in separate counters even though the amount is punched in the same field of the card. This is accomplished by means of an X or digit selection. In the example in Fig. 8-26, the item amount field represents sales on NX cards and returns on X cards.

In this report, the item amount is detail printed and the total is printed in the sales-amount column of the report for all NX cards and in the returns and allowances columns for all X78 cards.

The following wiring for control of the counters is shown in Fig. 8-27.

1. The amount is wired to both counter entries (8A and 8B). This allows both or either counter to receive the amount, depending on the counter control hubs.
2. The sales amount is detail and total printed by wiring counter 8B exit to alphameric print entry 36-43.
3. Returns and allowances are detail and total printed by wiring counter 8A exit to numeric print entry 1-8.
4. Pilot selector 2 is picked up from X78 at the second-reading station. This will cause the selector to be transferred on the next cycle when the returns and allowances card is at the third-reading station.
5. When this happens counter 8A will be impulsed to add. Otherwise counter 8B will be impulsed to add.
6. The wire from minor-total program to 8A and 8B totals will cause both counters to read-out and reset for every change in salesman number.
7. The machine is wired to detail print.

PROBLEM 6: Draw a diagram to produce a report using counter 8C to accumulate the amounts in the X80 electric cards and counter 8D to accumulate the amounts in the NX80 gas cards. The amount field is in columns 51-55. Compare on columns 7 to 9. Print the electric amounts in numeric print entry 10-17 and the gas amounts in normal alphameric print entry 10-17. Print both totals on a minor break.

DIGIT SELECTION

A digit punch as well as an X punch may be used to control pilot selectors. If the presence of any digit in a card column is sufficient to identify a particular type of transaction, then the column containing the digit may be wired directly to the D pickup of a pilot selector. If a specific digit is necessary to identify a particular type of transaction, then a digit selector is necessary.

DIGIT SELECTOR: A-D, 45-57

There are two optional digit selectors shown on the control panel - A and B. Each selector has a pair of C (common) entry hubs and exits for each of the digits 9 through 0 and for 11 and 12. When C is wired from a card column, the hubs 9-12 will emit impulses corresponding to the digits punched in the column. These digits may be used to pick up pilot selectors or to operate functions of the machine that may be controlled by digit impulses. Digit selectors are operative on card-feed cycles only.

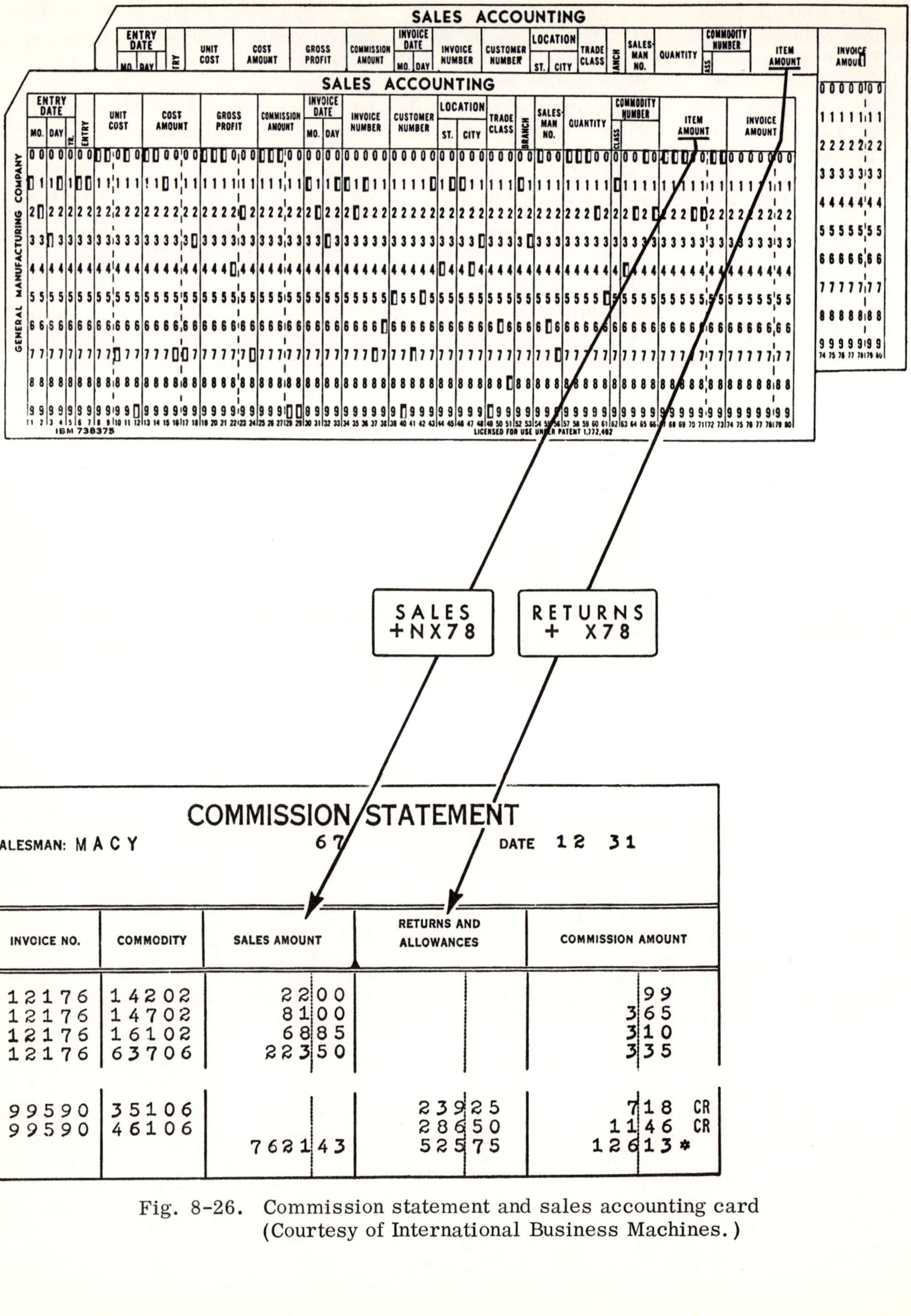

Fig. 8-26. Commission statement and sales accounting card (Courtesy of International Business Machines.)

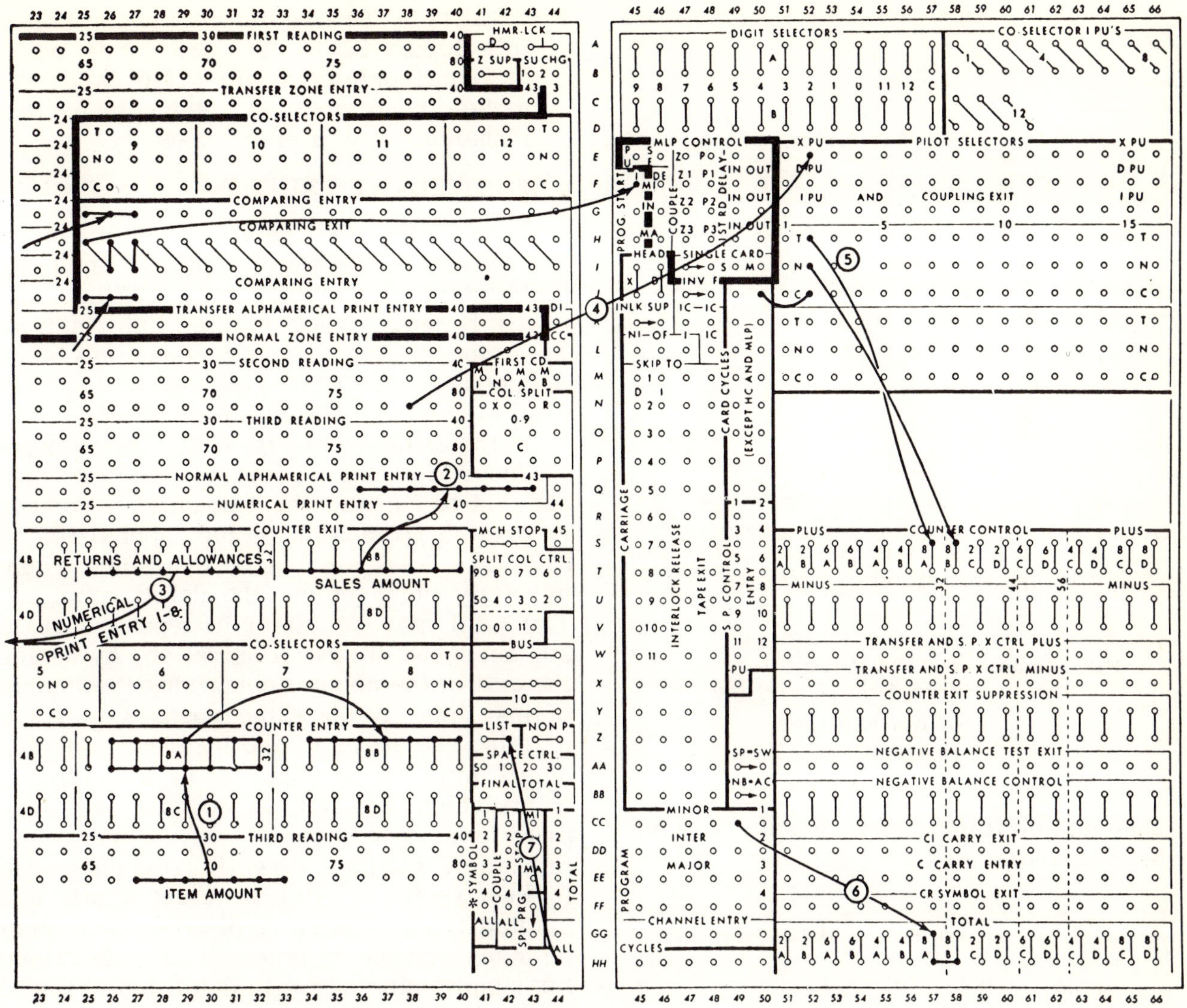

Fig. 8-27. Wiring for X-selection (Courtesy of International Business Machines.)

Figure 8-28 shows how a digit selector impulsed from the 7 hub of second reading can select only 5 impulses to pickup pilot selector 4 to control adding in counter 8A or 8B. Notice that the impulse from second reading is wired to the C hub of digit selector A and that the 5 impulse is available only from digit selector A.

DIGIT EMITTERS

You should be familiar with digit emitters from the 514 Reproducer. A digit emitter makes an impulse available at 0 to 9 and 11 and 12 time.

The digit selector can be used as a digit emitter when it is impulsed by the DI hub (K, 44). The DI (digit impulse) hub emits an impulse for every digit 9 through 0 and for 11 and 12 for every machine cycle including run-in and run-out cycles. When it is wired to the C hub of a digit selector, all digits are active for every card-feed cycle. The digit selector then becomes a digit emitter. (Cycles impulses should never be wired through a digit selector.)

PROBLEM 7: Draw a diagram showing the DI wired to C of digit selector A making it a digit emitter. SEP 13 is to be printed in alphameric typebars 31 to 36. The

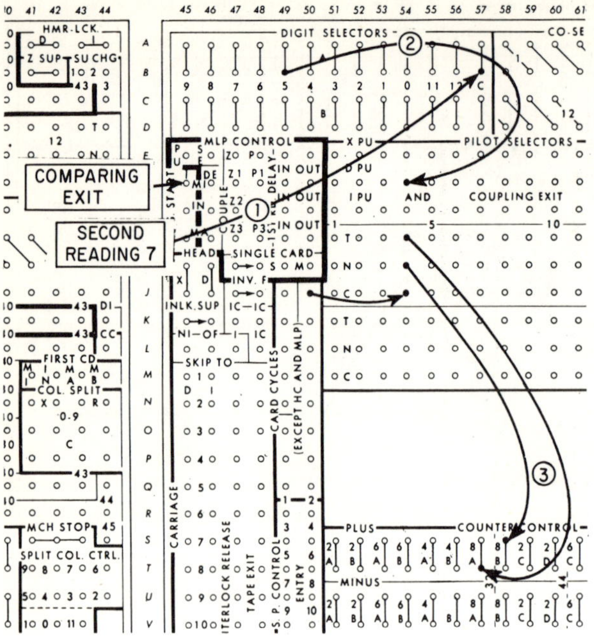

Fig. 8-28. Wiring for digit selection (Courtesy of International Business Machines.)

zone and digit punches necessary to print SEP 13 are:

	S	E	P	13
Zone	0	12	11	
Digit	2	5	7	13

SELECTIVE PRINTING

Certain cards of a group may be detail printed while other cards are group printed by the use of a pilot selector. The cards to be detail printed must be distinguished from those to be group printed by an X or digit, which is wired from the second-reading station to the pickup of a pilot selector. If X or digit cards are to be printed, a card-cycles impulse should be wired to the common of a pilot selector and out of the transferred side to LIST. If NX or no-digit cards are to be printed, the card cycles impulse is wired out of normal of the selector to LIST. All cards other than those to be selective printed will group print.

PROBLEM 8: Draw a diagram to list a field in columns 25 to 30. X80 cards are to be detail printed while NX80 cards are to be group printed. Print in normal alphameric print entry 38-43.

OFFSET TOTAL PRINTING

It is often necessary to detail print amounts from one set of typebars and print their total from another set of typebars directly beneath other printed information. This type of printing can be done only when the second- and third-reading stations are used to read alphabetic information.

In the example in Fig. 8-29, the name of the insured is printed from alphameric typebars 11 to 25, and the amount of insurance is printed from alphameric typebars 27 to 31. The total amount of insurance would normally print below the detail amounts. The total may be offset in typebars 16 to 20, as shown in the illustration, by wiring the exit of the counter containing the amount of insurance to the same typebars that are printing the name of the insured. Counter detail printing is suppressed by wiring a card-cycles impulse to counter exit suppression. The amount of insurance is printed by wiring it directly from third read to the typebars. (When offset totals are printed from numeric typebars, care must be taken that the hammersplit levers raised for suppressing zeros in detail printing will not interfere with the printing of zeros in the offset total.)

PROBLEM 9: Draw the diagram necessary to print the report illustrated in Fig.

POLICY NUMBER	NAME OF INSURED	AMOUNT OF INSURANCE
91846702	EVELYN SMITH	1500
60942301	DOROTHY GREEN	2500
66450398	ANDREW HERRON	5000
138149275	DONALD GREW	2000

POLICIES	TRANSFERS	TOTAL AMT. INSURANCE	REVIVALS
		11000	

Fig. 8-29. Offset total printed report (Courtesy of International Business Machines.)

8-29). The name of the insured is in columns 1 to 15 and is to be detail printed in normal alphameric print entry 11-25. The amount of insurance is in columns 16 to 20 and is to be detail printed in normal alphameric print entry 27-31. The total which is accumulated in counter 6B is to be printed in normal alphameric print entry 16-20. Totals are printed on a minor-program cycle. Comparison is made on columns 71 and 72, which contain the type of insurance.

HAMMERLOCK CONTROL

Each typebar on the 402 is equipped with two hammerlock levers, a short lever on the right and a long lever on the left. When both levers are down (Fig. 8-30A) the hammer will hit the typebar on every cycle. When the short hammerlock lever is raised (Fig. 8-30 B) the hammer will not hit the typebar, and therefore no printing will take place.

When the long hammerlock lever is raised, the firing of the hammer is under the control of the hammerlock hubs on the control panel. When the hammerlock hubs do not receive an impulse, the hammer will fire because the support bar remains in a normal position (Fig. 8-30C) When the hammerlock hubs do receive an impulse, the hammer will not fire because the support bar is tilted just enough to stop it from firing (Fig. 8-30D). (Hammerlock levers should not be raised while typebars are printing.)

In summary, short hammerlocks sup-

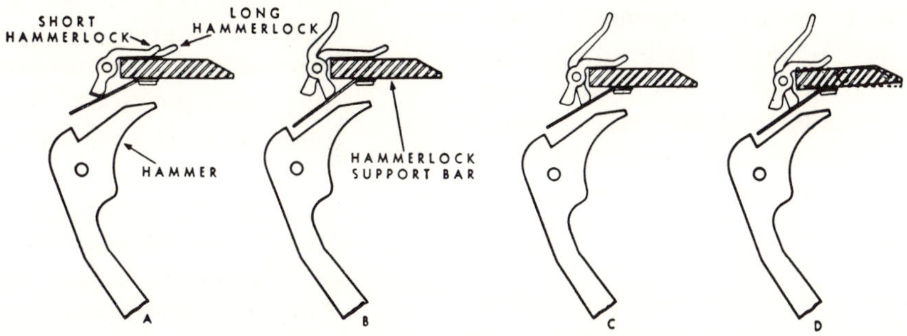

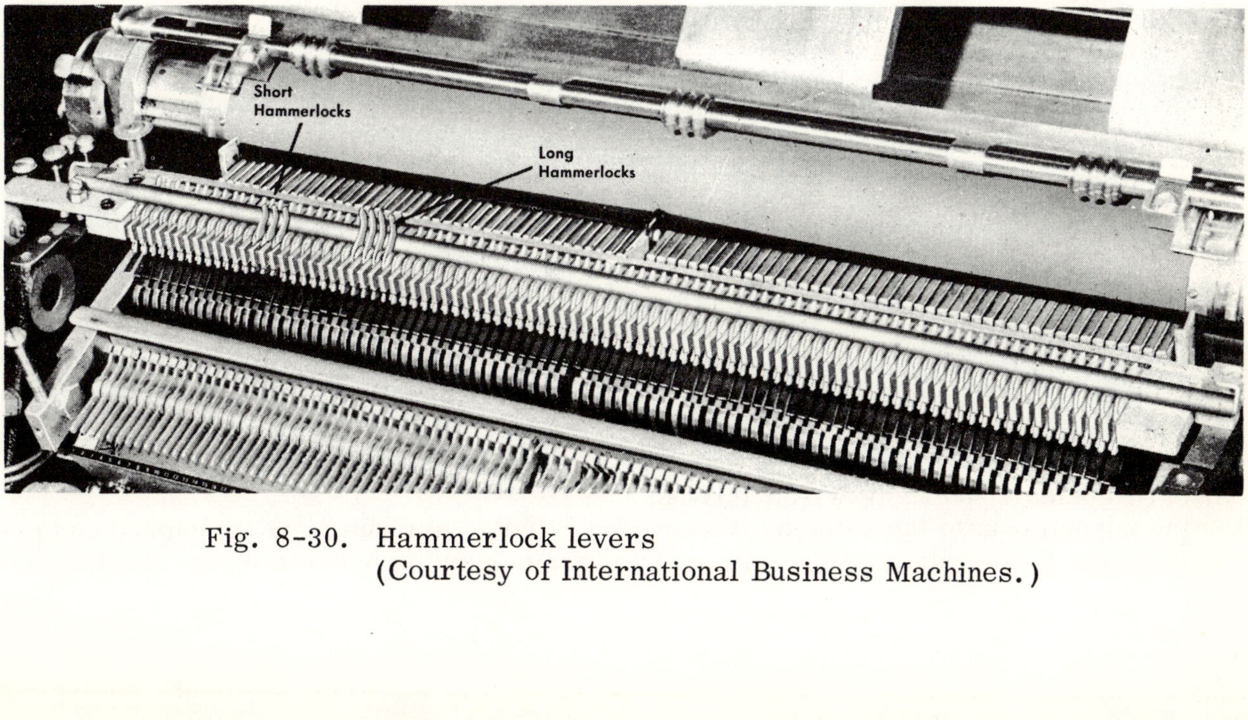

Fig. 8-30. Hammerlock levers
(Courtesy of International Business Machines.)

press printing all the time, and long hammerlocks suppress printing when wired to do so.

HAMMERLOCK HUBS: A, 41-44

When these hubs are impulsed, printing will be suppressed from those typebars for which the long hammerlock levers are raised. The D pickup hubs receive X or digit impulses to control hammerlocking on the following cycle. If the X is punched in a column which is also digit punched, a column split unit must be used. The immediate pickup hubs receive impulses to control hammerlocking on the same cycle and normally wired from total program to suppress printing on program cycles or from the first card hubs to suppress printing for the first card of a group. If hammerlocking is desired for NX or no digit cards, a card-cycles impulse must be controlled through a pilot selector. It is not possible to hammerlock some of the typebars with one kind of impulse and other typebars with another kind of impulse. All 88 typebars are subject to hammerlock control from a single impulse.

COLUMN SPLIT: N-P, 41-44

Column splits are active on card cycles only. Normally they are used to separate 11 and 12 impulses from 0 to 9 impulses read from a card column or the DI hub.

Figure 8-31 illustrates the use of hammerlocking and column splits with the following wiring:

1. Hammerlocking may be controlled from an X card by raising the long hammerlock levers for those typebars from which the information will print. For X hammerlock, the X is wired from the second reading station through a column split, to hammerlock D pickup. Hammerlocking will take place on the following cycle or as the card passes the third station.
2. Heavy lines on the diagram show the wiring for hammerlocking for NX cards. Column 40 is wired from second reading to the X pickup of a pilot selector. A card-cycles impulse is wired through the normal hubs of the selector to hammerlock immediate pickup. As each

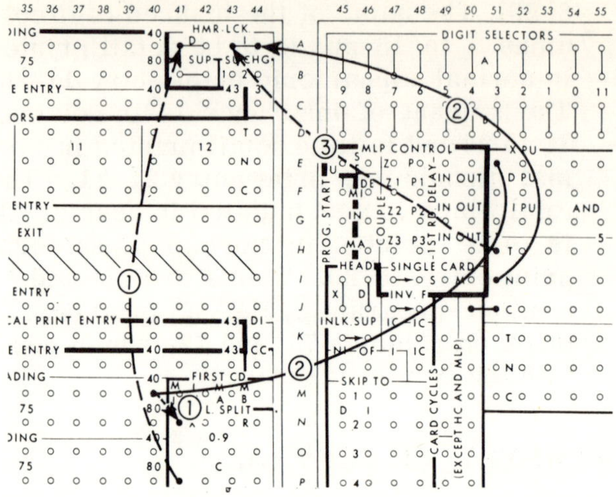

Fig. 8-31. Wiring for hammerlocking for X or NX cards (Courtesy of International Business Machines.)

NX card passes the third-reading station, a card-cycles impulse controls hammerlocking immediately, and if the long hammerlock levers are raised, printing will be suppressed.
3. The dotted wire from the transferred hub of the selector to I hammerlock shows the wiring for X cards. Whenever a card-cycles impulse is used to control hammerlocking, it must be wired to the I hub. Whenever X or digit impulses are used, they must be wired to the D hub.

PROBLEM 10: Draw a diagram for hammerlocking D or No D cards. (Just draw the necessary wires as in Fig. 8-31.) If there is a 2 in column 40, impulse the hammerlock D pickup hub. If there is no 2 in column 40, impulse the hammerlock I pickup hub.

PROBLEM 11: Draw a diagram for hammerlocking from a comparing exit. (Just draw the necessary wires as in Fig. 8-31.) On a comparing break impulse the hammerlock D pickup hub. If there is no comparing break, impulse the hammerlock I pickup hub.

GROUP PRINTING

If the list hub is not impulsed and program start is not wired, the typebars will rise only upon depression of the final-total key. If program start is wired, the typebars rise for the first card of each group for the purpose of group indication and for each program level for the purpose of total printing. Figure 8-4 shows a group printed report using the same cards that were used in Fig. 8-3. The group printed report eliminated the printing of detail items.

GROUP INDICATION

The printing of information from the first card of a group only, as shown in Fig. 8-32, is called ***group indication.*** In detail printing, the indicative information is normally printed repetitively from every card in the control group. This repetitive printing may be suppressed by selection, by hammerlocking, and by printing from counter exits. Each method will be discussed in detail, following the explanation of the hubs which are used for group indication.

FIRST CD (First card): M, 41-44

The MI (minor), IN (intermediate), and MA (major) first-card hubs emit impulses during the print cycle of the first card of their respective program groups. They are normally wired to counter plus to add the first card of a group, to a coselector pickup for group indication, to hammerlock control, or to carriage skip hubs to cause skipping before the first card of a group.

WIRING, GROUP INDICATION

Figure 8-33 demonstrates three methods of wiring for group indication:

A. *Selector method.* The commodity class is wired from third reading through the transferred points of coselector 6 to print entry. The coselector is picked up from minor first card, since commodity class is wired for minor-program start. The selector transfers for the first card of every minor group, at which time commodity class prints and is normal for all other cards in the same commodity class.

B. *Hammerlock method.* The trade class is wired from third reading directly to print entry. Intermediate first card is wired to the immediate pickup of a pilot selector. A card-cycles impulse is wired through normal of the selector to hammerlock immediate pickup, and the long hammerlock levers are

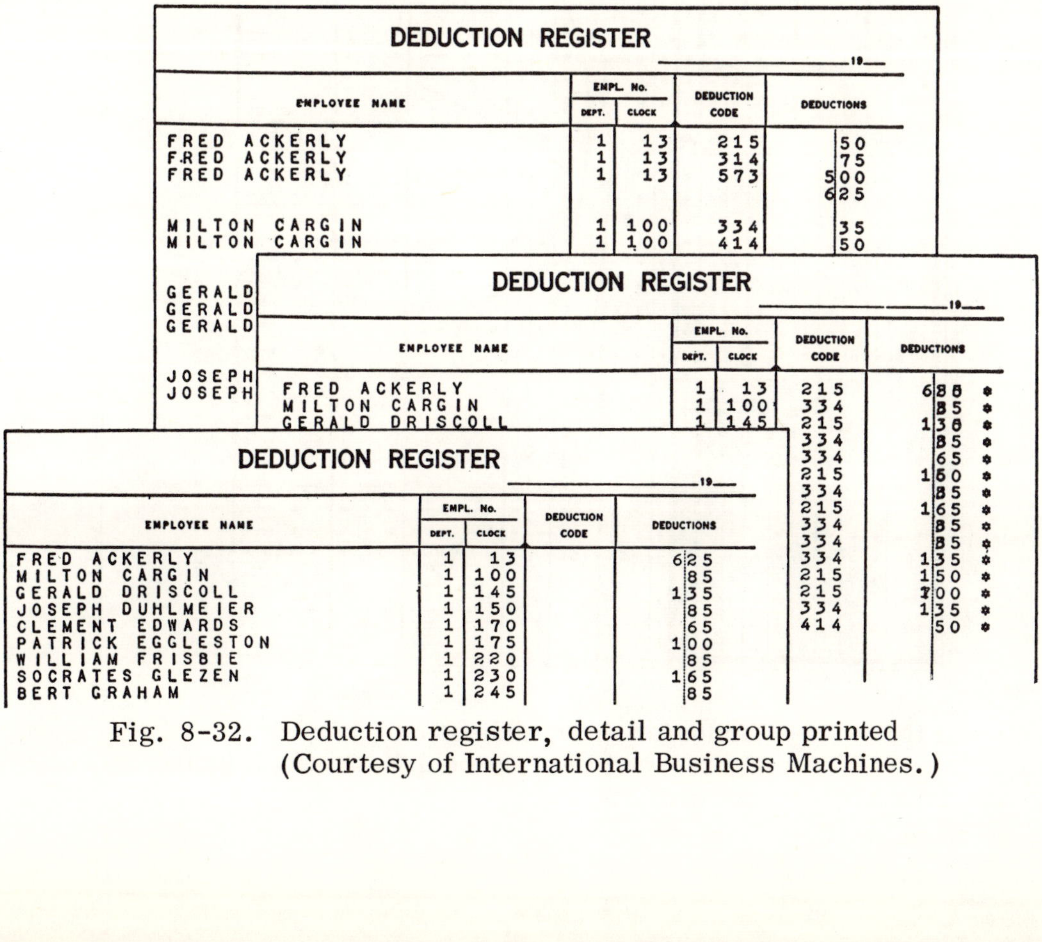

Fig. 8-32. Deduction register, detail and group printed (Courtesy of International Business Machines.)

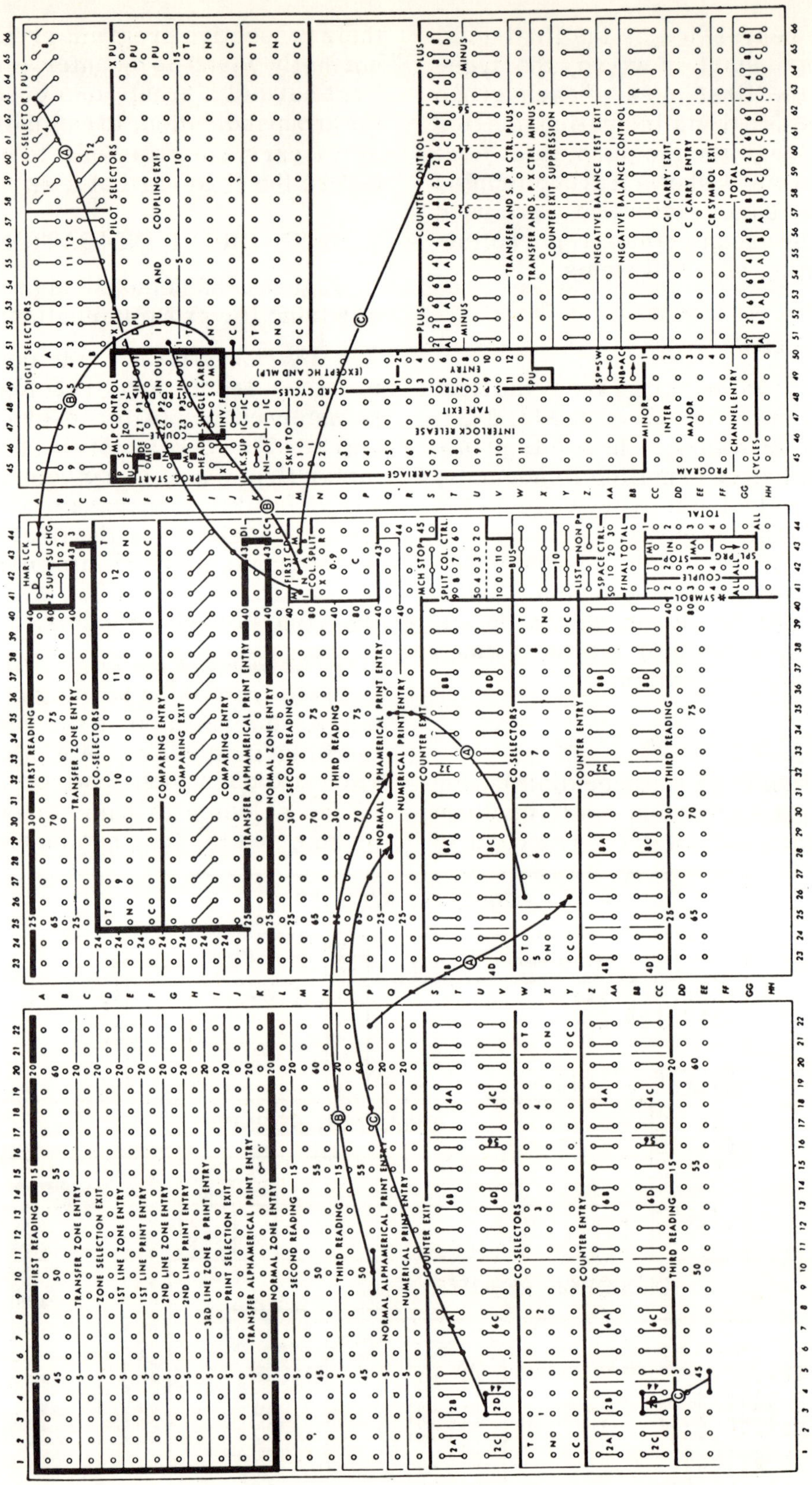

Fig. 8-33. Wiring for group indication
(Courtesy of International Business Machines.)

raised for the typebars to which trade class is wired. For every intermediate-program change, the pilot selector will pick up and the hammerlock will not be impulsed, thus allowing trade class to print once for each intermediate group.

C. *Counter method.* The state is wired to counter entry 2D, and the major first card is wired to the plus of that counter. The counter exits are wired to print entry. The counter will add the first card of a major group. Since counter exits are active when the counter is impulsed, the state will list once for every major group.

SETUP CHANGE: B, 43-44: C, 44

Within reasonable limitations one control panel may be used for several different reports, without any change in control-panel wiring, by the use of setup-change switches 1, 2, or 3, located on the side of the machine. Each setup-change switch has a corresponding hub on the control panel which emits an impulse on each machine cycle when the corresponding setup-change switch is turned on.

The setup-change exits may be wired directly to the list hubs or to the pickup of a coselector or a pilot selector. The selector can then be used to change machine functions according to the position of the setup-change switch.

In the example (Fig. 8-32), the first report is detail printed (all cycles to LIST) and the second and third reports are group printed (no wire to LIST). Without setup change this would necessitate the manual removal of the wire to LIST as well as the insertion of a card-cycles impulse to counter exit suppression to eliminate overprinting, as shown in the deduction column of the second report. The total of the group prints over the amount printed from the first card of the group.

These wiring changes can be made automatically by making use of the setup-change feature of the machine. There are many other uses of the setup change switches to vary machine function from one report to another, such as programming, hammerlocking, or counter clearing.

Figure 8-34 shows the following wiring for this operation when setup-change switch 1 is changed from off to on:

1. Setup-change hub 1 is wired to the immediate pickup of pilot selector 1 and switch 1 is turned on.
2. All cycles, wired through the normal side of this selector to list, is eliminated when the switch is on.
3. The card-cycles impulse, wired through the transferred side of the pilot selector, reaches counter exit suppression when the switch is on, to prevent printing of deductions from the first card of the group.

PROBLEM 12: Draw the following: When setup-change switch 2 is on, the I hub of hammerlock is impulsed and the minor total asterisk is not printed in numeric print entry 39.

TOTAL PRINTING FROM THE SAME TYPEBARS

More than one type of total may be printed from the same typebars, without the use of selectors. This operation is sometimes referred to as ***total transfer*** and is based on the principle of ***rolling totals,*** as they are obtained from one counter to another. Each total requires a separate counter. Only the minor counter adds or subtracts from the card, however. On the minor-program change, the minor total prints and rolls into the intermediate counter. On an intermediate-program change the intermediate total prints and rolls into the major counter. On a major program change, the major total prints. Thus, the major total is the sum of all the intermediate totals and the intermediate total is the sum of all the minor totals. This method of accumulating intermediate and major totals provides substantial proof that if the major total is correct, the intermediate and minor totals which contribute to the major total are also correct.

TRANSFER AND S. P. X CONTROL - PLUS AND MINUS: W-X, 51-66

These hubs emit impulses under the following conditions:

1. The transfer plus hub of a counter emits

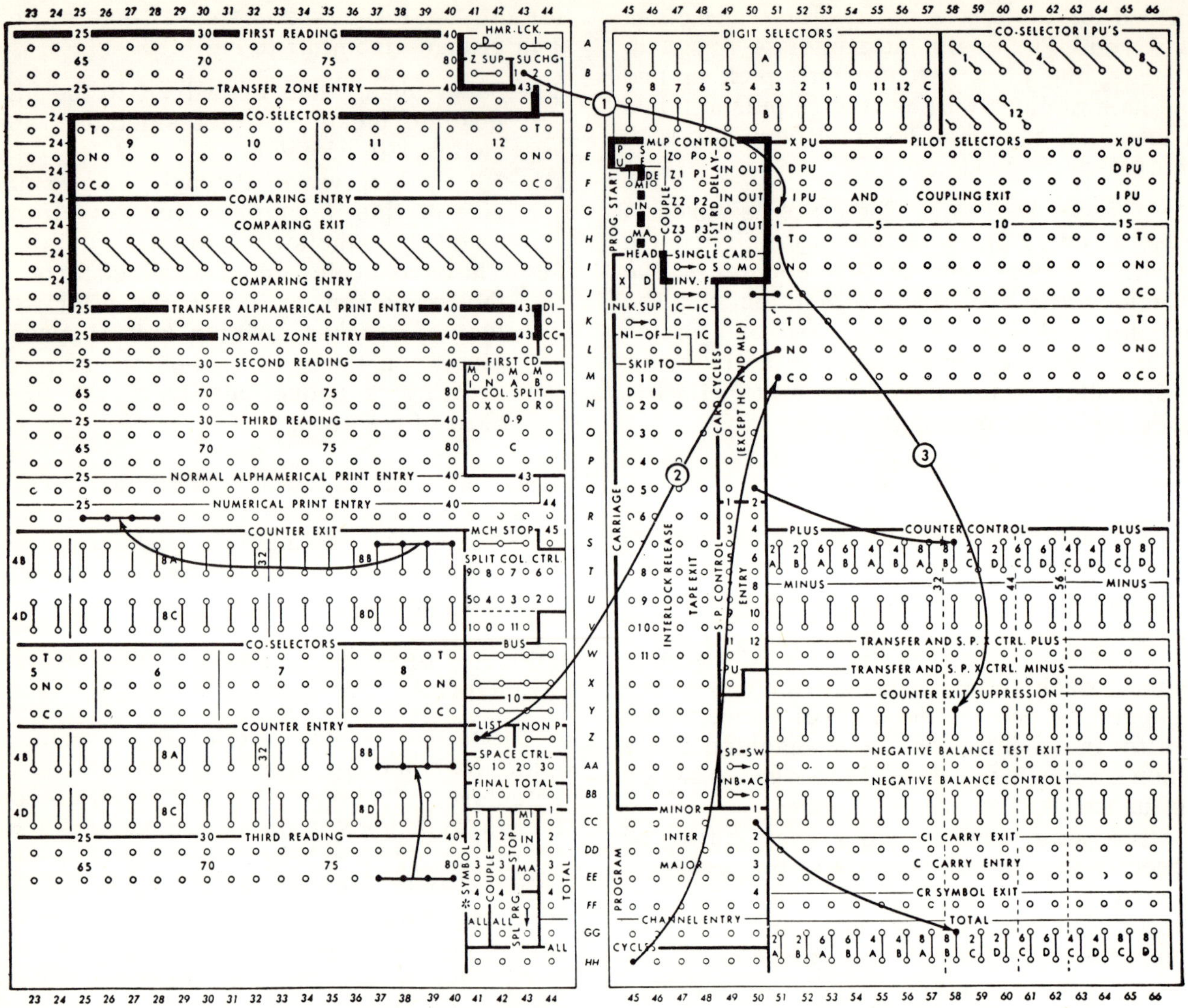

Fig. 8-34. Wiring for changing from detail print to group print (Courtesy of International Business Machines.)

an impulse whenever the total hub of that counter is impulsed and negative balance control is not wired. If negative balance control is wired, transfer plus emits for plus totals, and transfer minus emits for minus totals. They are normally wired to the counter control hubs of receiving counters.

2. When the accounting machine is connected to a summary punch, the summary-punch X control plus hub emits a summary-punch X impulse on every summary punch cycle. If negative balance control is also wired, summary-punch control X plus emits an X impulse for plus totals, and summary-punch control X minus emits an X impulse for minus totals. For summary-punch operations, these hubs are normally wired to the summary-punch control entries so that X's may be punched in summary cards for plus or minus balances.

Figure 8-35 illustrates the printing of minor, intermediate, and major totals from the same typebars. It is a group-printed report with a minor program on city, an intermediate program on county, and a major program on state. All three totals are printed from the same typebars, the intermediate totals being indicated by one asterisk and the major totals by two asterisks.

STATE	COUNTY	CITY	SALES	
1	1	1	100	Minor
		2	200	Totals
		3	95	
			395 *	Intermediate Total
	2	1	50	Minor
		2	49	Totals
		3	24	
			123 *	Intermediate Total
			518 * *	Major Total

Fig. 8-35. Printing three totals (same typebars) (Courtesy of International Business Machines.)

The wiring necessary for this report is illustrated in Fig. 8-36.

1. Sales amount is wired from third reading to counter entry 8A.
2. Returns are identified by an X punch in column 40. This column is wired from second reading to the X pickup of pilot selector 2. A card-cycles impulse is wired through the normal side of the pilot selector to the plus of 8A and through the transferred side to the minus of 8A.
3. Counters 8A, 8B, and 8D are controlled

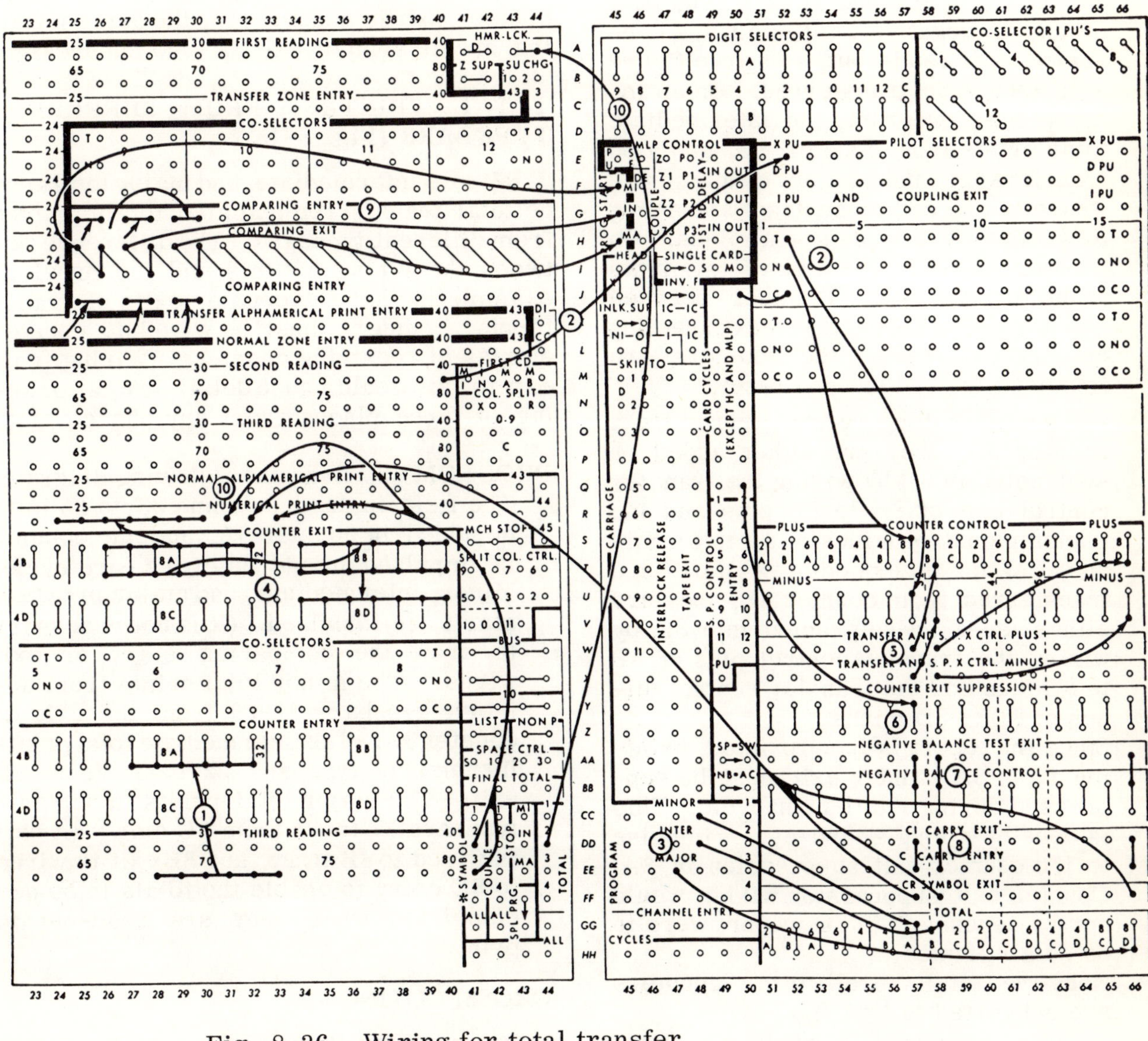

Fig. 8-36. Wiring for total transfer (Courtesy of International Business Machines.)

to read-out and reset on minor, intermediate, and major programs, respectively.

4. The exit of 8A is wired to the exit of 8B and the exit of 8B is wired to the exit of 8D. Counter 8A is also wired to numeric print entry 23-30. Counter 8A is the only counter that will add or subtract each individual card as it passes the third-reading station. Counters 8B and 8D will add or subtract totals only as they are transferred from one counter to the other. On a minor program, the total prints directly from counter 8A, but it also transfers to the intermediate counter 8B, where it adds or subtracts according to whether it is a plus or a minus. A negative total is always converted as it reads-out, so a true figure will always be transferred. On an intermediate program, the intermediate total prints from counter 8B, and also transfers to the major counter 8D, where it will add or subtract according to whether it is a plus or a minus. On a major program, the major total prints from counter 8D. Transfer between counters is made over wires connecting counter exits when the counters are impulsed to read out and reset.
5. When minor totals are transferred from counter 8A, they are either added or subtracted in 8B by wiring the transfer control plus of 8A to 8B plus and the transfer control minus of 8A to 8B minus. When intermediate totals are transferred from counter 8B, they are either added or subtracted into 8D by wiring the transfer control plus of 8B to 8D plus and the transfer control minus of 8B to 8D minus.
6. Since the report is group printed, printing from 8A counter exit must be suppressed during detail-print cycle. This is done by wiring a card-cycles impulse to the counter exit suppression of 8A. Counter exit suppression wiring would not be necessary if the report were to be detail printed.
7. Negative totals in all three counters are converted to true figures.
8. Each counter used is wired for carry back, because each is wired to subtract.
9. Program controls are wired normally.
10. One asterisk is printed for intermediate totals by wiring the asterisk symbol 2 to print entry 31. Two asterisks are printed for major totals by wiring asterisk symbol 3 to print entries 31 and 33. The asterisk in 33 is prevented from printing on an intermediate total by wiring the intermediate total-program exit to the immediate pickup of the hammerlock control and by raising the long hammerlock lever for typebar 33.

Credit symbols are printed for all negative totals by wiring the credit symbol exit of all three counters to print entry 32. When counter exit is suppressed, the corresponding credit symbol exit is also suppressed.

TOTAL PRINTING FROM DIFFERENT TYPEBARS (Fig. 8-18)

Minor, intermediate, and major totals can be total transferred and also totals printed from different typebars. The difference between the wiring for this and the previous example is that the counter exits of transferring counters must be wired to counter entries of receiving counters. Wiring from exit to exit would cause detail or total printing in three places from any one counter.

PROBLEM 13: Draw the following diagram: The field in card columns 33 to 35 is to be added in counter 8A, and the counter is impulsed to add on every card cycle. Minor, intermediate, and major program starts are impulsed. (It is not necessary to draw the comparing entry or exit wires.) The minor total prints from numeric typebars 27-30 from the exit of counter 8A. The intermediate total prints in numeric typebars 32 to 35 from 8B exit. The major total prints in numeric typebars 37 to 40 from 8C exit. 8A exit is wired to 8B entry, and 8B exit is wired to 8C entry to enable the totals to be accumulated when they are read-out to print.

CROSSFOOTING

As many as three fields may be crossfooted on the standard machine either from each individual card or from a group of cards. The three fields to be crossfooted are entered into three counters as the card passes the third-reading station. Three programs are used in three-field crossfooting, the minor level for crossfooting the first two fields, and the intermediate level for crossfooting the total of the first two fields with the third field. The major level is used to print the result. The typebars must be prevented from rising during the two crossfooting cycles, and this is one of the functions of the nonprint hubs.

NONPRINT: Z, 43-44

When these hubs are impulsed, the typebars will not rise, and spacing will be suppressed. If the print cycle is not needed for the first card of a group (group indicate elimination), the minor, intermediate, or major first card is wired directly to nonprint. To prevent printing and spacing (including skipping) on a total cycle, a total program is wired directly to nonprint. If printing is to be prevented for a particular card, the designating punch for that card must be wired to the X or D pickup of a pilot selector from the station preceding the printing station. A card-cycles impulse is then wired through the normal hubs of the pilot selector to nonprint, to suppress printing for NX cards or through the transferred hubs of the pilot selector to nonprint to suppress printing for X cards. The X or digit impulse itself cannot be wired directly to nonprint.

CARD COUNT: L, 44

This hub emits a 1 impulse as each card passes the third-reading station. It may be wired to a counter entry directly or through selectors to count cards, to numeric print entry hubs to force printing of zeros, or to program start to cause a program start for every card. By impulsing major program with a card count, all three levels will be operative for every card.

The example in Fig. 8-37 showing three-field crossfooting, adding two factors and subtracting a third (A+B-C-R), is explained by the following wiring:

1. Fields A, B, and C are wired from third reading to numeric print entry and are entered into counters 8A, 8B, and 8D.
2. All three counter exits are connected to provide a path for rolling factors from one counter into another. The exit of counter 8A is wired to print entry to print the result.
3. A card cycles impulse is wired to add in 8A and 8B and to subtract 8D.
4. Transfer control plus of 8A is wired to the plus of 8B. When the counter 8A is plus and the counter is read-out, factor A is added in 8B.
5. Detail printing from all counters is prevented by wiring a card-cycles impulse to counter exit suppression of each counter.
6. If the balance in 8D is negative, it will be converted to a true figure.
7. Since counter 8D is the only one subtracting, its CI to C is connected.
8. 8A is read out and cleared on a minor program 8B on an intermediate program and 8C on a major program.
9. Both printing and spacing for the minor and intermediate program levels are suppressed by wiring the corresponding program exit hubs to nonprint.
10. The CR symbol is printed for a negative total in numeric print entry 32.
11. All three programs are taken for each card by wiring a card count to major-program start. Since the card count hub emits a 1 impulse only at third reading, the first card through the machine will not print unless it is preceded by a blank card. The blank card serves to break control when it passes the third station, thus clearing out any totals which may be standing in any of the counters from a previous operation and providing a print cycle for the first punched card. Crossfooting of three totals at the end of a group may be done by wiring a comparing-exit impulse to major-program start.

PROBLEM 14: Draw the wiring necessary to perform the crossfooting of A + B + C = R.

Field A is in columns 15 to 19; add in counter 8A

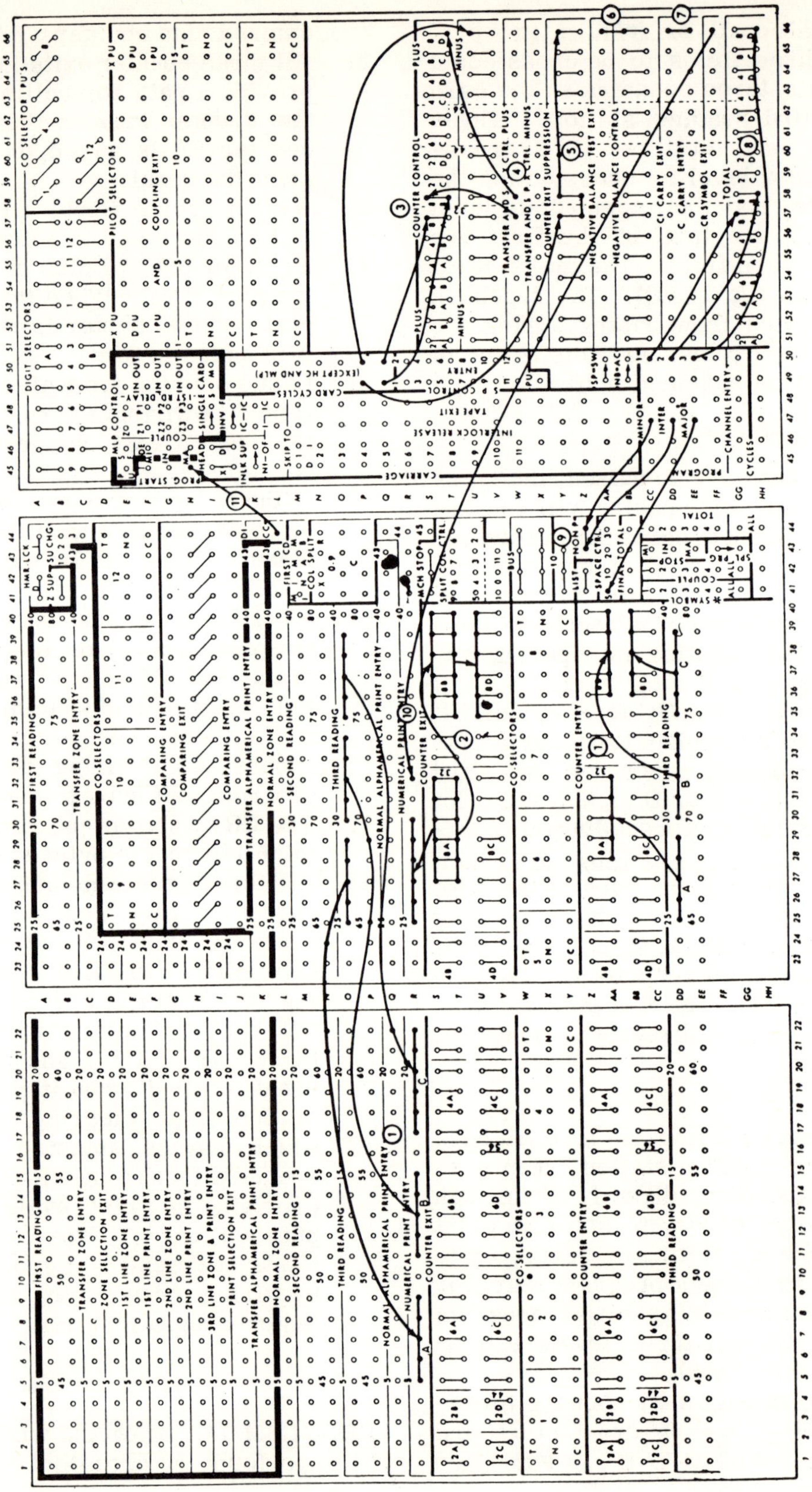

Fig. 8-37. Wiring for three-field crossfooting (Courtesy of International Business Machines.)

Field B is in columns 21 to 25; add in counter 8B
Field C is in columns 31 to 35; add in counter 8D
Print field A in numeric print entry 1-5
Print field B in numeric print entry 11-15
Print field C in numeric print entry 18-22
Print field R in numeric print entry 31-38
Print R from counter 8A
Take a major break on every card.
Print all the factors at major time only.
Print asterisks in print entries 39 and 41 on major cycles.

FIELD SELECTION

Field selection was encountered on the 548 Interpreter and the 514 Reproducer. The same principle applies on the 402 Accounting Machine. You wire impulses from two fields, but only print and/or add the selected one.

When a choice must be made between different fields on different cards, and the chosen field is to be printed from one set of typebars or entered into one counter, field selection is necessary. This is accomplished the same way as on the previous machines, by the use of selectors (coselectors). The selectors are controlled by an identifying punch in one of the cards. The field in the X or the digit card is then wired to the transferred row of the selector, the field in the NX or no-digit card to the normal row, and the common to the print entry or to a counter. We use the second-reading brushes instead of X-brushes to read the control punch. Figure 8-38 illustrates the wiring for numerical field selection by the following:

1. Regular rate is wired from 35-37 of the NX card to the normal side of coselector 8 and overtime rate from columns 38 to 41 of the X card to the transferred side of the coselector 8. The common side of the selector is wired to alphameric print entry 34-37.
2. The coselector is picked up by the controlling X punch which is wired from second reading to the X pickup of pilot selector 1. The coupling exit of the pilot selector is wired to the pickup of coselector 8. The coselector will transfer exactly like the pilot selector. When the NX card passes third reading, both selectors will be normal and the regular rate will print from card columns 35 to 37. When the X card passes third reading, both selectors will be transferred and the overtime rate will print from card columns 38 to 41.

ALPHABETIC FIELD SELECTION

Alphabetic as well as numeric information can be field selected, in which case one pilot selector and two coselectors are required. One coselector is needed to select zone impulses and another to select digit impulses. The selector used to select zone impulses must be picked up from second reading and in time to select the 0, 11, and 12 (zone) punches. Any identifying digit from 9 to 1 may be punched in the card and wired directly from second reading to the coselector immediate pickup. The coselector used to select the digit impulses must be controlled from the coupling exit of a pilot selector. Wiring for alphabetic field selection shown in Fig. 8-39 is given meaning by the following wiring:

1. Zone impulses are selected by wiring columns 70 to 74 of the digit card from second reading to the transferred side of coselector 8, and columns 65 to 69 of the no-digit card to the normal side of the same coselector. The common is wired to normal zone entry. The coselector is picked up from a control digit in column 40 wired from second reading.
2. Digit impulses are selected by wiring columns 70 to 74 of the digit card from third reading to the transferred side of coselector 6, and columns 65 to 69 of the no-digit card to the normal side of the same coselector. The common is wired to normal alphameric print entry. The coselector is picked up from the coupling exit of pilot selector 4. The same digit used to select zone impulses may be used to select the digit impulses. Column 40 is wired from second reading to the D pickup of pilot selector 4. When alphabetic and numeric fields are to be field selected, the zone impulses do not have to be selected be-

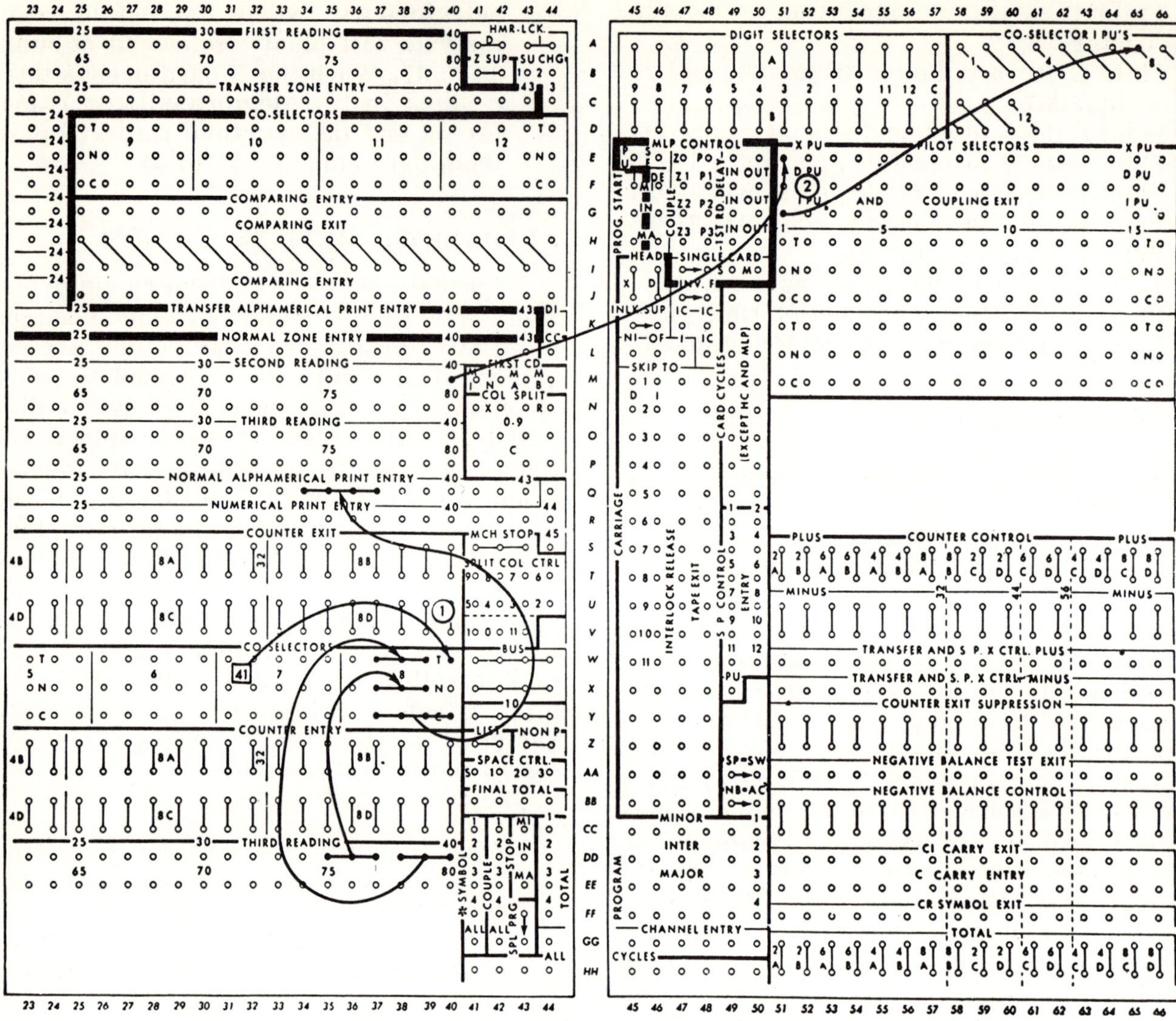

Fig. 8-38. Wiring for numeric field selection (Courtesy of International Business Machines.)

cause they can be controlled by zone suppression.

Z SUP (ZONE SUPPRESS): B, 41-42

These common hubs receive X, 12, all-cycles, or card-cycles impulses to suppress zoning for all 43 alphameric typebars. An X or 12 may be wired directly to Z-SUP to suppress zoning for all X or 12 punched cards. To suppress NX or No-12 punched cards you must use a card cycles wired through the normal hubs of a pilot selector to Z-SUP. A comparing exit may also be used to suppress zoning for NX cards by wiring DI through the X-R (11-12) side of a column split to one side of the comparing entry and the column containing the X to the other side of the comparing entry. The comparing exit is then wired to Z-SUP. A digit may be used to control-zone suppression if it is first wired to the D pickup of a pilot selector. A card cycles may then be wired through the selector to Z-SUP.

An example of this wiring can be seen in Fig. 8-40 where:

1. The alphabetic field in columns 30 to 34 is wired from the third-reading station to the normal side of coselector 8, since this field is to print for NX cards.
2. The numeric field in columns 35 to 39 is wired from the third-reading station to

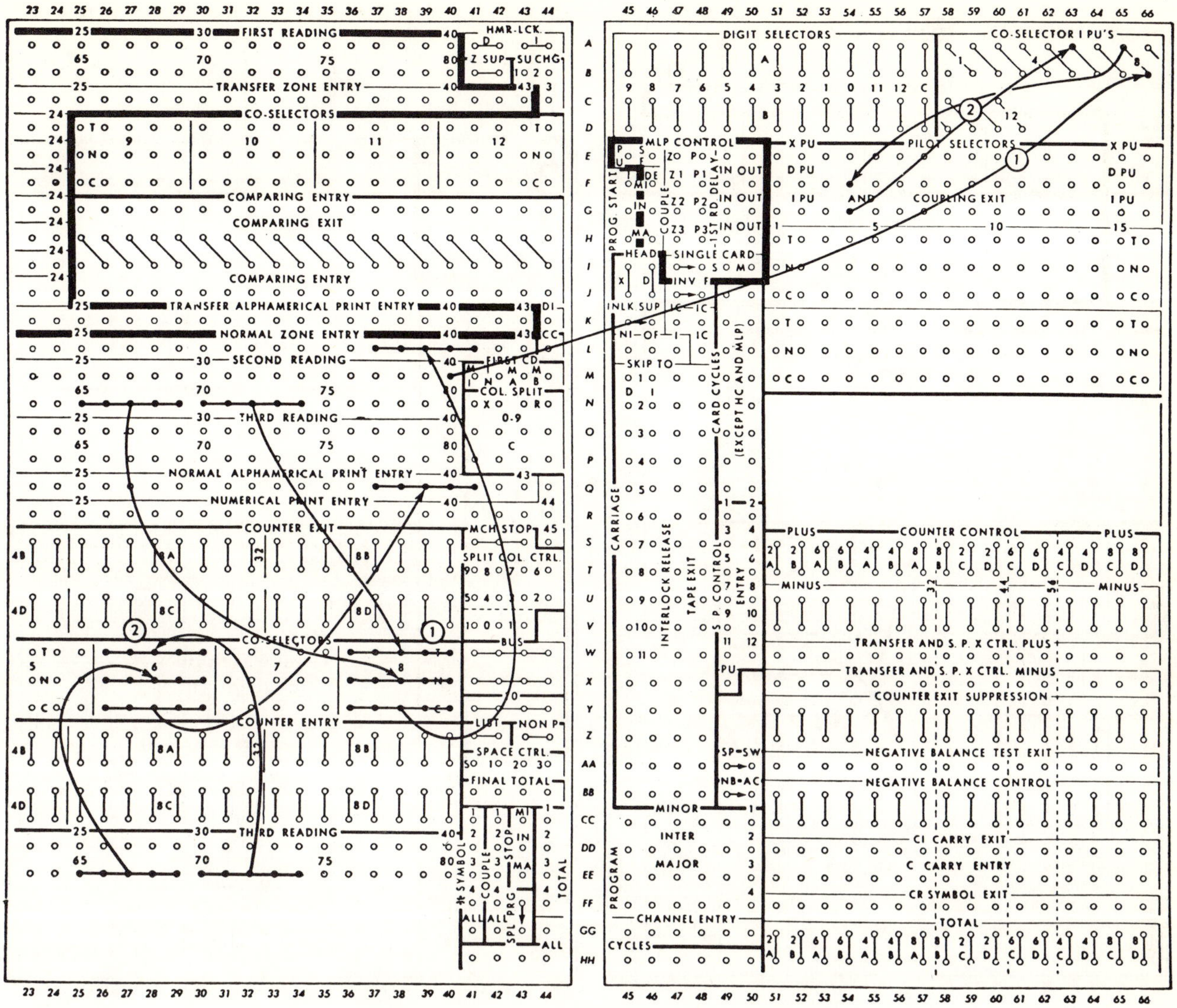

Fig. 8-39. Wiring for alphabetic field selection (Courtesy of International Business Machines.)

the transferred side of coselector 8, since this field is to print for X cards.

3. The common of this coselector is wired to normal alphameric print entry 31-35.
4. Typebars 31 to 35 are zoned by wiring directly from second reading columns 30 to 34.
5. Cards from which the numeric field is to print are X punched in column 40, which is wired from second reading to the X pickup of pilot selector 2. The coupling exit of pilot selector 2 is wired to the pickup of coselector 8.
6. When printing from the numeric field, zoning is suppressed by wiring the X in column 40 directly to Z-SUP, making it impossible for zone punches in columns 30 to 34 to interfere with digits in columns 35 to 39.

CLASS SELECTION

Class selection is necessary whenever a choice must be made between several printing locations wired from the same field in different cards. The different classes of cards must be identified by Xs or digits, which are used to control selection.

When a field is to be selected to one of two printing locations, the field punched in

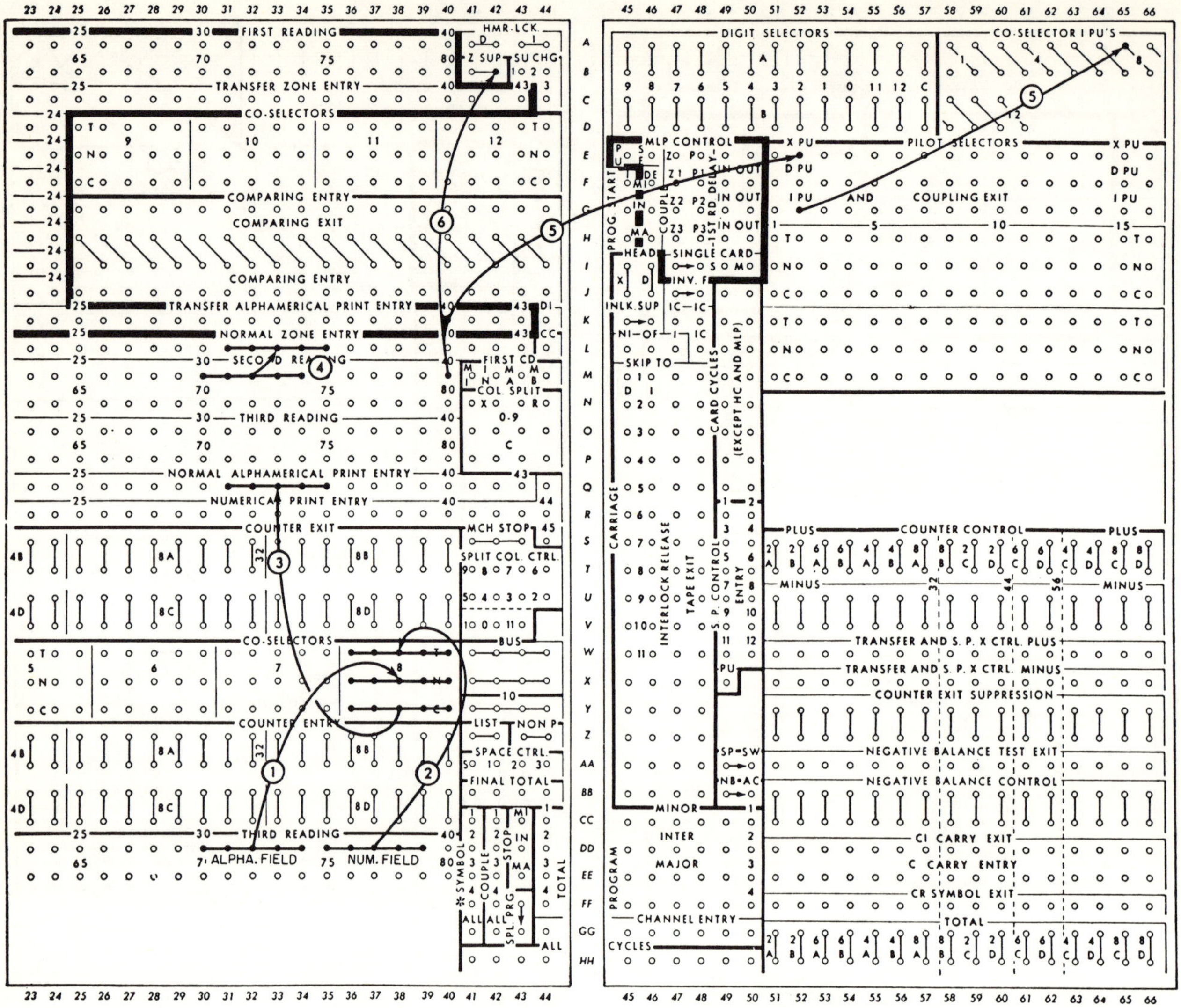

Fig. 8-40. Wiring for field selection of alphabetic and numeric fields (Courtesy of International Business Machines.)

the cards is wired to the common of a coselector, the normal to one set of print entry hubs, and the transferred to another set of print entry hubs. Although the information is punched in the same columns of two types of cards, the printing location will vary with the type of card being read.

PROBLEM 15: Prepare a diagram for numeric class selection. There are two types of daily time cards. The X76 cards contain the number of overtime hours in columns 69 to 71. The NX76 cards contain the number of regular hours in columns 69 to 71. Print the overtime hours in normal alphameric print entry 38-40 and the regular hours in normal alphameric print entry 34-36. Use pilot selector 1 and coselector 8.

PROBLEM 16: Prepare a diagram for alphabetic class selection. The alphabetic field is in columns 30 to 34. Print in normal alphameric print entry 37-41 for cards with a digit in column 80. Print in normal alphameric print entry 28-32 for cards without a digit in column 80. Use pilot selector 1 and coselectors 6 and 8.

SPACING

All printing is normally single spaced,

six lines to the inch. In detail printing, two spaces are taken before the first card of a group is printed. In group printing, the minor total will print on the same line as the group indication, and the intermediate and major totals will each single space. One space is taken before the first card of a minor group and two spaces before the first card of an intermediate or major group. Variations from this spacing may be obtained by the use of the space-control hubs.

SPACE CONTROL: AA, 41-44

Space-control hub 1 will receive an impulse to single space (6 lines to the inch); hub 2 will receive an impulse to double space (3 lines to the inch); hub 3 will receive an impulse to triple space (2 lines to the inch). The hub labeled S will receive an impulse to suppress all spacing. In Fig. 8-41 spacing is suppressed for all X40 cards.

These controls take precedence over all automatic spacing. If all printing is to be double or triple spaced, an all-cycles impulse is wired to space control 2 or 3. If spacing is to be varied for a particular card, an all-cycles or card-cycles impulse is wired through the transfer of a pilot selector picked up from the second-reading station. (The X or digit cannot be wired directly to space control (Fig. 8-42).

Normally a minor total prints directly beneath the last printed item, but it may be made to print three lines below the last item by wiring a minor-total program to space-control.

TOTAL PROGRAM COUPLE: CC-GG, 42

Each of these hubs emits an impulse at a specific program level. Hub 1 emits an impulse at the minor level, hub 2 at the intermediate level, hub 3 at the major level, hub 4 at the fourth level when special program is wired, and the A11 hub at all levels.

Two or more program totals may be made to print on the same line by joining their

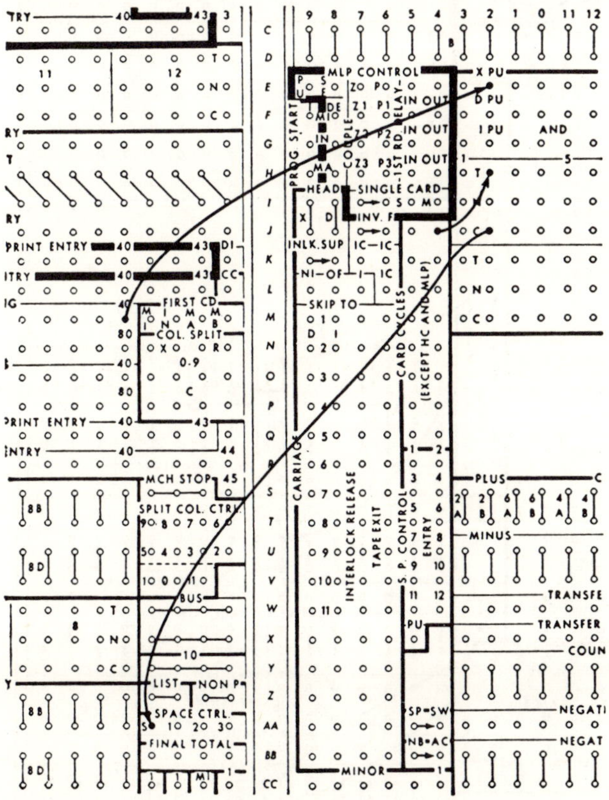

Fig. 8-41. Wiring for space suppress (Courtesy of International Business Machines.)

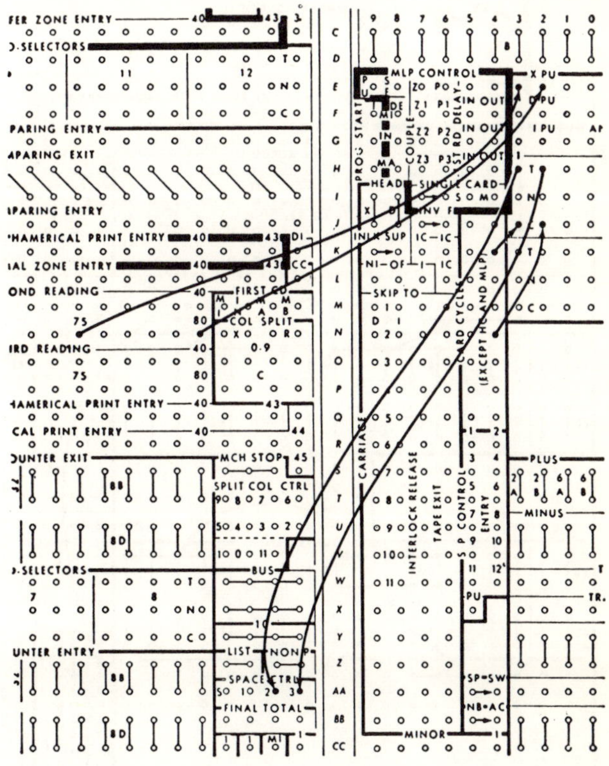

Fig. 8-42. Wiring for selected space control (Courtesy of International Business Machines.)

couple hubs. For example, if couples 1, 2, and 3 were joined, all three program totals will print on the same line and on the same cycle. When this method of total printing is used, it is not possible to transfer totals from one counter to another, because only one cycle is taken to print all totals. Therefore, the wiring must be from third reading to the counter entry of each of the counters in use, instead of from third reading to the counter entry of the minor counter and from the exits of the minor counter to the exit of the intermediate counter, and so on. This wiring is shown in Fig. 8-43. Notice that wire 3 joins couple hubs 1 and 2. As a result, the minor and intermediate totals are printed on the same line.

Normally the first card of a group prints two spaces from the previous total when the machine is wired to list. This spacing may be altered by wiring first-card control (minor, intermediate, or major) to space control.

EXPANDING PROGRAM EXITS

There are seven exits for each program level. The number of exits may be increased by controlling a coselector from a couple exit and by wiring all-cycles impulses through its transferred hub, as seen in Fig. 8-44.

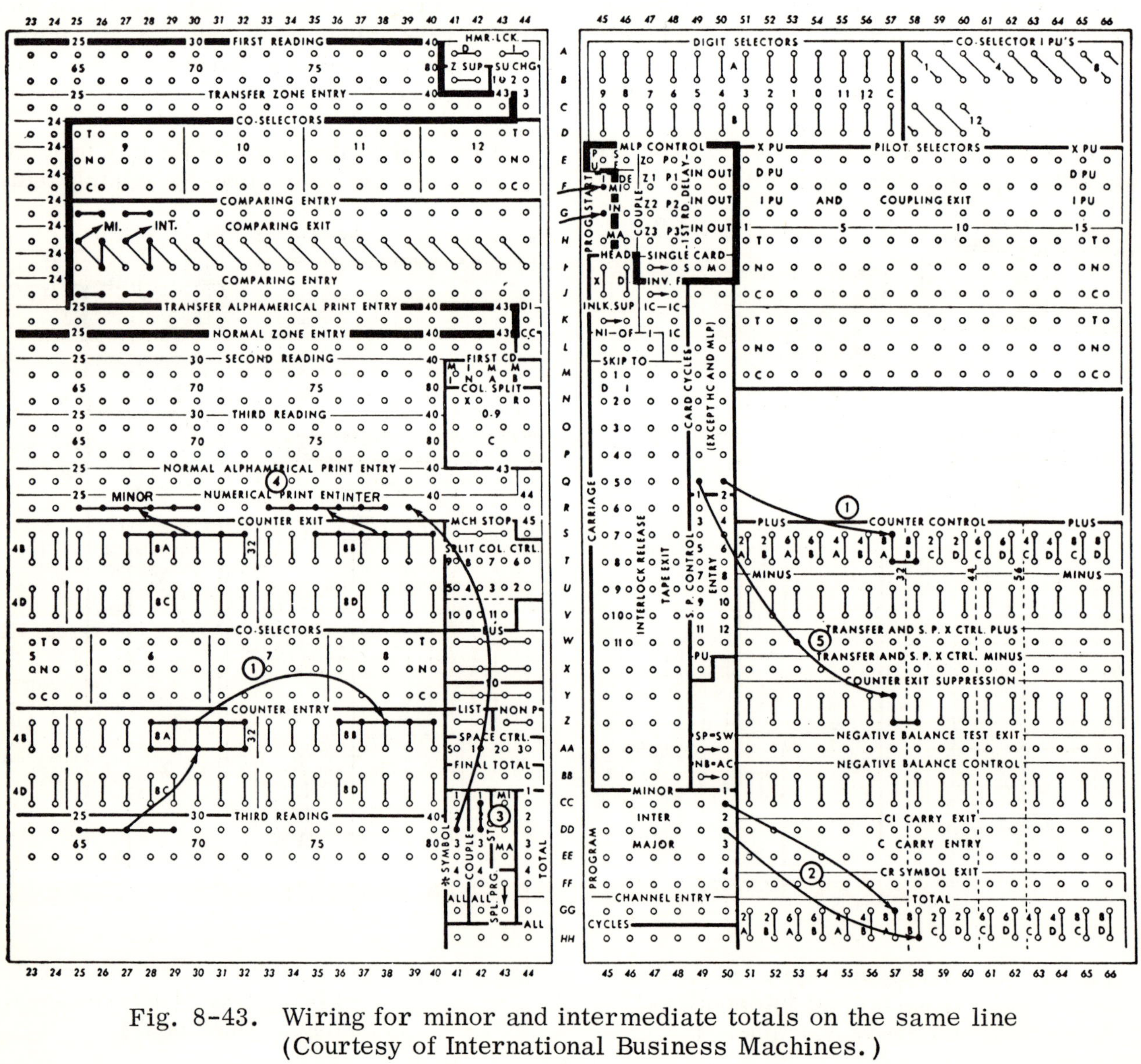

Fig. 8-43. Wiring for minor and intermediate totals on the same line (Courtesy of International Business Machines.)

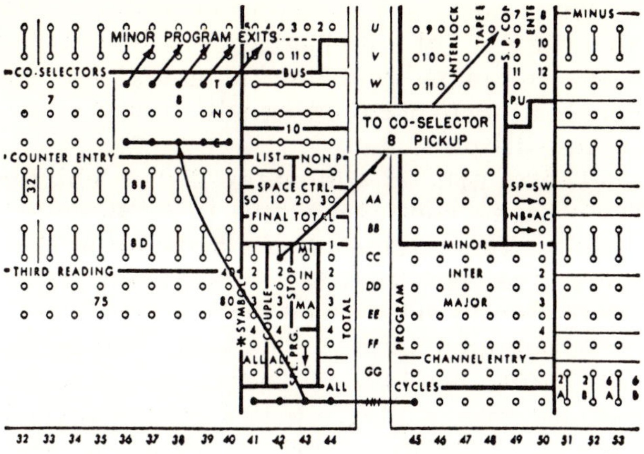

Fig. 8-44. Wiring for expanding program exit (Courtesy of International Business Machines.)

MACHINE STOP: S, 41-43

These three common stop hubs may be impulsed to stop the machine immediately and turn on the stop light. They have the following uses:

1. Stop the machine before total printing by wiring from a total-program exit.
2. Stop the machine before the first card of a group by wiring from a first-card minor, intermediate, or major.
3. Stop the machine when a counter turns negative by connecting NB-AC and wiring negative-balance-test exit to machine stop.

To restart the machine, the stop light must first be turned off by depressing the final-total key. Then the start key is pressed to continue.

NB-AC (NEGATIVE BALANCE ALL CYCLES): BB, 49-50

When the NB-AC hubs are connected, the negative-balance-test exit hub emits an impulse on every cycle during which a counter is negative, including zero balances.

Normally the negative-balance-test hubs emit an impulse when a counter is negative on a total program only. When NB-AC is connected, they emit impulses on any cycle during which a counter is negative.

Some of the uses for these hubs are:

1. Change from group print to detail print whenever a counter changes from positive to negative.
2. Change from detail to group print.
3. Stop the machine when a counter turns negative.
4. Cause a program to be initiated whenever a counter turns negative.

Figure 8-45 shows the wiring necessary to cause the machine to switch from group to detail printing when counter 8A turns negative.

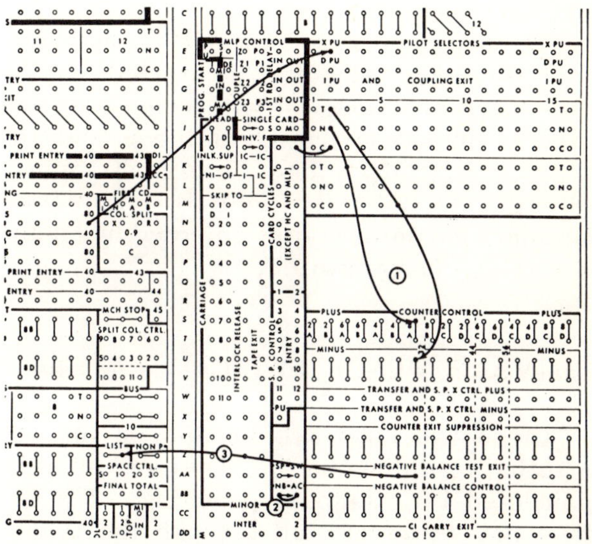

Fig. 8-45. Wiring for detail printing (NB - AC) (Courtesy of International Business Machines.)

SUMMARY PUNCHING

Summary punching is the automatic preparation of one total card to replace a group of detail cards. A total or summary card contains the identification of a group and one or more totals accumulated for that group. The primary purpose of summary cards is to reduce the card volume and thus accelerate the preparation of periodic reports. When totals or balances are carried forward from one period to another, as in stock-status summary or accounts receivable, the summary cards are called ***balance forward*** cards.

Summary cards are generally punched during the preparation of detail reports by a summary punch machine connected to the accounting machine by a cable.

The 514, 519, 523, 526, or 528 Summary Punch Machines may be used with the 402 Accounting Machine. The summary punch machine has a cable which must be connected to the receptacle provided for it on the accounting machine. When the control panels on both machines are properly wired, the exits of all the counters are made available on the summary punch control panel. Only information introduced into the counters of the accounting machine may be summary punched.

The card-feed stop light will go on whenever summary punching is started by the accounting machine. It will remain on and prevent further operation of the accounting machine if for any reason the summary punch operation is not satisfactorily completed. Summary punching may be selected by means of a setup change switch.

SUMMARY PUNCH SWITCH: AA, 49-50

These two hubs are located on the accounting machine control panel and must be connected for summary punching. The two hubs may be connected through the transferred side of a pilot or a coselector picked up by a setup change switch. The purpose of this switch is to synchronize the operation of both machines. If either machine runs out of cards, the operation stops. If the summary punch runs out of cards, the card-feed stop light remains on in the 402. If the 402 runs out of cards, the red (unlabeled) lights on the 402 turn on.

SUMMARY PUNCH CONTROL: R-W, 49-50

Summary punching may be initiated on any program change by impulsing the pickup (PU) hub (X, 49), directly or through selectors. If a total-program exit is wired to the pickup and the summary-punch switch hubs are connected, summary punching will take place just before the total prints. More than one type of total may be summary punched in the same run.

When summary punching is initiated, the advancement of the program will be delayed until summary punching is completed, at which time programming will continue and totals will print.

There are 12 summary punch entries from the accounting machine to the summary punch. The entries on the accounting machine are identified by 12 summary punch control entry hubs and on the summary punch by the column splits. The entry hub on the accounting machine is internally connected with a corresponding 11-12 column split hub on the summary punch as shown in Fig. 8-46. Entry 1 is connected to the 11-12 hub of column split 1; entry 2 is connected to the 11-12 hub of column split 2, and so on.

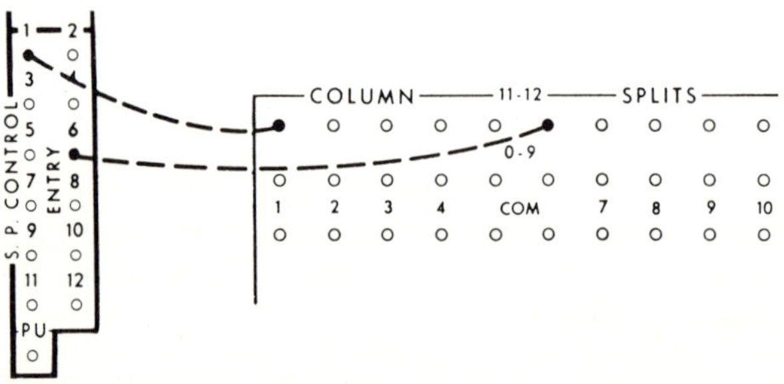

Fig. 8-46. Wiring for summary punch control (Courtesy of International Business Machines.)

There are eight (standard) column splits on the 514 Summary Punch Machine.

The SP entry hubs receive SP X control-plus or minus impulses for the purpose of punching an identifying X for positive or negative balances. The SP entry hubs may be used in any desired sequence.

The example in Fig. 8-47 is similar to that shown in Fig. 8-25, but only the summary punch wiring is explained.

1. The summary punch switch is turned on.
2. Summary punch control is picked up from the minor program level. A summary card will be punched for each salesman, since the minor program start is impulsed every time a group of cards changes from one salesman to another.

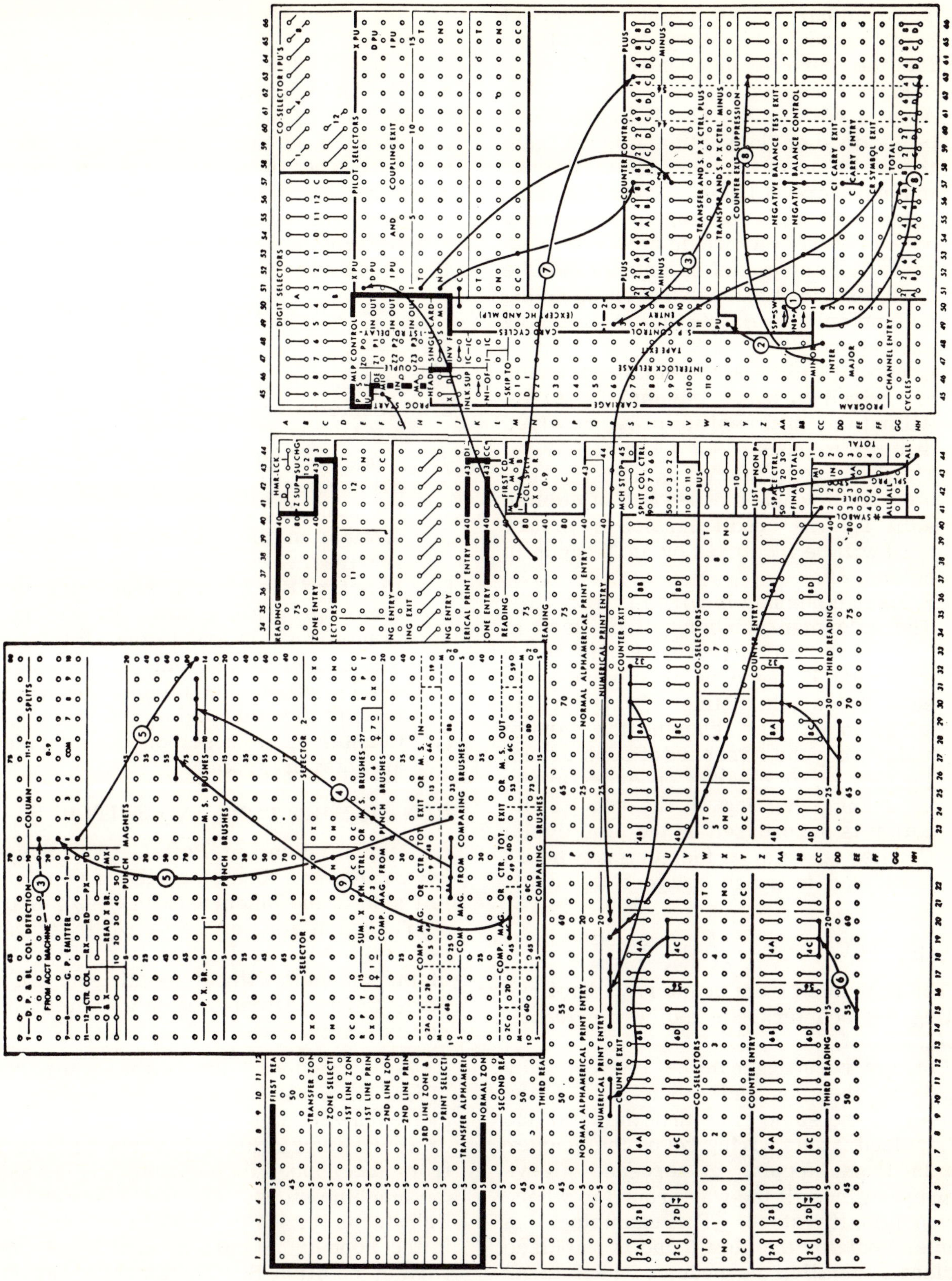

Fig. 8-47. Wiring for summary punching
(Courtesy of International Business Machines.)

3. The summary punch X control minus of 8A is wired to summary punch entry 1 for the purpose of identifying credit balances summary punched from that counter with an X. The X impulse can be obtained on the summary punch from the 11-12 hub of column split 1. If debit instead of credit balances are to be identified with an X punch, the summary punch control plus would be wired to SP entry 1. Any of the 12 entries may be used, provided there is a corresponding column split available on the summary punch panel.
4. Counter 8A exits on the summary punch are wired to punch columns 76 to 80. All but the units position of 8A are wired directly to punch.
5. The units position of 8A is wired to column 80 through the 0-9 hub of column split 1. The credit balance summary card will be identified by an X punch in column 80.
6. Salesman number is wired to 4C.
7. The salesman number will be used to identify the summary card, and hence must add in the counter only once for each salesman. Minor first card is wired to 4C plus, causing the card to add on only the first card of each group.
8. Counter 4C is cleared on every minor program. Printing on the group indication is suppressed on the total cycle.
9. Counter 4C exits on the summary punch are wired to punch columns 54 to 56.

PROGRESSIVE TOTAL PRINTING

Totals printed from counters without resetting the counters are called ***progressive totals.***

Counter resetting can be prevented by impulsing the plus and minus hub of the counter at the same time that the total hub is impulsed. This wiring keeps the counter wheels from stopping at zero and allows them to continue all the way around to where they originally stood. For example, if a counter contains the digit 6 and is impulsed to clear normally, the counter wheel turns from 6 to 7 to 8 and on to zero, where it stops. However, if the plus and minus hubs are impulsed, the stop at zero is suspended, and the wheel keeps turning until it reaches 6 again.

Although this feature is designed primarily for printing totals without clearing the counter, it may also be used for printing any common numeric information, such as a date. The information is stored in a counter from a master card and read out progressively whenever desired.

An example of this wiring can be seen in Fig. 8-48 where:

1. The field to be added is wired to counter entry 8B.
2. The totals are printed from 8B exit into print entry 36-40.
3. Counter 8B is impulsed to add from the card.
4. Since the operation is group printing, 8B counter exit must be suppressed on the indicated cycle.
5. A minor and intermediate program start is wired.
6. Counter 8B is wired to read-out on every minor program change by wiring the minor program exit to the 8B total hub. The counter is prevented from clearing out by wiring the minor program exit to both the plus and minus hubs of 8B.
7. Counter 8B is reset on the intermediate total program.

RUN-OUT BUTTONS AND SWITCHES

Nonprint Run-out Button - The ***nonprint run-out button,*** located on the far end of the left side of the machine (Fig. 8-49), may be depressed if for any reason (except card-feed failure) it is desired to run cards out of the machine without printing on the report. Cards will run out only when the hopper is empty.

Feed Interlock Start Button - The purpose of ***feed interlock*** is to stop the machine and prevent accidental total printing in the event of a card-feed failure. If a card fails to feed from the hopper to position A (Fig. 8-50), the machine stops, and the card-feed stop light turns on. At this point there are cards in the hopper, no card at position A, and a card at position B. The machine cannot be restarted except by removing cards from the hopper and depressing the feed-interlock start button. Card B then runs out into the

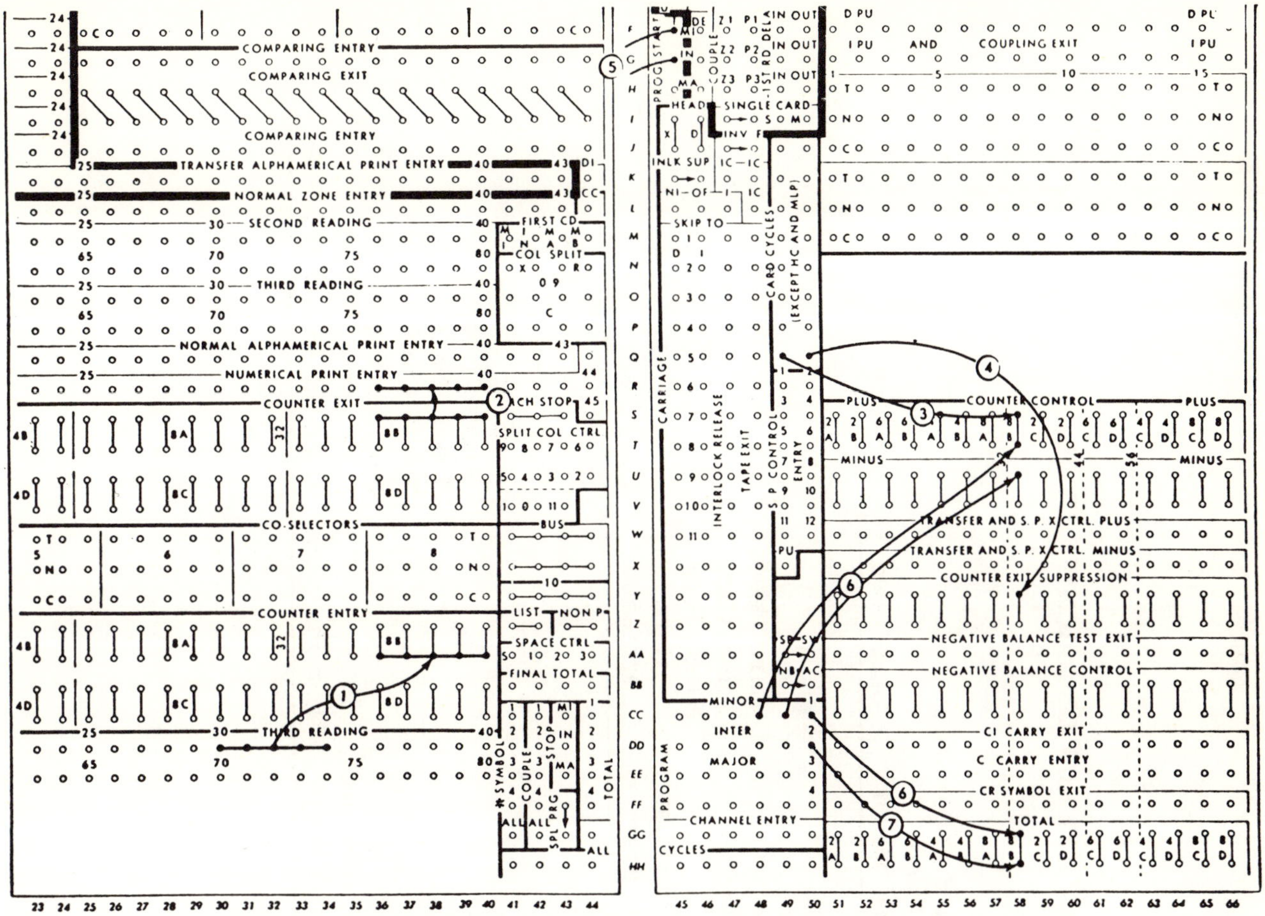

Fig. 8-48. Wiring for progressive total printing (Courtesy of International Business Machines.)

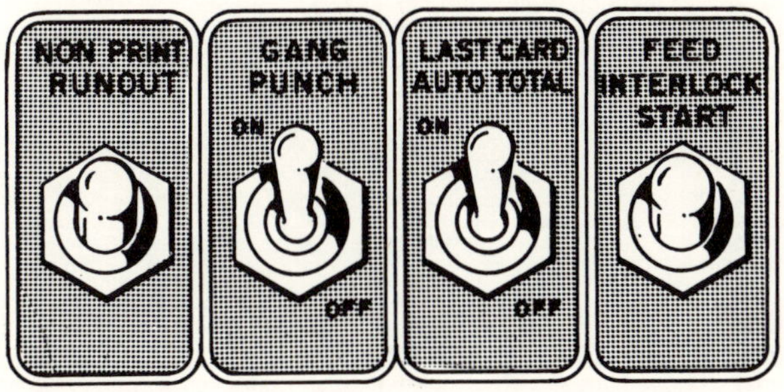

Fig. 8-49. Run-out buttons and switches (Courtesy of International Business Machines.)

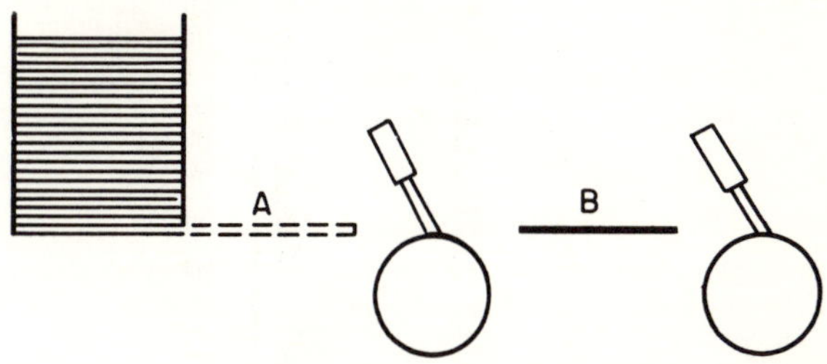

Fig. 8-50. Schematic of feed interlock (Courtesy of International Business Machines.)

stacker and performs all normal functions except programming.

The card in the hopper that failed to feed must be corrected. Card B must then be placed in front of the corrected card and the rest of the file and inserted in the hopper. To restart the machine the feed-interlock start button (Fig. 8-49) must be depressed. On the run-in, card B does not add, subtract, or print, but only compares. The operation for succeeding cards will be normal.

If it is not desirable to continue the run, after a card feed failure, it will be necessary to clear the feed interlock before a new run may be started. This is done by passing a blank card through the machine.

PROGRAM START EFFECT ON MACHINE CYCLE

MINOR START IMPULSE

Card Feed	Minor Program	Card Feed First Card Minor	Card Feed

INTERMEDIATE START IMPULSE

Card Feed	Minor Program	Intermediate Program	Card Feed First Card Minor First Card Intermediate	Card Feed

MAJOR START IMPULSE

Card Feed	Minor Program	Intermediate Program	Major Program	Card Feed First Card Minor First Card Intermediate First Card Major	Card Feed

MINOR PROGRAM START EXIT
- To CO. PU
- To I PU
- To X and D PU

INTERMEDIATE PROGRAM START

Minor Exit
- To CO. PU
- To I PU
- To X and D PU

Intermediate Exit
- To CO. PU
- To I PU
- To X and D PU

MAJOR PROGRAM START

Minor Exit
- To CO. PU
- To I PU
- To X and D PU

Intermediate Exit
- To CO. PU
- To I PU
- To X and D PU

Major Exit
- To CO. PU
- To I PU
- To X and D PU

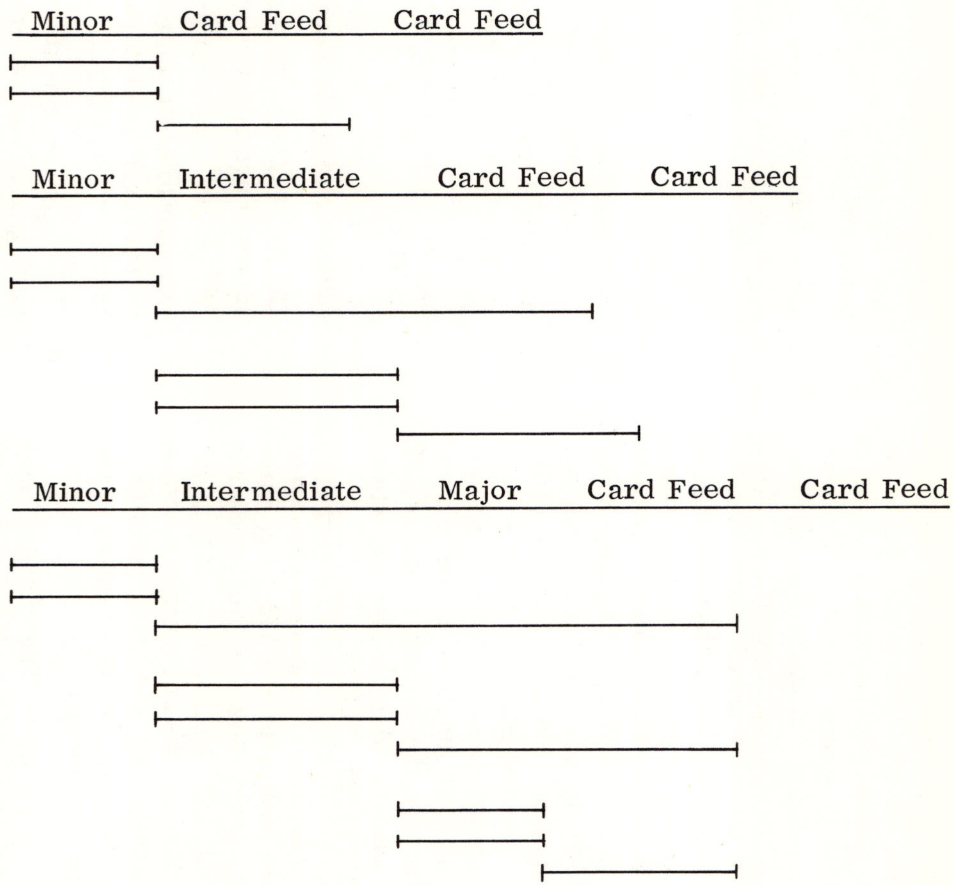

Last Card Auto-total Switch - The primary purpose of the *last card auto-total switch* (Fig. 8-49) is to provide a means of obtaining total program cycles on the run-out, thus permitting the automatic clearing of counters without program control. When the switch is on, comparing exits are inactive, and a major program change is forced on both the run-in and run-out, regardless of control-panel wiring. Detail printing will not be suspended for heading cards if the machine is set for group printing. Carriage skipping, if initiated by one of the cards being processed, will not be suspended. When the switch is off, program-control wiring will function in the normal manner. Whether the switch is on or off, only those counters will be cleared whose total hubs are wired to clear.

Gangpunch Switch - The *gangpunch switch* (Fig. 8-49) is used with the 523 Gang Summary Punch, when this machine does not operate under its own power. When the switch is turned on, the accounting machine will not operate, but the gang summary punch will, providing the cable between the two machines is connected.

Hopper stop switch - The *hopper stop switch* is not a standard feature, but it may be installed without charge. The purpose of this switch is as follows: 1. When on, the hopper stop contact is effective, and the machine will stop as the last card leaves the hopper. Cards must be run-out to print totals for the last control group. 2. When off, the hopper stop contact is ineffective, and the machine will stop as the last card is read by the third reading station. Totals for the last control group will print automatically.

Students interested in studying the IBM tape-controlled carriage or the IBM 403 Accounting Machine with the multiple-line printing feature can find these topics explained in the IBM manual A24-5654 IBM 402, 403, and 419 Accounting Machines, pages 93-112 and 113-134.

402-403 Accounting Machine Questions

Fill in blank spaces

1. Cards are fed______edge, face______.
2. To suppress printing by wiring, you must raise the corresponding________.
3. Card feeding stops and the form light goes on when the end of the form is ____ in. from the platen.
4. The 402 normal prints____line(s) from a card.
5. To suppress all printing from a typebar, an operator uses______________.
6. The standard 402 is capable of printing information from each card. This is known as______________________ and is the opposite of_________________ printing.
7. _____________________are used to suppress printing of unwanted zeros.
8. On the 402 the T, N, and C hubs (selectors) are controlled by ___________ and____________________punches.
9. In order to emit information on the 402, an operator must turn on the digit selector by wiring_________to__________.
10. The impulse manufactured by a comparing break is usually wired to______ _______ .
11. One counter can be controlled to add and subtract information on a card by wiring a ________________________ impulse through a____________________.
12. The purpose of jackplugging the CI to C hubs is to__________________________.
13. In order to print alphabetic information from one typebar, an operator must wire
    a. from_____________to_____________ of the typebar.
    b. and from___________to_____________ of the same typebar.
14. There are____alphameric typebars and _____numeric typebars on the standard 402.
15. There are____entry hubs for each comparing magnet on the 402.
16. The hub labeled D PU may receive____ impulses.

17. When the hub labeled XPU is impulsed the selector transfers on the ________ cycle.

18. The ________ switches allow an operator to wire one control panel for different types of reports.

19. The ________ button is used in the event of a card-feed failure.

20. ________________ is the automatic preparation of one total card to replace a group of detail cards.

21. - 23. List three conditions that must be satisfied before a final total is taken

21.
22.
23.

Answer True or False

24. ________ The XPU hub cannot pick up impulses from third read.

25. ________ The I hub of the pilot selector will emit an impulse when the selector is picked up.

26. ________ When coupling counters for addition, you wire the C of the low-order counter to CI of the high-order counter.

27. ________ Multiple-line print is accomplished on the 402 because cards are held at each reading station and read completely rather than digit by digit.

28. ________ Forms may be controlled by a combination of control-panel wiring and punched tape.

29. ________ The numeric designation of a counter indicates the position of the counter in relation to printing.

30. ________ The maximum number of counter positions on the machine is 64.

31. ________ The maximum number of counter positions that can be coupled is 12.

32. ________ Asterisk symbols may be wired to print from all typebars at total time.

33. ________ A counter may be wired to receive totals from another counter rather than items from a card.

Multiple choice

34. Card columns 55 to 59 (Fig. P8-1) will print for all cards with
    a. X or 12 punch in card column 80.
    b. 9-12 punch in card column 80.
    c. other than X or 12 punch in card column 80.
    d. other than 9-12 punch in card column 80 (card column 80 blank).

35. Pilot selector 4 (Fig. P8-2) will be transferred whenever
    a. a card with 765 in card columns 71 to 73 passes second reading.
    b. a card with 765 in card columns 71 to 73 passes third reading.
    c. a card with other than 765 in card columns 71 to 73 passes second reading.
    d. a card with other than 765 in card columns 71 to 73 passes third reading.

36. Pilot selector 8 (Fig. P8-2) will be transferred for cards with
    a. a 9-12 punch in card column 78.
    b. an X punch in card column 78.
    c. an 11-12 punch in card column 78.
    d. an 0-9 punch in card column 78.

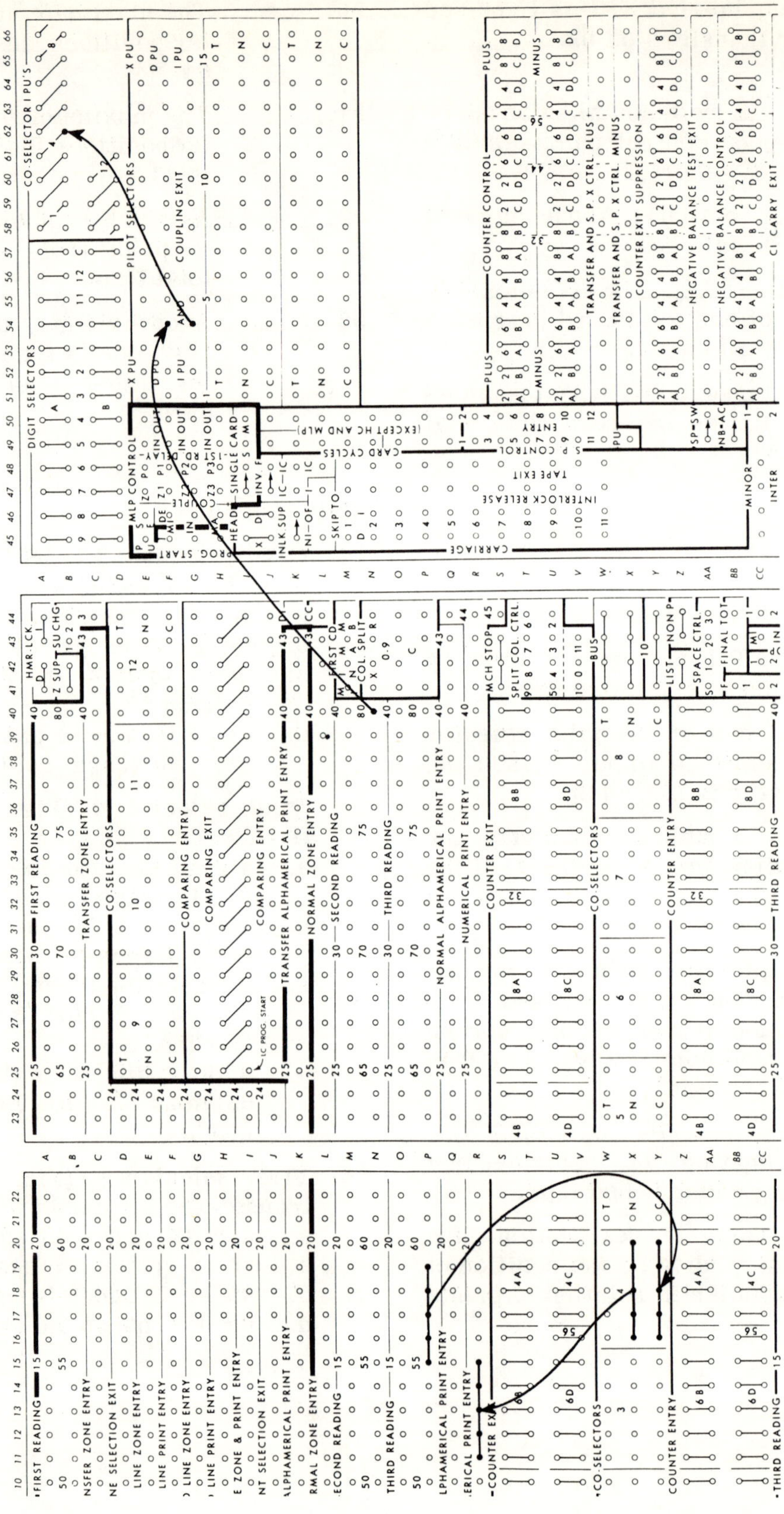

Fig. p8-1 (Courtesy of International Business Machines.)

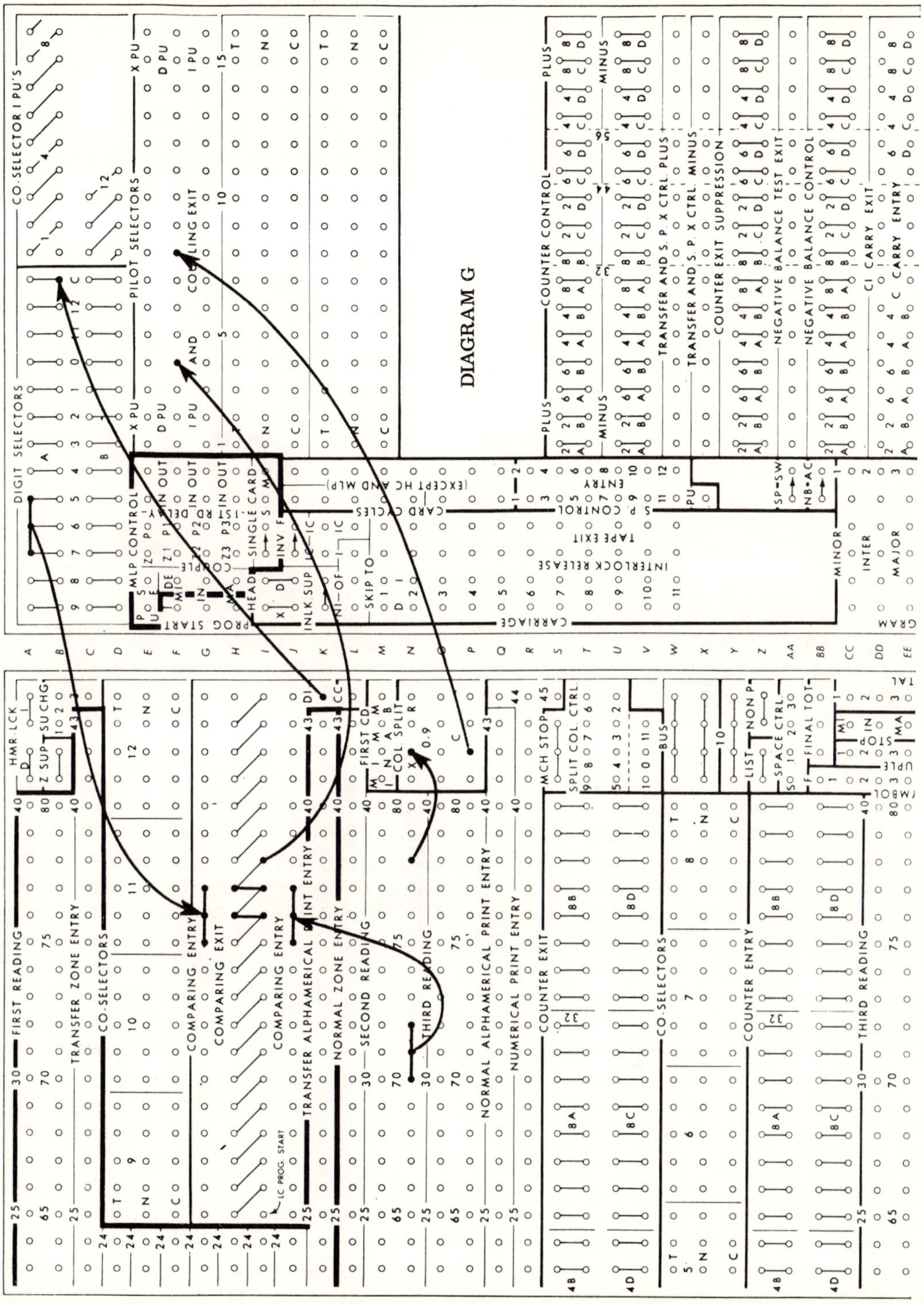

Fig. p8-2 (Courtesy of International Business Machines.)

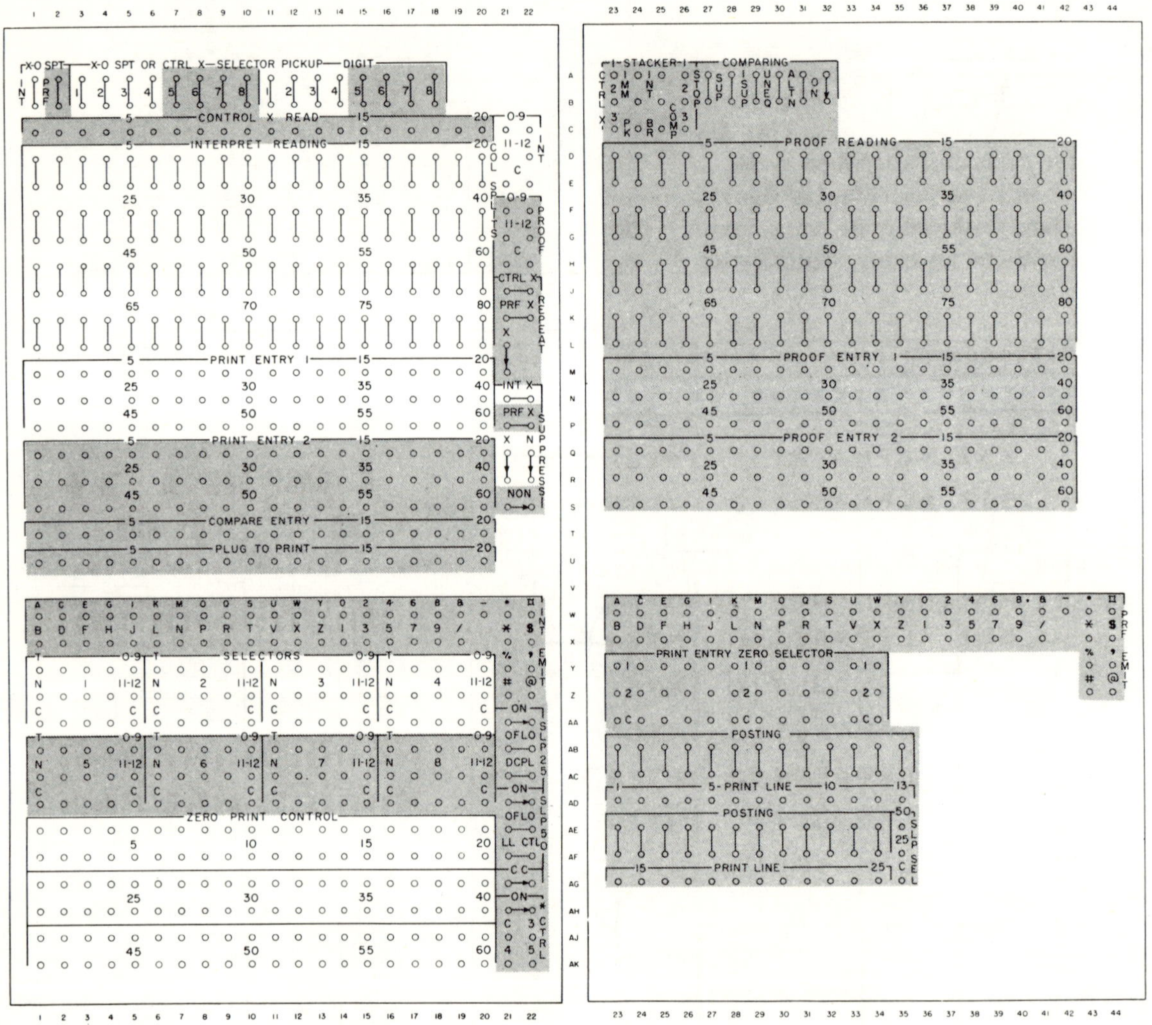

557 Control Panel. Shaded areas represent special features.

Section 9

THE 557 ALPHABETIC INTERPRETER

The student should be familiar with the IBM 548 Interpreter before beginning this section.

An interpreter is often considered to be the machine used only to eliminate the necessity for visual decoding. The IBM 557 (Fig. 9-1) Alphabetic Interpreter, however, has features which significantly increase

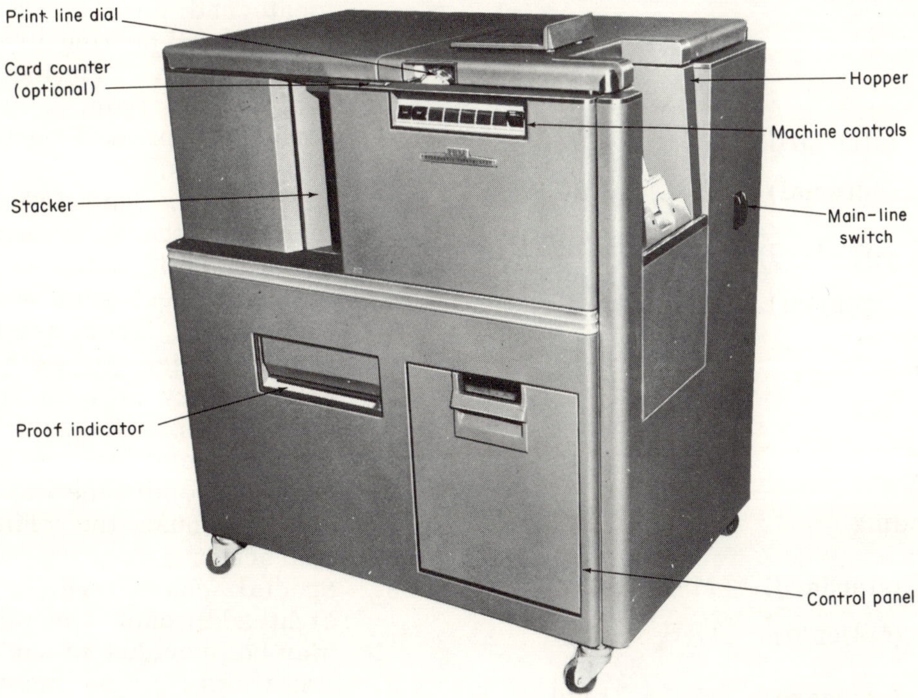

Fig. 9-1. IBM 557 Interpreter (Courtesy of International Business Machines.)

application potential. A variety of special features are available to tailor the machine to meet the demands of modern data-processing techniques. When equipped with several of the special features discussed in detail in this section, the 557 becomes an automatic line-finding, high-speed ledger-posting machine, while retaining all of the usual interpreter capabilities.

The 557 can not only accomplish the same functions as the 548 Interpreter, but is also equipped with the additional following features:

1. Zero print-control (electrical control of the printing of zeros provided on the control panel)
2. Print suppression (ability to suppress printing under the control of any X or NX condition)
3. Printing lines (twenty-five printing lines on the card selected by a manually operated printing position dial)

Control-panel hubs that perform the same functions can be found on the 557 and 548 Interpreters at the following locations:

548		Location
Reading brushes		A-D, 1-20
Print entry		M-S, 1-20
Selectors	(standard)	J-L, 1-10
	(optional)	J-L, 11-20
X-eliminators	(standard)	E-H, 1-10
	(optional)	E-H, 11-20
Read X-brushes		N-S, 21-22

557		Location
Interpret reading		D-L, 1-20
Print entry	(standard)	M-P, 1-20
	(optional)	Q-S, 1-20
Selectors	(standard)	Y-AA, 1-20
	(optional)	AB-AD, 1-20
Column split	(standard)	C-E, 21-22
	(optional)	F-H, 21-22
Control read	(optional)	C, 1-20

NOTE: No switch is necessary to make the column split operative.

In addition, the following special devices are available to increase the scope of applications that can be performed by the 557.

1. Card-to-card comparing. When printing from a master card to detail cards, comparison may be made of the control information in each to ensure that printing occurs only on matching cards. Comparing positions are furnished in groups of five, up to a total of four groups (20 positions). Three types of comparing can be supplied - numeric, alphabetic, and special character.
2. Selective stackers. A maximum of four stackers can be provided. Control-panel wiring allows separation of the cards into four groups.
3. Selective line printing. The 557 will locate and post the next available ledger-card posting line.
4. Repeat print. Printing information can be read from X or NX master cards and printed on the following detail cards.
5. Presensing. This station is required to permit the selectors to be used for alphabetic selection and to control the repeat-print device.
6. Print entry. There are two control-panel entries to each typewheel. Either entry may be selected by a manually operated switch.
7. Interpret emitter. A hub for each character emits the impulses necessary to cause the printing of that character.
8. Special characters. Printing of eight additional special characters may be provided in each typewheel.
9. Asterisks (*). As many as six asterisks adjacent to the left of the highest significant digit of a field in

specified preset positions can be printed. This feature is used for check protection.

10. Card counter. All cards except those for which the proof device has indicated an error are counted.
11. Selectors. Four additional selectors are available.
12. Proof. This is the ability to check the printing of characters punched in the card or set up by the emitter. Proof also can check print suppression, repeat print operations, and typewheel alignments.

The first six special features only will be explained in this section, since they are the ones most commonly encountered.

OPERATION

Cards are placed in a hopper, whose capacity is approximately 800 cards, 12 edge first, face down. The cards will stack in their original sequence in stackers which hold approximately 900 cards before they automatically stop card feeding. As on all other punched-card machines the 557 has a main-line switch and Start and Stop keys (Fig. 9-2). The running indicator is on

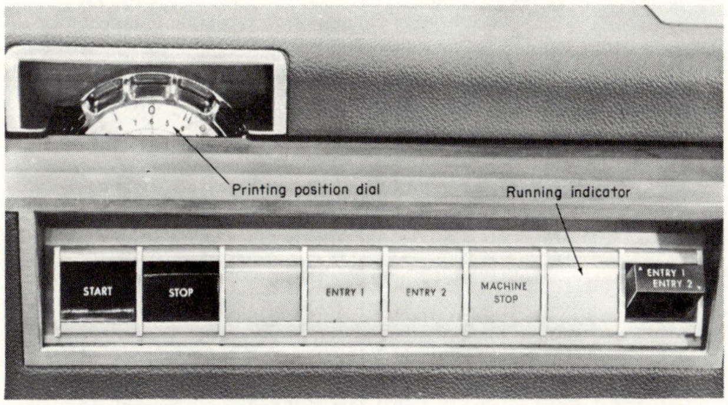

Fig. 9-2. Lights, keys, dial (Courtesy of International Business Machines.)

when the machine is on but not in use; it is off when the machine is in use. The machine prints at the rate of 100 cards per minute.

The printing-position dial may be set by the operator to any one of 25 possible positions. In Fig. 9-2, the dial is set for printing on line 6 which occurs on the zero punching position of the card. Figure 9-3 illustrates the 25 lines of printing. The stop light comes on when the proof device detects an error, and it is turned off by resetting the proof-indicator unit. The unit is reset by depressing the proof-indicator unit-reset cover on the front (Fig. 9-4).

PRINT ENTRIES 1 AND 2: M-P, 1-20, Q-S, 1-20

Print entries 1 and 2 provide for two different setups on one control panel. On the 548 not only did you need a separate control panel for each setup, but in order to interpret two lines you needed two panels. Selection of either one of the two setups is controlled by a manually operated switch (the *print-entry switch*) on the front of the machine.

Both sets of print-entry hubs cannot be made active at the same time. When print-entry 1 or 2 is active, the respective print-entry light on the front of the machine is on (Fig. 9-2).

PROBLEM 1: Print the information from columns 25 to 30 into print-entry 1, positions 30 to 35.

ZERO PRINT CONTROL

Additional panel wiring is necessary to print characters represented by 0, 11, or 12 punches. The impulse to accomplish this is called a zero print impulse and is controlled by wiring zero print control.

In addition to the print-entry hub for each typewheel, there is a pair of zero print-control hubs (AE-AK, 1-20). The hubs in the lower row are numbered from 1 to 60. These hubs control the printing of 0, 11, and 12 punches in the corresponding typewheel by jack plugging the corresponding hubs of a field and wiring the higher hub of the low-order position to the lower hub of the high-order position (Fig. 9-5, wire 6).

To eliminate the printing of zeros to the left of the highest significant digit, the zero print-control wire from the low-order position to the high-order position must be removed (Fig. 9-5, wire 7).

When a control panel is wired to print zeros to the left of print position 60, the

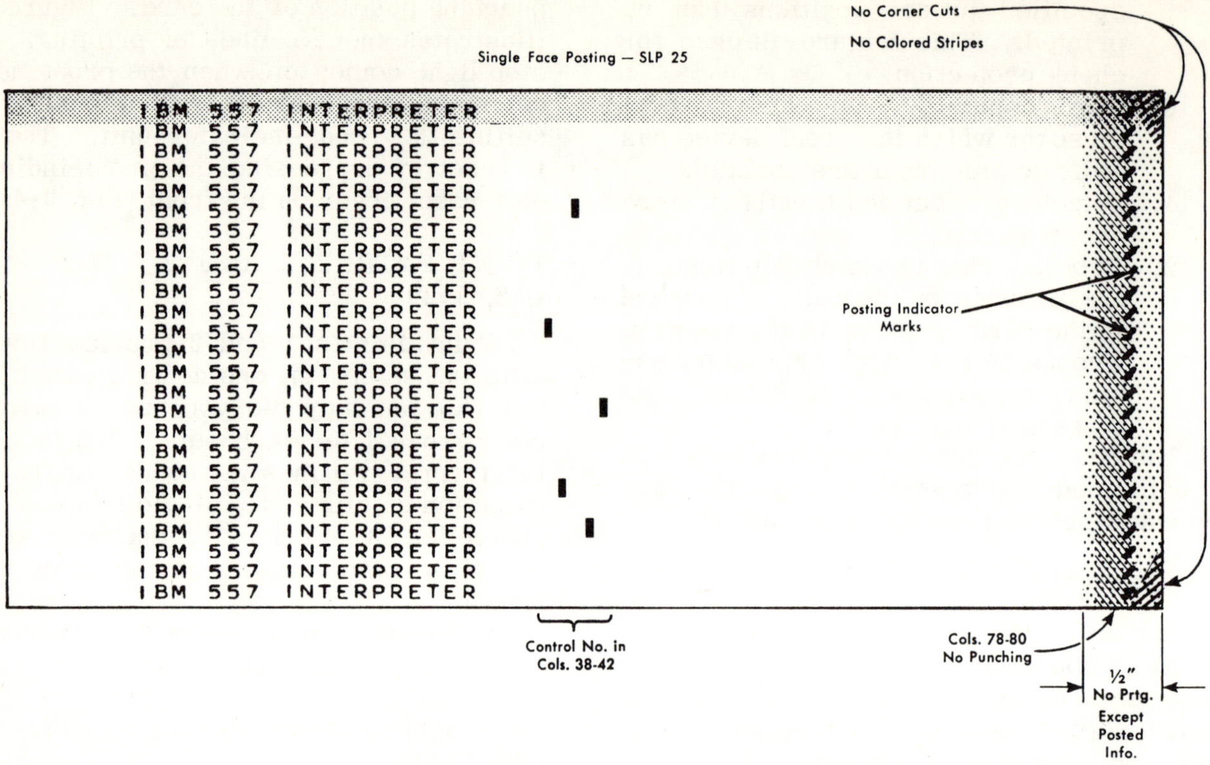

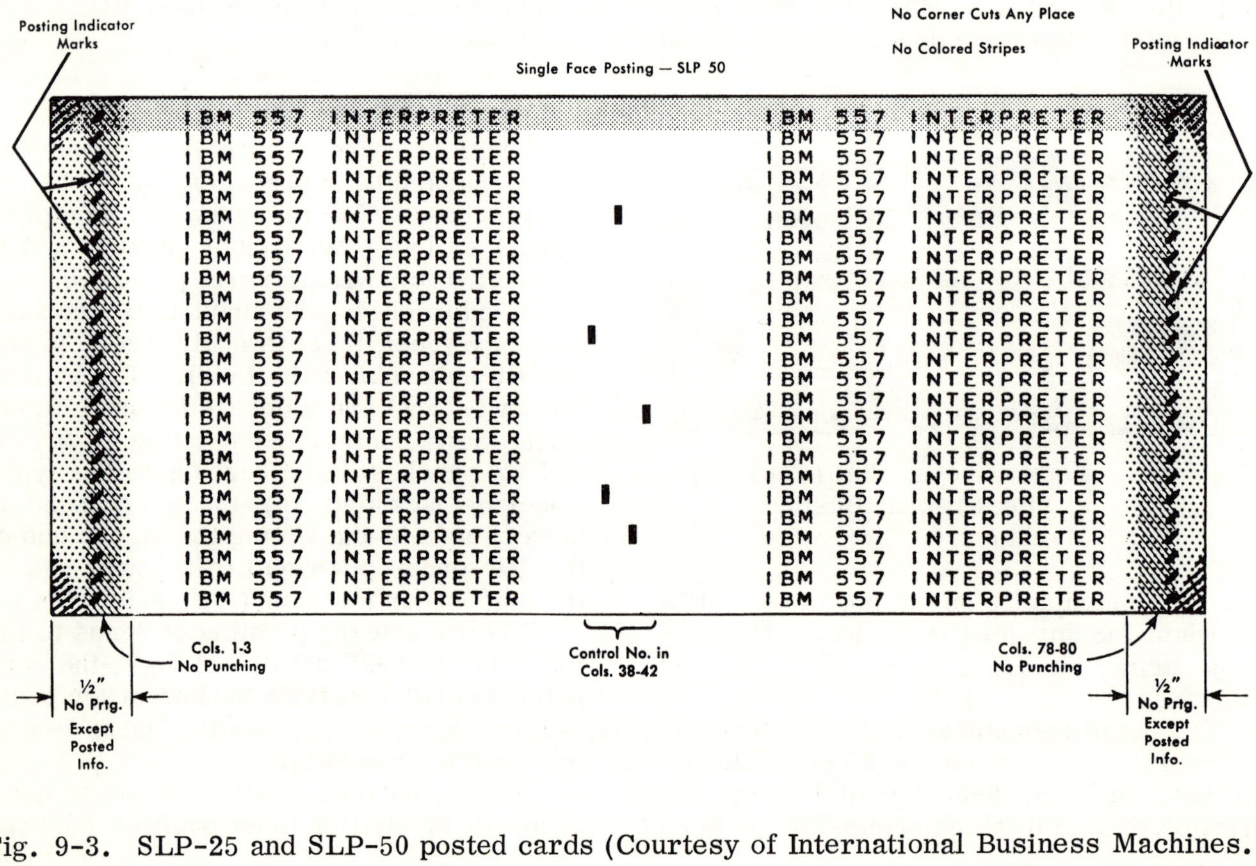

Fig. 9-3. SLP-25 and SLP-50 posted cards (Courtesy of International Business Machines.)

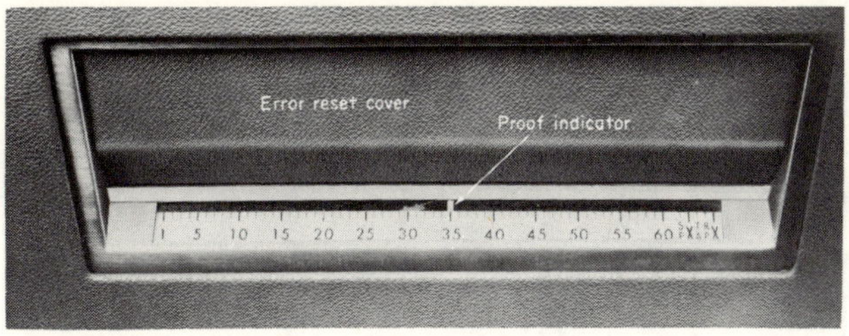

Fig. 9-4. Proof Indicator Unit (Courtesy of International Business Machines.)

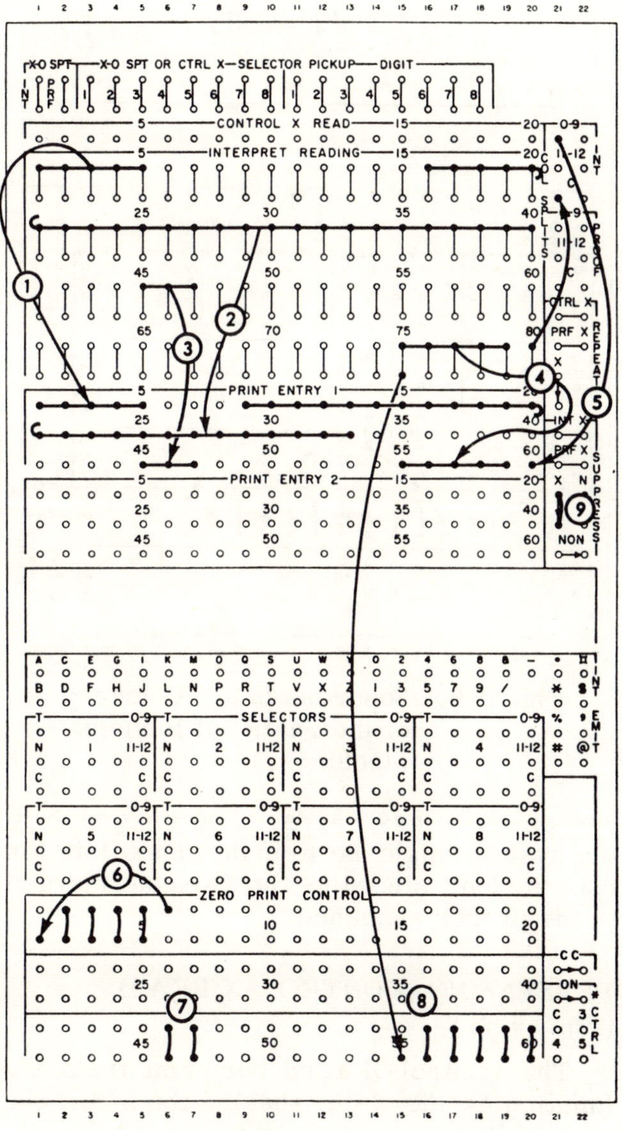

Fig. 9-5. Printing (Courtesy of International Business Machines.)

control-panel wire to the high-order position of the field is wired from the upper hub of zero print control 1. This hub is connected internally to print position 60.

When zeros are controlled to print to the right or left of a significant digit, ten consecutive zeros can be carried or controlled to print.

To print a field containing all zeros, such as a zero balance amount, the high-order position of the field must have an additional wire from interpret reading direct to the lower hub of the corresponding zero print-control position (Fig. 9-5, wire 8).

When a total of more than ten positions is to be controlled for zero printing, at least every tenth zero print-control position must be wired from interpret reading.

An example of zero print control plus regular interpreting and the use of column splits can be seen in Fig. 9-5. This example shows normal alphabetic printing, column splits, and control of zero printing:

1. Employee number is read from columns 1 to 5 and printed in typewheels 1 to 5.
2. Employee name is read from columns 16 to 40 and printed in typewheels 9 to 33.
3. Hours are read from columns 45 to 47 and printed in typewheels 45 to 47.
4. Amount is read from columns 75 to 80 and printed in typewheels 55 to 60.
5. The units position of the amount is wired through a column split to eliminate a control X punch in that column.
6. All zeros in employee number are controlled to print.
7. Zero print control is wired for the hours field to print all zeros except those to the left of the high-order significant digit.
8. Zero print control is wired for the amount field to print all zeros, including zero-balance amounts. If zero balances are to be identified, but zeros to the left of significant amounts are to be eliminated, interpret reading 79 can be wired to the lower hub of zero print-control po-

sition 59. With this wiring, 00 identifies zero balances.

9. The X-switch must be wired at all times except when suppressing printing on NX cards.

SUPPRESS PRINT

Selective printing of an entire card may be performed under the control of an X or NX condition. Although a 12 punch can be used as a control impulse in some circumstances, the basic control function is performed by an X punch, since the proof device treats all 12 punches in repeat and suppress print-control columns as errors. In this manner all of one type of card may be interpreted without separating the file or printing on the other cards in the file. Selective printing can be used in any application that has a merged master and detail file and that has to remain merged for processing by another machine.

The column containing the X control punch is wired from the interpret reading directly to the interpret X hub (N, 21-22). If suppression of the printing of X cards is desired, the X-switch (Q-R, 21) must be wired on. If, however, suppression of printing of the NX cards is wanted, the NX switch (Q-R, 22) must be wired instead.

The wiring example in Fig. 9-6 demonstrates the suppress-printing feature by printing only the NX80 cards. A field of the card is wired to print zeros to the left and right, and an X from column 80 is wired to the interpret X hub of the suppress-print device. The X-switch is wired to prevent printing of all cards containing the X punch in column 80.

A typical application would be after the creation of class cards from X master cards on a reproducer or computer, processing the merged file by the 557, where the information in the class cards would be interpreted. The file might next be listed on an accounting machine for a visual edit. Then at registration time the student leaves his name card plus a class card for each selected class. These cards are processed by the reproducer and the student's name and I.D. number are gangpunched into his class cards. This file then goes into the 557 to interpret the student's name and number on the class cards. The next step in the system might be to print class lists for each student, since the file is already merged in the proper sequence.

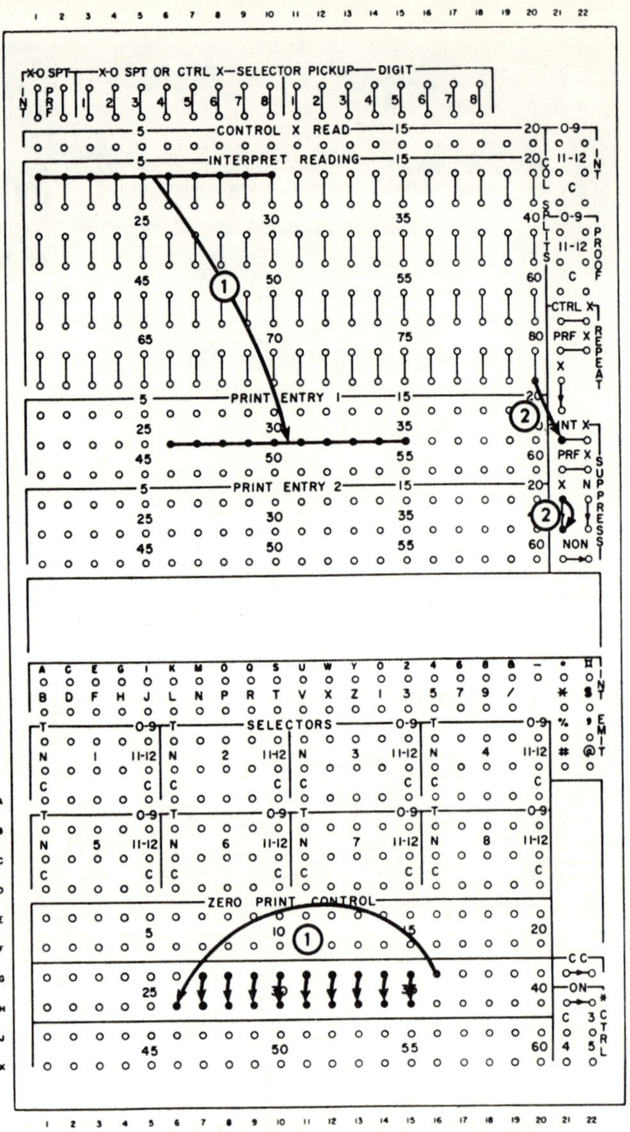

Fig. 9-6. Suppress print (Courtesy of International Business Machines.)

PRESENSING (CONTROL-X READ) (Fig. 9-7.)

The Control-X read performs the same function as the X-brushes of the 548. The control-X read controls selectors for alphabetic selection and is necessary to control the repeat-print feature.

The presensing station is composed of

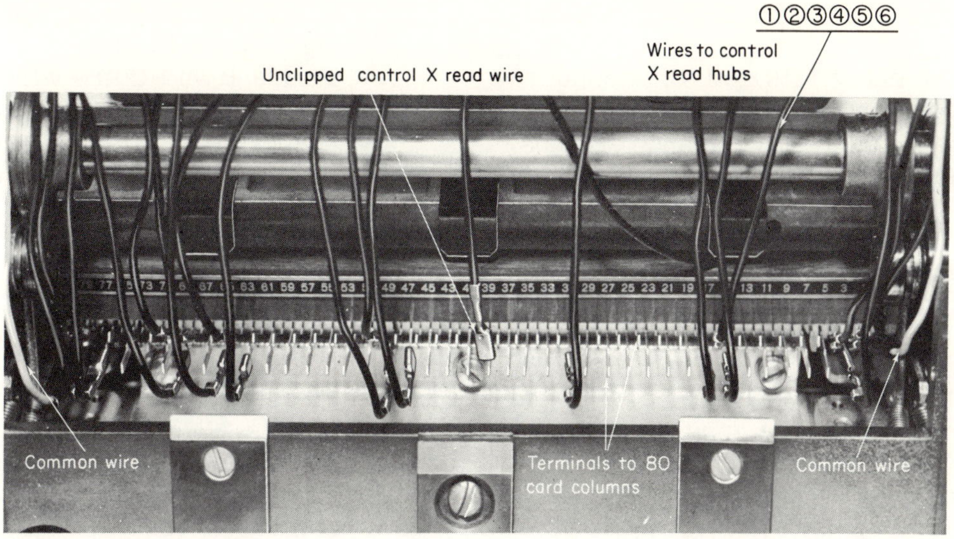

Fig. 9-7. Presenting (control-X read) (Courtesy of International Business Machines.)

80 contact pins. The terminals of these pins are arranged in two banks, odd numbers on the lower, even numbers on the upper. The lower bank is numbered, 1, 3, 5, 7, etc., from right to left. These terminals correspond to the 80 card columns.

The 20 Control-X read hubs are connected to the 20 presensing wires. The wires run consecutively from 1 to 20, right to left, and correspond to the 20 control-X hubs on the control panel at C, 1-20. They may be clipped by the machine operator to any of the 80 terminals.

REPEAT PRINT: J-M, 21-22

Information punched in a master card may be read and printed on the master card and succeeding details under the control of an X or NX condition recognized by the presensing station. However, it is not possible to read information from the detail cards and print it in addition to the information printing from the master cards during the same run.

This feature has applications whenever you desire to print information that is not punched in the card. Two common applications are to print pertinent information on cards that do not have the data punched in the card (for example, printing, "Make checks payable to___" on an accounts receivable card that is to be mailed to the customer), and to print instructions on how to answer questions that are also printed on the card.

The impulse from control X (C, 1-20) is wired to the control X hub (J, 21-22) of the repeat-print device. If the master card contains the X punch, the X-switch (L-M, 21) must be wired on. If the master card is an NX card the X-switch is *not* wired. When the cards run out, the typewheel setup is retained until a new master is sensed or the X-switch is disconnected. On machines equipped with the proof device (proof-X hub), K, 21-22, the column containing the control X, must be wired from proofreading to the proof X hub. The master card and/or selected details may be print suppressed during repeat printing.

PROBLEM 2: Print columns 25 to 30 in print entry 1, positions 25 to 30. Show the wiring for zero printing of zeros to the right of a significant digit and the wiring to print all zeros.

PROBLEM 3: Draw a diagram to interpret the information punched in columns 11 to 16 into print positions 25 to 30 of NX detail cards. Wire zero print control to print all zeros in print positions 25 to 30.

In operations where it is necessary to alter the zero print-control wiring from the print entry 1 setup to the print entry 2 setup, you must use the 12-position print-entry zero selector.

PRINT ENTRY ZERO SELECTOR: Y-AA, 23-34

When print entry 1 is active, a connection exists between the C (common) row of hubs and the 1 (print entry 1) row of hubs. When print entry 2 is active, the connection between the C and 1 rows is broken, and a connection is established between the C and 2 (print entry 2). These hubs may also be used to change the setup of control wiring, such as print suppression or repeat print.

Two setups are wired on the same control panel (Fig. 9-8) through the use of the print-entry switch and the print-entry zero-selector:

1. Field A is printed in typewheels 2 to 6 in both print entries. Zero print control is wired to eliminate zeros to the left of the highest significant digit in the field.
2. Fields B and C are wired to print in typewheels 24 to 28 and 30 to 34, respectively, through print entry 1.
3. Zero print control is wired through the C and 1 side of the print entry zero-selector to print all the zeros in field B.
4. Similarly, field C is wired to print all the zeros through the C and 1 sides of the selector.
5. Field D is wired to print in typewheels 27 to 31 through print entry 2.
6. Zero print-control wiring used to control fields B and C on the print entry 1 setup is broken when print

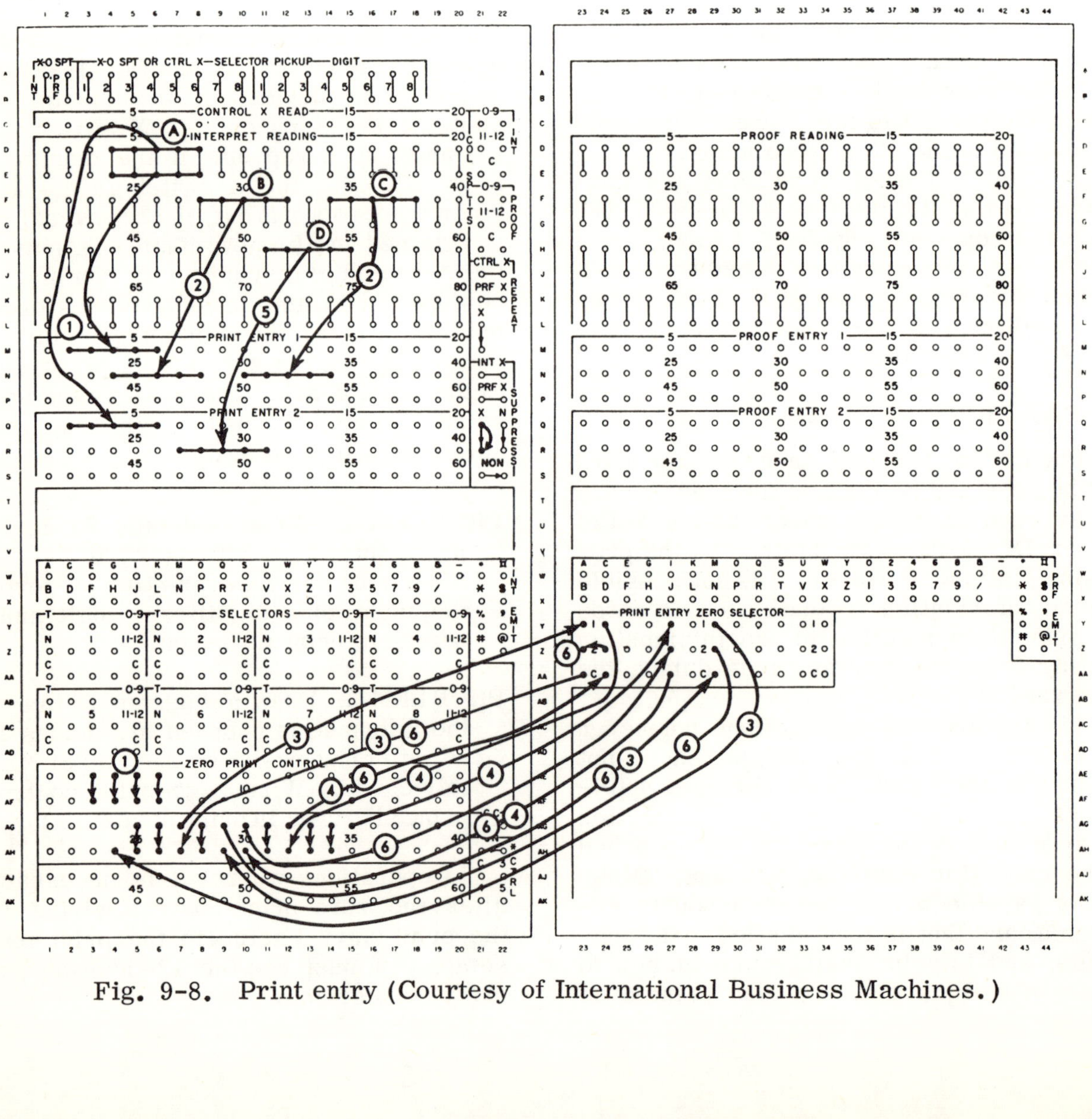

Fig. 9-8. Print entry (Courtesy of International Business Machines.)

entry 2 is made active. New zero print control wiring is established through the C and 2 sides of the selector to control the printing of zeros in field D.

SELECTORS: Y-AA, 1-20, AB-AD, 1-20

Four five-position selectors are standard on the basic machine. Four additional selectors can be added as a special feature. These selectors may be used for numeric selection, alphabetic selection (if presensing (control X) is installed), or as column splits.

SELECTOR PICKUP: A-B, 1-4; A-B, 11-14; A-B, 5-8; A-B, 15-18

Each selector has two separate pickups which should *never* be connected together. Each pickup should be activated by a specific impulse for a specific function. Both pickups will transfer the selector immediately and hold it until the completion of that cycle.

X-O SPLIT OR CONTROL X: A-B, 1-4; A-B, 5-8

This pickup can be wired from X-O split hubs (A-B, 1-2), to use the selector as a column split, or from control X read for selection. The interpret X-O split hub (A-B, 1) when wired to X-O split pickup, causes that selector to function as a column split for use with the interpret reading brushes. The normal side of the selector becomes the exit for any 11 or 12 impulses that enter the common hub, and the transferred side becomes the exit for 0 to 9 impulses. The proof X-O split hub (A-B, 2) controls the selector in the same manner in time with the proofreading brushes.

Wiring from control-X read to this pickup transfers the selector for the entire cycle in the same manner that the X-brushes transfer the selectors on the 548 Interpreter.

DIGIT PICKUP: A-B, 1-4; A-B, 5-8

These hubs are normally impulsed by an X impulse from the interpret or proofreading stations. Since the hubs accept any impulse from 12 to 9, a column split is required to select out the X-control punch. If the selector is being used to select zero print-control wiring, the X impulse from the interpret reading station must be filtered through the 12 and 11 side of a column split to prevent the zero print impulse from transferring the selector.

CARD-TO-CARD COMPARING AND SELECTIVE STACKING

The comparing feature provides a means of verifying operations when information from a master card is transferred to detail cards. With selective stacking, cards can be separated or selected into a maximum of four stackers. The normal stacker on the extreme left is numbered 4. The selective stackers are numbered 1 to 3, right to left.

In a compare operation, data read from the master card is stored for comparison with successive detail cards. The data in the master card can be held for repeat printing. Printing can be suppressed on unmatched detail cards and continued on the following matched detail cards. Machine operation can be stopped and printing can be suppressed whenever unmatched or duplicate cards are recognized.

Comparing positions are furnished in groups of five, up to a total of four groups (20 positions). Three types of comparing can be supplied.

1. Numeric. In each position comparison takes place only on single numeric characters, 0 through 9. A zero compared with a blank is recognized as unequal.
2. Alphabetic. Comparison can be made on single numeric punches, the 0 to 1 code, single zone punches, or any single alphabetic character A to Z.
3. Special character. Comparison can be made on all numerals, letters, codes, and special characters that can be printed on the 557. A maximum of ten positions is available for special-character comparing.

On machines with selective stackers, control-panel wiring determines which cards fall into the extra pockets. Unmatched cards, duplicate master or detail cards, cards preceding unmatched and duplicate cards, and cards with punching in a given column can be selected.

Any application that processes a mixed file or a file containing alternating master and detail cards on the 557 could make use of this feature.

As you will learn shortly, when the compare stop hub (A-B, 27) receives an impulse from the unequal, alternate, or immediate suppress hubs (A-B, 28-31), the machine will stop and the compare stop light will go on. To resume processing, you must turn off the compare stop light by depressing the stop key, and then depressing the start key for three cycles.

COMPARE OPERATIONS

The compare unit recognizes alternating master and detail cards with matching control fields as a normal condition. In the normal condition, the compare operation alternates storing from the master card and comparing from the detail card. Under the normal condition, neither the unequal nor the alternate hub emits an impulse (Fig. 9-9).

The alternate hub emits whenever storing and comparing do not occur on alternate cycles, that is, whenever a master card is not followed by a detail card (Fig. 9-10). Notice that in Fig. 9-10) the cards have the same control number.

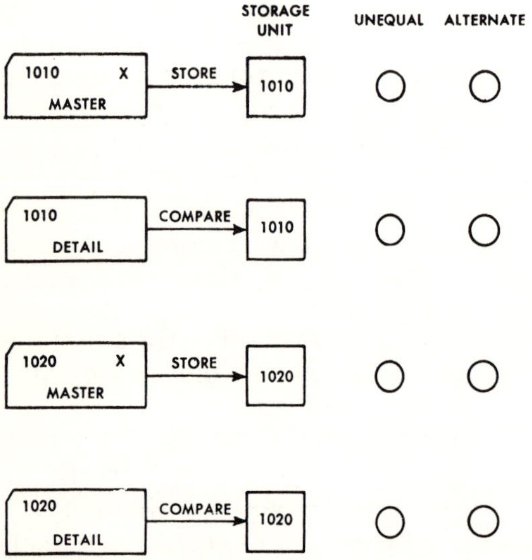

Fig. 9-9. Normal comparing (Courtesy of International Business Machines.)

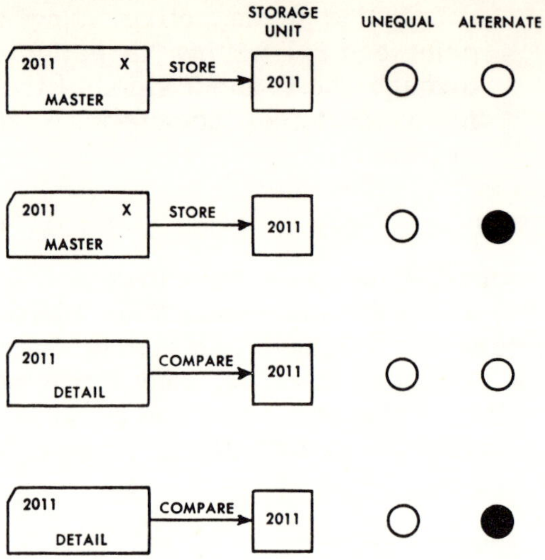

Fig. 9-10. Comparing (alternate emitting) (Courtesy of International Business Machines.)

The unequal hub emits only on comparing cycles when the compared fields are unequal, that is, whenever a detail card does not match the preceding master card (Fig. 9-11).

If, during a compare cycle, storing and comparing have not occurred alternately and the compared fields are unequal, both the alternate and unequal hubs emit an impulse, that is, whenever a second detail card follows a master card and does not match the master. The first detail card may or may not match the master (Fig. 9-12).

CARD-TO-CARD COMPARING

Information from a detail card read by

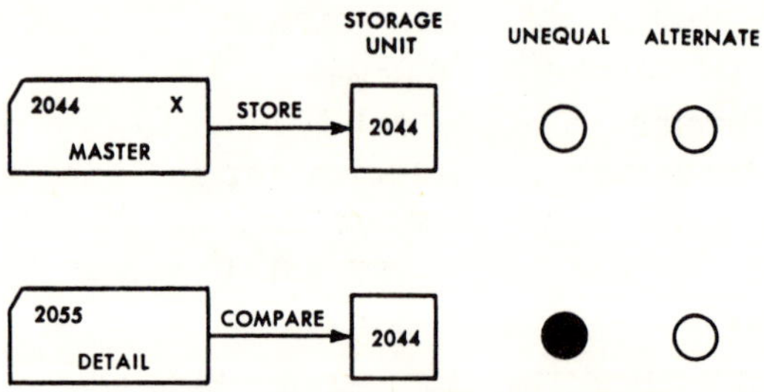

Fig. 9-11. Comparing (unequal emitting) (Courtesy of International Business Machines.)

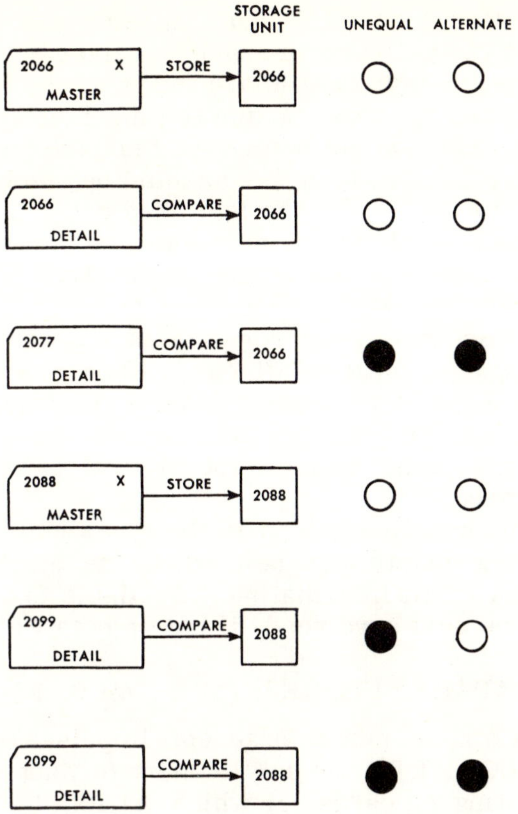

Fig. 9-12. Comparing (unequal and alternate emitting) (Courtesy of International Business Machines.)

the interpret brushes is compared with information stored from the preceding master card. As the master card is read by the interpret brushes, the control field enters storage where it is held until the next master card is read. Information in each detail is compared with the master information in storage. Therefore, during comparing, the arrangement of a file composed of a single master and single detail cards can be checked. If the sequence is not alternately master and detail cards, the machine can be made to operate as follows:

1. The machine can be stopped.
2. Printing can be suppressed.
3. Duplicate cards can be selected.

The above operations can be performed separately or in combinations.

The compare unit enables the operator to check the alternating sequence of the file. It is *not* possible on the 557 to check numeric sequence as done by the collator. The fields being compared, as well as other information in the master, can be printed on the master and following detail cards under an X or NX control.

Machines having the card-to-card comparing feature must also have control-X read (presensing) and repeat-print features. Comparing operates in conjunction with the following two features: Master cards are distinguished by the presence or absence of an X punch in a given column; and a control-X read contact is used to read the X-punched column.

The following is the necessary wiring for the interpreter to recognize a master card for comparing:

1. A control-X read contact is wired to control-X repeat.
2. The X-switch is wired if master cards are X punched; it is unwired if detail cards are X punched.

COMPARE ENTRY: T, 1-20

The field to be compared is wired from interpret read to compare entry. Information read from the master card to compare entry is placed in storage and held for comparison with succeeding detail cards. Information read from the detail cards is compared with the stored data.

Each time a new master card is read by the interpret reading brushes, the storage unit is cleared and the new control information is placed in storage for comparison with successive detail cards. Comparing does not take place between two master cards or the last detail card in a group and the following master card. The fields being compared must *not* be wired to print entry directly from interpret read. The plug-to-print hubs must be used.

PLUG-TO-PRINT: U, 1-20

The compare entry hubs are connected internally to the plug-to-print exit hubs. Information received by the compare entry hubs is available from the corresponding plug-to-print hubs. These hubs can be wired to print entry 1 or 2 to print the control information on the master and/or detail card. Information to be printed can be selected only at the time a master card is being read.

The following hubs allow predetermined operations as a result of comparison.

COMPARING UNEQUAL (UNEQ): A-B, 30

The unequal hub emits an impulse on the compare cycle when detail information compared to master information in storage is unequal (Fig. 9-11). An unequal impulse can be:

1. Wired to compare stop to interrupt a machine operation.
2. Wired to compare suppress to prevent printing on the unequal detail card.
3. Wired to stacker compare to select the unequal detail card or to immediate pick to select the card immediately preceding the unequal detail card.
4. Controlled by a selector.

COMPARING ALTERNATE (ALTN): A-B, 31

When the 557 is wired from control-X read to repeat print and the repeat print-X switch is wired on, the comparing alternate hub emits if the card sequence is not alternately master and detail. An impulse is available from ALTN when a detail card immediately follows a detail, or a master immediately follows a master. In the sequence M1 - D1 - D1 - D2 - M3 - M3 - M4 - D4, ALTN emits for the cards underlined as they pass interpret reading (Fig. 9-10), ALTN can be wired to:

1. Compare stop hub to stop machine operation
2. Compare suppress to prevent printing
3. Stacker compare to select all multiple-detail or master cards except the first in a series or to stacker immediate pick to select all multiple-detail or master cards except the last in the series
4. Digit pickup of a selector to control the UNEQ impulse

COMPARING STOP (STOP): A-B, 27

Comparing stop is normally wired from the UNEQ or ALTN hubs to stop machine operation. When this hub receives an impulse, no more cards are fed from the hopper, and the cards inside the machine automatically run out before the machine stops. The card for which the machine has stopped will be the next to the last card out. On the runout, cards are read, compared, printed, and selected according to control-panel wiring. Master information from the last master-card read remains in storage for comparing with detail cards when machine operation is resumed. Master information remains in storage until another master card is read or until the control panel is changed.

Information stored in the typewheels for repeat printing is held when the machine stops. This information is available to print on the next card read, if it is a detail card.

COMPARE SUPPRESS (SUP): A-B, 28

Compare suppress accepts impulses from UNEQ, ALTN, or I SUP hubs to suppress printing on cards for which ALTN, UNEQ, or I SUP emit. Wiring to the nonsuppress switch has no effect when SUP is impulsed.

COMPARE SUPPRESS IMMEDIATE (I SUP): A-B, 29

Compare suppress immediate emits impulses when two or more master cards immediately follow each other. I SUP wired to SUP suppresses printing on all master cards except the last in the series. For instance, in the sequence M5-D6-M7-M8-M9, if I SUP was wired to SUP, printing would be suppressed on M7 and M8.

Wiring the nonsuppress switch has no effect when I SUP is wired to compare suppress.

COMPARE OU (OU): A-B, 32

The compare on hubs must be jackplugged to make this feature active. In Fig. 9-13, the 557 is controlled to compare detail cards with the preceding master card. If the result of comparing is unequal, printing is suppressed and the machine stops as wired by the following:

1. Control-X contact 20 is used to read

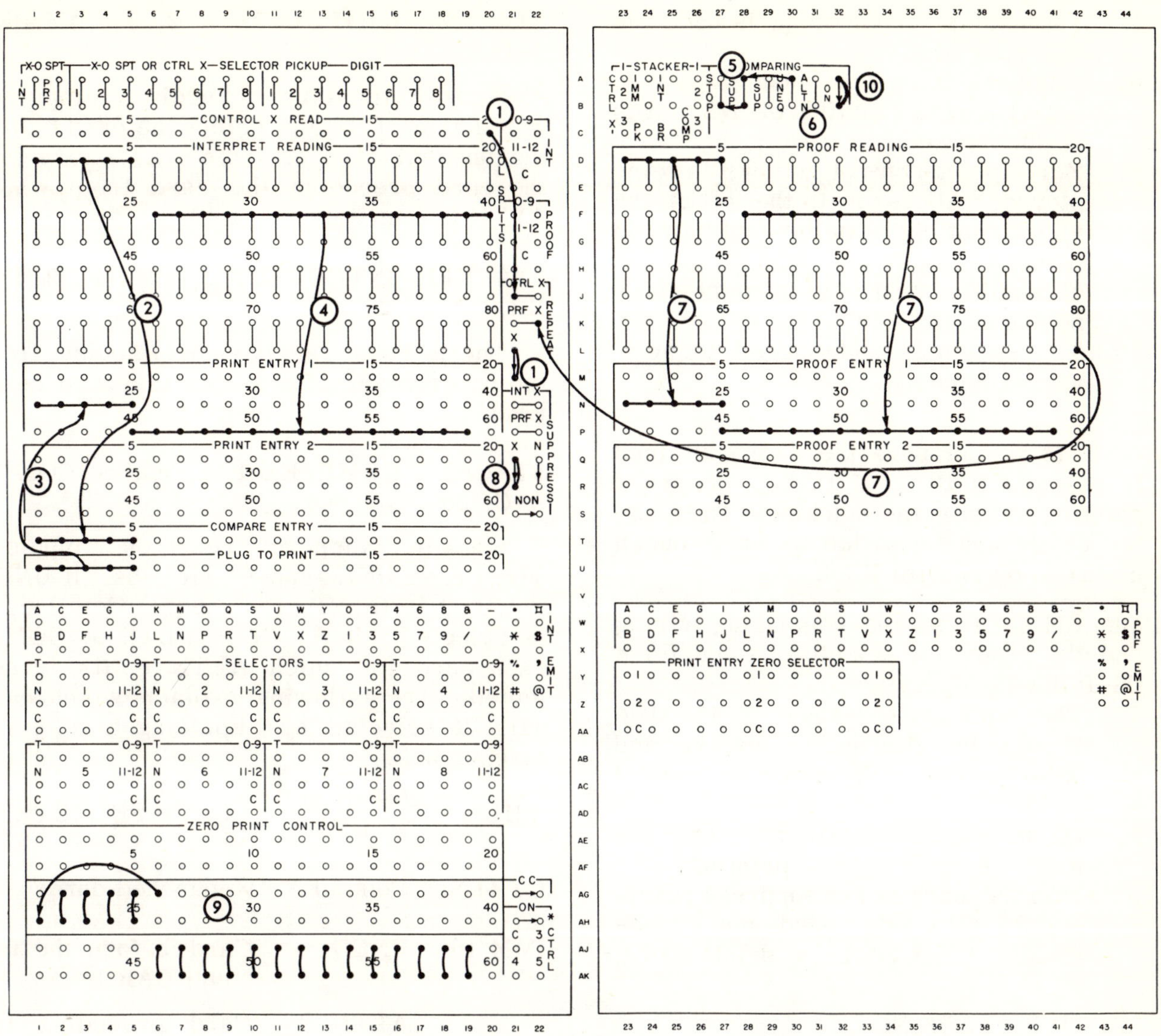

Fig. 9-13. Suppressing printing on unmatched detail cards (Courtesy of International Business Machines.)

master cards that are X punched in column 80. Control-X read 20 is wired to repeat control X, and the X-switch is wired on. With this wiring, the master cards are recognized. Also, control is set up for repeat print and comparing operations.

2. The control field to be compared is wired from interpret reading to comparing entry.
3. Plug-to-print is wired to print entry 1 to repeat-print the control field on the master and following detail cards.
4. Wiring from interpret reading to print entry 1 sends master-card information to the typewheels for the repeat-print operation. This field is not used in the compare operation, so it is wired directly to print entry 1.
5. Wiring from UNEQ to SUP and STOP stops the machine operation and suppresses printing on unmatched detail cards.
6. The ALTN hub is not wired because in this problem multiple-detail cards are the normal condition.

7. The normal proofwiring is used for this operation.
8. Suppress-X switch must always be wired unless printing of NX cards is suppressed.
9. Zero print-control wiring is employed. All zeros to the left of the significant digits in the control field print; zeros do not print to the left of significant digits in print-entry positions 45 to 59.
10. The switch is jackplugged to activate comparing.

PROBLEM 4: Compare the data contained in columns 1 to 5; if UNEQ, suppress printing and stop the machine. The master cards are identified by an X punch and read by control X 20.

PROBLEM 5: Draw the comparing wiring and the wiring for selector 1 to perform the following operation:

1. The normal sequence of the file should be alternating master and detail cards with matching control fields.
2. On all multiple detail cards stop the machine and suppress printing.
3. Stop the machine and suppress printing for all master cards not immediately followed by a detail card.

SELECTIVE STACKING

Each of the selective stackers (3, 2, and 1) has four control hubs used to determine which cards fall into each stacker. The control hubs are labeled CTRLX, IMM PK, INT BR, and COMP (A-C, 23-26). If a card is directed by panel wiring to fall into two stackers at the same time, the card goes to the first one it reaches.

STACKER CONTROL X, 1, 2, and 3 (CTRLX): A-C, 23

The 1, 2, and 3 hubs represent the corresponding stackers. These hubs accept impulses from control-X read to select the cards that are X punched in a given column. A control-X contact must be wired to read the column.

STACKER IMMEDIATE 1, 2, 3 (IMM PK): A-C, 24

Stacker immediate receives impulses wired from UNEQ to select the card before the unequal card or from ALTN to select the card preceding the card from which ALTN is emitting.

STACKER INTERPRET 1, 2, and 3 (INT BR): A-C, 25

These hubs receive any impulse from interpret reading to select the card being read.

STACKER COMPARE 1, 2, and 3 (COMP): A-C, 26

Stacker compare receives impulses wired from UNEQ and ALTN hubs. If UNEQ is wired to COMP, the unequal detail card is selected. If ALTN is wired to COMP, each card for which ALTN emits is selected. The following explains which card will be selected by impulsing a selective stacker hub.

HUB	IMPULSED BY	CARD SELECTED
CTRLX	Control X	X-punched cards
IMM PK	UNEQ	Card before the unequal CARD
	ALTN	Card preceding the card for which ALTN is emitting
INT BR	Interpret reading	Card being read
COMP	UNEQ	Unequal detail card
	ALTN	Each card for which ALTN emits

The wiring in Fig. 9-14 illustrates the use of selective stacking.

1. Control-X contact 20 senses the X in column 80. Wiring control-X read 20 to repeat control X and wiring the X-switch indicates when a master card is being read.
2. The control field is wired from interpret reading to compare entry.

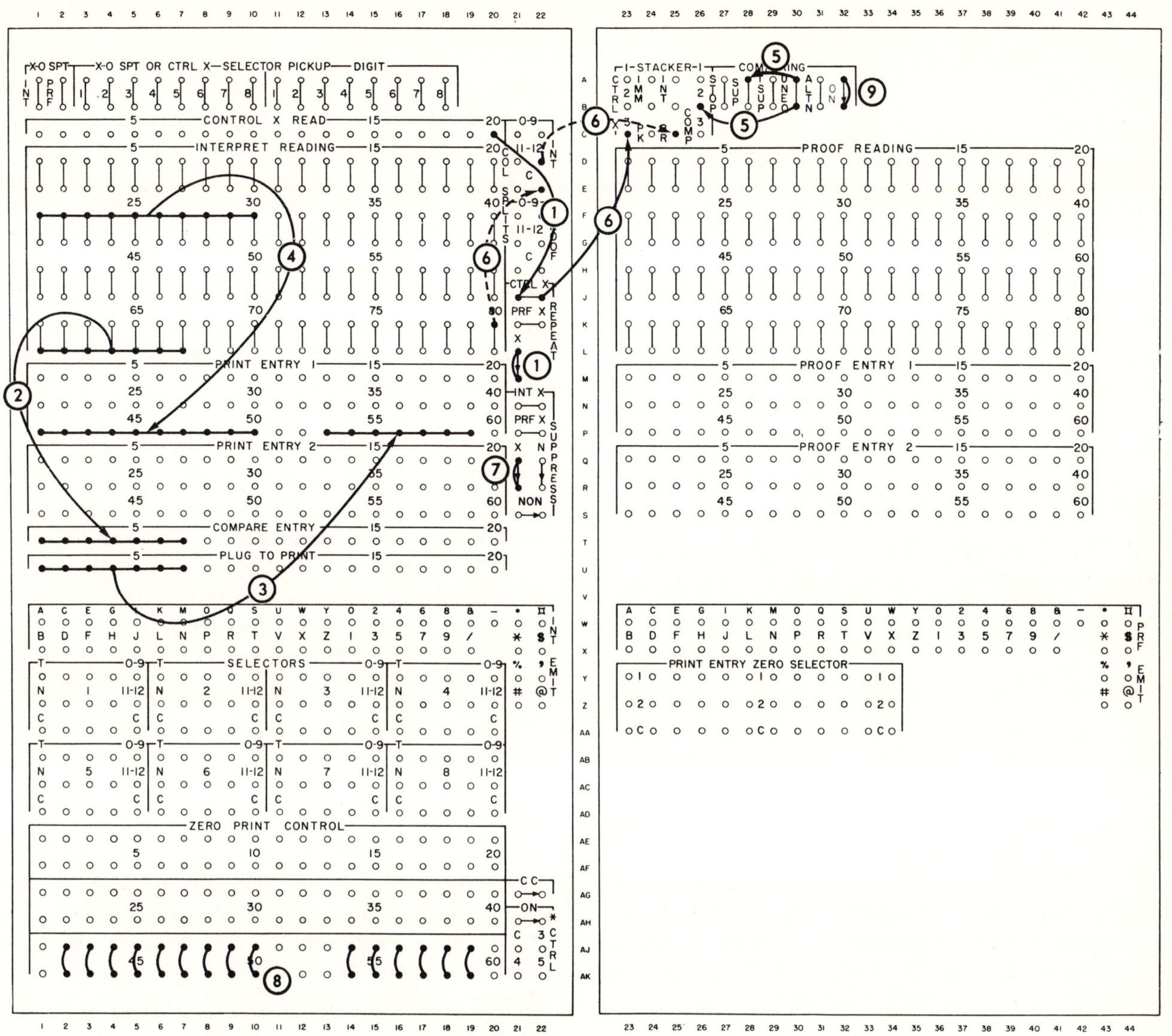

Fig. 9-14. Print suppression and card selection
(Courtesy of International Business Machines.)

3. Wiring from plug-to-print to print entry 1 allows the control information to print on the master card and repeat print on detail cards.

4. Wiring from interpret reading to print entry 1 enables master card information *not* being compared to repeat print in detail cards.

5. UNEQ wired to SUP prevents printing on unmatched detail cards. UNEQ wired to stacker 2 COMP directs unmatched detail cards to stacker 2.

6. Wiring from control-X read contact 20 to stacker 3, CTRLX, causes the machine to stack all master cards in stacker 3. No column split is necessary with this wiring. The dotted line shows an alternate wiring to select X-punched master cards by wiring from interpret read brush 80 through a column split to stacker 3 INT BR.

7. Suppress-X switch must be wired unless printing on NX cards is suppressed.

8. Normal zero print-control wiring is used. NOTE: For a machine with a proof device, wiring should be added for proofreading each field being printed.

9. The switch is jackplugged to activate comparing.

PROBLEM 6: Draw a diagram showing only the wiring for comparing and selection to perform the following:
1. Suppress printing for unmatched detail cards
2. Select to stacker 1 unmatched and duplicate master cards
3. Select to stacker 2 unmatched detail cards
4. All other cards to stacker 4 (the normal stacker)

SELECTIVE LINE PRINTING

If the selective line printing device is installed on the 557 Interpreter, the following devices must also be installed:
1. Control-X read (presense)
2. Repeat print
3. A minimum of five positions of comparing
4. A minimum of one selective stacker

Selective line printing is available in two models to post a maximum of either 25 lines (SLP-25) or 50 lines (SLP-50) from a data card to each face of a ledger card. By reversing the card, a maximum of either 50 or 100 lines can be posted from a data card to a ledger card. Print control is maintained by control-panel wiring.

OPERATION

Any application that uses a ledger card can utilize this feature. For example, the posting of cash receipts cards on a ledger card could be accomplished after the ledger card was merged behind the corresponding receipts card.

The 557 can print information from a master card on the same master card and/or subsequent detail card or cards. Therefore, in a posting operation, the data cards would be identified as master cards and the ledger cards as detail cards. The terminology ***master - data cards*** and ***detail - ledger cards*** will be used for the remainder of this section. Information can be posted from a master-data card to an immediately following detail-ledger card. Card-to-card comparing should be performed at the same time. The multiple stackers can be impulsed to select out cards from both the card-to-card comparing and posting operations. If suppress print is being used in the card-to-card comparing process, this device operates the same for all repeat-print processes. For example, if we are repeat printing the control-compare field on NX cards only, we can post by selective-line printing on NX ledger cards only. Each printed line requires a separate pass of the data and ledger cards.

Ledger cards can be posted in any sequence on the 25 or 50 printing lines through control-panel wiring. The posting sequence must be the same during any specific run of the cards. For instance, if we wire the 557 to post ledger cards three times on lines 5, 10, and 25, all ledger cards must be posted on those lines and in that order. The print-position dial is inoperative during selective line printing. The data card is positioned for printing by means of control-panel wiring.

SENSING UNIT

Certain print positions on ledger cards are reserved for the posting-indicator mark only. This (diagonal) mark is printed from the 0 to 1 section of the typewheel. The posting-indicator marks are sensed by a photosensitive unit. This unit recognizes the posting-indicator marks printed on the ledger card during the previous posting run. The mark is in line with, and printed at the same time as, the posted information (Fig. 9-3).

After the mark or marks made during the previous posting or postings have been read at the sensing station, the card is automatically positioned to be printed on the next posting line. This line has been determined by control-panel wiring. The card then moves to the printing station where the next line is posted, and a new indicator mark is printed.

SLP-25 COMPONENTS: AB-AG, 23-35

Fifty posting hubs are provided, two common-exit hubs for each of the 25 posting passes. They are usually wired to print-line entry hubs or the comparing (comp) hub of a selective stacker. After all indicator marks on the ledger card have been scanned, one set of posting hubs emits. These hubs emit consecutively and in sequence, one set at a time. For instance, if a ledger card has been posted three times previously, the fourth set of posting hubs emits regardless of where the previous three lines have been printed.

Ledger cards may be selected to stackers 1, 2, or 3 after the desired number of posting entries has been made. An impulse from the posting hub designating the last printed posting of the overflow-25 hub (AB, 21-22) must be wired to the COMP hub of a selective stacker. The fully posted card can be selected to one of the multiple stackers on either the twenty-fifth or twenty-sixth pass of the file. If ledger cards which have been posted 25 times are to be selected out directly after the twenty-fifth posting, posting hub 25 must be wired to the COMP hub of one of the selective stackers. If the ledger cards are to be selected on the twenty-sixth pass of the file, OFLO-25 must be wired to the COMP hub of one selective stacker. If fewer than 25 lines are being printed, the ledger card can be selected directly after the last posting or on the pass of the file following the last posting. For instance, if we are posting ten times and wish to select the ledger card on the tenth pass of the file, posting hub 10 would be wired to the COMP hub of a selective stacker. If the ledger card is to be selected on the eleventh pass of the file, the following wiring would be necessary:

1. Posting hub 11 to the COMP hub of a selective stacker
2. Posting hub 11 to COMPARING SUP hub to suppress printing on the ledger card during the eleventh pass of the file.

Twenty-five print-line entry hubs are provided, one for each print line on the card. These hubs accept impulses to cause printing on a specific line of the card. They are usually wired from the posting exit hubs. Any single-posting impulse can be wired to any single print-line hub.

The overflow-25 hub (OFLO-25) is an exit hub that emits only after all 25 lines of the card have been posted, i.e., on the twenty-sixth pass of the card. This impulse can be used to select the filled card to one of the selective stackers or to stop the machine. Print suppression is automatic when OFLO-25 emits.

The data card print-line hubs (DCPL) (AC, 21-22) are exit hubs that control printing on the master card. They must be wired to a specific print-line hub to print all data cards during a specific pass of the file. If a posting hub has already been wired to the desired print-line hub, the DCPL impulse can be wired to one of the two common posting hubs. For example, if we wire posting hub 3 to print-line hub 5, we print information on the fifth line of the ledger card during the third pass of the file. If we also wish to print on line 5 of the data card we wire from DCPL to print-line hub 5 to one of the common hubs of posting hub 3.

Print suppression on the data card is accomplished in the normal manner under an X or NX control in the print-suppression unit. If the proof device is installed, the DCPL hub must always be wired to a print-line hub. If printing is being suppressed on the data card, the DCPL hub must still be wired to a print-line hub, or a proof error will occur.

CARD AND PRINT ADJUSTMENT

Because the photosensing unit is sensitive to punching, printing, and coloring, certain adjustments in these areas must be made for the ledger card only. Because the data card prints under a separate control, it can be punched and printed in the normal manner. In SLP-25 with single-face posting, the following restrictions must be observed for all ledger cards:

1. No printing or marking of any kind other than the posted information can occur within one-half in. of the right edge of the card. A maximum of 57 characters can be printed on any single pass of the card.
2. Columns 78, 79, and 80 must not be punched.
3. The card must be free of colored stripes; white or natural stock is recommended.

4. Corner cuts cannot be made in the upper or lower right-hand corners of the card.

If both faces of the card are being posted in SLP-25, the following restrictions must be observed for the ledger card:

1. No printing or marking of any kind other than the posted information can occur within one-half in. of the right edge of both faces of the card. A maximum of 59 characters can be printed on any single pass of a card.
2. Columns 1, 2, 3 and 78, 79, 80 must not be punched.
3. The card must be free of colored stripes; white or natural stock is recommended.
4. The card cannot have corner cuts.

Fig. 9-15 is a combined SLP-25 and card-to-card comparing operation. The ledger card is posted on all 25 lines. Matching control fields for master and detail cards are punched in columns 21 to 25. The sequence of the file is alternating data and ledger cards. Information to be posted is punched in columns 45 to 60 of the master card; it is X punched in column 50. The wiring to accomplish this follows:

1. The control field is used in the compare operation only; it is not printed on either data cards or ledger cards. Wiring from columns 21 to 25 to compare entry checks the related fields in master and detail cards.
2. Posted information is read from

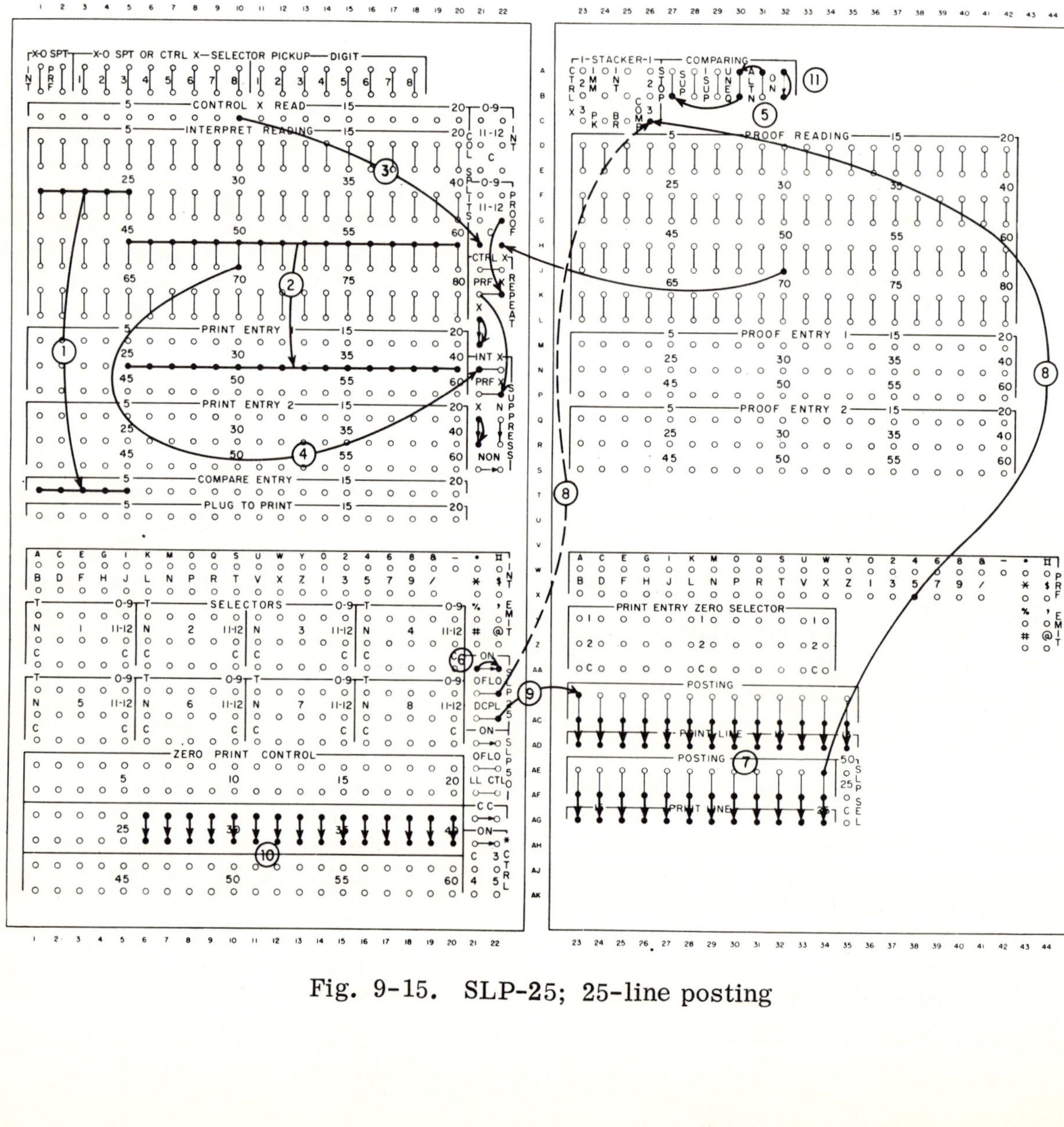

Fig. 9-15. SLP-25; 25-line posting

columns 45 to 60 in master cards and printed in position 25 to 40 on detail cards.

3. The control-X read station 10 is set to read column 50 of master cards and impulses the repeat-print unit. Master cards are X punched, so the X-switch is wired.
4. Wiring interpret read brush 50 to suppress print, with X-switch wired, suppresses printing on master data cards.
5. Unequal and alternate hubs are jack-plugged and wired to the STOP hub. If control fields do not match or the sequence of the file is not alternately master and detail, the machine stops. The error card is the next to the last card in the stacker.
6. The SLP-25 switch must be wired.
7. Posting hubs 1 to 25 are wired to print lines 1 to 25. The first pass of the card is printed on line 1, the second on line 2, etc.
8. Posting hub 25 is wired to stacker 3 COMP. Completely posted cards are selected out on the twenty-fifth pass of the file. The dotted line from OFLO-25 to stacker 3 COMP shows the alternate method of selecting fully posted ledger cards on the twenty-sixth pass of the file. Cards with less than 25 posted lines stack normally in stacker 4.

NOTE: Selection on both the twenty-fifth and twenty-sixth passes of the ledger card can be combined at the same time by wiring OFLO-25 to the INT BR hub of stacker 3 and posting hub 25 to COMP hub of stacker 3.

9. Although printing is suppressed on the data card, DCPL must still be wired. DCPL is wired to print line 1.
10. Normal zero print-control is wired for the posted field.
11. Jackplug the ON hubs to make comparing active.

PROBLEM 7: Draw the wiring for comparing, stacker selection, and selective line posting to accomplish the following:

1. X-switch is wired.
2. The card is to be posted only five times on print lines 1, 2, 5, 7, and 10, successively.
3. Select the ledger card to stacker 3 on the fifth pass of the file.
4. Activate comparing.

There are many variations of the sample applications in addition to those applications not mentioned in this section. The only limitation to the interpreting capabilities of the 557 is the application and the user's imagination. The other special features are not explained because they lack the wide adaptability of those explained and therefore are less likely to be encountered.

IBM 557 Alphabetic Interpreter Questions

Multiple choice

1. The basic function of the 557 is to read
   a. printed data on a card and translate it into punched data on the same card
   b. punched data on a card and translate it into printed data on the same card
   c. printed data on a card and translate it into punched data on a different card
   d. punched data on a card and translate it into printed data on a different card

2. How many characters can be printed on one line of a card?
   a. 20
   b. 80
   c. 60
   d. 120

3. On how many lines can printing be performed?
   a. one
   b. two
   c. 13
   d. 25

4. Cards are put into the hopper
   a. face down, 9 edge toward the throat
   b. face down, 12 edge toward the throat
   c. face up, 9 edge toward the throat
   d. face up, 12 edge toward the throat

5. Which of the following cards have been interpreted correctly, according to the interpreter instructions? (See Fig. p9-1.)

   a. A
   b. B
   c. C
   d. D

6. Which is the correct wiring diagram for this instruction? (See Fig. p9-2.)

   a. A
   b. B
   c. C
   d. D

7. Which is the correct wiring diagram for this instruction? (See Fig. p9-3.)

   a. A
   b. B
   c. C
   d. D

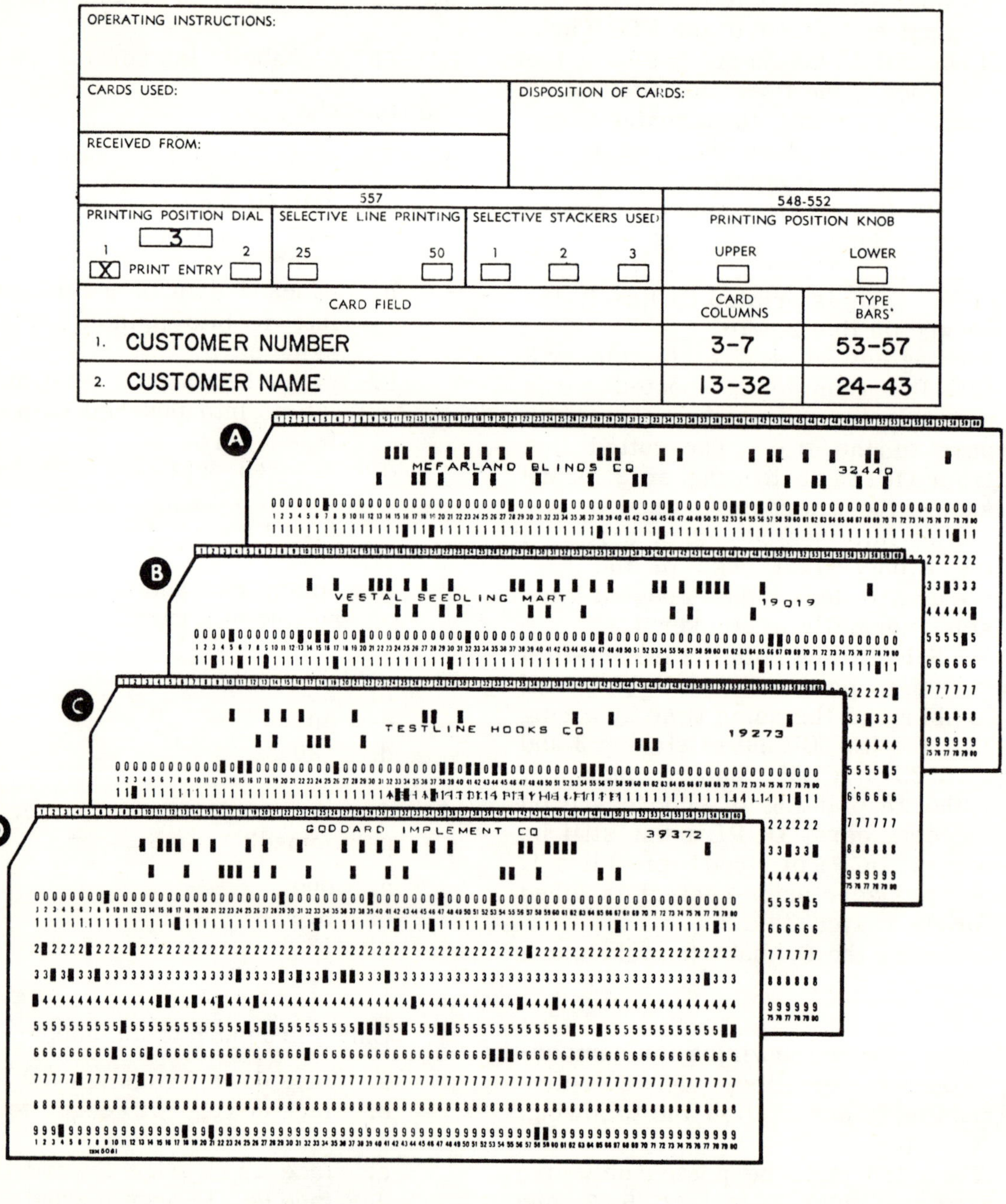

Fig. p9-1. (Courtesy of International Business Machines.)

CARD FIELD	CARD COLUMNS	TYPE BARS
1. CUSTOMER NUMBER (INTERPRET ALL ZEROS)	1-5	3-7
2. CUSTOMER NAME	15-34	17-36

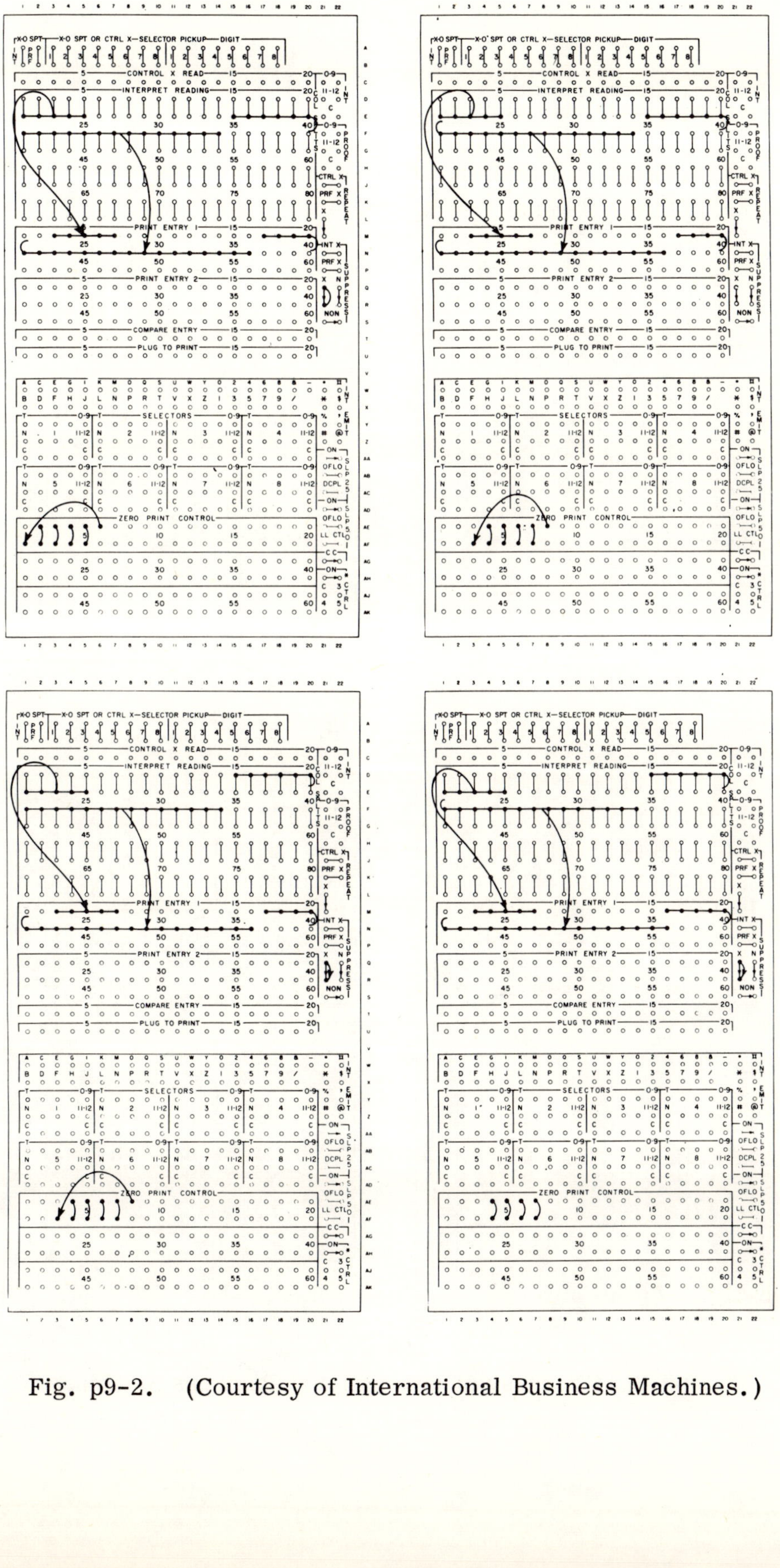

Fig. p9-2. (Courtesy of International Business Machines.)

CARD FIELD	CARD COLUMNS	TYPE BARS
1. INVOICE NO. (INTERPRET ALL ZEROS)	5-9	1-5
2. INVOICE NO. (INTERPRET LOW-ORDER ZEROS)	5-9	55-59
3. NAME	17-25	9-17

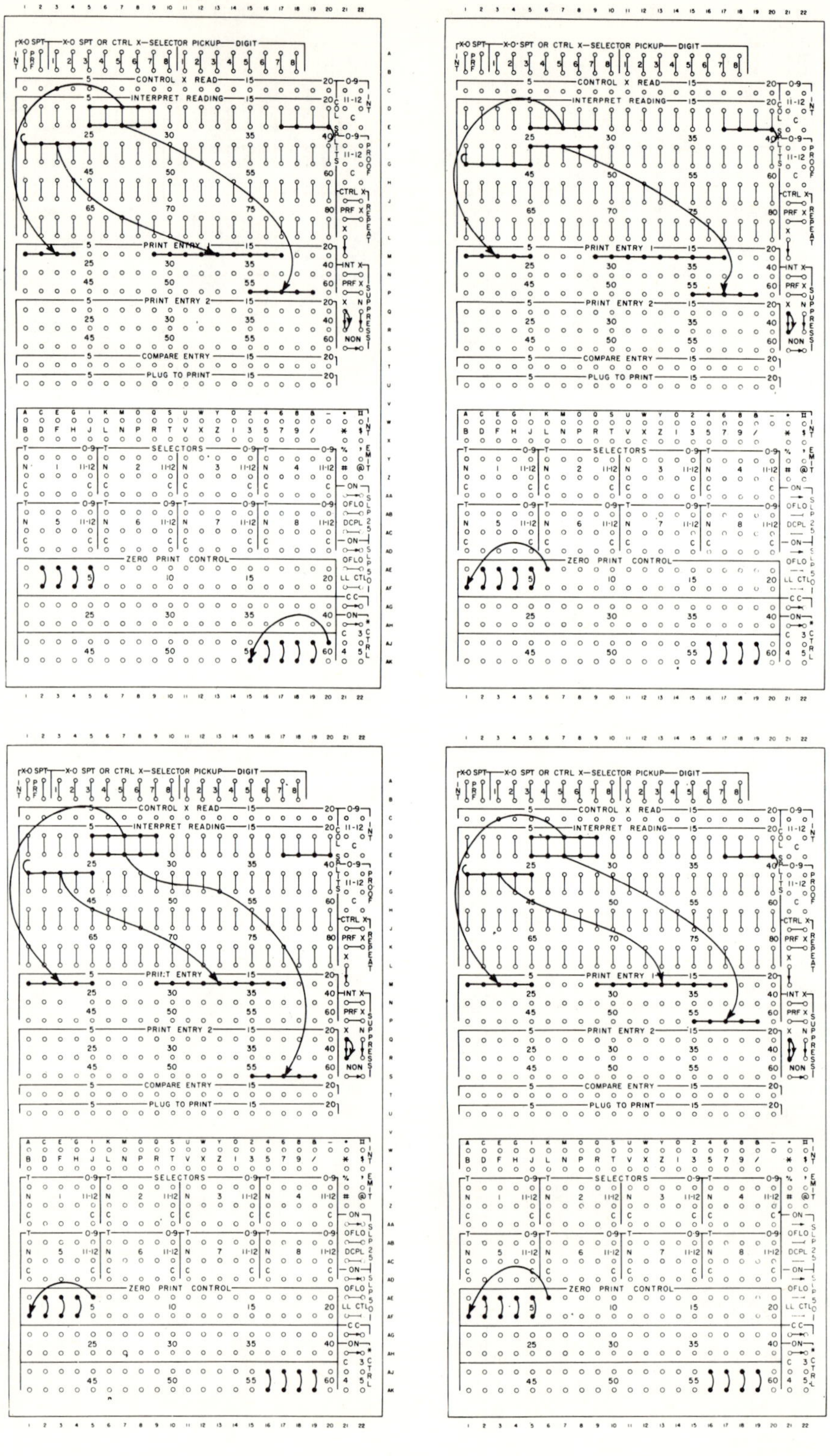

Fig. p9-3. (Courtesy of International Business Machines.)

8. Which would be the correct interpreter instructions for Fig. p9-4?

a. A
b. B
c. C
d. D

9. Which of the following diagrams (Fig. p9-5) shows the control panel wired correctly to carry out the instructions?

a. A
b. B
c. C
d. D

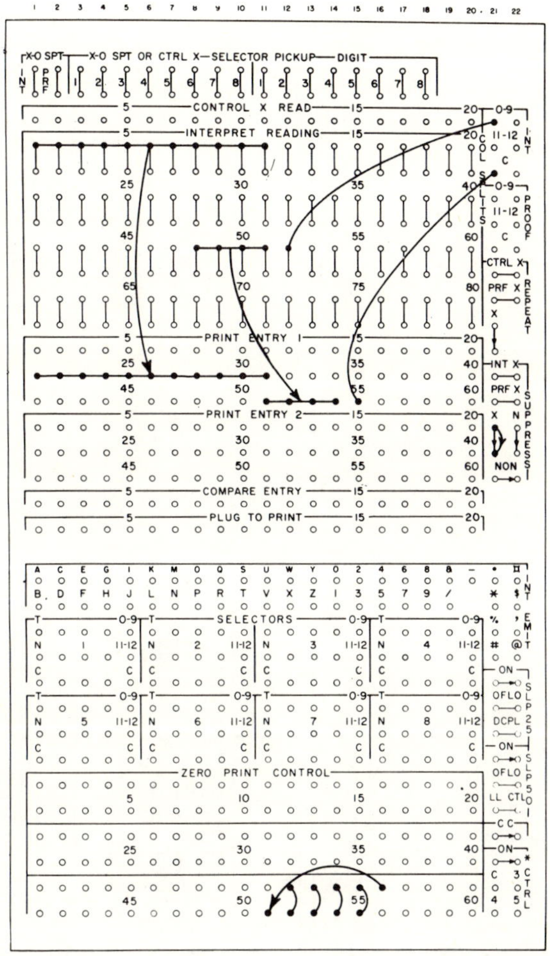

CARD FIELD	CARD COLUMNS	TYPE BARS
1. NAME	1-11	21-31
2. LOCATION (ELIMINATE X52)	48-52	51-54

1. NAME	1-11	21-31
2. LOCATION (ELIMINATE X55)	48-52	51-55

1. NAME	1-11	21-31
2. LOCATION (ELIMINATE X 52)	48-52	51-55

1. NAME (ELIMINATE X52)	1-11	21-31
2. LOCATION	48-52	51-54

Fig. p9-4. (Courtesy of International Business Machines.)

	CARD FIELD	CARD COLUMNS	TYPE BARS
1	COST AMOUNT (IN NX60 CARDS)	33-37	14-18
2	COST AMOUNT (IN X60 CARDS)	33-37	1-5

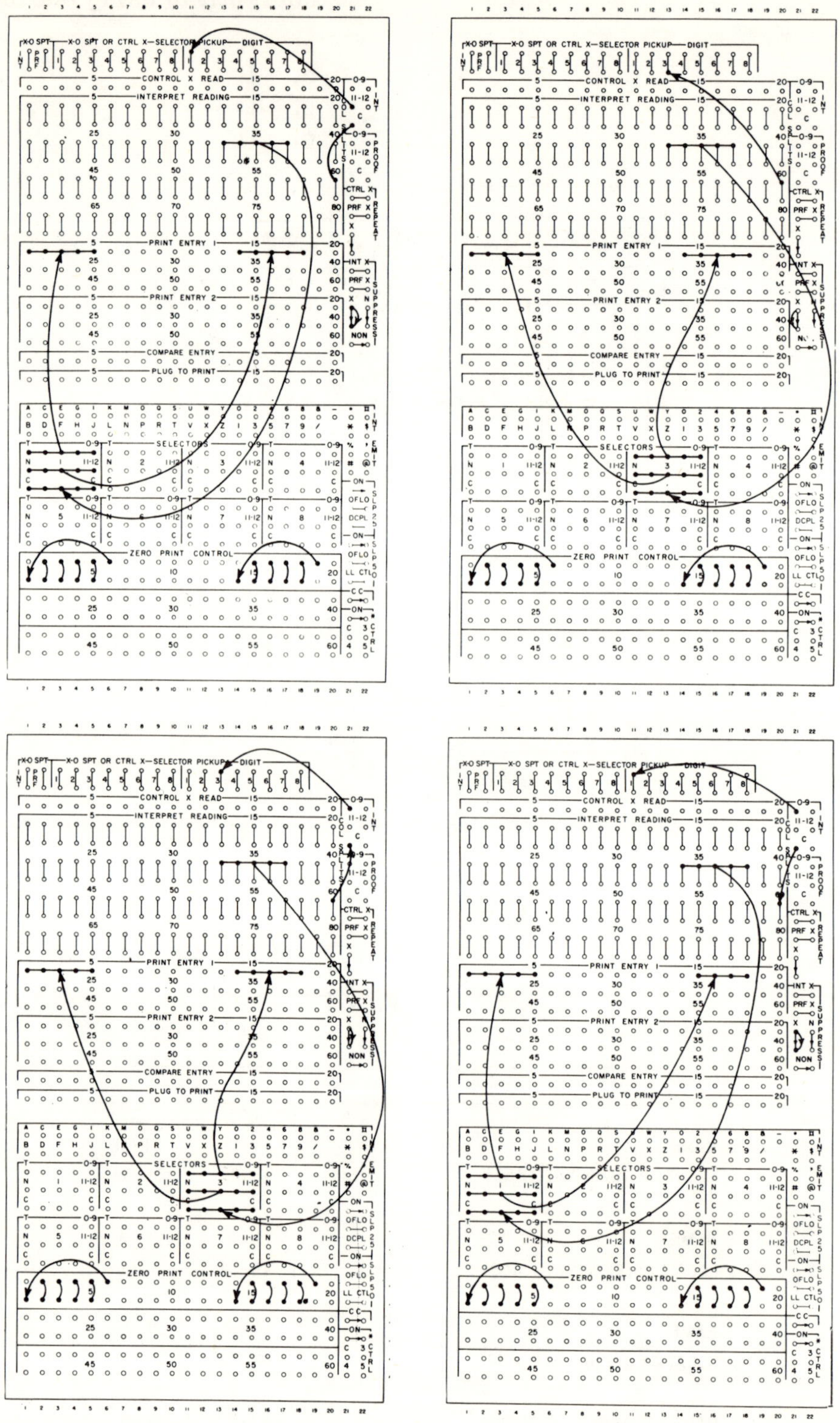

Fig. p9-5. (Courtesy of International Business Machines.)

Answer True or False

10. All 80 columns of a card can be interpreted on one pass through the machine.

11. The line on which printing is performed is controlled by the print-entry switch.

12. All zeros will be interpreted unless specifically wired not to interpret.

13. The setting of the printing position dial determines in what printing position on a line a character will be printed.

14. It is possible on one pass through the machine to interpret a field in two places on the card.

15. Card row 11 corresponds to printing line 4.

16. The diagram (Fig. p9-6) shows the wiring required to interpret all zeros read in columns 35 to 38.

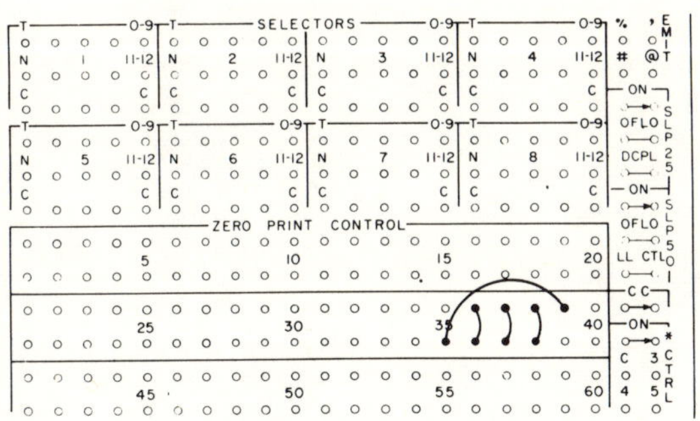

Fig. p9-6. (Courtesy of International Business Machines.)

17. The diagram (Fig. p9-7) shows the correct method for wiring the suppress X hubs.

18. The diagram (Fig. p9-8) shows wiring for interpreting low-order zeros only.

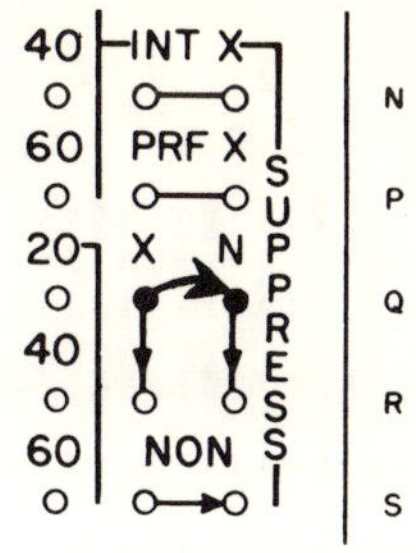

Fig. p9-7. (Courtesy of International Business Machines.)

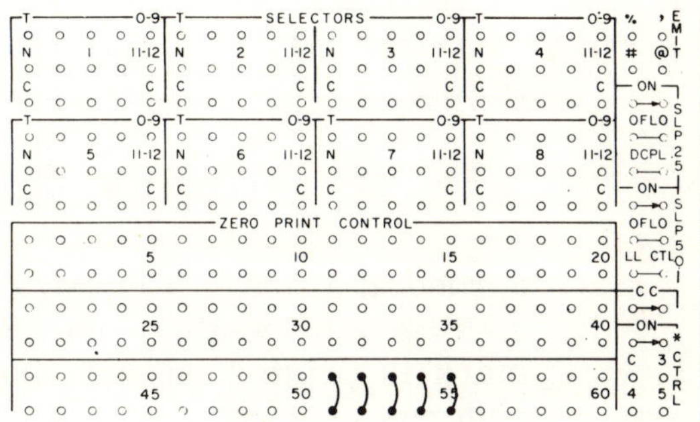

Fig. p9-8. (Courtesy of International Business Machines.)

19. If the control punch is in a numeric field you would not wire through the column split hubs.

20. In class selection you would need to perform zero print-control wiring for two sets of printing positions.

21. If only some cards in a file are to be interpreted, it is necessary before the machine run to separate out those cards which are not to be interpreted.

22. If only NX40 cards are to be interpreted, the cards in Fig. p9-9 have been interpreted correctly.

23. The posting of a card requires a different control-panel wiring setup for each posting line.

24. Each time a transaction is re-

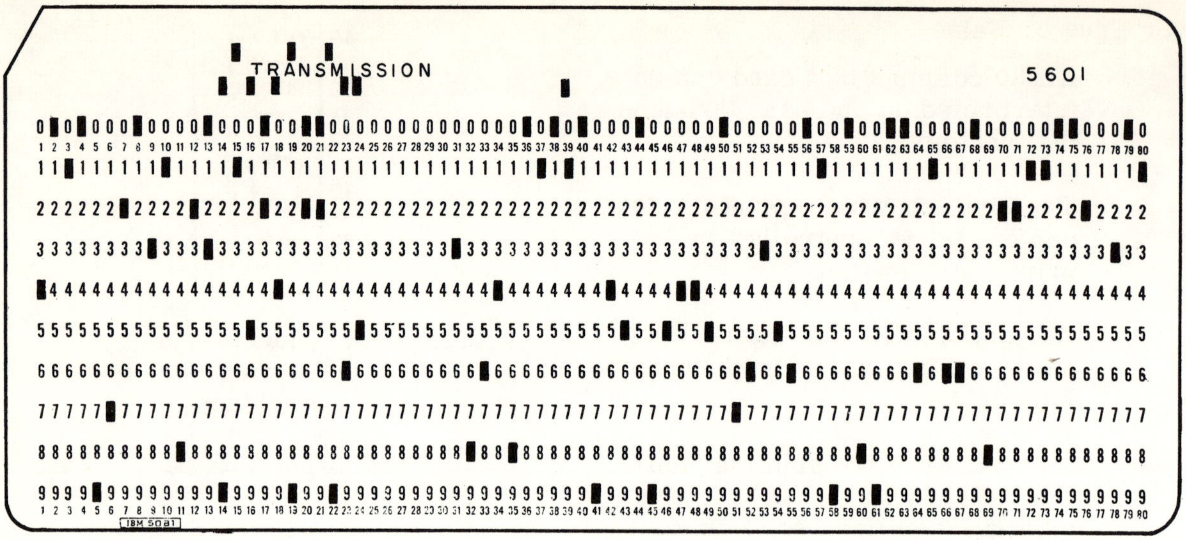

Fig. p9-9. (Courtesy of International Business Machines.)

corded on a line of a ledger card a diagonal posting indicator mark is printed on that line in columns 78 to 80.

25. Completely posted cards can be directed into a selective stacker by means of control-panel wiring.

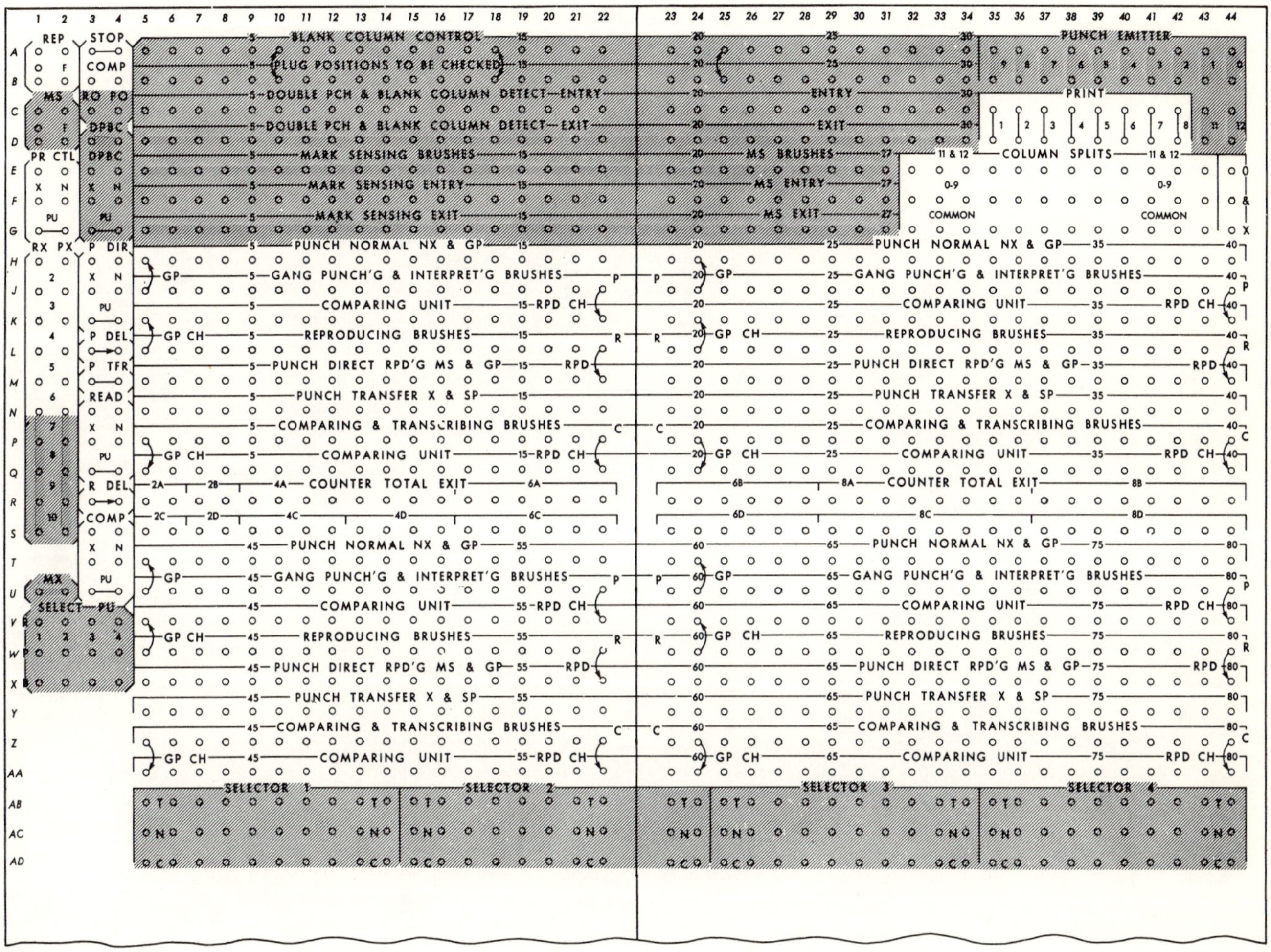

519 Control Panel. Shaded areas represent special features.

Section 10

THE 519 DOCUMENT ORIGINATING MACHINE

It is assumed that the student has become familiar with the 514 Reproducing Punch before beginning this section.

The 519 Document-Originating Machine (Fig. 10-1) permits the rapid, automatic preparation of IBM punched card documents. Reproducing, gangpunching, and end printing are the basic functions of the

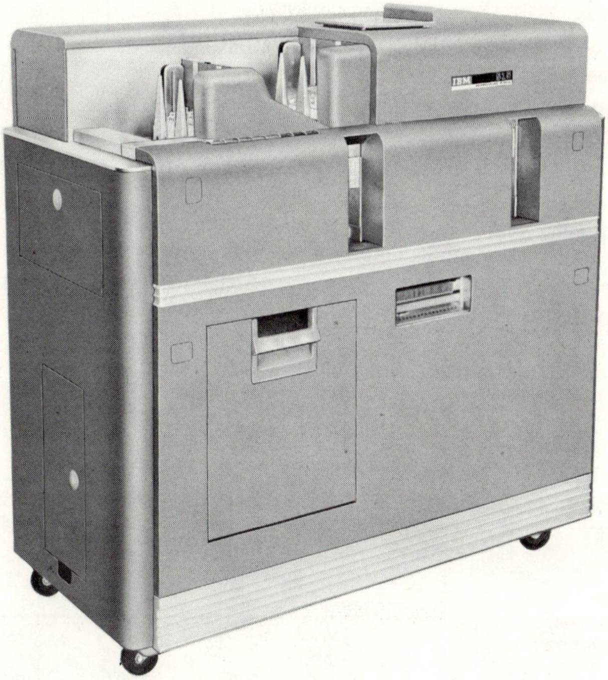

Fig. 10-1. IBM 519 Document-Originating Machine (Courtesy of International Business Machines.)

machine. The 519 performs all of the operations of the 514:

- Reproducing
- Reproducing and comparing
- Selective reproducing
- Selective reproducing and comparing
- Field-selected reproducing
- Class-selected reproducing
- Comparing of class and field-selected reproducing
- Gangpunching
- Gangpunching and comparing
- Interspersed master-card gangpunching (Masters can be in either the read or punch unit.)
- Interspersed master-card gangpunching and comparing
- Offset gangpunching
- Offset gangpunching and comparing
- Reproducing and gangpunching
- Reproducing, gangpunching, and comparing
- Double punch and blank-column detection (special features)
- Mark sensing (special features)

In addition to all of these, the standard 519 is capable of end printing, which enables printing of up to eight digits on the face of the card during a single run through the machine. These digits can be printed on the face of the card in which they are punched (interpreting) or printed on one set of cards from the punched holes in another set of cards (transcribing).

OPERATING KEYS, SWITCHES, AND SIGNALS

The 519 possesses a complement of keys and lights similar to the 514.

Switch Key Light	Function
Main-line switch	Supplies power
Start key	Causes the machine to start feeding
Stop key	Stops card feeding
Reset key	Pressed to resume operations after an error
Ready light	Indicates the machine is ready, but that there are no cards feeding
Comparing light	Comes on as the result of a comparing error, goes off when the Reset key is pressed
DPBC detection light	Comes on as the result of a double-punch or blank-column error
Print light	Comes on when the print unit is engaged and ready to print

SCHEMATIC (Fig. 10-2)

The schematic of the 519 is identical to that of the 514, the only difference being the names of two reading stations. The following chart compares the 514 control panel with the 519 control panel.

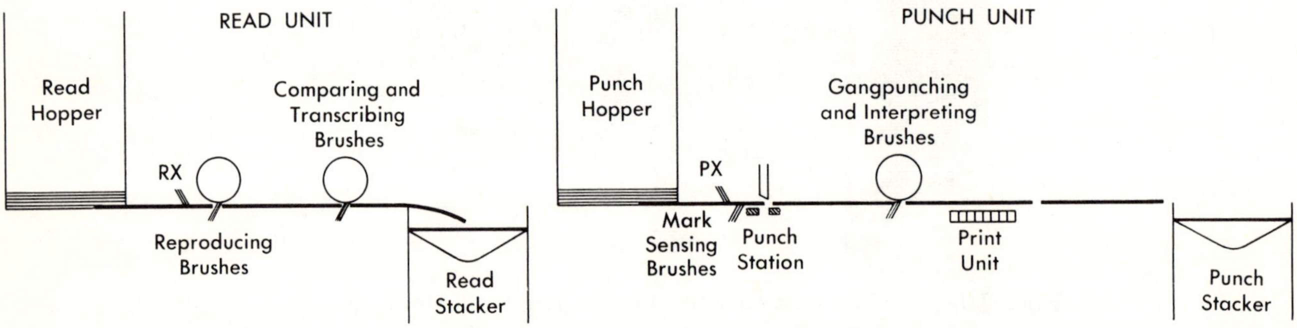

Fig. 10-2. 519 schematic (Courtesy of International Business Machines.)

514	Location	519	Location
RX-brush hubs	J, 5-9	RX-brush hubs	H-N, 1
Reproducing brushes	A-D, 1-20	Reproducing brushes	L, W, 5-44
Comparing brushes	AG-AK, 1-20	Comparing and transcribing brushes	P, Z, 5-44
PX-brush hubs	P, 1-6	PX-brush hubs	H-N, 2
Mark-sensing brushes	X, 4-17	Mark-sensing brushes	E, 5-44
Punch magnets	K-N, 1-20	Punch direct	M, X, 5-44
		Punch normal	H, T, 5-44
		Punch transfer	N, Y, 5-44
RX-hub	H, 5-6	Read	N-Q, 3-4
PX-hub	H, 8-9	P Dir pickup	K, 3-4
O & X	J, 1-4	O & X	E-G, 44
Selectors	U-W, 1-20	Selectors	AB-AD,5-44
Comparing magnets	Y-AF, 1-20	Comparing unit	K, Q, 5-44
PD-hub	H, 10	P Del	L, 3-4
RD-hub	H, 7	R Del	R, 3-4

The manual switches on the 514 are replaced on the 519 by control-panel wired switches.

514 Switch	519 Hubs	Location
Reproduce	REP (Reproduce)	A-B, 1-2
Detail-master	P DIR XN	H-J, 3-4
Sel Repd and GP Comp	COMP	S-U, 3-4

Since the functions and the basic wiring on the 519 are similar to those of the 514, only the control panel hubs that are unique to the 519 will be explained. Figure 10-3 is an example of reproducing and comparing. Card columns 1 to 10 are reproduced into columns 1 to 10 and the reproduced columns are then compared to the columns in the

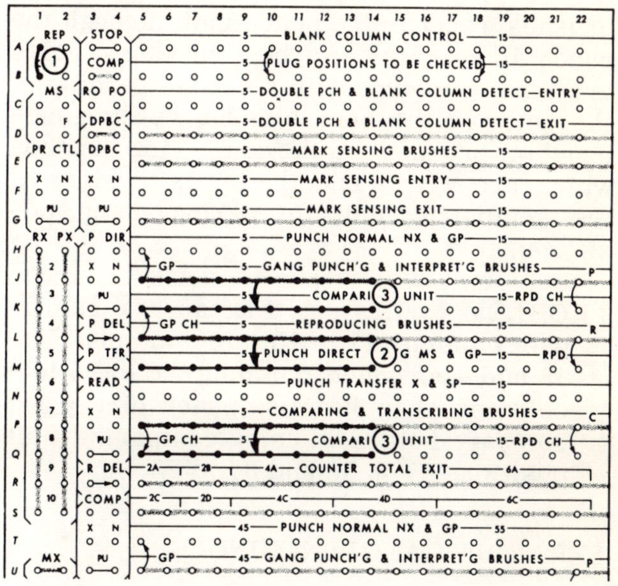

Fig. 10-3. Reproducing and comparing (Courtesy of International Business Machines.)

source card. *Comparing* and *verification* are interchangeable terms.

REP (REPRODUCE SWITCH): A-B, 1-2

This switch must be wired on to cause the read and punch units to operate together. This function was accomplished by the manual reproduce switch on the 514.

COMPARING UNIT: K, Q, V, AA, 5-44

This unit acts the same as the comparing magnets on the 514, but because there are 80 positions, it is advisable to use the positions corresponding to the columns being compared. As a result, the indicator in the comparing-indicator unit will not only indicate which comparing magnet detected an error, but also which card column was in error.

PUNCH DIRECT RPD'G MS AND GP: M, X, 5-44

These 80 hubs are direct entries to the punch magnets for punching the corresponding columns of the card. Impulses wired to these hubs cause punching unless punching is suspended by the punch-direct switch. Because the read and punch units are being used together, REP is wired on. Information from the card passing the reproducing brushes reaches the punch unit through the punch direct entries. The reproduced holes are then compared with a second reading of the holes in the source cards by the gangpunching brushes and the comparing brushes which are wired into the opposite sides of the comparing unit in corresponding positions.

PROBLEM 1: Draw a diagram to reproduce columns 11 to 15 into columns 11 to 15 and reproduce columns 21 to 25 into columns 31 to 35. Use punch direct and compare both field using comparing-unit positions 11 to 15 and 31 to 35.

STRAIGHT GANGPUNCHING

In straight gangpunching you can wire from the gangpunch and interpreting brushes to either punch normal or punch direct as seen in Fig. 10-4. Both sets of wiring will

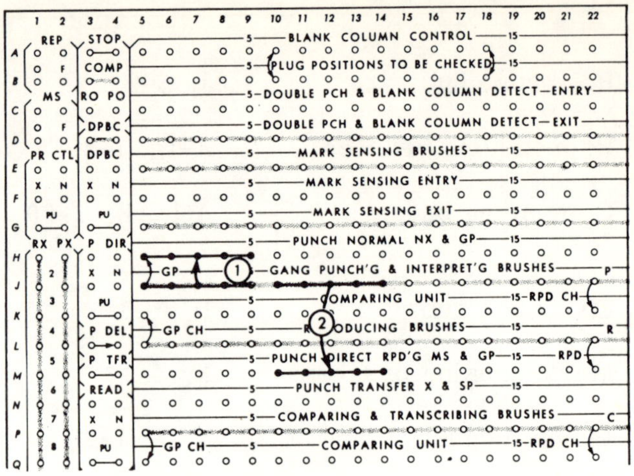

Fig. 10-4. Gangpunching (Courtesy of International Business Machines.)

cause straight gangpunching. Comparing of straight gangpunching can be done visually by looking through the gangpunched columns of the entire file, if small enough, or by comparing the first and last cards of the file. The read unit can also be used for comparing while gangpunching is taking place in the punch unit. Columns 1 to 5 are gangpunched by wiring from the gangpunching brushes to the punch-normal entries. Columns 6 to 10 are gangpunched by wiring from the gangpunching brushes to the punch-direct entries.

PROBLEM 2: Draw a diagram to gangpunch information from columns 17 to 22, of an X master card into columns 17 to 22 of the NX detail cards. Use the punch-normal method, and compare in the read unit using comparing entries 17 to 22.

INTERSPERSED-MASTER-CARD GANGPUNCHING

On the 514 you learned that in interspersed-master-card gangpunching, punching had to be suspended whenever a master card was under the punch magnets. This was necessary to prevent punching data from the last detail card of the preceding group into the master card of the next group. This was accomplished by the use of a PX-brush, the detail-master switch, the PX-hub, the punch brushes, and the punch magnets. The same controls are available on the 519.

P DIR (PUNCH DIRECT): H-K, 3-4

This switch permits punching for either X or NX cards. If the X hubs are jackplugged only X cards will be punched. If the N hubs are jackplugged only the NX cards will be punched. This switch is normally activated by an impulse from a PX hub to the pickup of the switch. Figure 10-5 is an illustration of interspersed-master-card gangpunching (punch direct method).

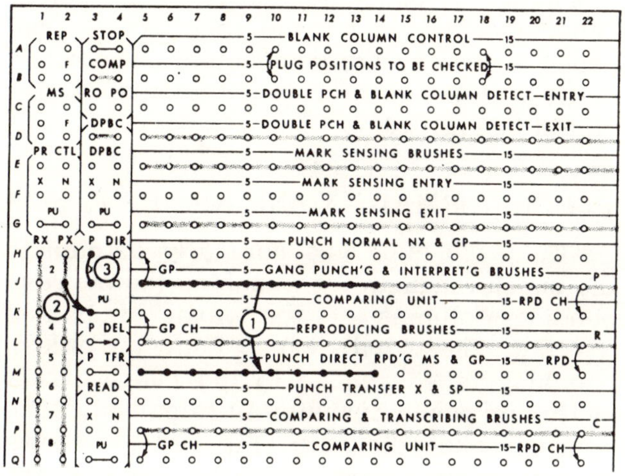

Fig. 10-5. Interspersed-master-gangpunching (punch-direct method) (Courtesy of International Business Machines.)

Notice that

1. Impulses from the holes read at the gangpunching and interpreting are wired to the punch direct entries (the punch normal entries are also receptive).
2. PX-brush 2 is placed to read the X in each detail card. Punch direct pickup is impulsed from the PX-brush for each X detail card.
3. Because the X detail cards are to be punched, P DIR X is jackplugged. To control this operation for X-master cards, remove the jackplug from the P DIR X switch and either wire P DIR N or leave both X and N unwired.

As on the 514, the comparing of interspersed-master-card gangpunching can be accomplished in the read unit while still gangpunching in the punch unit.

Figure 10-6 shows only the wiring necessary for comparing a file of gangpunched cards containing interspersed masters. The reproducing brushes and the comparing and transcribing brushes for the gangpunched columns (Fig. 10-5) are wired to the entries of the comparing unit. As on the 514, you can use any of the comparing entries as long as you use the corresponding entries of the other unit. RX-brush 2 is placed to read the X in each detail card. The RX-brush reading is wired to the COMPARING pickup. Because the detail cards are to be compared, COMP X is wired.

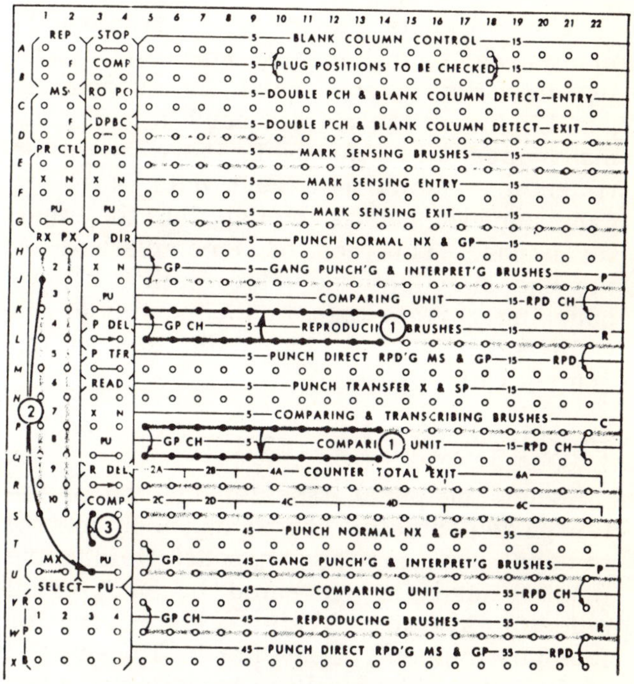

Fig. 10-6. Interspersed-master-gangpunching; comparing (Courtesy of International Business Machines.)

COMP (COMPARING) (S-U, 3-4)

This switch can be wired to make comparing effective for only one type of card X or NX. This is done to avoid comparing the last detail card of a group with the master of the next group.

The PU (pickup) hubs are normally wired from the RX-brush that is set to read the identifying X in the card. Then, if the X hubs are jackplugged, cards are compared only when an X card is at the reproducing brushes. If the pickup hubs are wired and neither the X nor N hubs are jackplugged, cards are compared only when an NX card is at the reproducing brushes. If the pickup hubs are not wired and the X hubs are jackplugged, no comparing occurs.

PROBLEM 3: Draw a diagram to perform interspersed-master-card gangpunching. The master cards are X punched and are read by PX-brush 1. The data to be gangpunched is in columns 54 to 62. Use the punch-direct method. Compare the gangpunched cards in the read unit. Use RX 1 and comparing entries 54 to 62.

The previous method of interspersed-master-card gangpunching prevents punching into the master card by suspending punching when the master card is under the punch magnets. However, there might be times when some pertinent data is to be gangpunched, such as the date into the master cards. This can be accomplished by the use of selectors. This method allows punching certain data in the master cards while selecting out other data such as the control field.

PUNCH-TRANSFER METHOD

When the punch-transfer method of interspersed-master-card gangpunch control is used, punching the gangpunch field in the master cards is prevented by an internal selector system. This selector can be found on the control panel at H, T, 5-44 and N, Y, 5-44. The punch is transferred when the punch transfer pickup is impulsed (M, 3-4). To identify the master cards, the PX reading is wired to the pickup. If the detail cards are X punched, the gangpunch field is wired to the punch-transfer entries; if the master cards are X punched, the gangpunch field is wired to the punch normal entries. Because punching the gangpunch field in the master cards is prevented by selection rather than by suspension of all punching, other fields can be punched in the master card, if desired. This method of interspersed-master-card-gangpunch control must be used whenever a field that is punched is also wired to some other entry, such as print or DPBC detection. If the PUNCH DIRECT method of X-NX control is used, incorrect punching and printing can occur.

P TFR (PUNCH TRANSFER): M, 3-4

These pickup hubs control the 80-position internal selector that permits either the punch normal entries or the punch transfer entries to be connected to the punch magnets. When P TFR is impulsed, punch transfer becomes the entry to the punch magnets, and punch normal is disconnected. Otherwise, punch normal is effective, and punch transfer is disconnected. The schematic of the punch-transfer feature is depicted in Fig. 10-7.

PUNCH NORMAL NX AND GP: H, T, 5-44

These 80 hubs are normally entries to the punch magnets for punching the corresponding columns of the card. Impulses wired to these hubs cause punching unless punching is suspended by the punch-direct switch or punch transfer is impulsed. The control-panel diagram (Fig. 10-8) shows the necessary wiring when columns that are wired to punch must also be wired to another entry. In this diagram, the columns being gangpunched are also being interpreted on the card as follows:

1. The gangpunching and interpreting brushes are wired to both punch-transfer entry and print entry.
2. PX-brush 2 is wired to P TFR. This makes the punch-transfer hubs entries for punching the X detail cards.

The other wiring is the same as for Fig. 10-6.

SELECTIVE REPRODUCING

Selective reproducing allows you to reproduce selectively only X or NX cards by control-panel wiring. The selectively reproduced cards can then be compared to ensure the accuracy of the reproduced card. The following wiring to selectively reproduce X 18 cards can be seen in Fig. 10-9.

1. Because the units are being used together, REP is wired on.
2. When an X 18 card reaches the RX-brushes, P TFR is impulsed. This

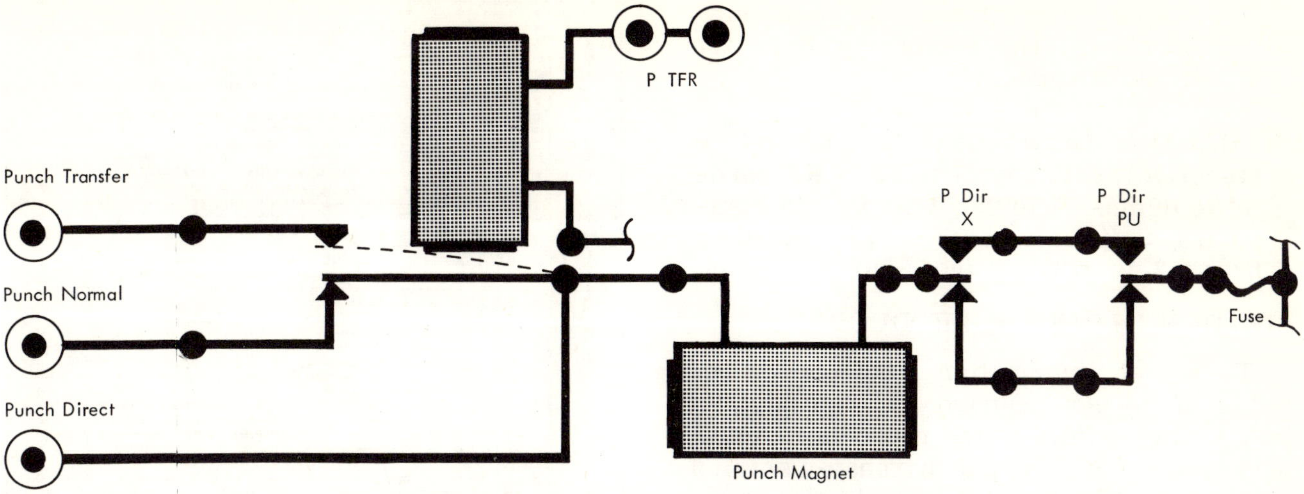

Fig. 10-7. Operation of the punch-transfer feature (Courtesy of International Business Machines.)

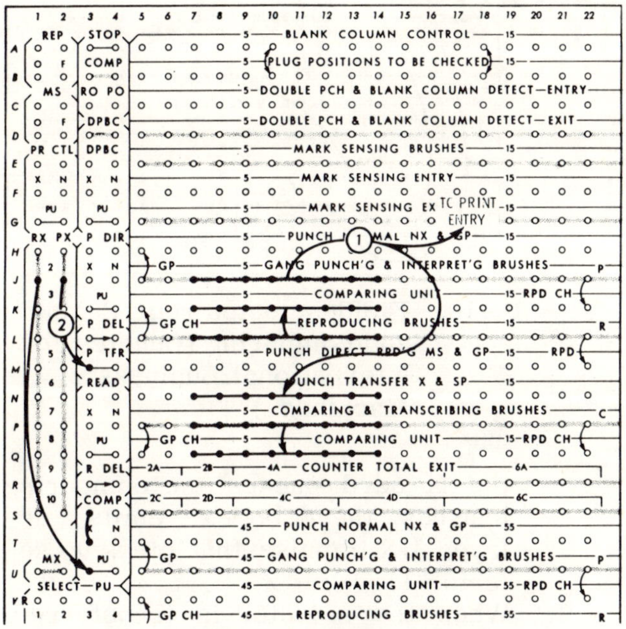

Fig. 10-8. Interspersed-master-gangpunching and comparing (punch-transfer method) (Courtesy of International Business Machines.)

makes the punch-transfer entries receptive as the source card passes the reproducing brushes.

3. Reproducing takes place through this wiring.
4. The reproduced cards are compared on the following cycle. The comparing control is wired through the read delay unit to be effective as the

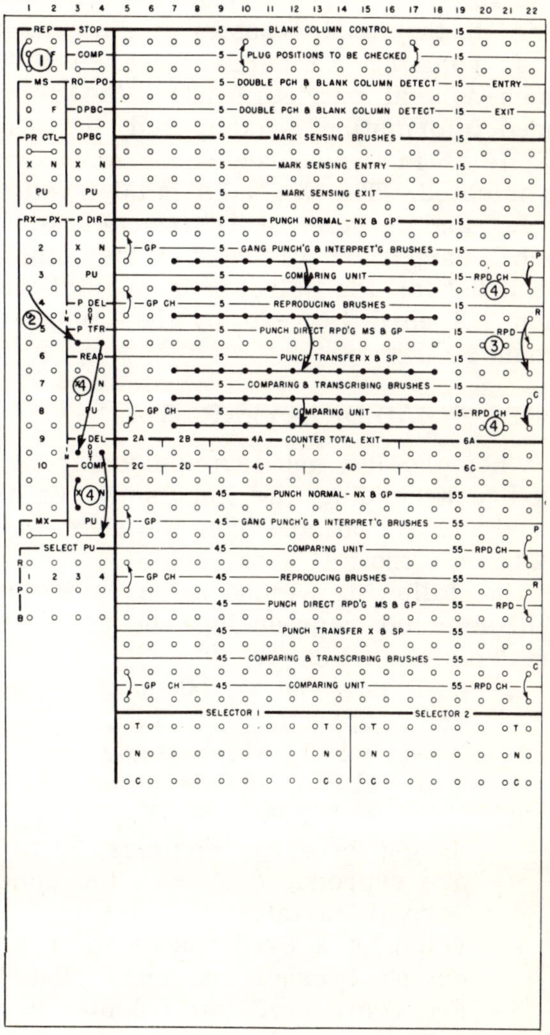

Fig. 10-9. Selective reproducing and comparing

X source card passes the comparing brushes. The comparing X-switch is jackplugged.

PROBLEM 4: Draw a diagram to reproduce selectively columns 17 to 22 of NX cards into columns 17 to 22. Compare in comparing unit entries 17 to 22. Reading brush 2 is reading the control column.

FIELD-SELECTED REPRODUCING

To select information from one of two fields in the source card and reproduce it into a single field of the reproduced card, the punch normal and punch transfer entries are used. Selection is made by the presence or absence of an X punch in a specified column that is read by an RX-brush. The field to be reproduced from the X cards is wired to the punch-transfer entries and the field from the NX cards is wired to the punch-normal entries. When the reproduced information is compared, the X and NX fields in the source cards must again be selected. The X reading is delayed one cycle, and a selector is transferred for each X card when it is read by the comparing brushes; the selector is normal when each NX card is read by the comparing brushes.

R DEL (READ DELAY): R, 3-4

When the left hub is impulsed from an RX-brush reading, the impulse is remembered and is available from the right hub at RX time of the following cycle.

The following wiring is an example of field-selected reproducing and comparing and depicted in Fig. 10-10:

1. REP is wired on, because the units are to operate together.
2. RX-brush 2, which reads the control column, is wired to P TFR.
3. When an NX card passes the reproducing brushes, columns 50 to 54 are reproduced through the punch-normal entries.
4. When an X card passes the reproducing brushes, columns 50 to 54 are reproduced into columns 3 to 7 through the punch-transfer entries.
5. The RX-brush reading is also wired to the read delay entry. Just before the X card passes the comparing brushes, the delay exit emits a delayed RX impulse that picks up selector 1.
6. When the selector is transferred, columns 50 to 54 of the X source card at the comparing brushes are compared with columns 3 to 7 of the card passing the gangpunching brushes. Otherwise, the selector is normal, and columns 3 to 7 of the NX source card are compared with columns 3 to 7 of the card passing the gangpunching brushes.

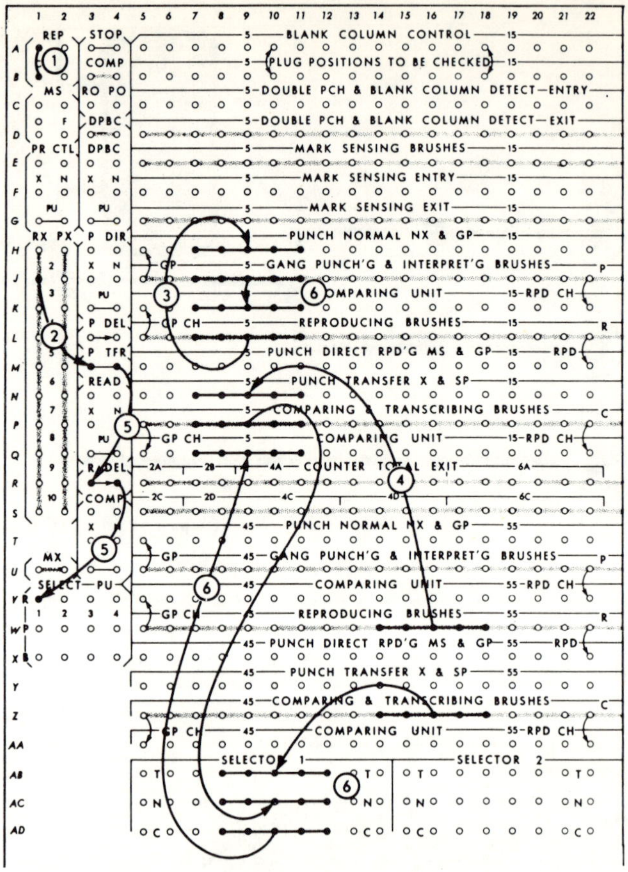

Fig. 10-10. Field-selected reproducing and comparing (Courtesy of International Business Machines.)

OFFSET GANGPUNCHING

Whenever data from certain columns in the master cards is to be gangpunched into different columns in the detail cards, the operation is known as *offset gangpunching*.

When a master card follows a detail card, punching must be suspended as in normal gangpunching, to prevent punching into the master card.

Because this operation requires that information be read from either of two card fields, selection is required. The punch normal and punch transfer entries to the punch magnets are used for this selection and are controlled by the identifying X punch in the cards. The X can be punched in either the master cards or the detail cards.

In order to compare the selected fields, the master card impulse must be remembered. This is accomplished by the P DEL hubs.

P DEL (PUNCH DELAY): L, 3-4

When the left hub is impulsed from the PX-brush, the impulse is remembered and is available at the right hub one cycle later, just before the X card passes the gangpunching brushes.

Figure 10-11 illustrates the necessary wiring for offset gangpunching:

1. PX-brush 2 is wired to the punch direct pickup to suspend punching as the master card passes the punch station. Because the X cards are detail cards, the punch direct X-hubs are jackplugged.
2. PX-brush 2 is also wired to punch delay. Just before each detail card passes the gangpunching brushes, the delay exit (right hub) emits an impulse that picks up punch transfer.
3. The punch-normal entries are receptive when a master card passes the gangpunching brushes; therefore, gangpunching brushes 50 to 54 are wired to punch-normal entries 3 to 7 for master to detail gangpunching.
4. Normal gangpunching from detail to detail is wired from gangpunching brushes 3 to 7 to punch-transfer entries 3 to 7.

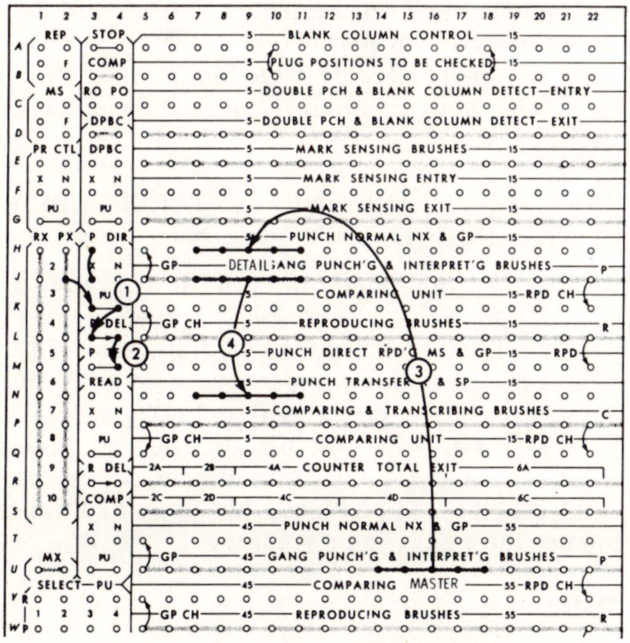

Fig. 10-11. Offset gangpunching; X-detail operation (Courtesy of International Business Machines.)

PROBLEM 6: Draw a diagram using the same columns as Fig. 10-11. In this problem the master cards are X punched and detail cards are not.

COMPARING

When offset gangpunching is compared, field selection similar to that required when the cards are punched is necessary. The selection must be made to read the proper field from the card at the comparing brushes. When a master card is at the comparing brushes, the master field must be read for comparison with the detail card at the reproducing brushes; when a detail card is at the comparing brushes, the detail field must be read for comparison with the following detail card at the reproducing brushes. The features available to accomplish offset gangpunch comparing are: Selectors: AB-AD, 5-44.

These selectors function exactly as the selectors on the 514; when the selector pickup is impulsed the connection between common (C) and normal (N) is broken and a connection is made between common (C) and transfer (T).

SELECT PU (SELECTOR PICKUP): V-X, 1-4

The selectors have three pickup hubs:

1. The R (READ) pickup hub is normally wired from an RX-brush to

cause the selector to transfer and remain transferred until the X card that caused the selector to transfer passes the REPRODUCING BRUSHES.

2. The P (PUNCH) pickup hub is normally wired from a PX-brush to cause the selector to transfer and remain transferred until the X card that caused the selector to transfer passes the punch station.
3. The B (BALANCE) pickup hub is receptive to a balance test impulse from the accounting machine for non-net-balance summary punching operations.

NOTE: R and P pickups can be used interchangeably when both feeds are being used.

R DEL (READ DELAY): R, 3-4

The above hubs are used in Fig. 10-12 to perform offset gangpunch comparing of X detail cards. RX-brush 2 is wired to the comparing pickup. Because X detail cards are to be compared, the comparing X hubs are jackplugged. RX-brush 2 is also wired to the read-delay entry. When an X card passes the comparing brushes, the exit hub emits and transfers selector 1. The detail field (columns 3 to 7) is wired from the comparing brushes through the transferred side of the selector to the comparing entries. The offset field from the NX master cards (columns 50 to 54) is wired from the comparing brushes through the normal side of the selector to the comparing entries. Comparing is effective only when X detail cards are passing the reproducing brushes; thus, the other side of the comparing unit is wired from the reproducing brushes directly from the detail field (columns 3 to 7). For X master cards the jackplug must be removed from the comparing X hubs.

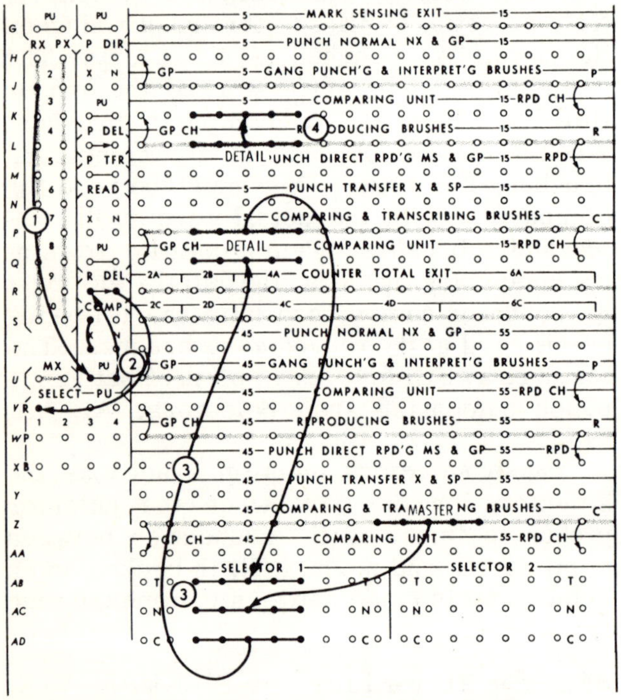

Fig. 10-12. Offset gangpunch comparing; X-detail operation (Courtesy of International Business Machines.)

COMBINED REPRODUCING AND GANGPUNCHING

For all combined reproducing and gangpunching operations, the read and punch units operate together. If gangpunching is to be performed from a single master card and no master card control is used, a blank card should precede the cards in the read unit. This is necessary because the master gangpunch card in the punch unit should be one card cycle in advance of the first source card in the read unit to avoid reproducing the first source card into the gangpunch master card.

GANGPUNCH MASTERS INTERSPERSED IN THE PUNCH UNIT

With the gangpunch masters interspersed in the punch unit, whenever a new master card arrives at the punch station, punching must be suspended for one cycle so that the master card can be passed and not punched. At the same time, feeding in the read unit must be stopped, so that the next source card can be reproduced into the card following the gangpunch master.

READ: N-Q, 3-4

This switch can be wired to control feeding in the read unit, so that feeding is permitted for only one type of card (X or NX) in the punch unit.

The PU (pickup) hubs are normally wired

from the PX-brush that is set to read the identifying X. Then, if the X hubs are jack-plugged, a card is fed past the reproducing brushes whenever an X card is fed past the punch station; if the N hubs are jackplugged, a card is fed past the reproducing brushes whenever an NX card is fed past the punch station. If the pickup is wired and neither the X nor N hubs are jackplugged, the operation is the same as when the N hubs are jackplugged.

The following wiring in which the gang-punch masters are X punched is illustrated in Fig. 10-13:

1. Because the two units are operated together, REP is jackplugged.
2. Gangpunching takes place through this wiring.
3. Reproducing takes place through this wiring.
4. When an X master card is read by PX-brush 6, P TFR is impulsed to suspend all punching. The read control pickup is impulsed (and neither the X nor N hubs are jackplugged) to suspend feeding of the next card in the read unit. The PX impulse is also wired to the punch-delay unit so that the impulse is available for control when the master card passes the gangpunching brushes.
5. The reproduced information is compared by wiring to the comparing unit from the comparing brushes and the gangpunching brushes. After the new master card passes the punch station, feeding is resumed in the read unit. Because no card passes the comparing brushes when the master card passes the gangpunching brushes, comparing must be suspended to prevent the machine from signaling an error when the master card is read. Cards are compared only when an NX card is read, by wiring from punch delay to comparing pickup.

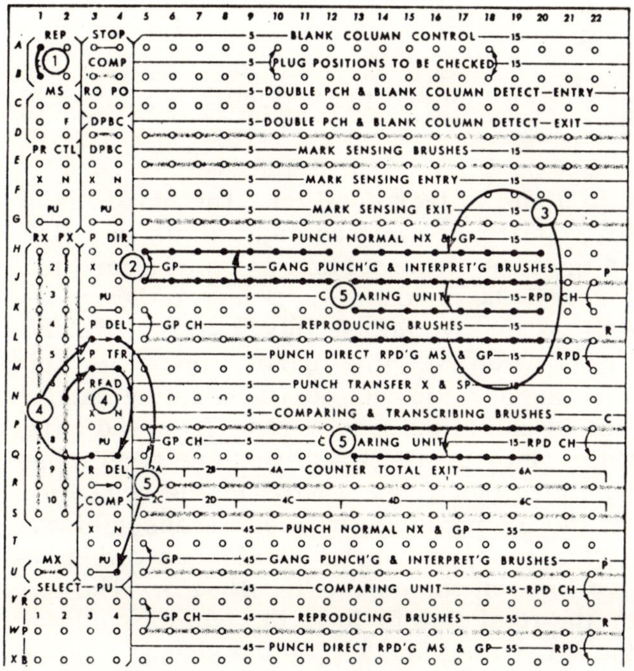

Fig. 10-13. Reproducing and gang-punching (masters in punch unit) (Courtesy of International Business Machines.)

GANGPUNCH MASTERS INTERSPERSED IN THE READ UNIT

Whenever a new master card passes the reproducing brushes with the gangpunch masters interspersed in the read unit, it is reproduced into the card passing the punch station. This card becomes the setup card for gangpunching into the next group of detail cards. The reproduction of the master card is compared in this operation, and the gangpunching is compared in a later operation. For gangpunch comparing purposes the master X must be reproduced.

The wiring to gangpunch masters interspersed in the read unit can be seen in Fig. 10-14:

1. Because the units are used together, REP is jackplugged.
2. The X 7 master cards in the read unit are sensed by RX-brush 4. This is wired to pick up punch transfer.
3. When punch transfer is receptive, the gangpunch master information is reproduced from the master card by wiring from reproducing brushes to punch transfer.
4. For detail cards, the punch normal hubs are receptive, and gangpunching is therefore wired from the gang-punching brushes to punch normal. Column 7 is wired through a column

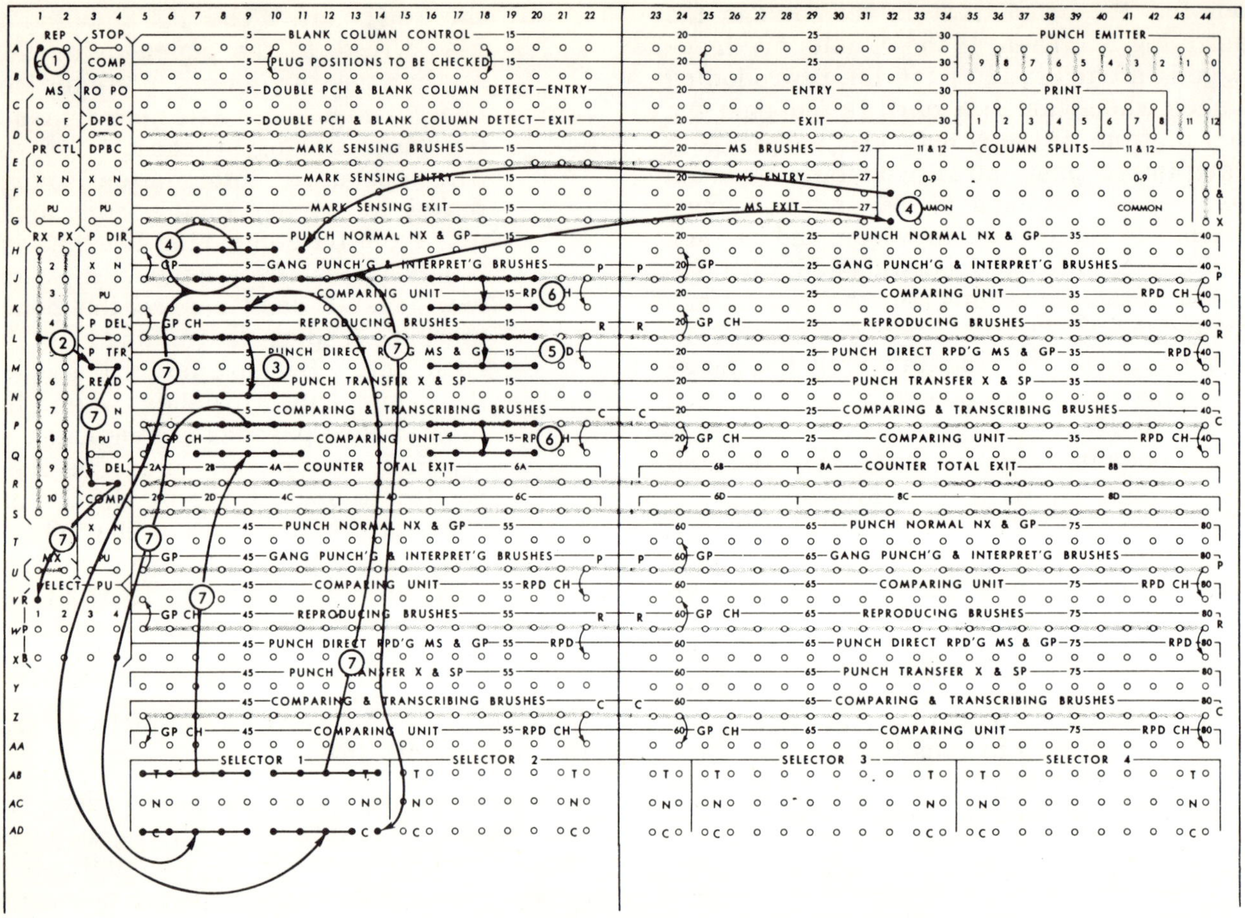

Fig. 10-14. Reproducing and gangpunching (masters in read unit) (Courtesy of International Business Machines.)

split to prevent gangpunching the master X in the detail cards.

5. Other information can be reproduced during either of these cycles (master or detail); therefore, the field is wired to the punch direct entries.
6. Reproduced fields are compared in the normal manner.
7. The gangpunch master information is compared on the cycle through the use of a selector after it is reproduced. The selector is transferred through the read delay unit as the master source card passes the comparing brushes and the reproduced master card passes the gangpunching brushes.

END PRINTING

The print unit consists of eight print wheels, each of which contains the digits 0 to 9 and a blank position. The unit is used for printing as many as eight digits in a line on the face of the column 1 end of a card fed through the punch unit. Some of the applications that would use this feature are the preparation of time cards, inventory tub file cards, or job lot cost accounting cards. The information can be read from the card itself (interpreting), or it can be read from an emitter or from a card in the read unit at the comparing brushes (transcribing).

Information can be printed on either of two lines of the card (Fig. 10-15). The top of the first line is 5/16 in. from the end of the card, and the top of the second line is 5/8 in. from the end of the card. Printing on two lines requires two runs of the cards through the machine. The printing line is selected by latching the printing unit in one of three notches in the rail on which the unit slides. The middle notch causes printing

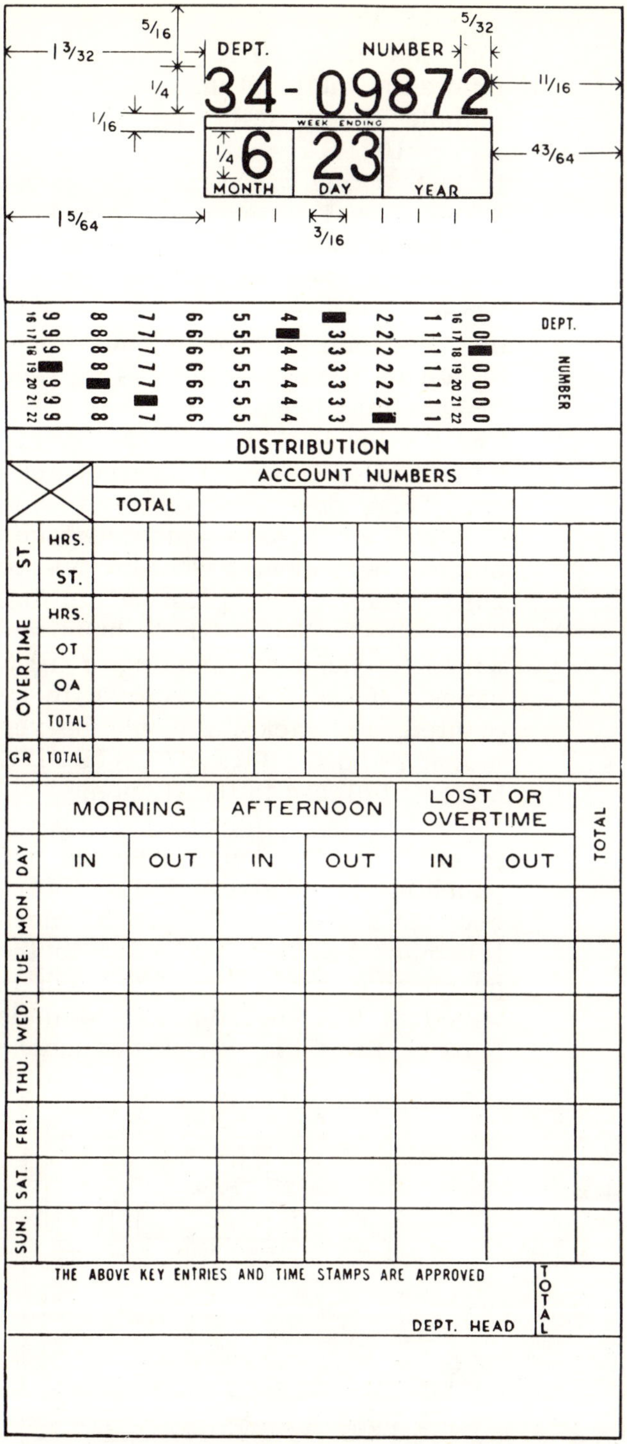

Fig. 10-15. End printing (Courtesy of International Business Machines.)

on the first line; the notch furthest from the operator causes printing on the second line; the notch nearest the operator disengages the unit. The print unit should be disengaged when not in use to prevent unnecessary wear on the moving parts.

PRINT UNIT

If the print unit cannot be readily engaged, these steps should be taken:

1. Draw the unit toward the front of the machine.
2. Turn the knurled knob on the left side of the unit until the letter D on the index wheel is in line with the arrow scribed on the unit (Fig. 10-16).
3. Hold the wheel in this position and slide the unit toward the rear of the machine, stopping at the notch desired.

Fig. 10-16. Print unit (left side) (Courtesy of International Business Machines.)

If the unit is engaged in one of the printing notches, and if the control-panel entry hubs are wired to a source of information, all cards are printed. If desired, printing can be controlled to print only X cards or only NX cards.

A zero wired to the right of a significant digit is always printed, even if blank positions intervene; a zero to the left of the first significant digit is not printed. Blank columns and positions not wired are not printed.

In Fig. 10-17 X detail cards in the punch unit are to be end printed during a gangpunching operation. The same X is used for both print control and gangpunch control, but two different X's could be used if desired.

PRINT: C-D, 35-42

These eight pairs of hubs are entries to the eight print wheels; the 1 hubs are the entry to the left (high order) print wheel; the 2 hubs to the wheel that is second from the left, etc.; and the 8 hubs to the right (units position) print wheel. If all cards are to be printed, only the N hubs of the print control unit must be wired.

PR CTL (PRINT CONTROL): E-G, 1-2

When the print hubs are wired, all cards are printed if only the N hubs are wired. This feature also permits the printing of only one type of card, X or NX.

The PU (pickup) hubs are wired from an X-brush that is set to read the identifying X in the card. Then, if the X hubs are jackplugged, only NX cards are printed. If the pickup hubs are wired and neither the X nor N hubs are jackplugged, no cards are printed. This control has a built-in delay unit to compensate for the difference in time when the PU is impulsed from an X-brush and the card is printed at the print unit.

An example of the following wiring is shown in Fig. 10-17.

1. Print hubs are wired from the gangpunching and interpreting brushes, because it is desired to print information punched in the card itself. (To print information from a card in the read unit, the print hubs would be wired from the comparing and transcribing brushes.)
2. The PX-brush that reads the identifying X is wired to print control pickup. Then, depending on the wiring of the X or N hubs, printing takes place or is suspended when the source card reaches the printing station.
3. The PRINT CONTROL X hubs are wired to cause the printing of all X cards. If the NX cards were to be printed, the jackplug would be removed from the PRINT CONTROL X hubs and placed in the N hubs.
4. Because the information being printed is also being punched and punching is controlled for interspersed master cards, punch transfer must be used for entry to the punch magnets. The PX-brush is wired to P TFR from the common hubs of PR CTL PU. If the punch-

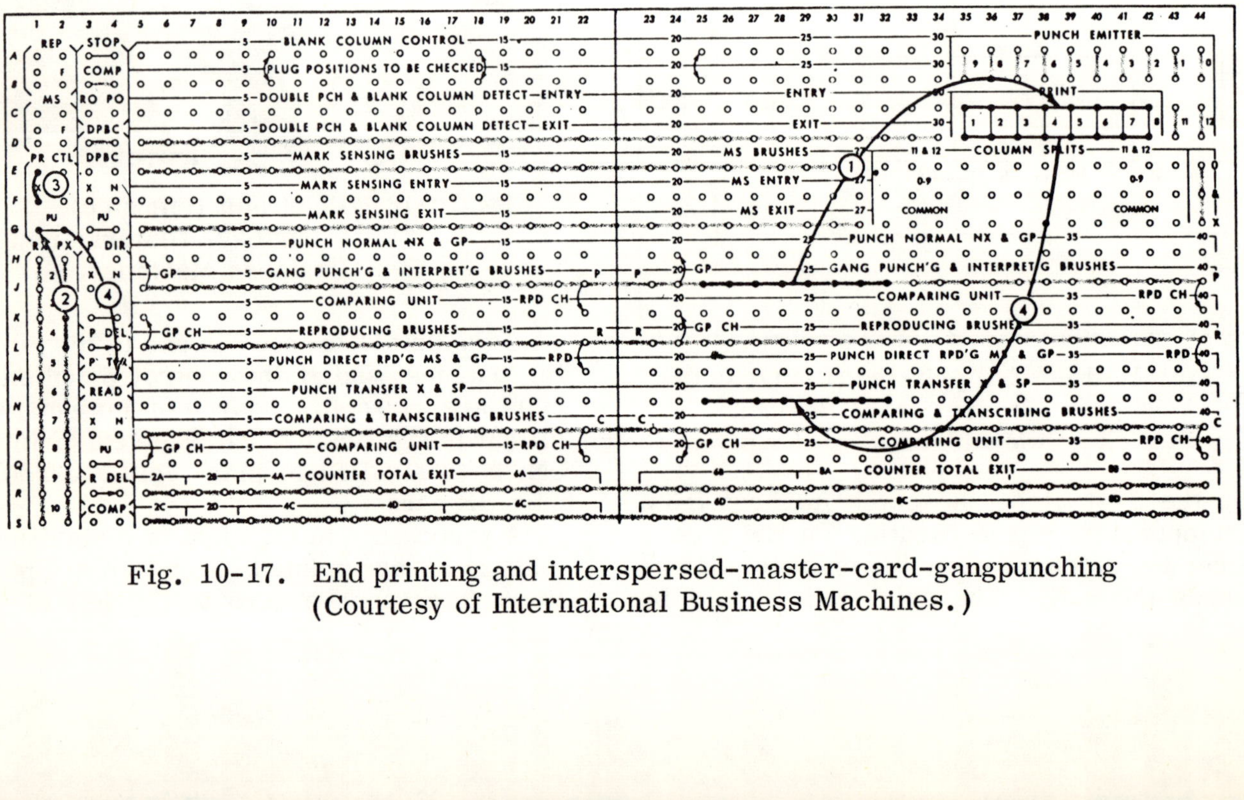

Fig. 10-17. End printing and interspersed-master-card-gangpunching (Courtesy of International Business Machines.)

direct method were used for gangpunch control, back circuits through the punch magnets might cause erroneous punching or printing.

PROBLEM 5: Draw a wiring diagram to perform reproducing, gangpunching, and end printing.

1. Reproduce columns 8 to 22 into columns 8 to 22, column 30 into column 30, columns 35 to 37 into columns 35 to 37, columns 41 to 43 into columns 41 to 43, and columns 65 to 69 into columns 65 to 69. Use the punch-direct method.
2. Compare the information that has been reproduced. Use comparing entry positions 8-22, 30, 35-37, 41-43, and 65-69.
3. Gangpunch columns 23 to 28 into columns 23 to 28. Use the punch-direct method.
4. Compare the gangpunched information in comparing entry positions 23-28.
5. Interpret columns 65 to 69 in the five high-order print positions for all cards.

PROBLEM 6: Draw a wiring diagram to perform offset gangpunching with end printing.

1. Gangpunch from columns 14 to 18 into columns 31 to 35. Use the punch-transfer method.
2. PX-brush 1 is wired to P DIR PU to suspend punching for X masters.
3. Gangpunch selective information from columns 31 to 35 into columns 31 to 35 for detail cards only. Use the punch-normal method.
4. Interpret the information in columns 31 to 35 in print positions 4-8 for all cards.

Now that you have finished this section you have learned that the 519 performs all of the functions of a reproducer plus the very important function of end printing. End printing is an essential part of any system that uses the punched card as a source document and where a visual control number can add to the efficiency of a system.

Questions on the IBM 519 Document-Originating Machine

Multiple choice

1. In a gangpunching operation, one pass of the cards will
   a. not allow punching of all information into the detail cards
   b. allow only one field of information to be punched
   c. allow all information to be punched
   d. allow only 60 columns of information to be punched

2. During a gangpunching operation, the machine stops. The cause could be
   a. a card jam
   b. a misfeed
   c. empty hopper(s) or full stacker(s)
   d. any of the above

3. Gangpunching from a single master card is verified by
   a. running the master card and the detail cards through the IBM 56 Card Verifier
   b. sight checking the master card and the last detail card
   c. using a special control panel
   d. running the cards through the punch unit again

4. To load cards in the machine for a gangpunching operation:
   a. place the master card in front of the detail cards, and place the deck into the punch-unit hopper
   b. place the detail cards in front of the master card, and place the deck into the punch-unit hopper
   c. place the master card in front of the detail cards, and place the deck into the read-unit hopper
   d. place the detail cards in front of the master card, and place the deck into the read unit hopper

5. The diagram in Fig. p10-1 shows wiring to gangpunch
   a. columns 11 to 16 of the detail cards

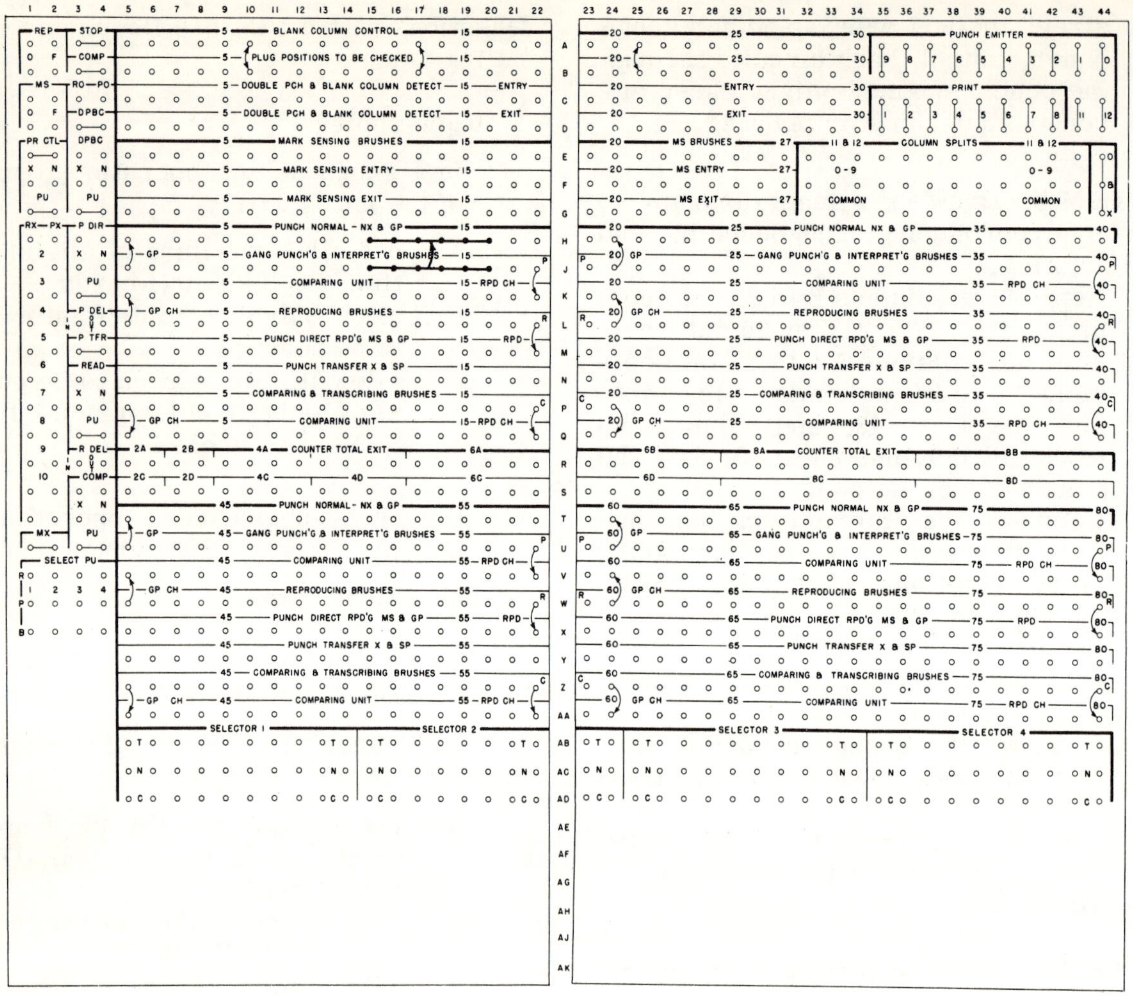

Fig. p10-1. (Courtesy of International Business Machines.)

into columns 11 to 16 of the master cards

b. columns 11 to 16 of the master cards into columns 11 to 16 of the detail cards

c. columns 5 to 10 of the master cards into columns 5 to 10 of the detail cards

d. columns 5 to 10 of the detail cards into columns 5 to 10 of the master cards

6. What does the diagram in Fig. p10-2 show?

   a. Card columns 1 to 14 of the master card will be gangpunched into columns 58 to 71 of the detail cards.
   b. Card columns 1 to 14 of the detail card will be gangpunched into columns 58 to 71 of the master cards.
   c. Incorrect gangpunching wiring.
   d. Card columns 58 to 71 of the master card will be gangpunched into columns 1 to 14 of the detail cards.

7. During reproducing and comparing, assume that an error has been indicated. The specific location of the error is indicated by

   a. the error reset light
   b. the comparing-unit indicator
   c. the restoring lever on the comparing-unit indicator
   d. the COMP light

8. The Comparing Indicator always shows

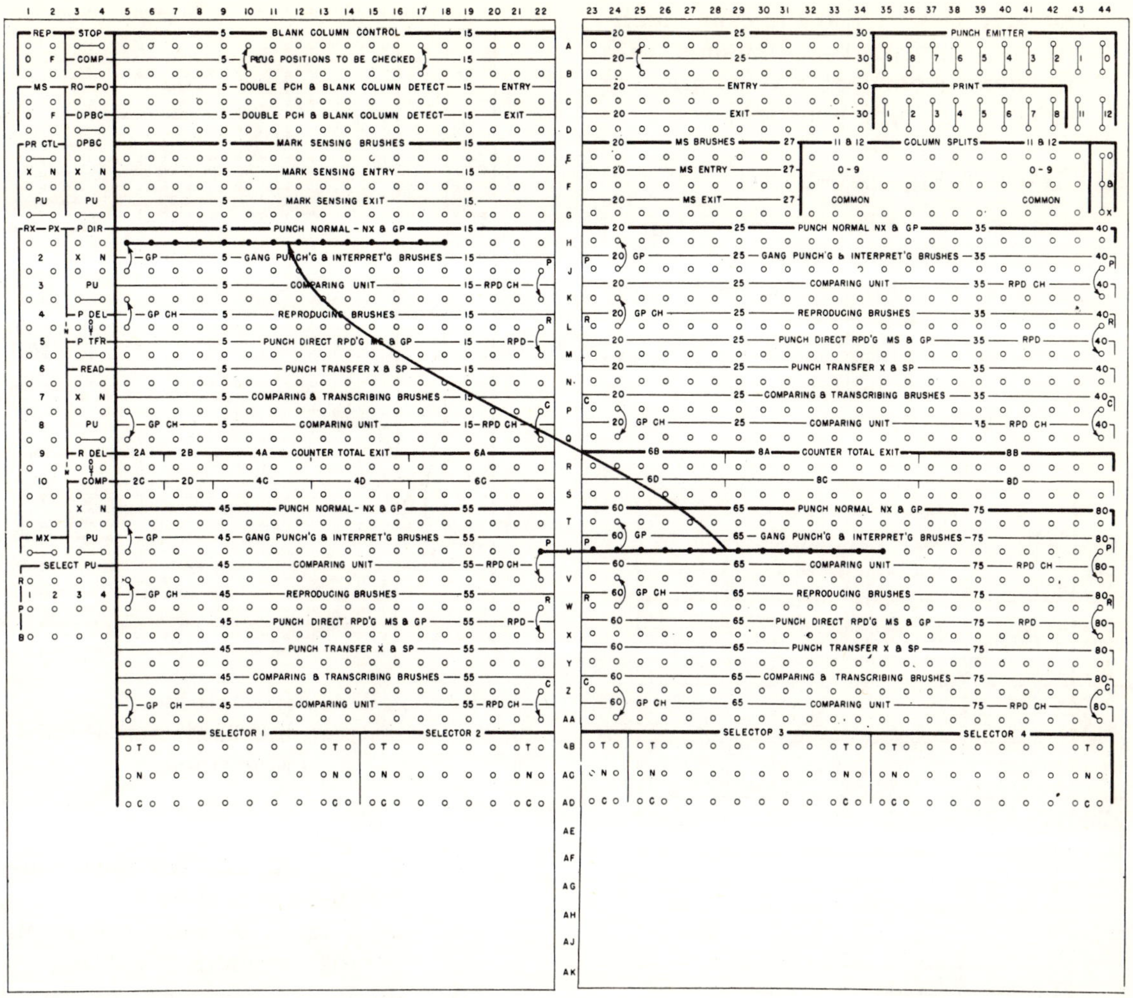

Fig. p10-2. (Courtesy of International Business Machines.)

a. the card column in which the punching is incorrect.
b. the number of the comparing magnets that do not match.
c. the punch brush that read the error.
d. the punch that punched the error.

9. To load cards in the machine for a reproducing operation

a. place the source deck in front of the new deck, and place both decks into the punch-unit hopper.
b. place the new deck in front of the source deck, and place both decks into the read-unit hopper.
c. place the source deck in the read-unit hopper and the new deck in the punch-unit hopper.
d. place the new deck in the read-unit hopper and the source deck in the punch-unit hopper.

10. Reproducing is verified by

a. sight checking the first source card and the last new card.
b. automatically comparing the newly punched card at the comparing and transcribing brushes with its source card at the gangpunching and interpreting brushes.
c. placing the new deck into the read-unit hopper, the source deck into the punch-unit hopper, and running the decks through the machine again.
d. automatically comparing the

punched new card at the gangpunching and interpreting brushes with its source card at the comparing and transcribing brushes.

11. The wiring in Fig. p10-3 will
    a. suspend comparison when an X master card is detected.
    b. suspend punching when an X master card is detected.
    c. continue punching when an X master card is detected.
    d. none of the above.

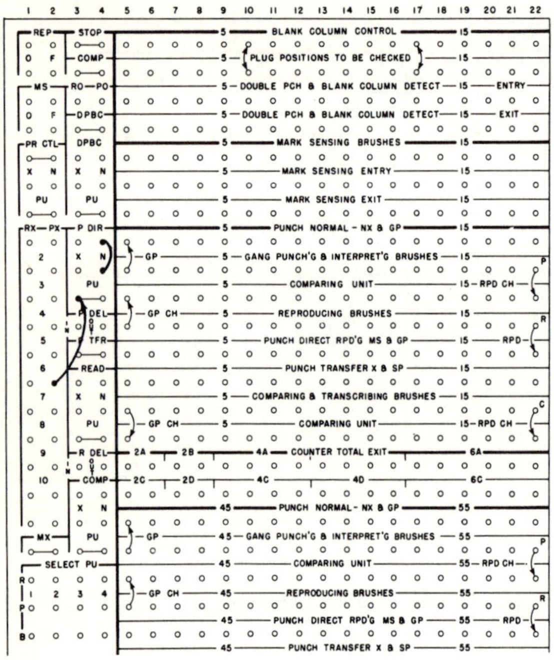

Fig. p10-3. (Courtesy of International Business Machines.)

12. The wiring in Fig. p10-4 will
    a. suspend comparing when an X master card is detected.
    b. suspend punching when an X master card is detected.
    c. continue punching when an X master card is detected.
    d. none of the above.

13. In Fig. p10-5 compare on card field 25-30; suspend comparison whenever an X master card is detected by the RX-Brushes. This wiring is

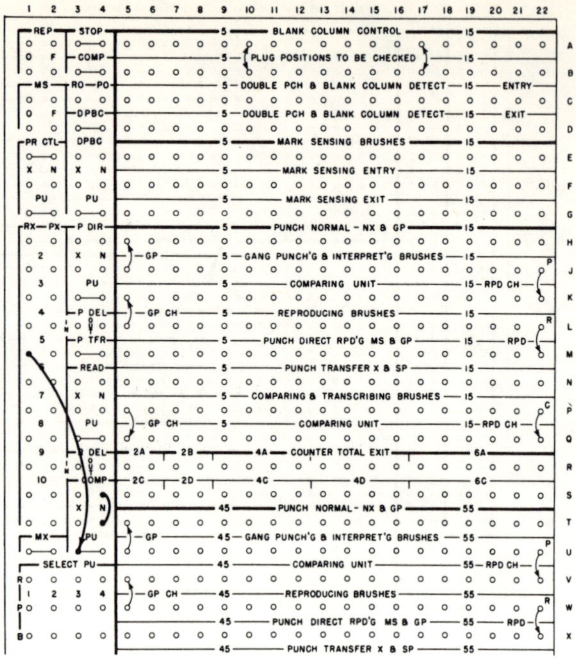

Fig. p10-4. (Courtesy of International Business Machines.)

    a. correct.
    b. incorrect, because the wrong punch magnets are used.
    c. incorrect, because the wrong comparing magnets are used.
    d. incorrect, but not for any of the reasons stated.

14. A control X punch is:
    a. an 11 punch not meant as one of the punches in an alphabetic character.
    b. an 11 punch in the X column.
    c. a 12 punch not meant as one of the punches in an alphabetic character.
    d. a 0 punch not meant as one of the punches in an alphabetic character.

15. A control X punch is often put into an unused card field, but it can be put into a field with:
    a. alphabetic data.
    b. numeric data.
    c. alphameric data.
    d. special characters.

16. For both field and class selection, veri-

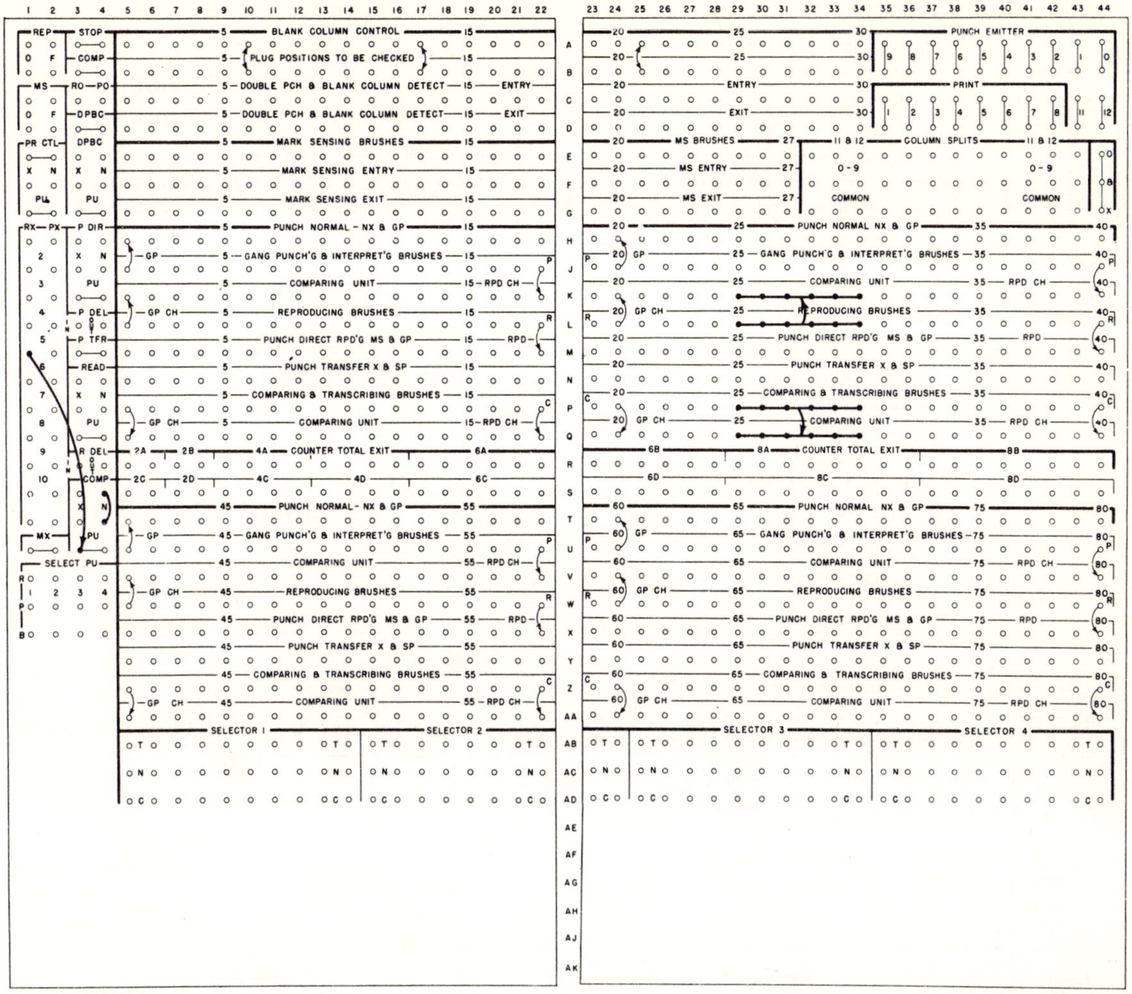

Fig. p10-5. (Courtesy of International Business Machines.)

fication is done by

a. sight checking the first and last cards.
b. manual comparing.
c. automatic comparing.
d. sight checking the first two cards.

17. The wiring diagram in Fig. p10-6 shows

a. the detection of an X punch by Read X-brush 2 will activate selector 2 one cycle after activating selector 1.
b. the detection of an X punch by Read X-brush 2 will activate selector 1 one cycle after activating selector 2.
c. the detection of an NX condition by the R Del hub will activate selector 2.
d. only selector 1 will be activated.

18. The print unit can print information

a. punched in the same card.
b. punched in another card.
c. not contained in any card.
d. from any of the above sources.

19. The print unit can print information

a. on the column 1 end of the card.
b. in any of eight print positions.
c. on one of two lines, as cards pass once through the machine.
d. any of the above.

20. The wiring in the above diagram in Fig. p10-7 will cause

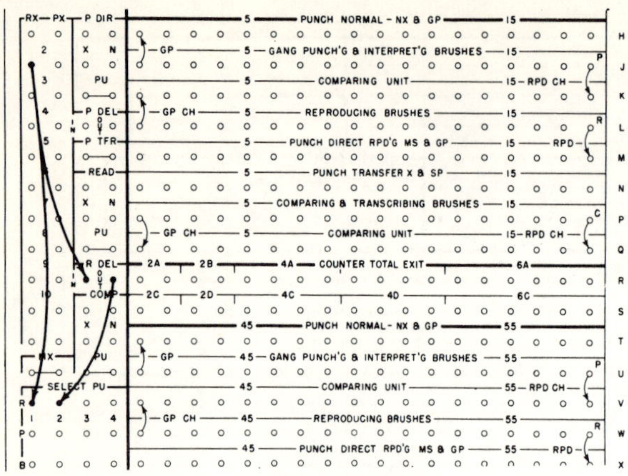

Fig. p10-6. (Courtesy of International Business Machines.)

a. printing of "1264" in print positions 1 to 4.
b. printing of alphabetic information punched in columns 35 to 38 of each card.
c. printing of X cards only.
d. printing of "5678" in positions 5-8.

21. According to the diagram in Fig. p10-7, the wiring that determines which card will be printed is

a. 1.
b. 1 and 2.
c. 4.
d. none of the above.

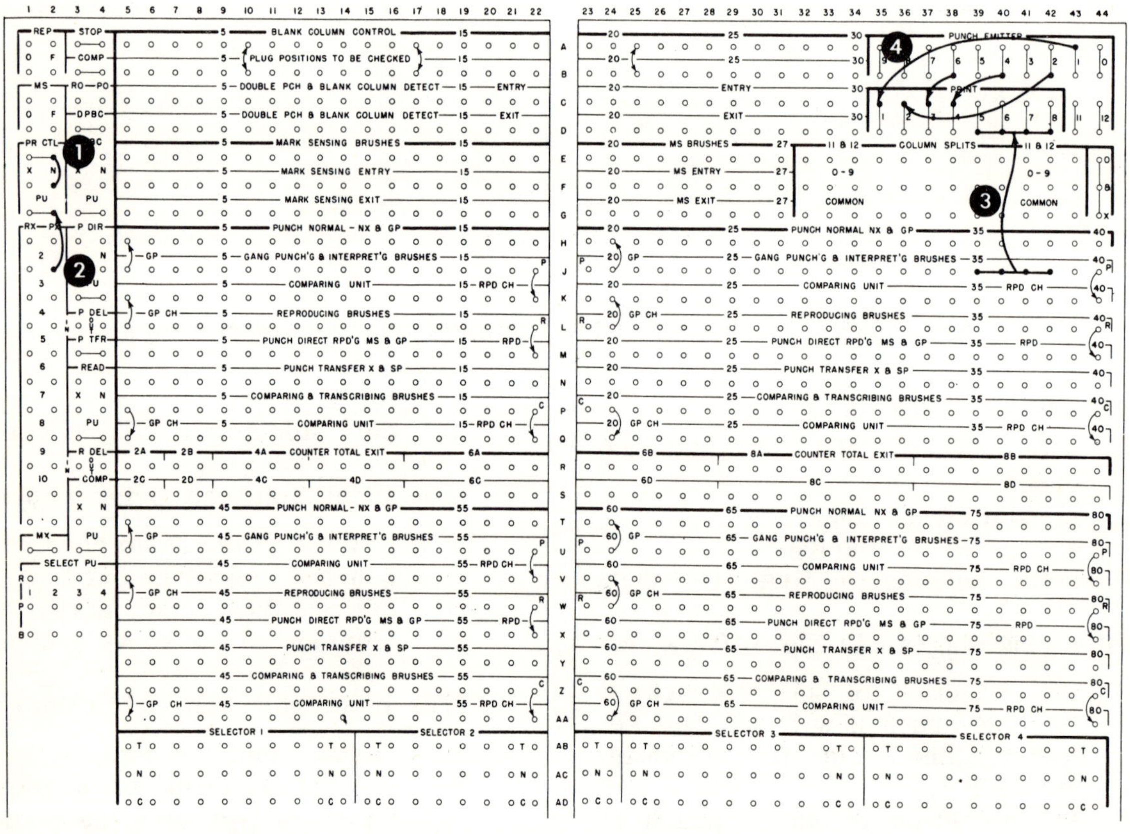

Fig. p10-7. (Courtesy of International Business Machines.)

GLOSSARY

Accumulating - Adding or subtracting in a counter to obtain a total.

Alphabetic character - Any of the 26 letters of the alphabet, A to Z, are represented by a combination of a zone punch (12, 11, or 0) and a digit punch (1 to 9) in the same card column.

Alteration switch (Set-up change switch) - A toggle switch mounted on the machine to change control-panel wiring so that a single panel can perform different operations.

Block sorting - Separating large decks into meaningful blocks and then sorting each block independently in order to allow for overlap of machine processing.

Brush - An electrical conductor for reading information from a punched card. Normally, each brush has a corresponding hub on the control panel.

Bus hubs - Hubs that are internally connected. They are used to obtain more than one impulse from an exit hub.

Cable - A group of wires bound together and used to connect machine units (for example, summary-punch cables).

Card-to-card comparing - Comparison of control information when printing from a master card to detail cards.

Card column - One of the eighty vertical divisions of a card, normally accommodating one letter, digit, or special character. Each column contains twelve punching positions.

Card feed - The path of the card from the hopper to the stacker.

Carriage - A device on the accounting machine for controlled feeding of continuous forms.

Carriage tape - A 12-channel paper band punched with holes to stop skipping of forms at a predetermined printing position.

Chute blades - Metal strips that guide a card along the card path to the selected pocket.

Collating - Arranging two files of cards into a single file according to a predetermined pattern.

Column indicator - The pointer showing the column to be punched or read in the key punch or verifier.

Common hubs - Hubs that are internally connected. Therefore, any impulse accepted by one hub is available from the other hubs.

Comparing - Examination of fields (usually in two cards) for equality of data punched.

Control panel - The removable device which contains external wiring which causes data to be processed in the desired fashion.

Control punch - A punched hole (usually the 11 punch) for controlling machine operations.

Corner cut - A diagonal cut at the corner of a card as one means of visual identification.

Coupling-exit impulse - Impulse available from the 1 pickup of a pilot selector if the X or D pickup of that selector has been impulsed. It is used to pick up a coselector. The coselector will transfer at the same time and for the same duration as the pilot selector.

Crossfooting - Accumulating numbers in different fields in the same card.

Cycle - A complete series of operations at the end of which the entire series can be repeated.

Deck - A set of cards used to perform a particular operation.

Detail card - A term applied to a punch card to distinguish it from a master card.

Detail printing (Listing) - Printing information from each card passing through the machine.

Digit - Any of the ten digits 0 to 9 are represented by a punch in the corresponding row.

Digit punch - Punches in the 0, 1, 2, 3, 4, 5, 6, 7, 8, or 9 positions of a card column, used to code the corresponding digit or used in combination with a zone punch (12, 11, or 0) to code alphabetic or special characters.

Digit row - The 0, 1, 2, 3, 4, 5, 6, 7, 8, or 9 row.

Ejection - Movement of a card from the card bed to a stacker.

Emitting - Originating digits, letters, and special characters electrically within the machine rather than from a punched card.

End printing - Prints as many as eight digits in a line on the face of the column 1 end of a card fed through the punch unit of the 519 Document-Originating Machine.

Entry hub - A hub that accepts an impulse from a wire.

Exit hub - A hub that emits an impulse to a wire.

Field - A column or group of consecutive columns in a card allocated for punching specific information.

Finder card - A card containing a control field whose number is used to locate cards in a file that has equal, lower, or higher fields.

Form stop - A device for sensing when the last continuous form feeds in an accounting machine.

Gangpunching - Punching information read from a master card into the succeeding detail cards. Each card then serves as the master card for the succeeding card.

Group printing (tabulating) - Printing group totals and group indication as cards pass through an accounting machine.

Grouping - The arranging together of data of the same classification.

Hammerlock levers - Two levers for each printing position in the 402 that can prevent printing in that position. Printing regulated by one of the levers is governed by control-panel wiring.

Hammersplits - A lever for each printing position in a 402 that can be raised to prevent printing zeros to the right of that position.

Heading cards - Cards punched with significant information used to print headings on forms such as invoices or checks.

High order - The left, or high position of a field.

Hopper - The receptacle for holding cards to be fed into a machine.

Interpreting - Printing on a card the data that is punched in it.

Interspersed master gangpunching - Gangpunching with more than one master card.

Interspersed X-finder cards - Finder cards, each containing a unique control field, positioned throughout a file of cards. As each X-finder card is read, its control field is used to search the following cards until the next X-finder card.

Lacing - Extra multiple punching in a card column, giving the appearance of lacework.

Line finder - The scribed mark on the forms tractor pressure finders serving as a guide for positioning the first printing line on a preprinted form.

Low order - The right, or low position of a field.

Mark sensing - Punching information marked on a card with an electrographic pencil.

Master card - The first card of a group containing fixed or indicative information for that group (for example, gangpunch master card).

Matching - Checking two files to see if there is a corresponding card or group of cards in each file.

Merging - Combining two files, already in sequence, into a single file.

MLP (Multiple-line printing) - Printing more than one line from a card passing through a 402.

Needle checking - Verifying that all cards in a deck contain the same punch in a given column. The needle is pushed through the punched hole and stops at a card containing a different punch.

Overpunch - Punch (usually control punch) over the significant digit in a column.

Pockets - Receptacles (stackers) for receiving cards from the card feed in a multiple-stacker machine (for example, sorter or collator).

Presensing - Similar to X-brushes. On the 557 Interpreter it permits the selectors to be used for selection.

Program card - A card, punched with specific coding, placed around a program drum to control automatic operations in a card punch or verifier.

Program drum - The card-controlled mechanism on a key punch or verifier for controlling such automatic operations as skipping and duplicating.

Punch station - The position in the card feed where punching occurs.

Punching position - One of the twelve divisions of a card column into which a hole may be punched.

Reading - Converting punched holes into electrical impulses.

Read station - The position in the card feed where reading occurs.

Repeat print - Information punched in a master card may be read and printed on the master card and succeeding details under the control of an X or NX condition recognized by the presensing station.

Restore - To clear or return a unit to its normal starting position (for example, comparing unit or carriage tape).

Run-out - Moving the last cards in the machine to the stacker.

Selecting - Removing cards from a file or processing cards according to predetermined conditions.

Selection - The ability of a machine to perform an operation based upon what is punched in a card. Almost all IBM machines have the ability to select.

Selective line printing - The 557 will locate and post the next available ledger-card positing time.

Sequence checking - Checking cards to ensure that they are all in ascending (or descending) order.

Sight checking - Examining a group of cards for identical punching by viewing a light source through the punched holes.

Sorting - Arranging cards in a predetermined sequence according to the punching in the card.

Source document - The original paper on which the details of a transaction are recorded.

Special character - Any of the special characters such as -, &, *, $, etc. are represented by one, two, or three punches in the same column.

Stacker - A receptacle for receiving cards through the machine.

Starwheels - Rotating contact wheels reading the program card in a key punch or verifier. They are lowered by the program-control lever.

Station - Any position along a card feed where a card is processed (for example, a reading station or punching station).

Stripe - A narrow band of a different color across a card for identification.

Summary punching - Punching summary of total information in cards automatically while printing a report or calculating.

Tape punch - A device for punching the 12-channel carriage tape.

Typebars - A movable bar containing letters, digits, and special characters for printing. A demountable typebar is one that can be readily removed by the operator and replaced with a different type bar.

Vernier - A device for making fine adjustments (for example, vertical positioning of printing on a form).

X-brushes - Adjustable reading brushes for sensing control punches.

X-panel - A small panel for connecting the X-brushes to the main control panel.

X-punch - A control punch in the 11 row.

Zero-carry clips - Clips mounted on hammersplit levers to force zeros to print to the left of a significant digit.

Zone punches - Punches in the 12, 11, or 0 position of a card column, used in combination with digit punches 1 to 9, to code an alphabetic or special character.

Zone rows - The 12, 11, and 0 rows.

INDEX

BLANK WIRING DIAGRAMS FOR USE WITH PROBLEMS

548 INTERPRETER DIAGRAM

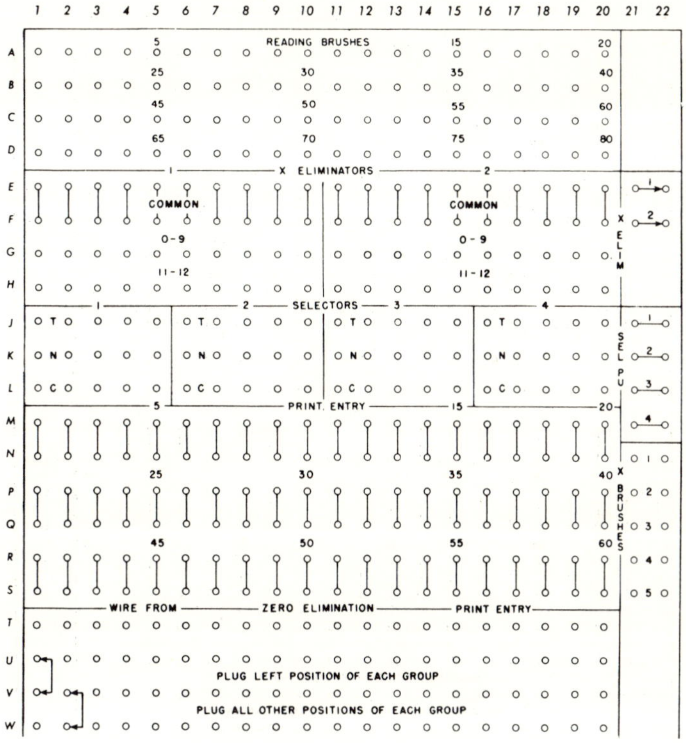

548 INTERPRETER DIAGRAM

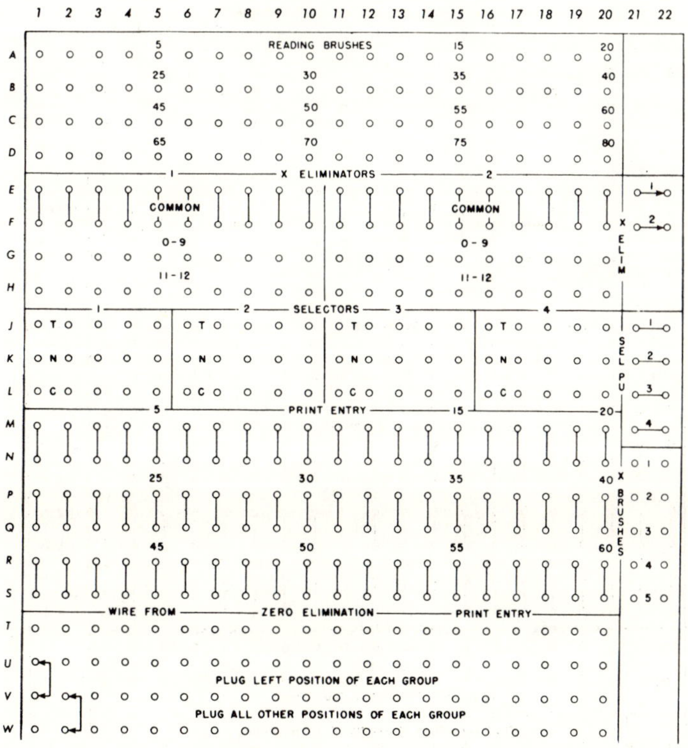

548 INTERPRETER DIAGRAM

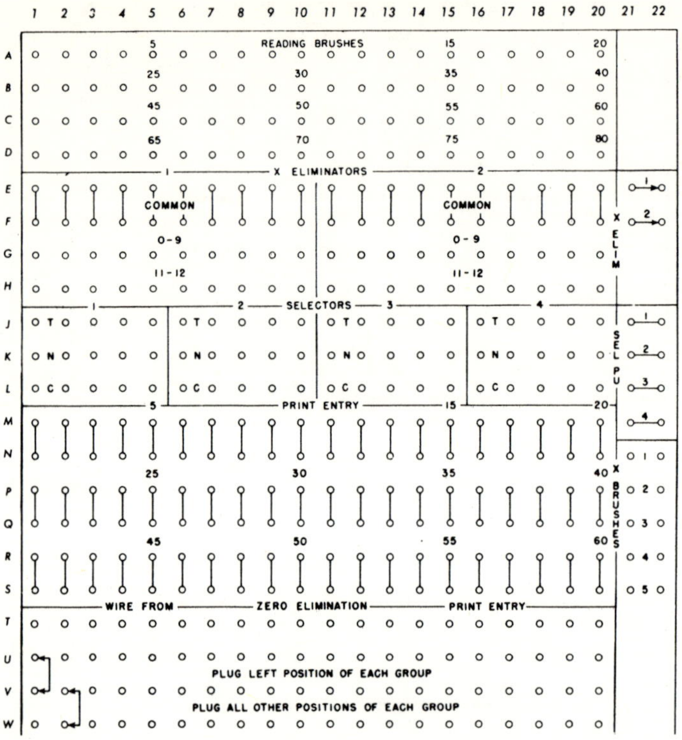

548 INTERPRETER DIAGRAM

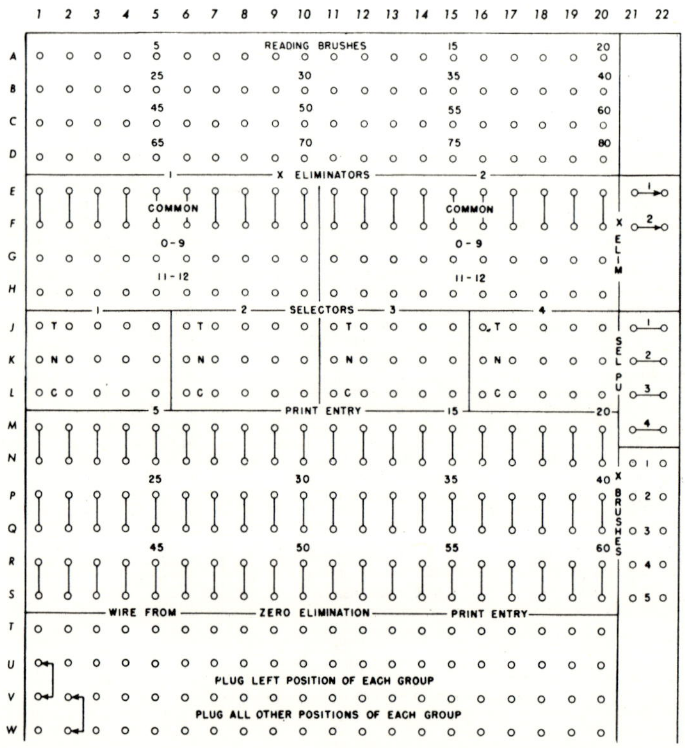

548 INTERPRETER DIAGRAM

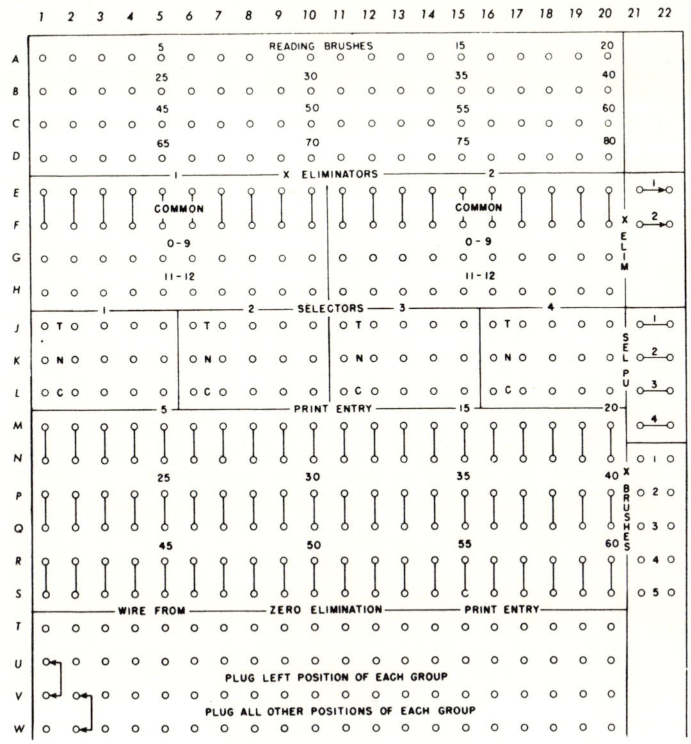

548 INTERPRETER DIAGRAM

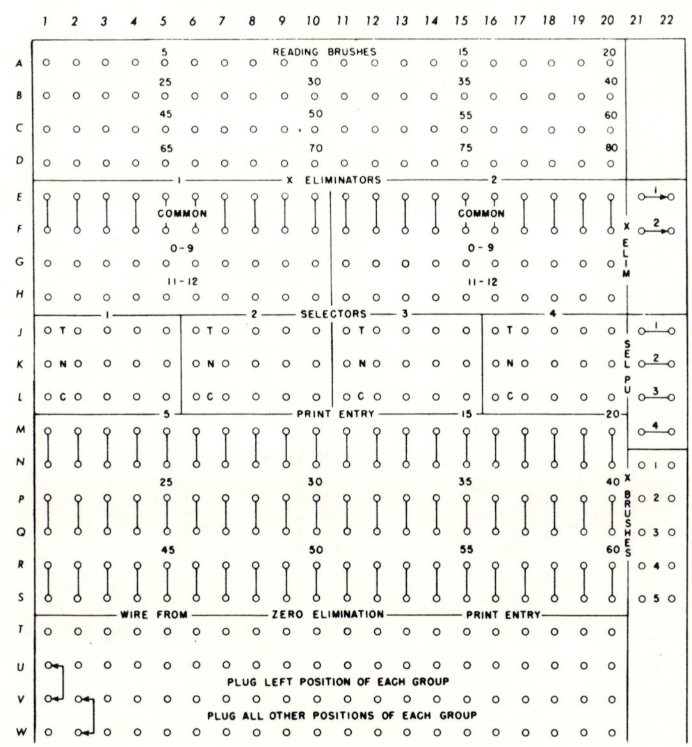

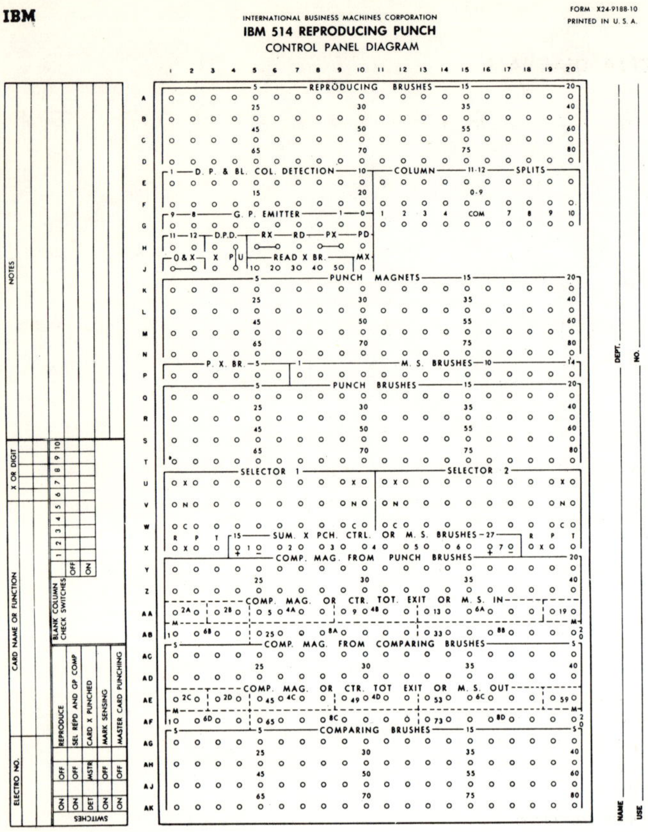
IBM
INTERNATIONAL BUSINESS MACHINES CORPORATION
IBM 514 REPRODUCING PUNCH
CONTROL PANEL DIAGRAM
FORM X24-9188-10
PRINTED IN U. S. A.
REPRODUCING BRUSHES
D. P. & BL. COL. DETECTION
COLUMN
SPLITS
G. P. EMITTER
PUNCH MAGNETS
P. X. BR.
M. S. BRUSHES
PUNCH BRUSHES
SELECTOR 1
SELECTOR 2
SUM. X PCH. CTRL. OR M. S. BRUSHES
COMP. MAG. FROM PUNCH BRUSHES
COMP. MAG. OR CTR. TOT. EXIT OR M. S. IN
COMP. MAG. FROM COMPARING BRUSHES
COMP. MAG. OR CTR. TOT. EXIT OR M. S. OUT
COMPARING BRUSHES
NOTES
X OR DIGIT
CARD NAME OR FUNCTION
BLANK COLUMN CHECK SWITCHES
ELECTRO NO.
REPRODUCE
SEL REPD AND GP COMP
CARD X PUNCHED
MARK SENSING
MASTER CARD PUNCHING
SWITCHES
DEPT.
NO.
NAME
USE

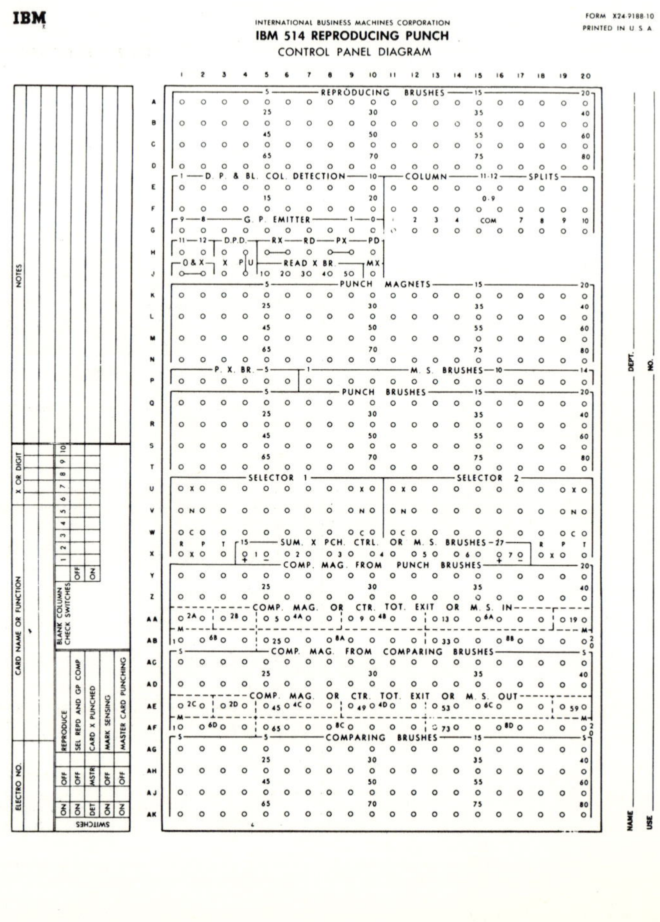
IBM
INTERNATIONAL BUSINESS MACHINES CORPORATION
IBM 514 REPRODUCING PUNCH
CONTROL PANEL DIAGRAM
FORM X24-9188-10
PRINTED IN U. S. A.

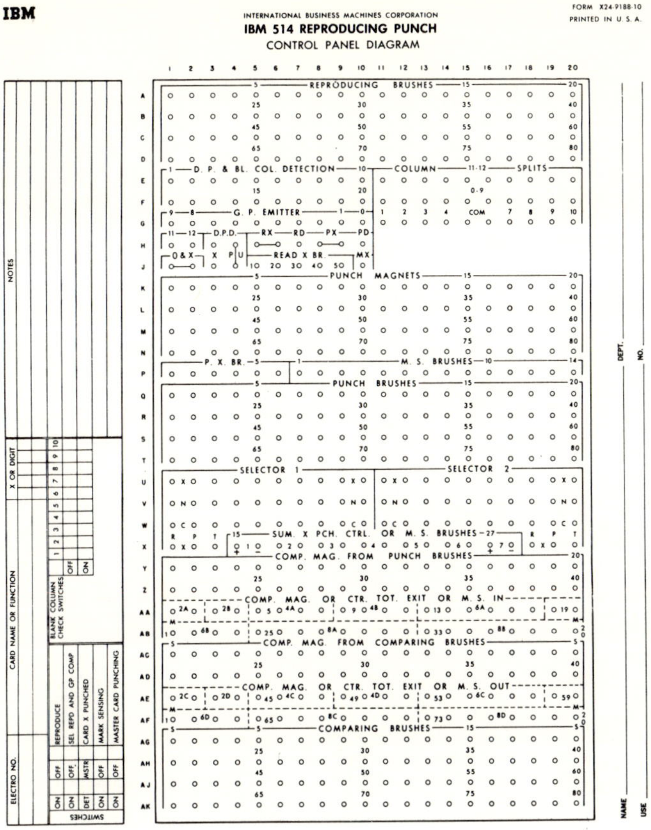
IBM
INTERNATIONAL BUSINESS MACHINES CORPORATION
IBM 514 REPRODUCING PUNCH
CONTROL PANEL DIAGRAM
FORM X24-9188-10
PRINTED IN U. S. A.

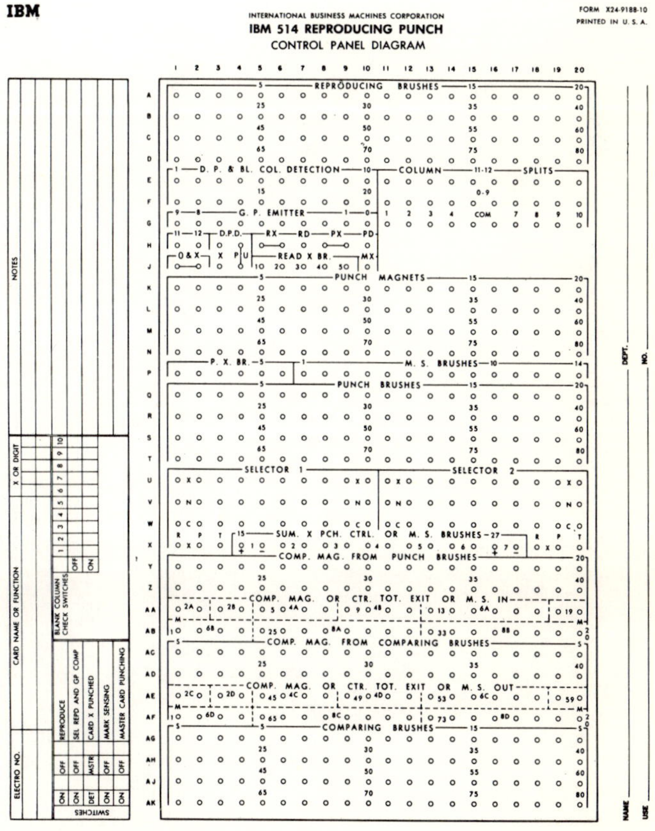
IBM
INTERNATIONAL BUSINESS MACHINES CORPORATION
IBM 514 REPRODUCING PUNCH
CONTROL PANEL DIAGRAM
FORM X24-9188-10
PRINTED IN U. S. A.

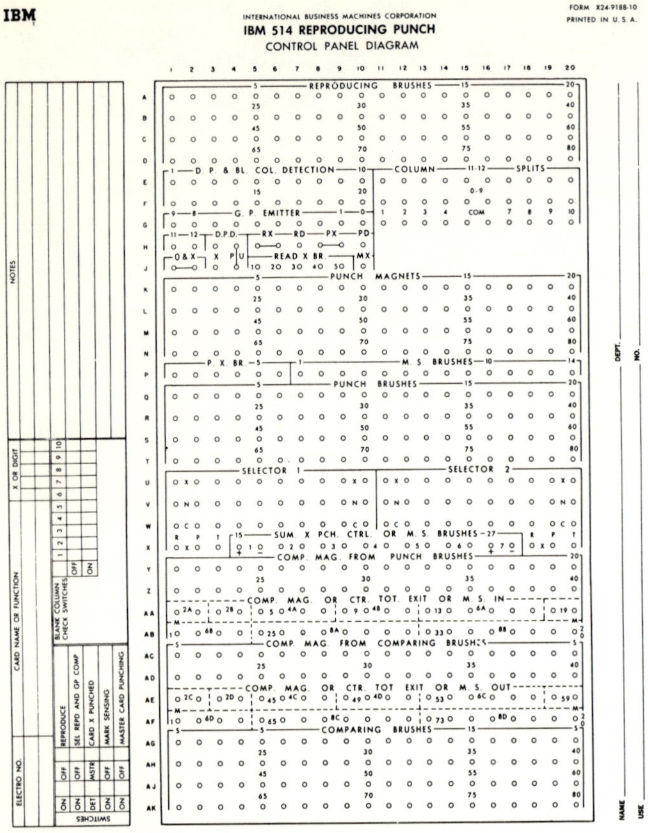
IBM
INTERNATIONAL BUSINESS MACHINES CORPORATION
IBM 514 REPRODUCING PUNCH
CONTROL PANEL DIAGRAM
FORM X24-9188-10
PRINTED IN U. S. A.
REPRODUCING BRUSHES
D. P. & BL. COL. DETECTION
COLUMN
SPLITS
G. P. EMITTER
D.P.D.
READ X BR.
PUNCH MAGNETS
P. X. BR.
M. S. BRUSHES
PUNCH BRUSHES
SELECTOR 1
SELECTOR 2
SUM. X PCH. CTRL. OR M. S. BRUSHES
COMP. MAG. FROM PUNCH BRUSHES
COMP. MAG. OR CTR. TOT. EXIT OR M. S. IN
COMP. MAG. FROM COMPARING BRUSHES
COMP. MAG. OR CTR. TOT. EXIT OR M. S. OUT
COMPARING BRUSHES
NOTES
CARD NAME OR FUNCTION
ELECTRO NO.
X OR DIGIT
BLANK COLUMN CHECK SWITCHES
REPRODUCE
SEL. REPD AND GP COMP
CARD X PUNCHED
MARK SENSING
MASTER CARD PUNCHING
SWITCHES
DEPT.
NO.
NAME
USE

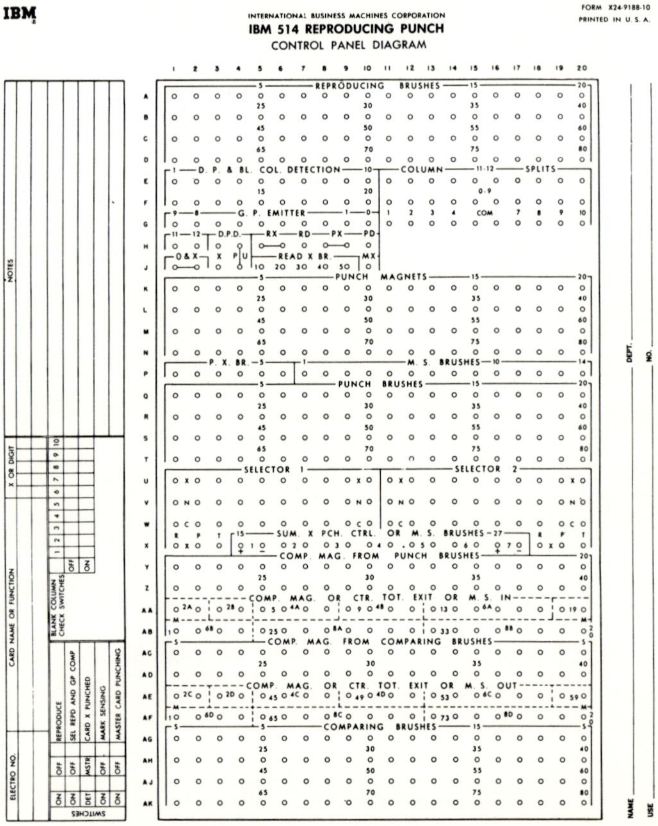
IBM
INTERNATIONAL BUSINESS MACHINES CORPORATION
IBM 514 REPRODUCING PUNCH
CONTROL PANEL DIAGRAM
FORM X24-9188-10
PRINTED IN U. S. A.
REPRODUCING BRUSHES
D. P. & BL. COL. DETECTION
COLUMN
SPLITS
G. P. EMITTER
D.P.D.
READ X BR.
PUNCH MAGNETS
P. X. BR.
M. S. BRUSHES
PUNCH BRUSHES
SELECTOR 1
SELECTOR 2
SUM. X PCH. CTRL. OR M. S. BRUSHES
COMP. MAG. FROM PUNCH BRUSHES
COMP. MAG. OR CTR. TOT. EXIT OR M. S. IN
COMP. MAG. FROM COMPARING BRUSHES
COMP. MAG. OR CTR. TOT. EXIT OR M. S. OUT
COMPARING BRUSHES
NOTES
CARD NAME OR FUNCTION
ELECTRO NO.
X OR DIGIT
BLANK COLUMN CHECK SWITCHES
REPRODUCE
SEL. REPD AND GP COMP
CARD X PUNCHED
MARK SENSING
MASTER CARD PUNCHING
SWITCHES
DEPT.
NO.
NAME
USE

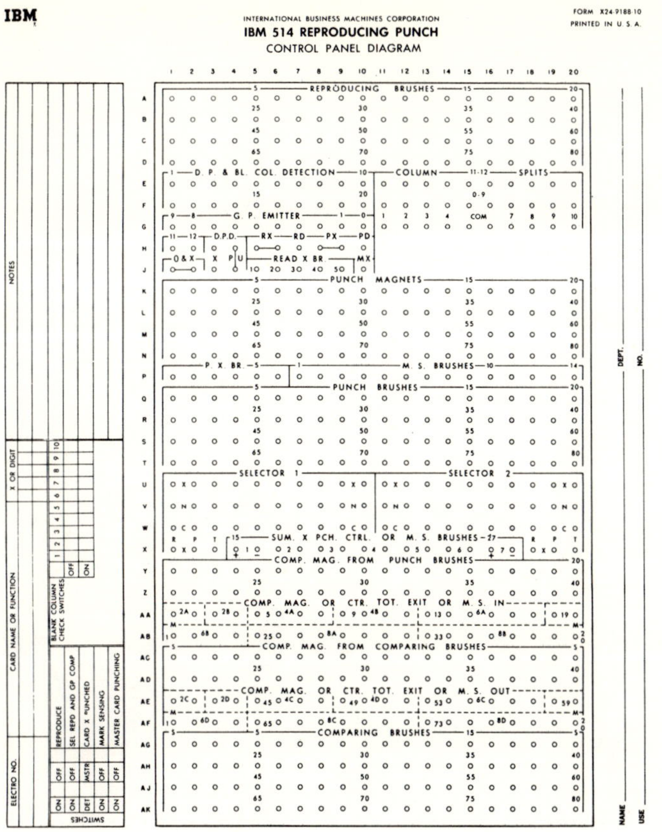
IBM
INTERNATIONAL BUSINESS MACHINES CORPORATION
IBM 514 REPRODUCING PUNCH
CONTROL PANEL DIAGRAM
FORM X24-9188-10
PRINTED IN U. S. A.

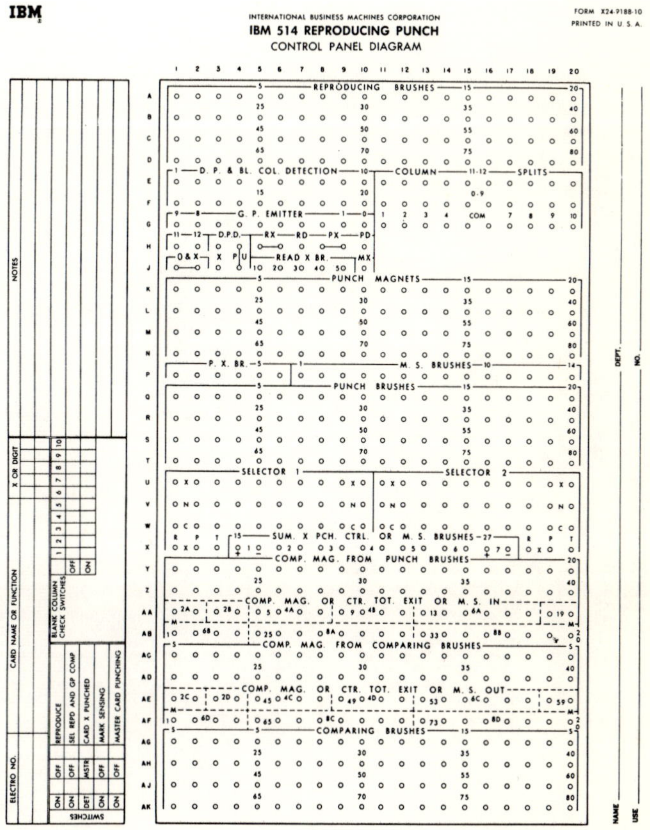
IBM
INTERNATIONAL BUSINESS MACHINES CORPORATION
IBM 514 REPRODUCING PUNCH
CONTROL PANEL DIAGRAM
FORM X24-9188-10
PRINTED IN U. S. A.

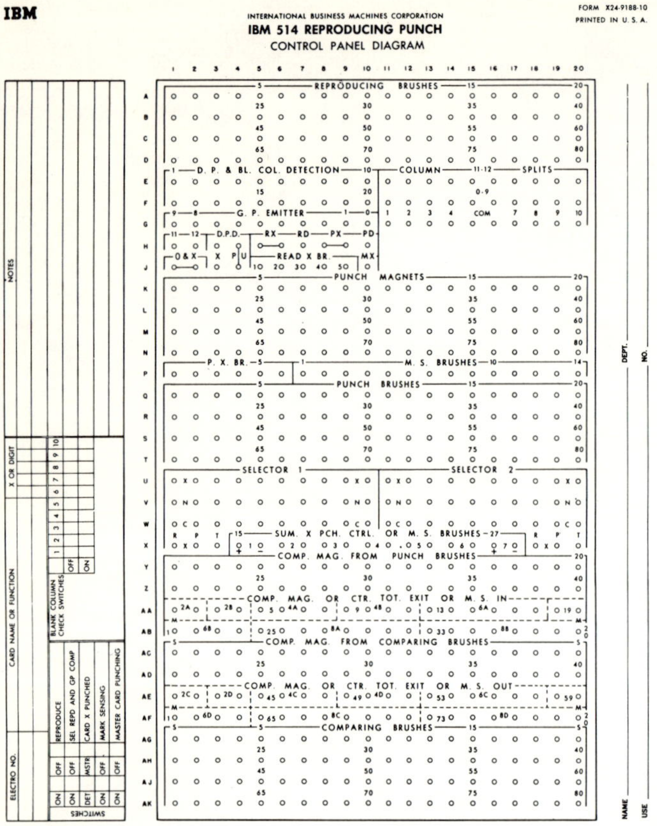
IBM
INTERNATIONAL BUSINESS MACHINES CORPORATION
IBM 514 REPRODUCING PUNCH
CONTROL PANEL DIAGRAM
FORM X24-9188-10
PRINTED IN U. S. A.

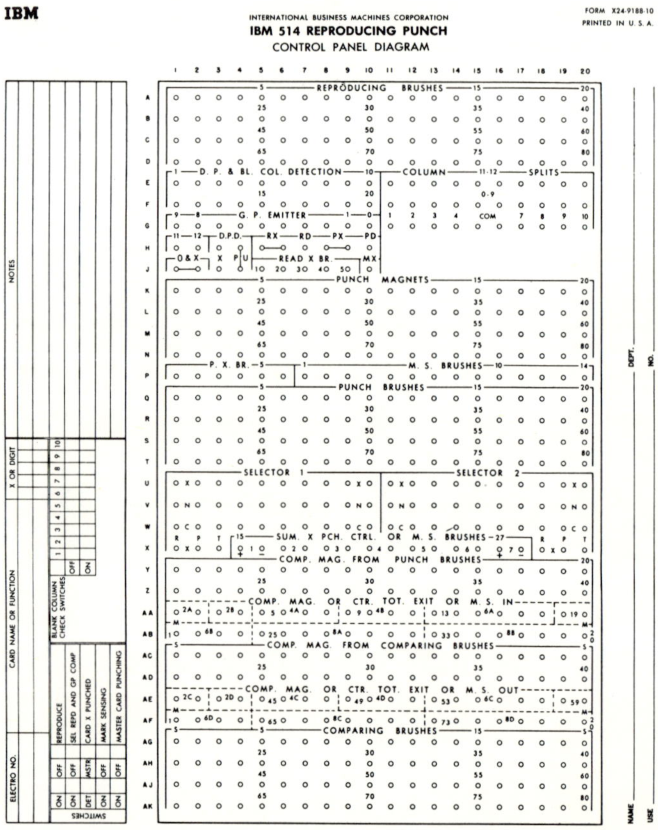
IBM
INTERNATIONAL BUSINESS MACHINES CORPORATION
IBM 514 REPRODUCING PUNCH
CONTROL PANEL DIAGRAM
FORM X24-9188-10
PRINTED IN U. S. A.

IBM

INTERNATIONAL BUSINESS MACHINES CORPORATION

IBM 77, 85 COLLATORS

IBM 85 CONTROL PANEL

Form X24-6395-2
Printed in U. S. A.

INSTRUCTIONS

JOB NAME:			JOB NO.
CTRL. PANEL NO.	OPERATION NAME:		OP. CODE:

FREQUENCY:

- ☐ DAILY
- ☐ WEEKLY
- ☐ BI-WEEKLY
- ☐ SEMI-MONTHLY
- ☐ MONTHLY
- ☐ QUARTERLY
- ☐ ANNUALLY
- ☐ OTHER

DUE IN		DUE OUT	
TIME	DATE	TIME	DATE

ESTIMATED VOLUME:	ESTIMATED TIME:	
	HOURS	TENTHS

CARDS USED:

RECEIVED FROM:

OPERATING INSTRUCTIONS:

TYPE OF CARD:

PRI. FEED ________

SEC. FEED ________

	FIELDS	COLUMNS
CONTROL SEQ.		
MAJOR		
INTER.		
MINOR		
BL. COL. DET.		

POCKETS:

4 SEL. SECDY.	3 SEL. SECDY.	2 MERGED	1 SEL. PRI.

- - - Fold to Here - - -

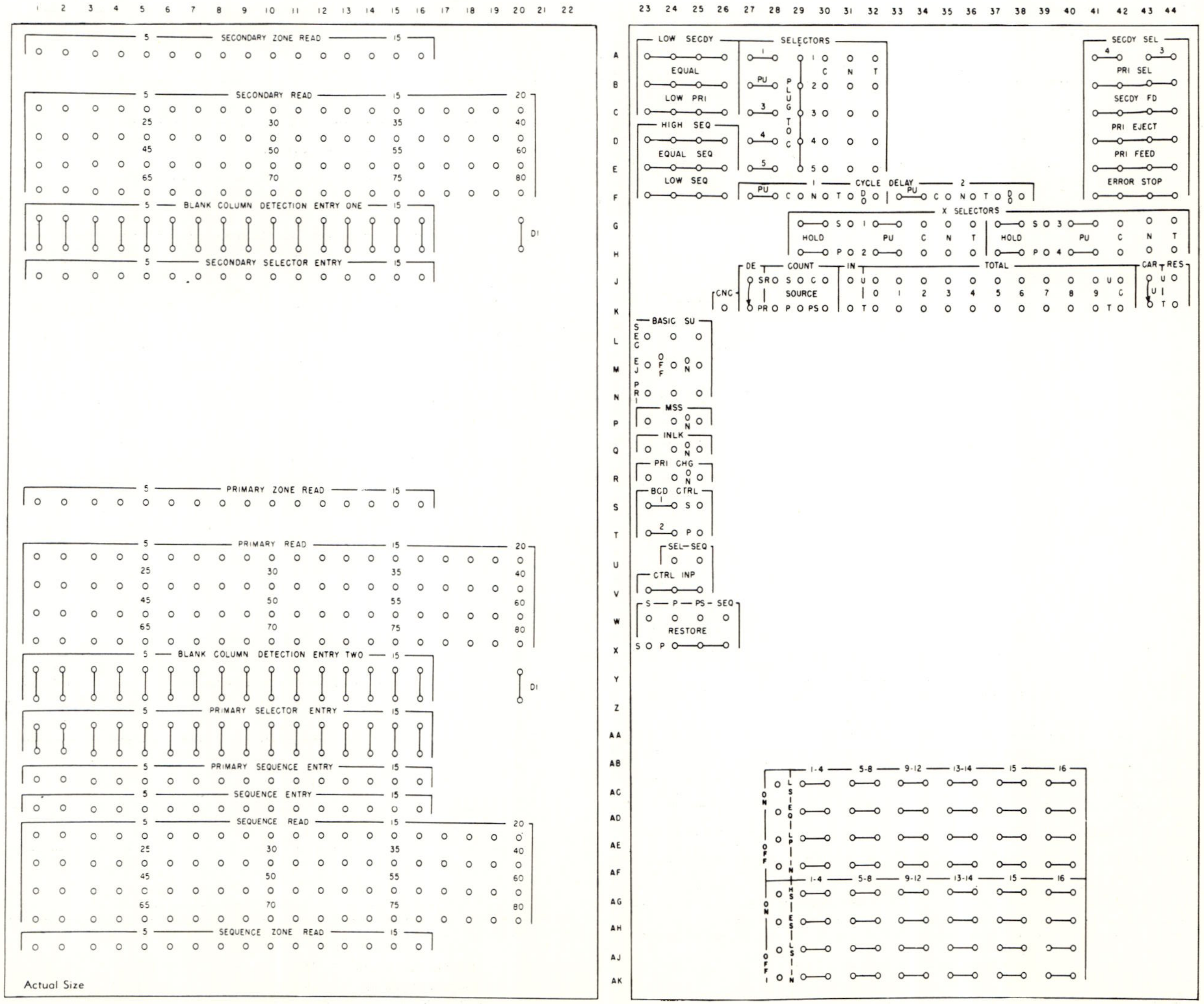

IBM

INTERNATIONAL BUSINESS MACHINES CORPORATION

IBM 77, 85 COLLATORS

IBM 85 CONTROL PANEL

Form X24-6395-2
Printed in U. S. A.

INSTRUCTIONS

JOB NAME:		JOB NO.
CTRL. PANEL NO.	OPERATION NAME:	OP. CODE:

FREQUENCY:
- ☐ DAILY
- ☐ WEEKLY
- ☐ BI-WEEKLY
- ☐ SEMI-MONTHLY
- ☐ MONTHLY
- ☐ QUARTERLY
- ☐ ANNUALLY
- ☐ OTHER

DUE IN		DUE OUT	
TIME	DATE	TIME	DATE

ESTIMATED VOLUME:	ESTIMATED TIME: HOURS	TENTHS

CARDS USED:

RECEIVED FROM:

OPERATING INSTRUCTIONS:

TYPE OF CARD:

PRI. FEED

SEC. FEED

	FIELDS	COLUMNS
CONTROL SEQ.		
MAJOR		
INTER.		
MINOR		
BL. COL. DET.		

POCKETS:

4 SEL. SECDY.	3 SEL. SECDY.	2 MERGED	1 SEL. PRI.

Fold to Here

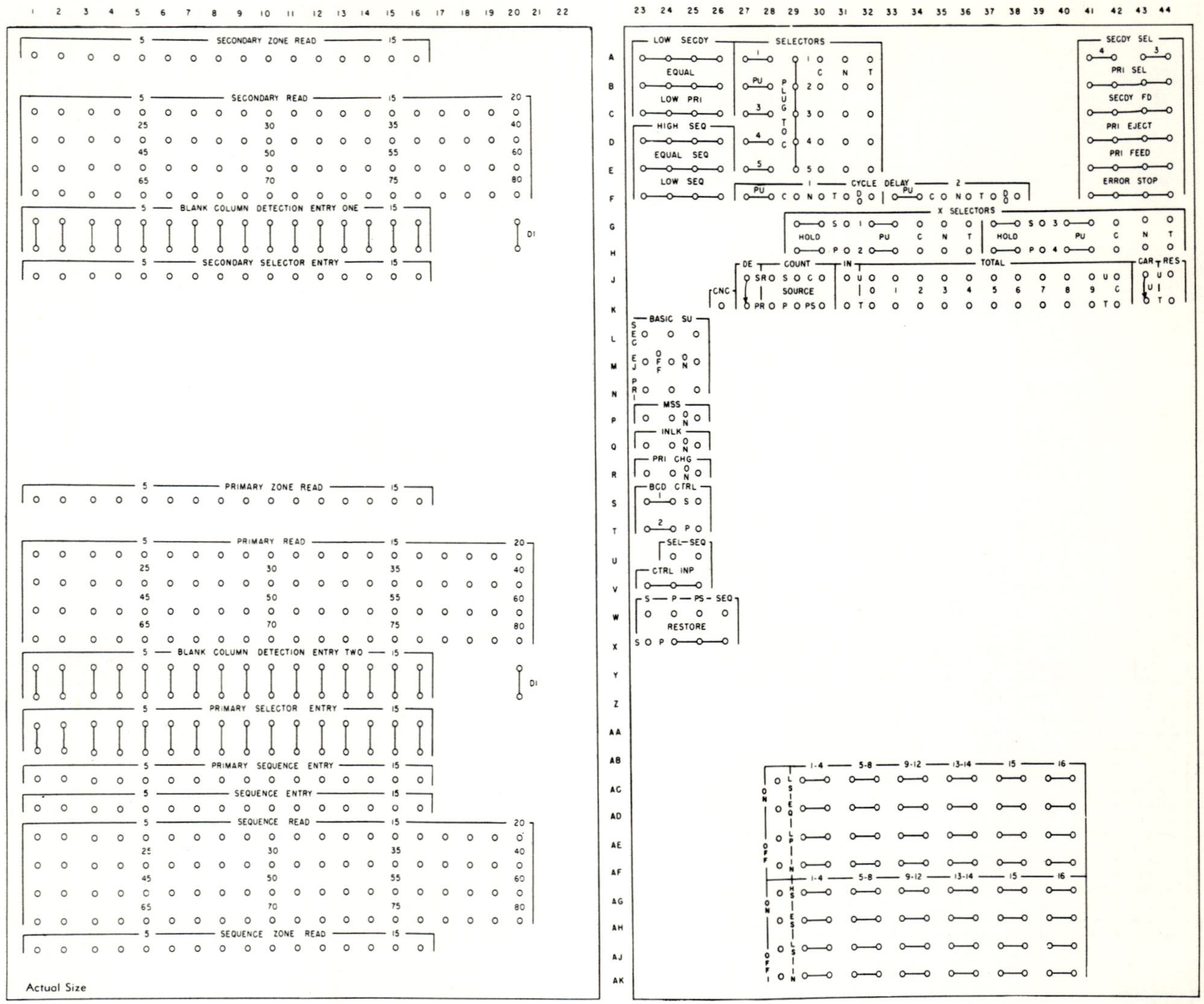

Actual Size

IBM

INTERNATIONAL BUSINESS MACHINES CORPORATION

IBM 77, 85 COLLATORS

IBM 85 CONTROL PANEL

Form X24-6395-2
Printed in U. S. A.

INSTRUCTIONS

JOB NAME:		JOB NO.
CTRL. PANEL NO.	OPERATION NAME:	OP. CODE:

FREQUENCY:

- ☐ DAILY
- ☐ WEEKLY
- ☐ BI-WEEKLY
- ☐ SEMI-MONTHLY
- ☐ MONTHLY
- ☐ QUARTERLY
- ☐ ANNUALLY
- ☐ OTHER

DUE IN		DUE OUT	
TIME	DATE	TIME	DATE

ESTIMATED VOLUME:	ESTIMATED TIME:	
	HOURS	TENTHS

CARDS USED:

RECEIVED FROM:

OPERATING INSTRUCTIONS:

TYPE OF CARD:

PRI. FEED

SEC. FEED

	FIELDS	COLUMNS
CONTROL SEQ.		
MAJOR		
INTER.		
MINOR		
BL. COL. DET.		

POCKETS:

4 SEL. SECDY.	3 SEL. SECDY.	2 MERGED	1 SEL. PRI.

- - - Fold to Here - - -

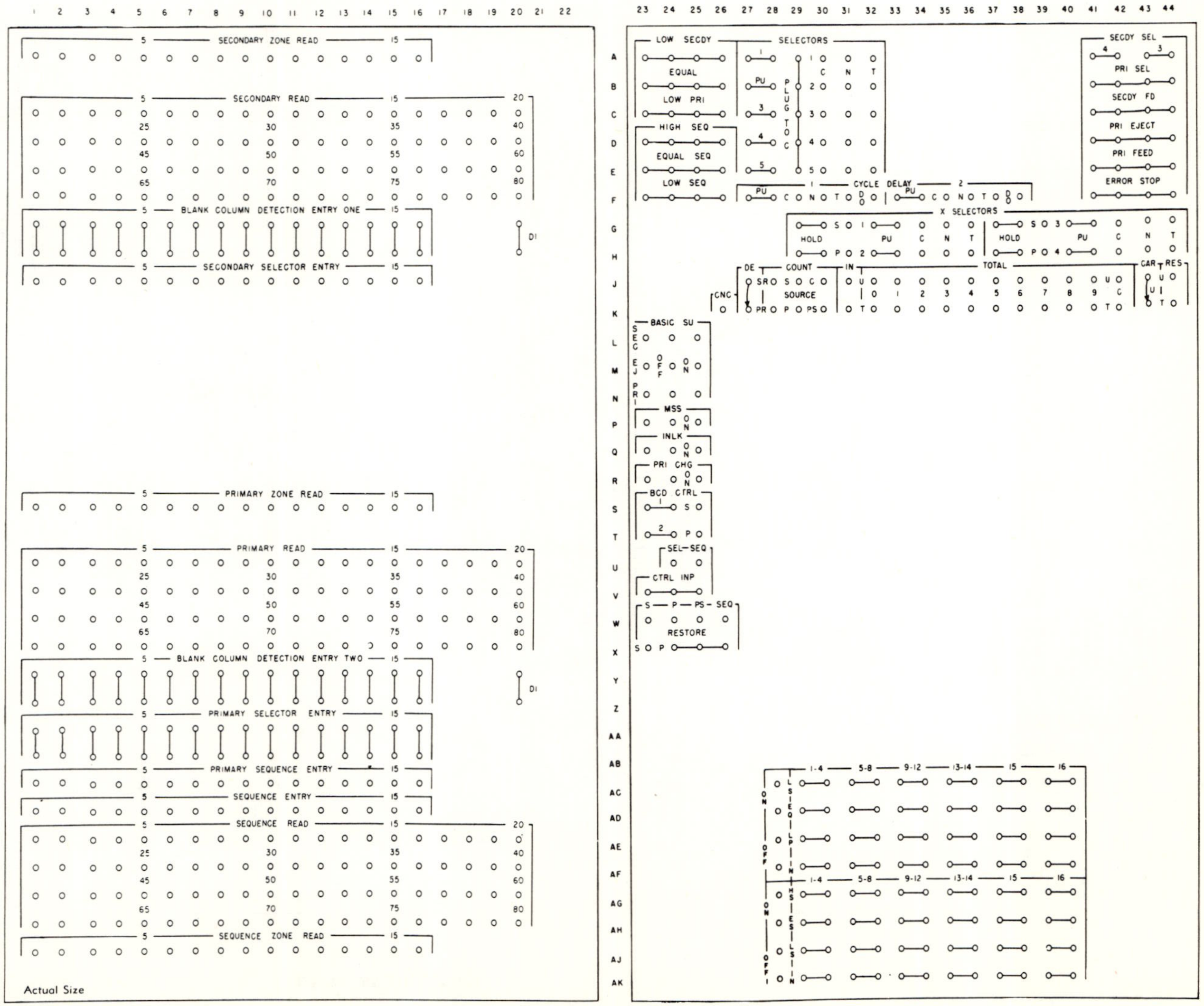

Actual Size

IBM

INTERNATIONAL BUSINESS MACHINES CORPORATION
IBM 77, 85 COLLATORS
IBM 85 CONTROL PANEL

Form X24-6395-2
Printed in U. S. A.

INSTRUCTIONS

JOB NAME: | JOB NO.

CTRL. PANEL NO. | OPERATION NAME: | OP. CODE:

FREQUENCY:
- ☐ DAILY
- ☐ WEEKLY
- ☐ BI-WEEKLY
- ☐ SEMI-MONTHLY
- ☐ MONTHLY
- ☐ QUARTERLY
- ☐ ANNUALLY
- ☐ OTHER

DUE IN		DUE OUT	
TIME	DATE	TIME	DATE

ESTIMATED VOLUME: | ESTIMATED TIME: HOURS | TENTHS

CARDS USED:

RECEIVED FROM:

OPERATING INSTRUCTIONS:

TYPE OF CARD:

PRI. FEED

SEC. FEED

	FIELDS	COLUMNS
CONTROL SEQ.		
MAJOR		
INTER.		
MINOR		
BL. COL. DET.		

POCKETS:

4 SEL. SECDY.	3 SEL. SECDY.	2 MERGED	1 SEL. PRI.

- - - Fold to Here - - -

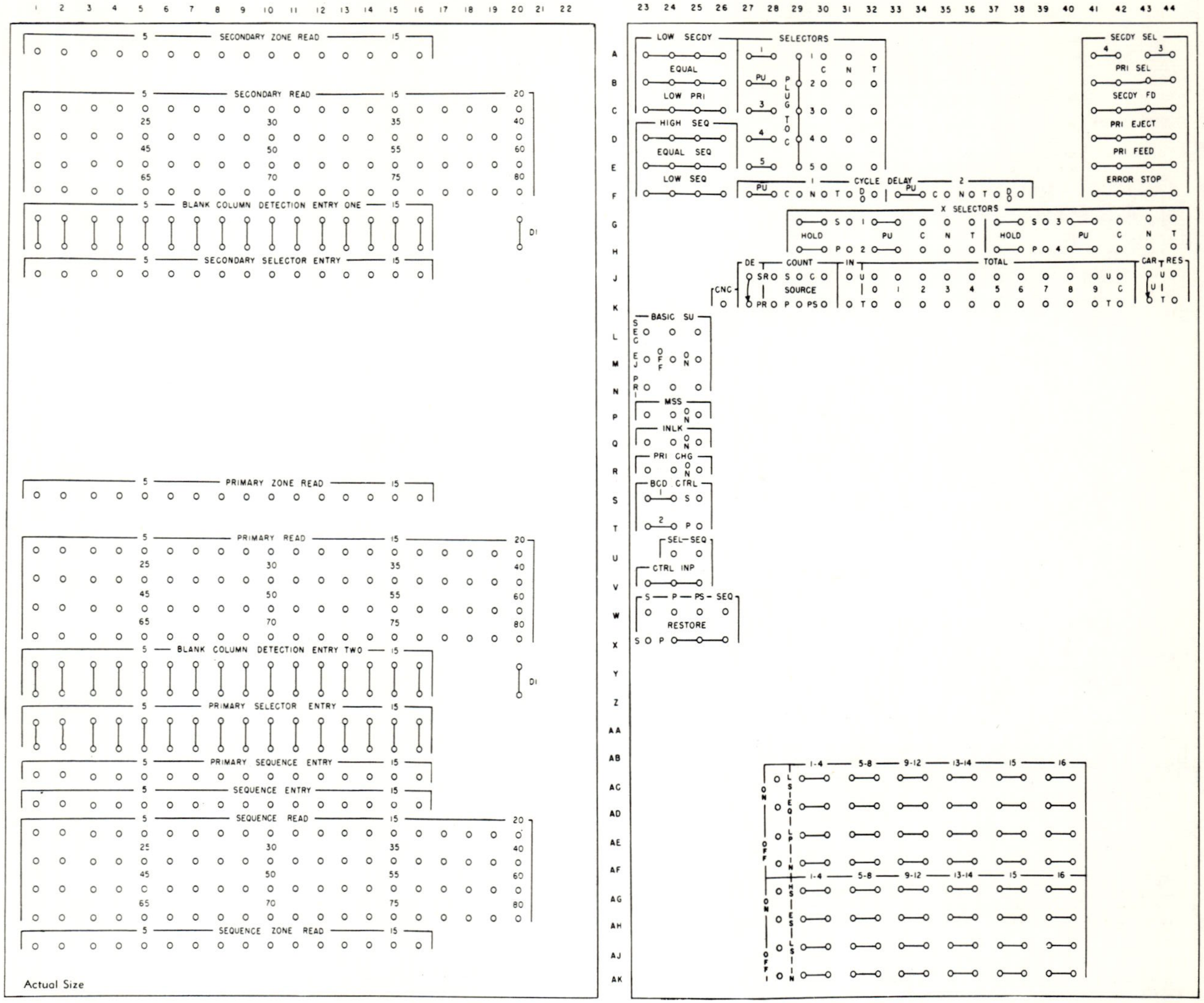

IBM

INTERNATIONAL BUSINESS MACHINES CORPORATION

IBM 77, 85 COLLATORS

IBM 85 CONTROL PANEL

Form X24-6395-2
Printed in U. S. A.

INSTRUCTIONS

JOB NAME:		JOB NO.
CTRL. PANEL NO.	OPERATION NAME:	OP. CODE:

FREQUENCY:

- ☐ DAILY
- ☐ WEEKLY
- ☐ BI-WEEKLY
- ☐ SEMI-MONTHLY
- ☐ MONTHLY
- ☐ QUARTERLY
- ☐ ANNUALLY
- ☐ OTHER

DUE IN		DUE OUT	
TIME	DATE	TIME	DATE

ESTIMATED VOLUME:	ESTIMATED TIME: HOURS	TENTHS

CARDS USED:

RECEIVED FROM:

OPERATING INSTRUCTIONS:

TYPE OF CARD:

PRI. FEED

SEC. FEED

	FIELDS	COLUMNS
CONTROL SEQ.		
MAJOR		
INTER.		
MINOR		
BL. COL. DET.		

POCKETS:

4 SEL. SECDY.	3 SEL. SECDY.	2 MERGED	1 SEL. PRI.

- - - Fold to Here - - -

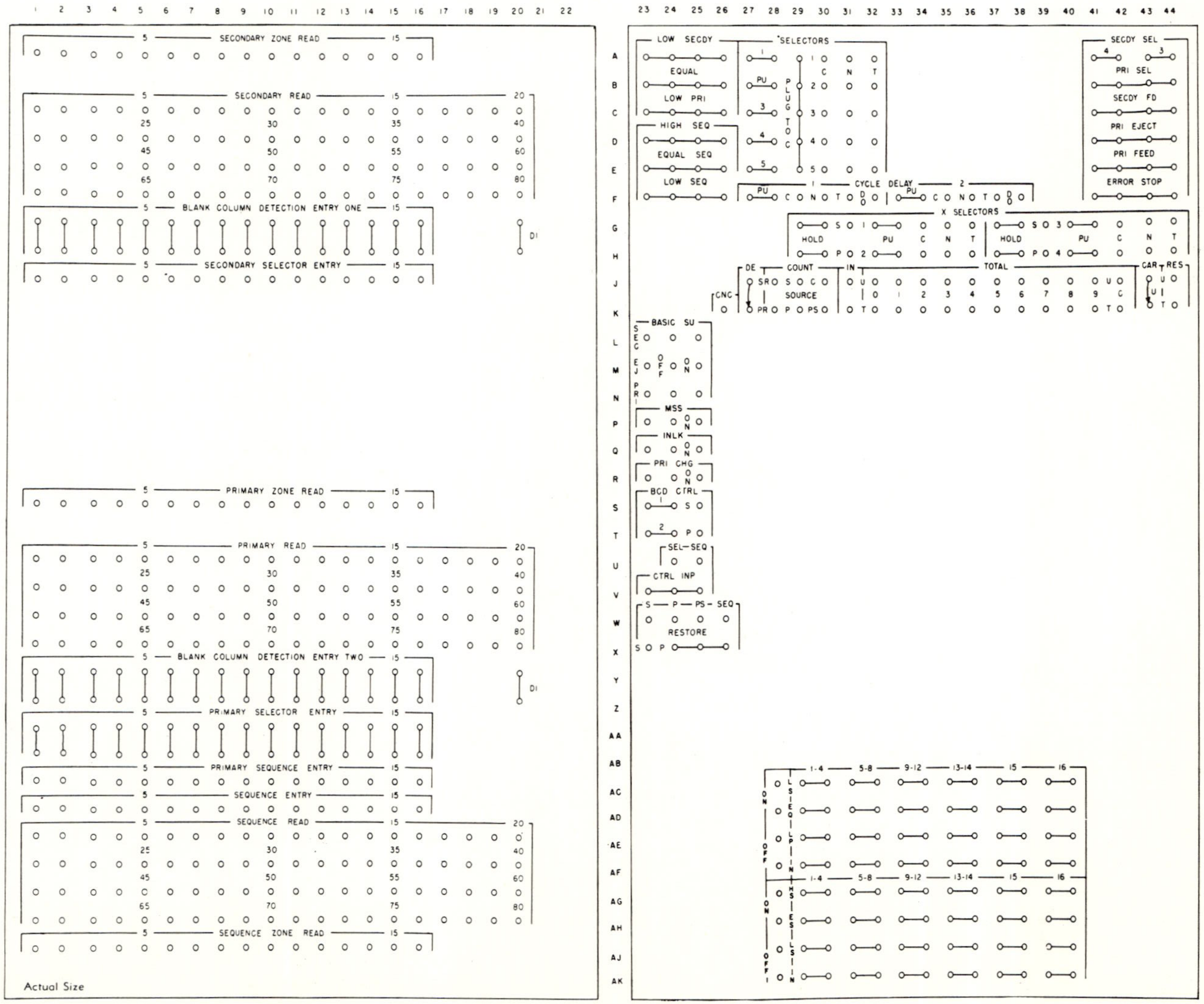

IBM

INTERNATIONAL BUSINESS MACHINES CORPORATION

IBM 77, 85 COLLATORS

IBM 85 CONTROL PANEL

Form X24-6395-2
Printed in U. S. A.

INSTRUCTIONS

JOB NAME:			JOB NO.
CTRL. PANEL NO.	OPERATION NAME:		OP. CODE:

FREQUENCY:
- ☐ DAILY
- ☐ WEEKLY
- ☐ BI-WEEKLY
- ☐ SEMI-MONTHLY
- ☐ MONTHLY
- ☐ QUARTERLY
- ☐ ANNUALLY
- ☐ OTHER

DUE IN		DUE OUT	
TIME	DATE	TIME	DATE

ESTIMATED VOLUME:	ESTIMATED TIME:	
	HOURS	TENTHS

CARDS USED:

RECEIVED FROM:

OPERATING INSTRUCTIONS:

TYPE OF CARD:

PRI. FEED

SEC. FEED

	FIELDS	COLUMNS
CONTROL SEQ.		
MAJOR		
INTER.		
MINOR		
BL. COL. DET.		

POCKETS:

4 SEL. SECDY.	3 SEL. SECDY.	2 MERGED	1 SEL. PRI.

- - - Fold to Here - - -

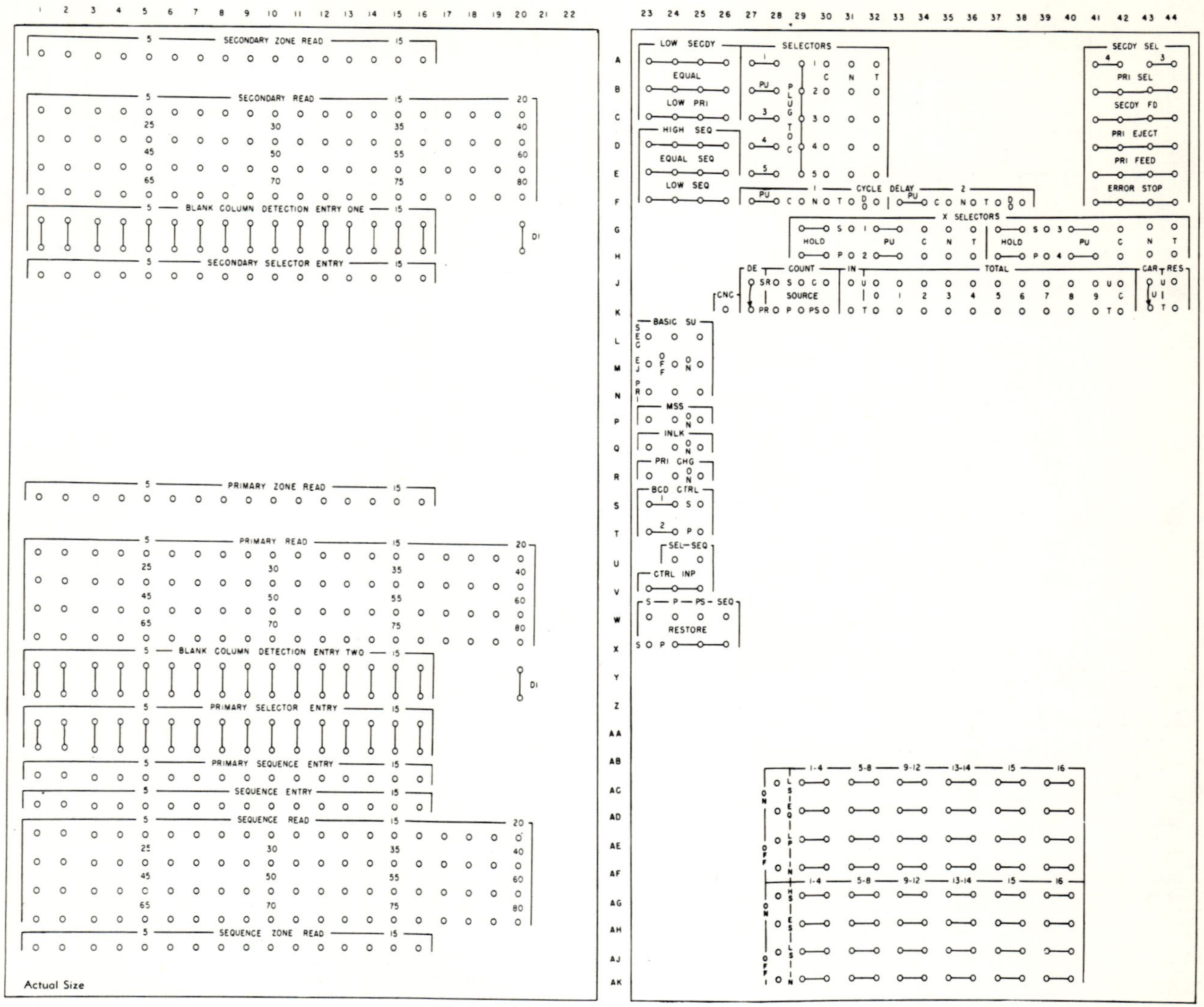

IBM

INTERNATIONAL BUSINESS MACHINES CORPORATION

IBM 77, 85 COLLATORS

IBM 85 CONTROL PANEL

Form X24-6395-2
Printed in U. S. A.

INSTRUCTIONS

JOB NAME: | JOB NO.

CTRL. PANEL NO. | OPERATION NAME: | OP. CODE:

FREQUENCY:
- ☐ DAILY
- ☐ WEEKLY
- ☐ BI-WEEKLY
- ☐ SEMI-MONTHLY
- ☐ MONTHLY
- ☐ QUARTERLY
- ☐ ANNUALLY
- ☐ OTHER

DUE IN		DUE OUT	
TIME	DATE	TIME	DATE

ESTIMATED VOLUME: | ESTIMATED TIME: HOURS | TENTHS

CARDS USED:

RECEIVED FROM:

OPERATING INSTRUCTIONS:

TYPE OF CARD:

PRI. FEED

SEC. FEED

	FIELDS	COLUMNS
CONTROL SEQ.		
MAJOR		
INTER.		
MINOR		
BL. COL. DET.		

POCKETS:

4 SEL. SECDY.	3 SEL. SECDY.	2 MERGED	1 SEL. PRI.

- - - Fold to Here - - -

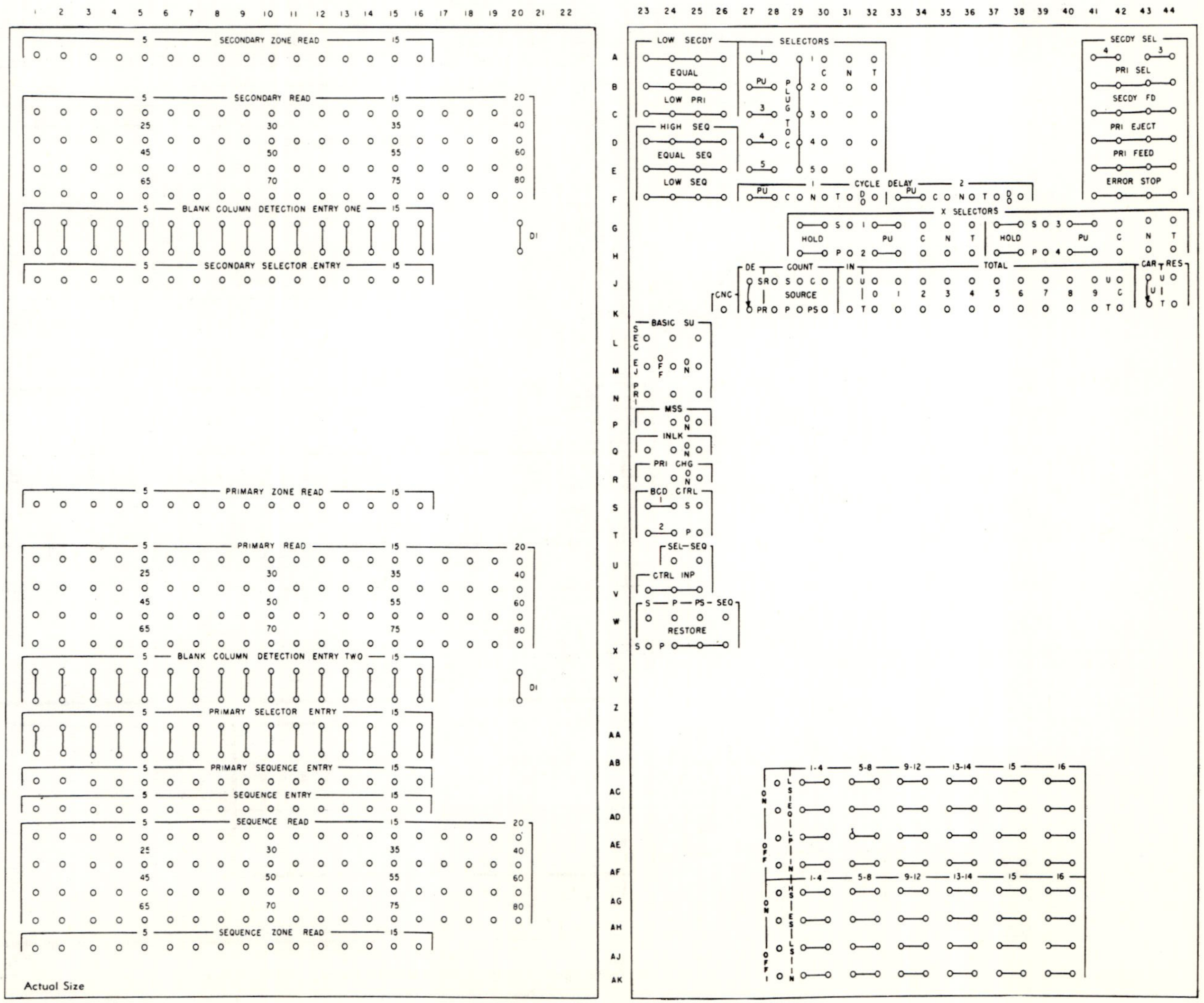

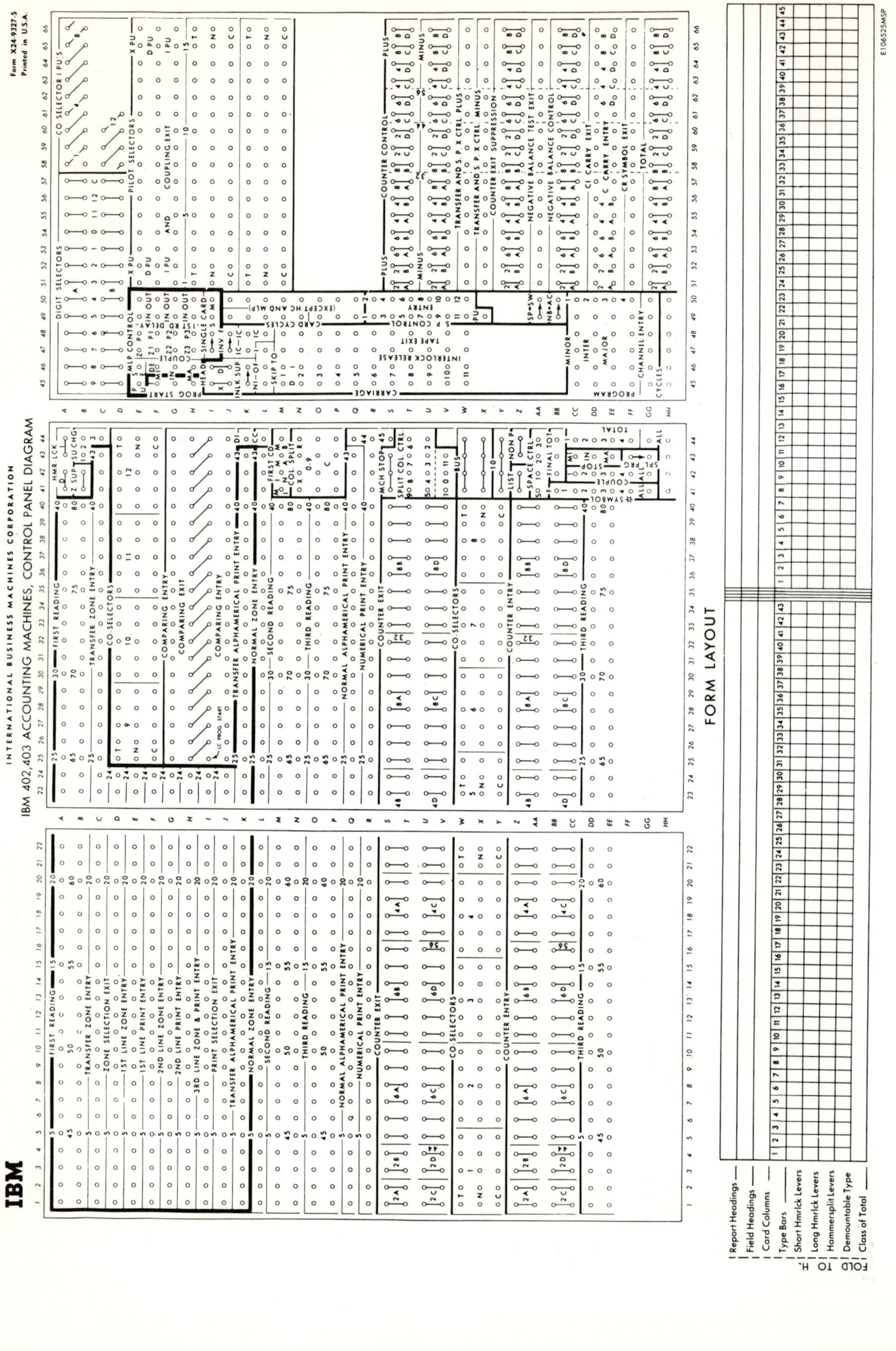
IBM
INTERNATIONAL BUSINESS MACHINES CORPORATION
IBM 402,403 ACCOUNTING MACHINES, CONTROL PANEL DIAGRAM
Form X24-9327-5
Printed in U.S.A.
FORM LAYOUT
Report Headings
Field Headings
Card Columns
Type Bars
Short Hmrlck Levers
Long Hmrlck Levers
Hammersplit Levers
Demountable Type
Class of Total
FOLD TO H.

IBM

INTERNATIONAL BUSINESS MACHINES CORPORATION

IBM 402,403 ACCOUNTING MACHINES, CONTROL PANEL DIAGRAM

Form X24-9327-5
Printed in U.S.A.

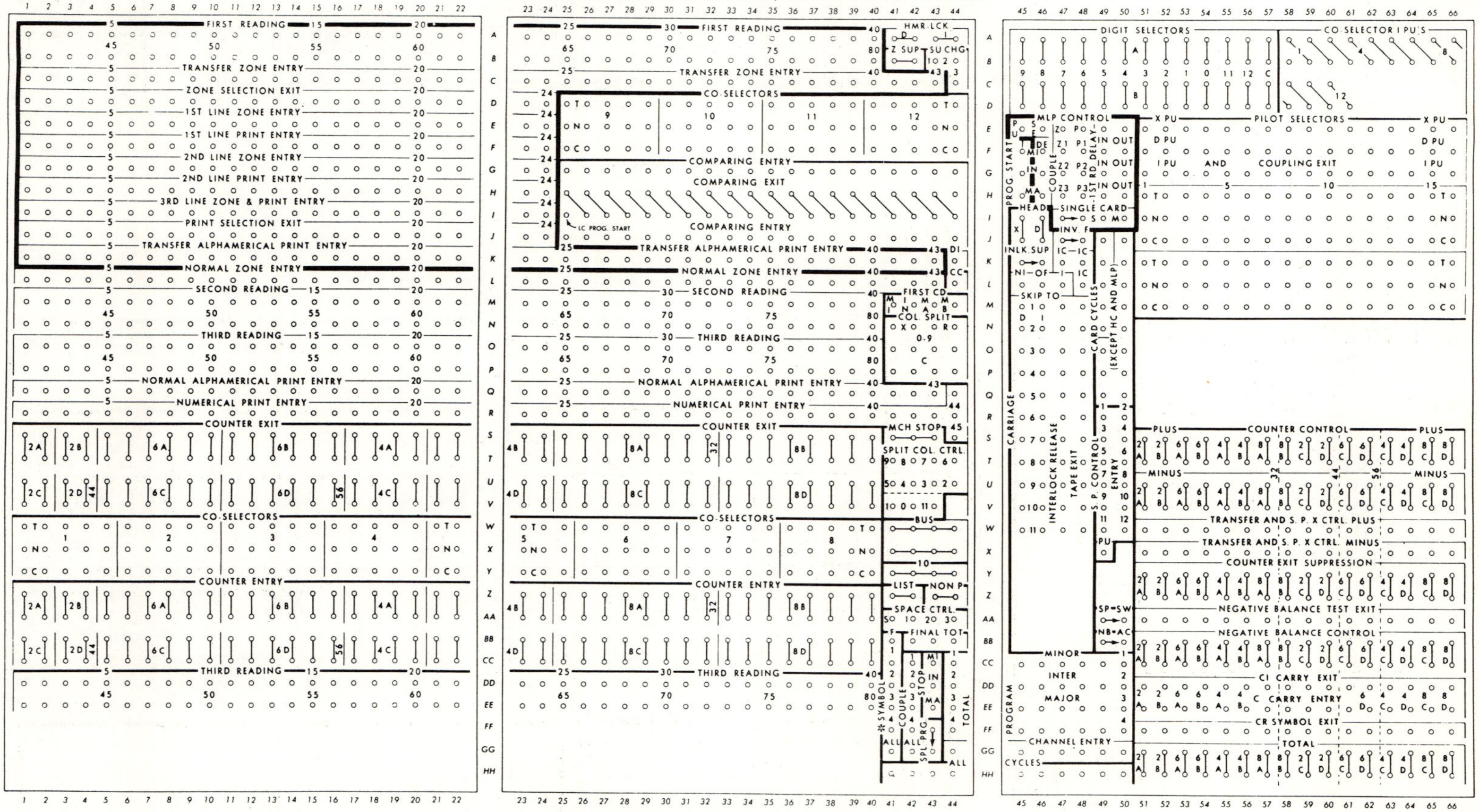

FORM LAYOUT

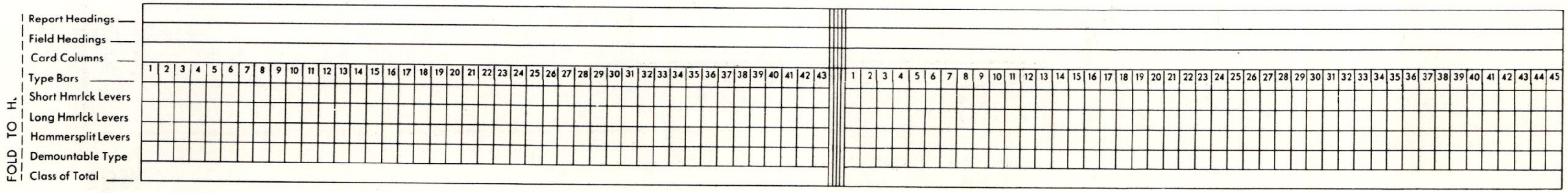

E106525MSP

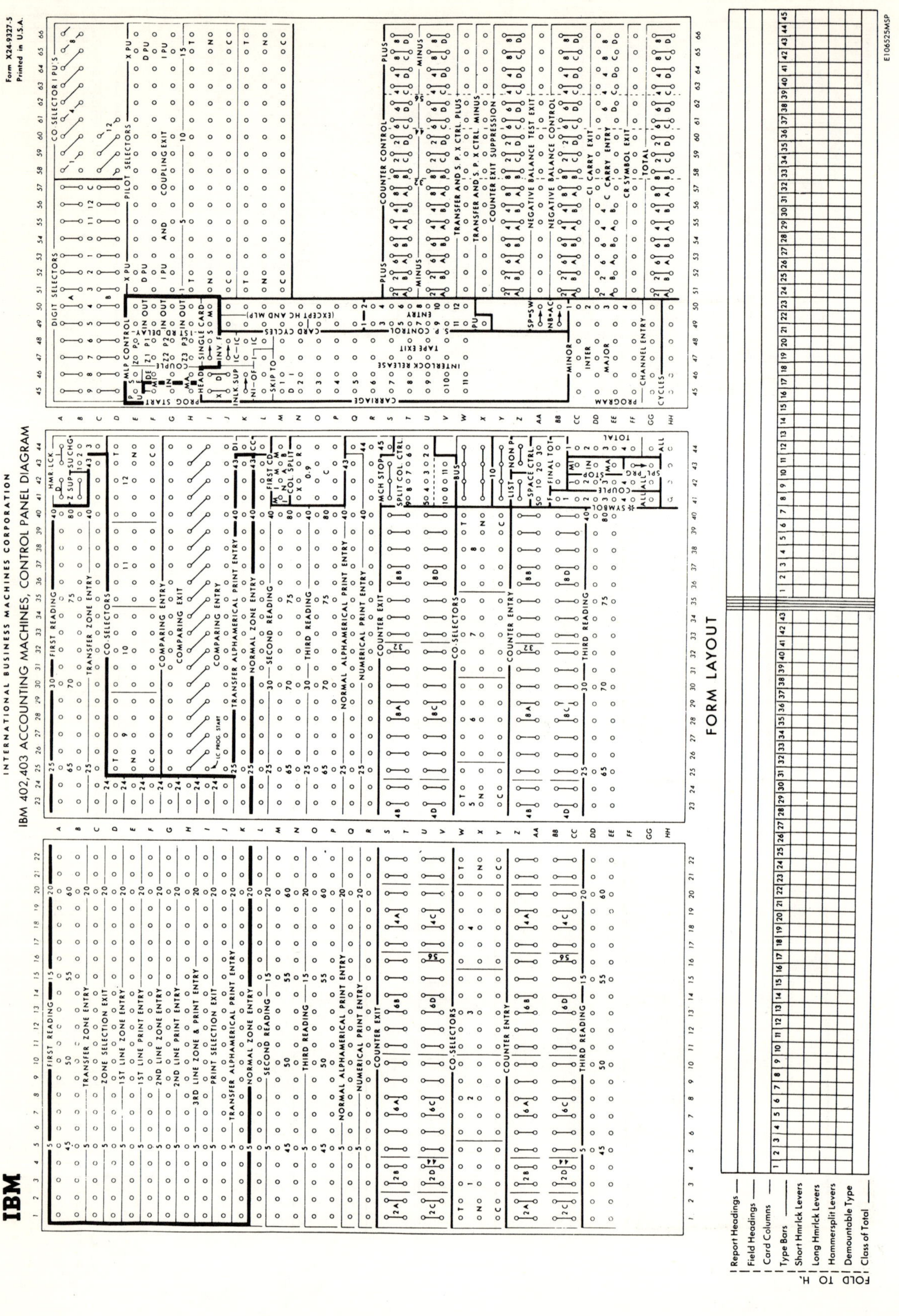

IBM

INTERNATIONAL BUSINESS MACHINES CORPORATION

IBM 402,403 ACCOUNTING MACHINES, CONTROL PANEL DIAGRAM

Form X24-9327-5
Printed in U.S.A.

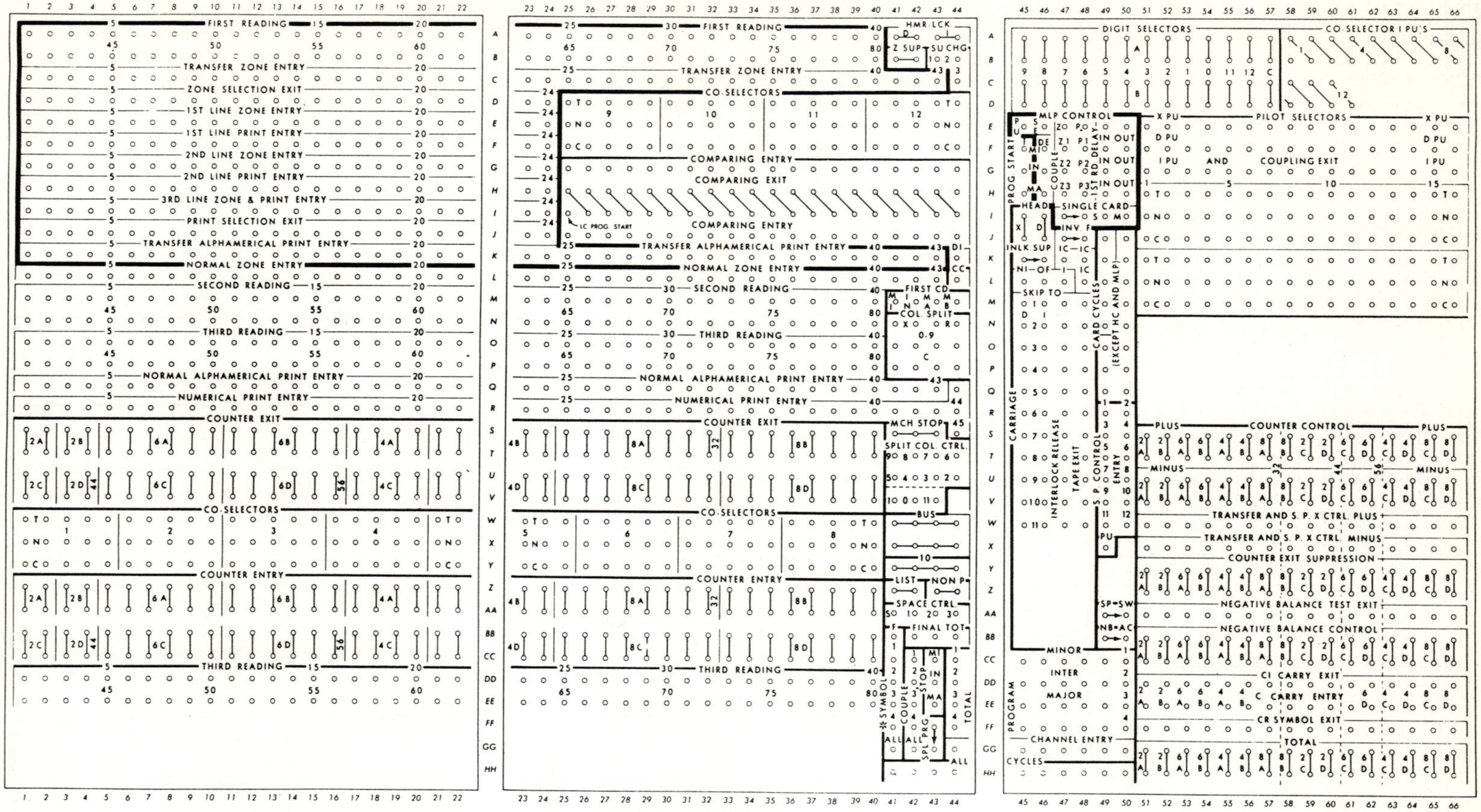

FORM LAYOUT

Report Headings	
Field Headings	
Card Columns	
Type Bars	1 2 3 4 5 6 7 8 9 10 11 12 13 14 15 16 17 18 19 20 21 22 23 24 25 26 27 28 29 30 31 32 33 34 35 36 37 38 39 40 41 42 43 ‖ 1 2 3 4 5 6 7 8 9 10 11 12 13 14 15 16 17 18 19 20 21 22 23 24 25 26 27 28 29 30 31 32 33 34 35 36 37 38 39 40 41 42 43 44 45
Short Hmrlck Levers	
Long Hmrlck Levers	
Hammersplit Levers	
Demountable Type	
Class of Total	

FOLD TO H.

E106525MSP

IBM

INTERNATIONAL BUSINESS MACHINES CORPORATION

IBM 402,403 ACCOUNTING MACHINES, CONTROL PANEL DIAGRAM

Form X24-9327-5
Printed in U.S.A.

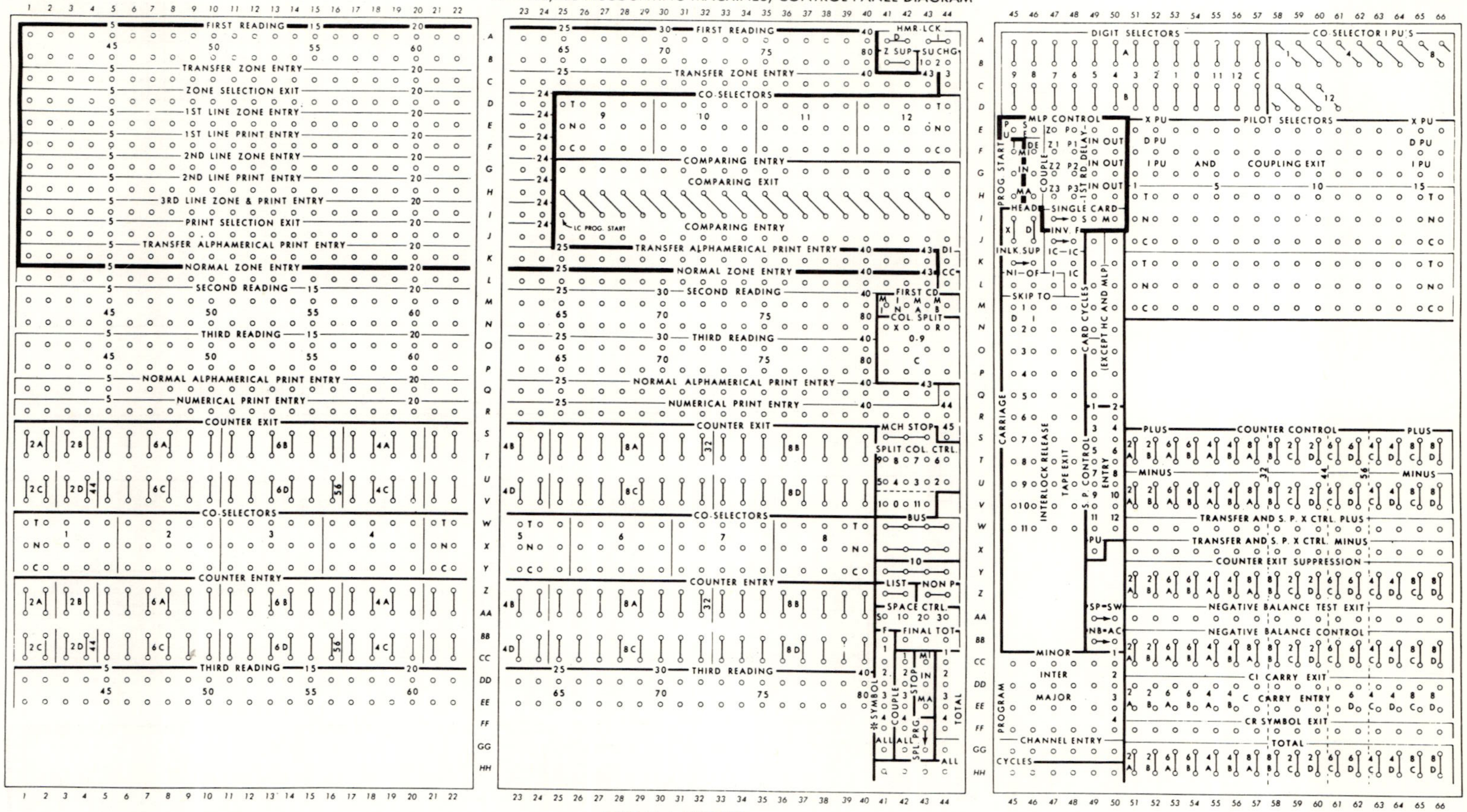

FORM LAYOUT

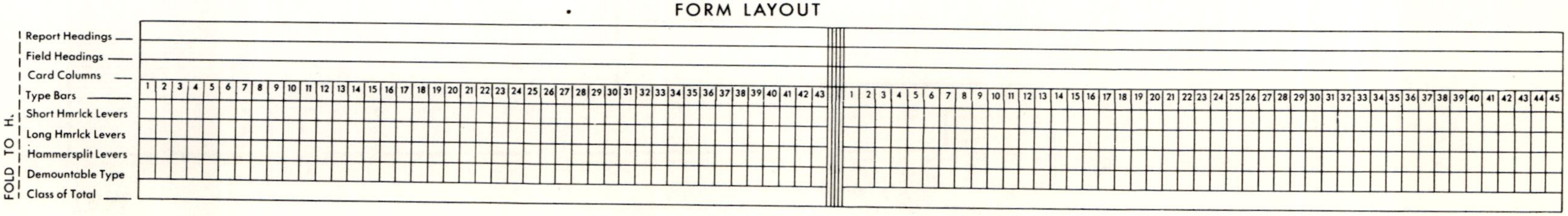

E106525MSP

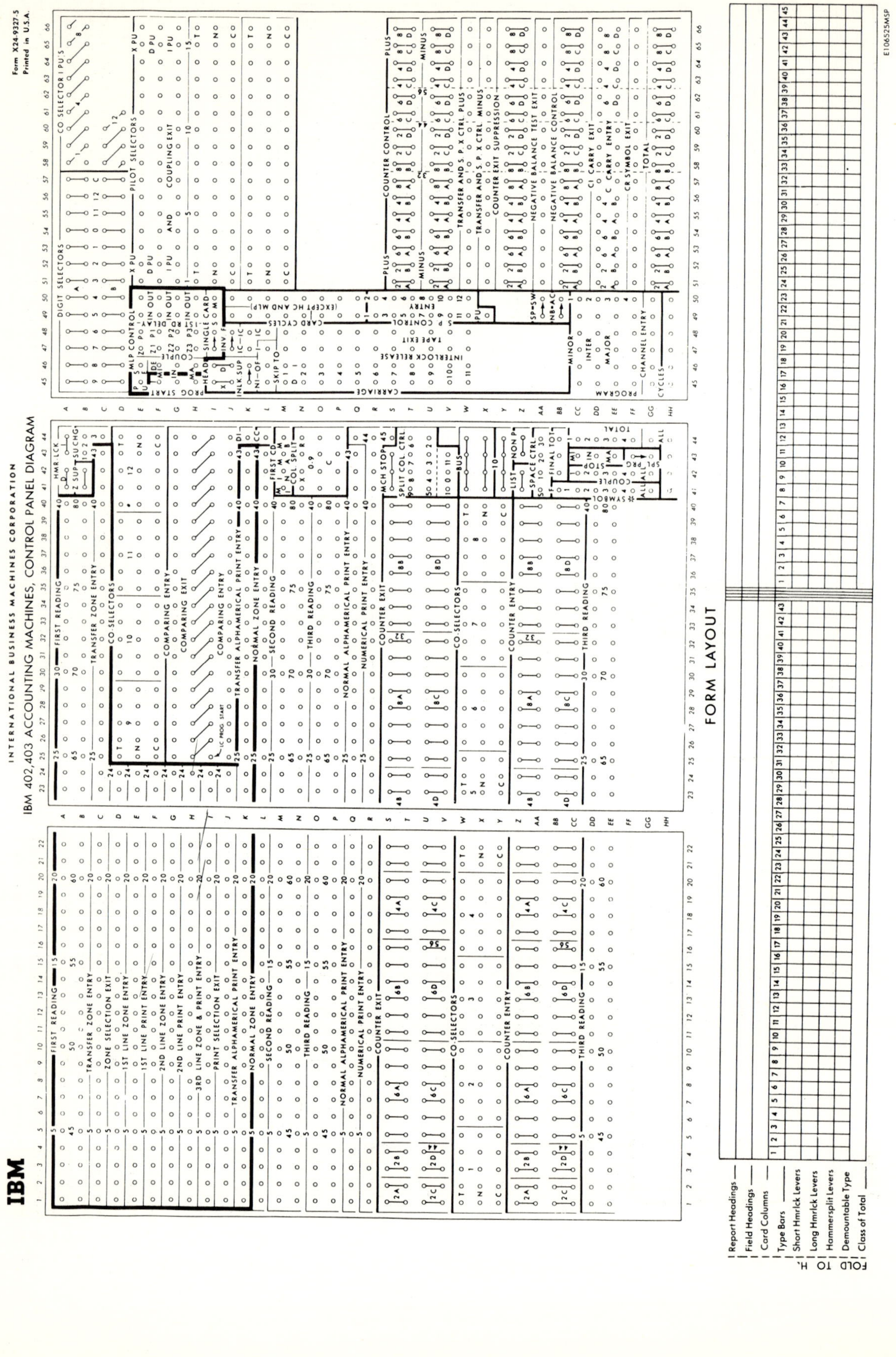
IBM
INTERNATIONAL BUSINESS MACHINES CORPORATION
IBM 402, 403 ACCOUNTING MACHINES, CONTROL PANEL DIAGRAM
Form X24-9327-5
Printed in U.S.A.
FORM LAYOUT
Report Headings
Field Headings
Card Columns
Type Bars
Short Hmrlck Levers
Long Hmrlck Levers
Hammersplit Levers
Demountable Type
Class of Total
FOLD TO H.
E10652SMSP

IBM

INTERNATIONAL BUSINESS MACHINES CORPORATION

IBM 402,403 ACCOUNTING MACHINES, CONTROL PANEL DIAGRAM

Form X24-9327-5
Printed in U.S.A.

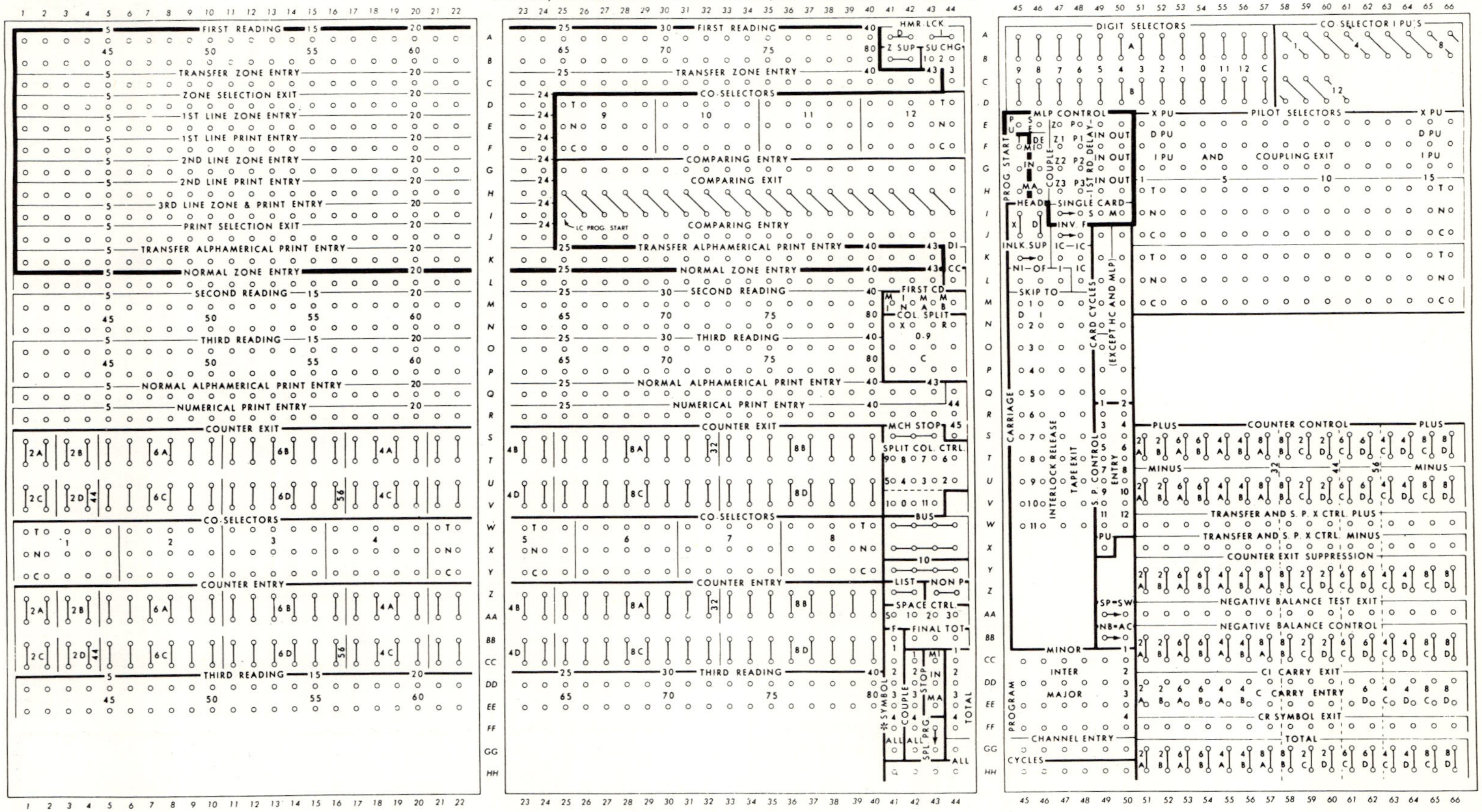

FORM LAYOUT

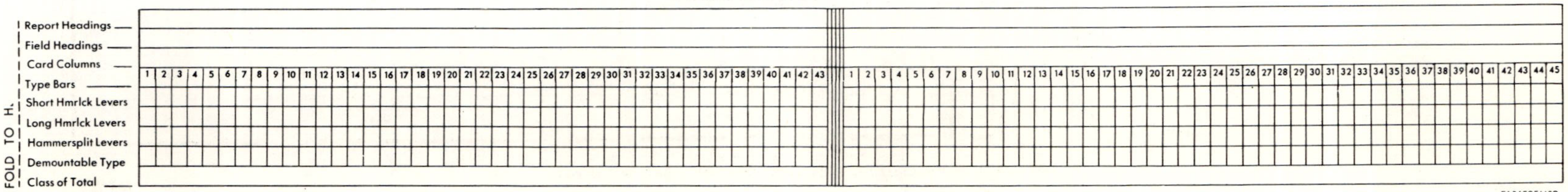

E106525MSP

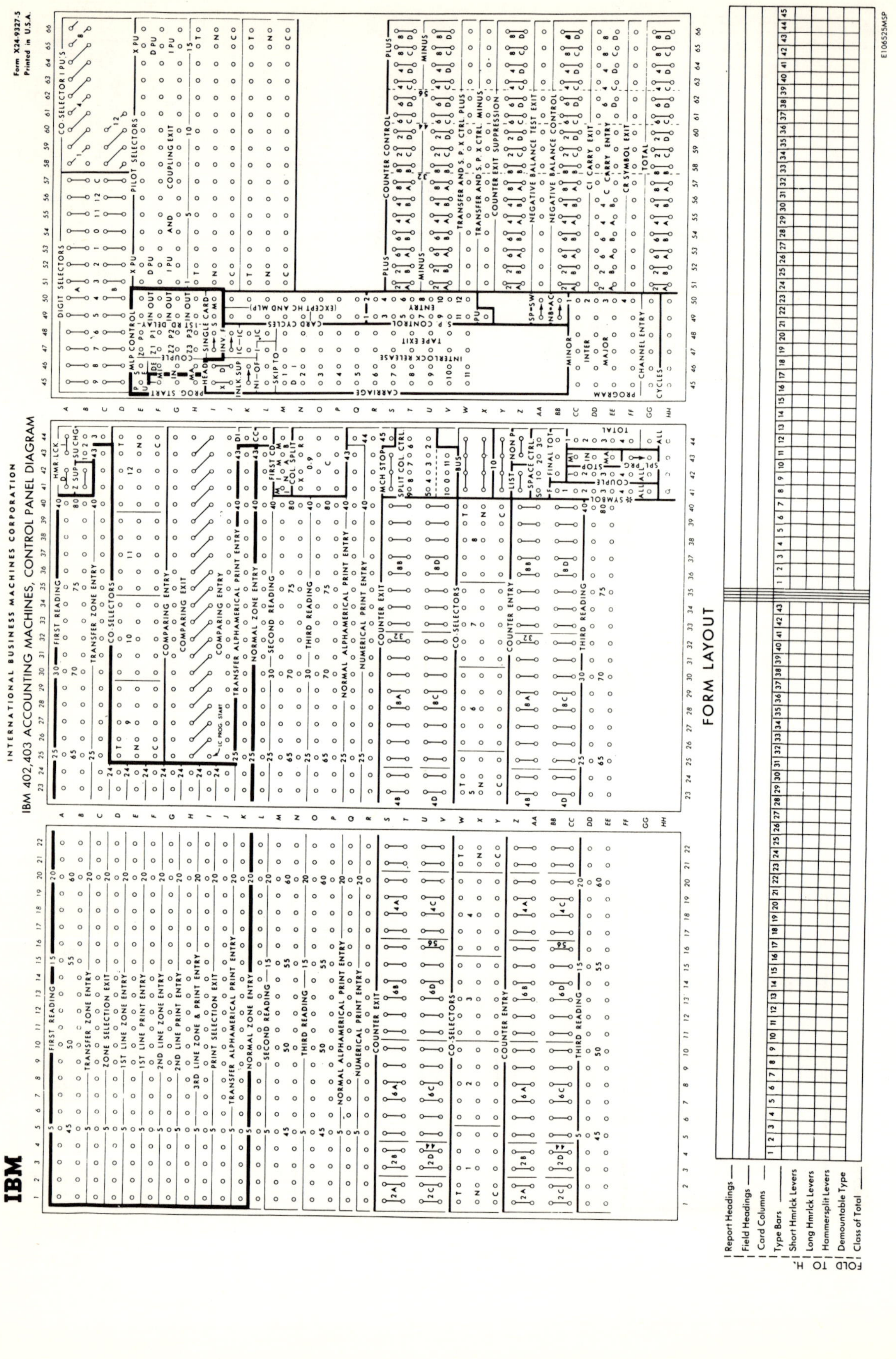

IBM
INTERNATIONAL BUSINESS MACHINES CORPORATION
IBM 402, 403 ACCOUNTING MACHINES, CONTROL PANEL DIAGRAM
Form X24-9327-5
Printed in U.S.A.
FORM LAYOUT
Report Headings
Field Headings
Card Columns
Type Bars
Short Hmrlck Levers
Long Hmrlck Levers
Hammersplit Levers
Demountable Type
Class of Total
FOLD TO H.
E106525MSP

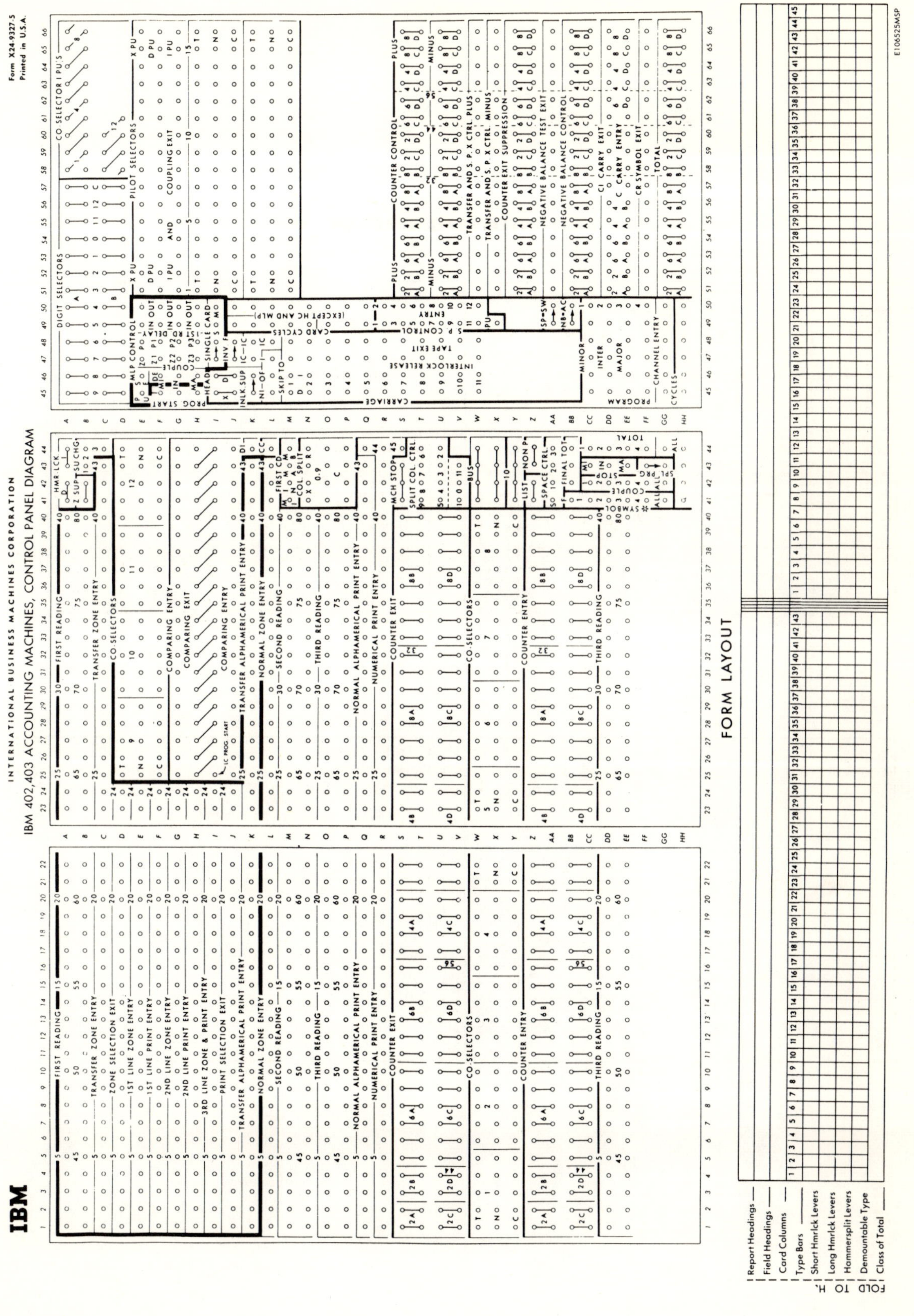
IBM
INTERNATIONAL BUSINESS MACHINES CORPORATION
IBM 402,403 ACCOUNTING MACHINES, CONTROL PANEL DIAGRAM
FORM LAYOUT
Form X24-9327-5
Printed in U.S.A.
E106525MSP

557 INTERPRETER DIAGRAM

557 INTERPRETER DIAGRAM

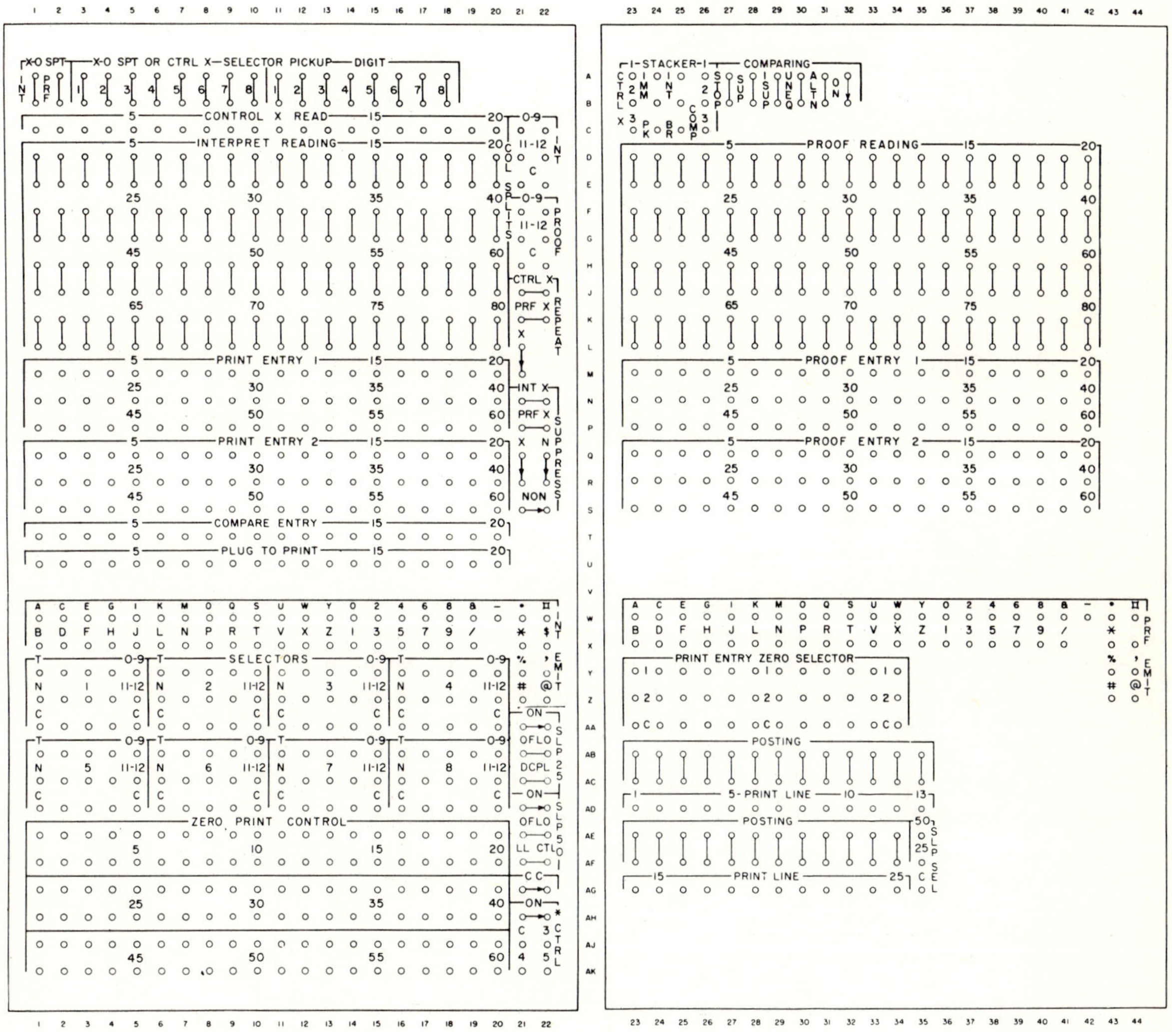

557 INTERPRETER DIAGRAM

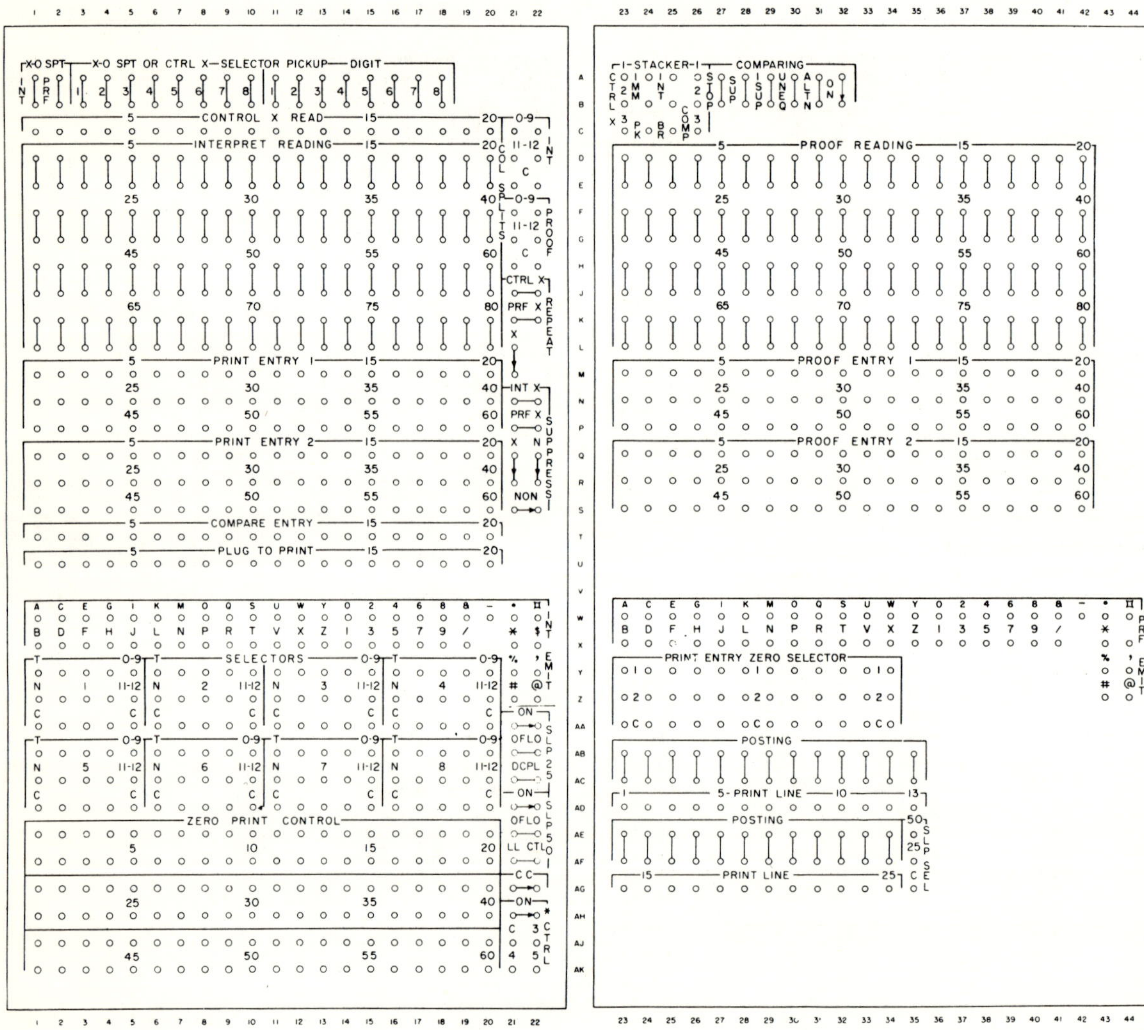

557 INTERPRETER DIAGRAM

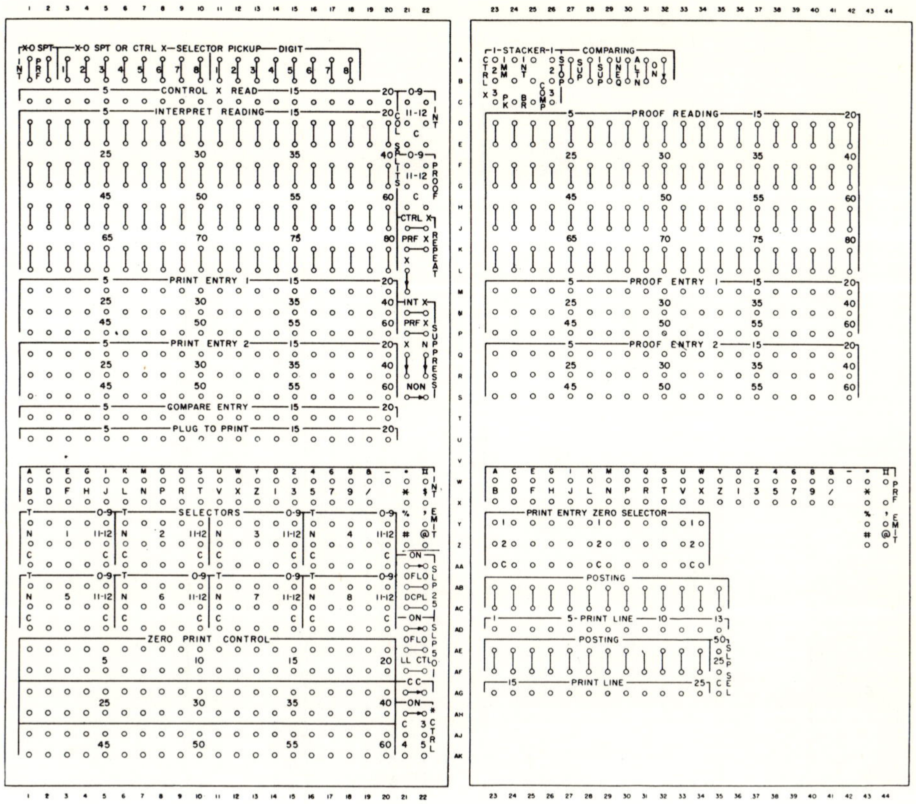

557 INTERPRETER DIAGRAM

IBM

INSTRUCTIONS

JOB NAME: JOB NO.

CTRL. PANEL NO. OPERATION NAME: OP. CODE:

FREQUENCY:

DAILY	MONTHLY
WEEKLY	QUARTERLY
BI WEEKLY	ANNUALLY
SEMI MONTHLY	OTHER

DUE IN		DUE OUT	
TIME	DATE	TIME	DATE

ESTIMATED VOLUME: ESTIMATED TIME: HOURS TENTHS

CARDS USED:

RECEIVED FROM:

OPERATION

☐ REPRODUCE	☐ INTERSPERSED G. P.
☐ GANG PUNCH	☐ END PRINT
☐ DPBCD	☐ SUMMARY PUNCH
☐ COMPARE	☐ M. S. PUNCH

READ FEED CARDS X-D CTL

RX BRUSH	1	2	3	4	5
CARD COL.					

PUNCH FEED CARDS X-D CTL

PX BRUSH	1	2	3	4	5	6
CARD COL.						

END PRINTING

☐ 1st LINE
☐ 2nd LINE
☐ OFF

PRINTING POSITIONS

								U
								L
1	2	3	4	5	6	7	8	

← Fold to Here

INTERNATIONAL BUSINESS MACHINES CORPORATION

IBM 519 DOCUMENT-ORIGINATING MACHINE

CONTROL PANEL

Form X24-9317-3
Printed in U.S.A.

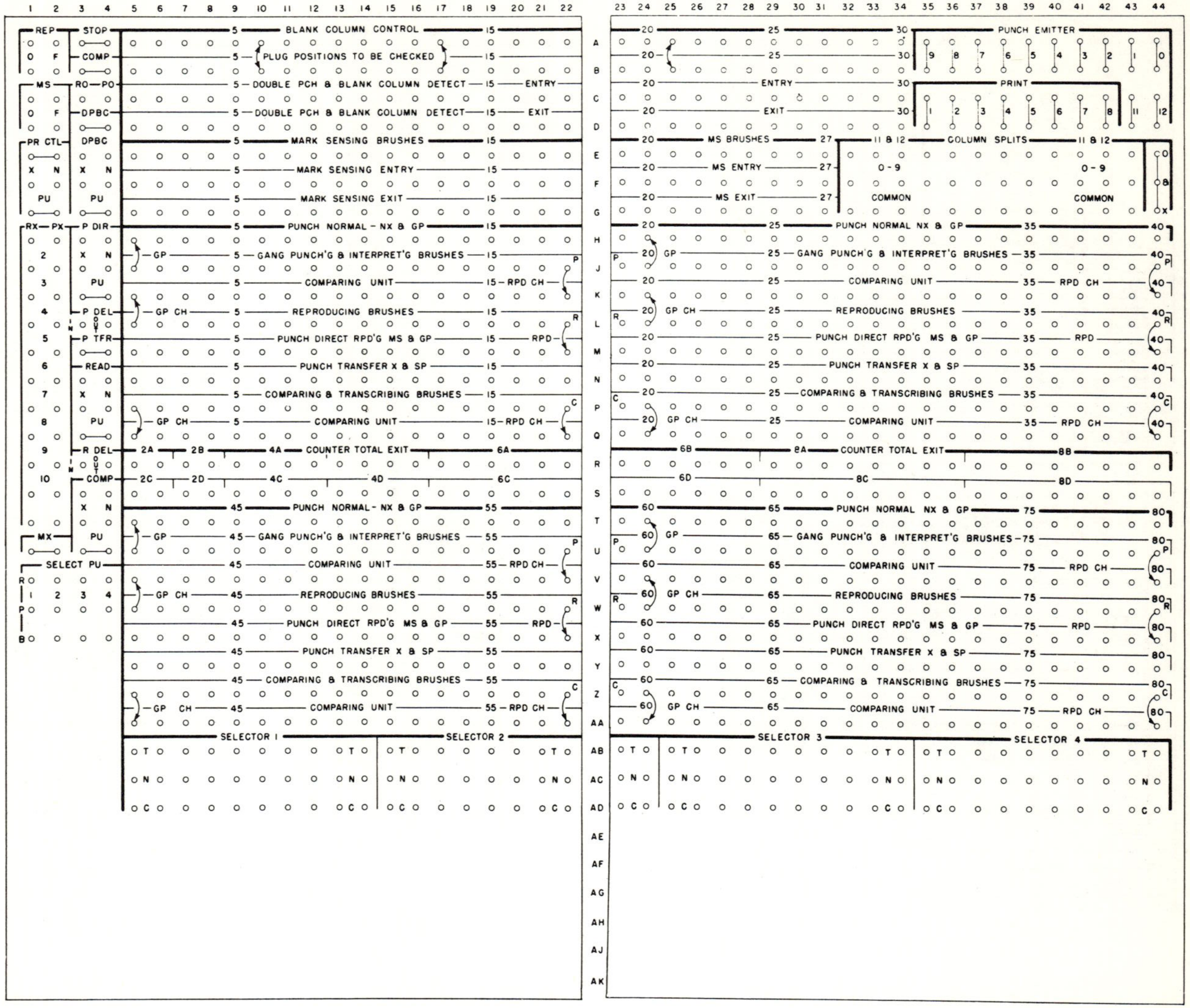

IBM

INTERNATIONAL BUSINESS MACHINES CORPORATION

IBM 519 DOCUMENT-ORIGINATING MACHINE

CONTROL PANEL

Form X24-9317-3
Printed in U.S.A.

INSTRUCTIONS

JOB NAME: JOB NO.

CTRL. PANEL NO. OPERATION NAME: OP. CODE:

FREQUENCY:

DAILY	MONTHLY
WEEKLY	QUARTERLY
BI WEEKLY	ANNUALLY
SEMI MONTHLY	OTHER

DUE IN		DUE OUT	
TIME	DATE	TIME	DATE

ESTIMATED VOLUME: ESTIMATED TIME: HOURS TENTHS

CARDS USED:

RECEIVED FROM:

OPERATION

- ☐ REPRODUCE
- ☐ GANG PUNCH
- ☐ DPBCD
- ☐ COMPARE
- ☐ INTERSPERSED G. P.
- ☐ END PRINT
- ☐ SUMMARY PUNCH
- ☐ M. S. PUNCH

READ FEED CARDS X-D CTL

RX BRUSH	1	2	3	4	5
CARD COL.					

PUNCH FEED CARDS X-D CTL

PX BRUSH	1	2	3	4	5	6
CARD COL.						

END PRINTING

- ☐ 1st LINE
- ☐ 2nd LINE
- ☐ OFF

PRINTING POSITIONS

1	2	3	4	5	6	7	8	
								U
								L

Fold to Here

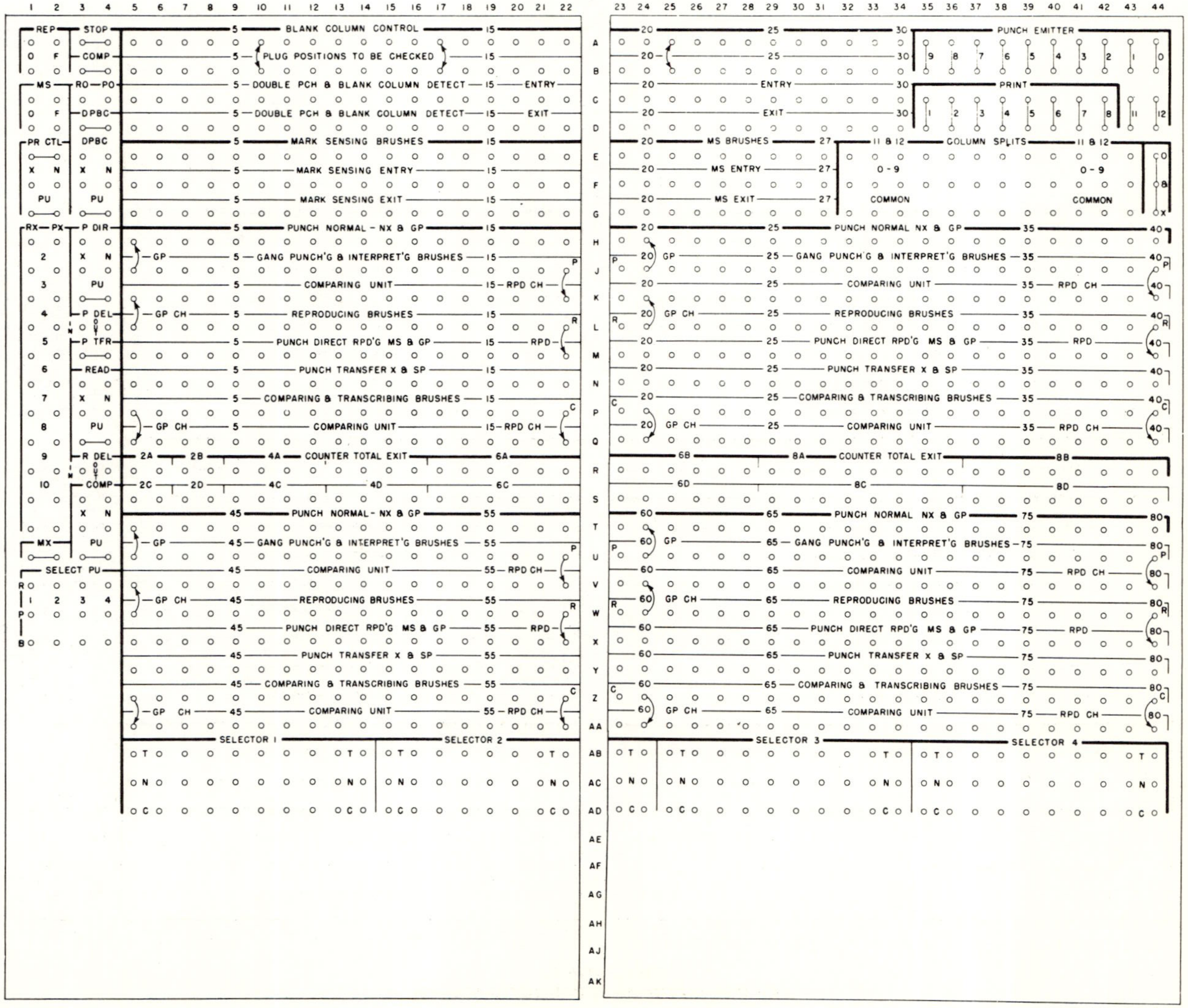

IBM

INTERNATIONAL BUSINESS MACHINES CORPORATION

IBM 519 DOCUMENT-ORIGINATING MACHINE

CONTROL PANEL

Form X24-9317-3
Printed in U.S.A.

INSTRUCTIONS

JOB NAME: JOB NO.

CTRL. PANEL NO. OPERATION NAME: OP. CODE:

FREQUENCY:

DAILY	MONTHLY
WEEKLY	QUARTERLY
BI WEEKLY	ANNUALLY
SEMI MONTHLY	OTHER

DUE IN		DUE OUT	
TIME	DATE	TIME	DATE

ESTIMATED VOLUME: ESTIMATED TIME: HOURS TENTHS

CARDS USED:

RECEIVED FROM:

OPERATION

☐ REPRODUCE ☐ INTERSPERSED G. P.
☐ GANG PUNCH ☐ END PRINT
☐ DPBCD ☐ SUMMARY PUNCH
☐ COMPARE ☐ M. S. PUNCH

READ FEED CARDS X-D CTL

RX BRUSH	1	2	3	4	5
CARD COL.					

PUNCH FEED CARDS X-D CTL

PX BRUSH	1	2	3	4	5	6
CARD COL.						

END PRINTING

☐ 1st LINE
☐ 2nd LINE
☐ OFF

PRINTING POSITIONS

								U
								L
1	2	3	4	5	6	7	8	

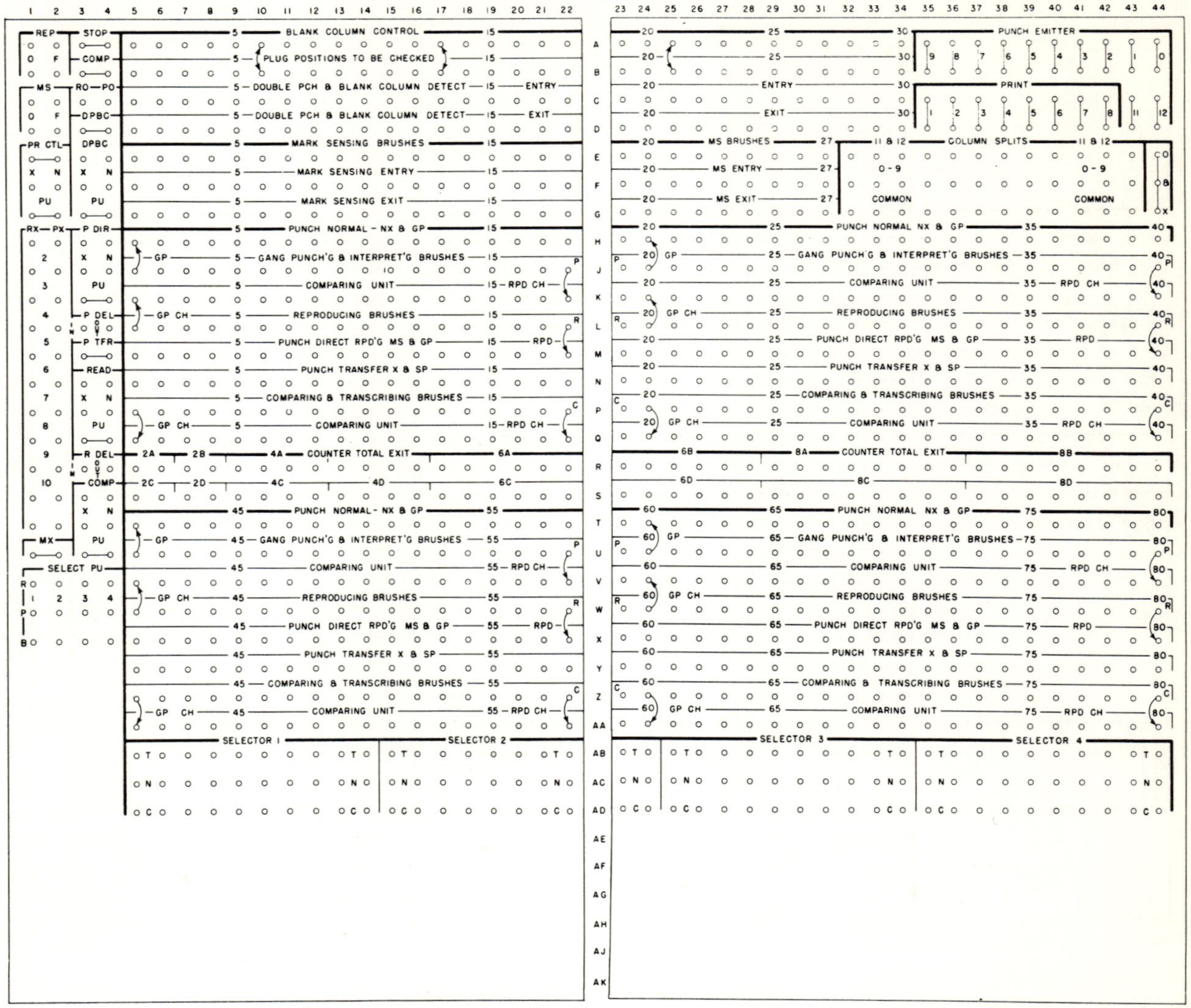

← Fold to Here

IBM

INTERNATIONAL BUSINESS MACHINES CORPORATION

IBM 519 DOCUMENT-ORIGINATING MACHINE

CONTROL PANEL

Form X24-9317-3
Printed in U.S.A.

INSTRUCTIONS

JOB NAME: JOB NO.

CTRL. PANEL NO. OPERATION NAME: OP. CODE:

FREQUENCY:

DAILY	MONTHLY
WEEKLY	QUARTERLY
BI WEEKLY	ANNUALLY
SEMI MONTHLY	OTHER

DUE IN		DUE OUT	
TIME	DATE	TIME	DATE

ESTIMATED VOLUME: ESTIMATED TIME: HOURS TENTHS

CARDS USED:

RECEIVED FROM:

OPERATION

☐ REPRODUCE	☐ INTERSPERSED G. P.
☐ GANG PUNCH	☐ END PRINT
☐ DPBCD	☐ SUMMARY PUNCH
☐ COMPARE	☐ M. S. PUNCH

READ FEED CARDS X-D CTL

RX BRUSH	1	2	3	4	5
CARD COL.					

PUNCH FEED CARDS X-D CTL

PX BRUSH	1	2	3	4	5	6
CARD COL.						

END PRINTING

☐ 1st LINE
☐ 2nd LINE
☐ OFF

PRINTING POSITIONS								
								U
								L
1	2	3	4	5	6	7	8	

Fold to Here

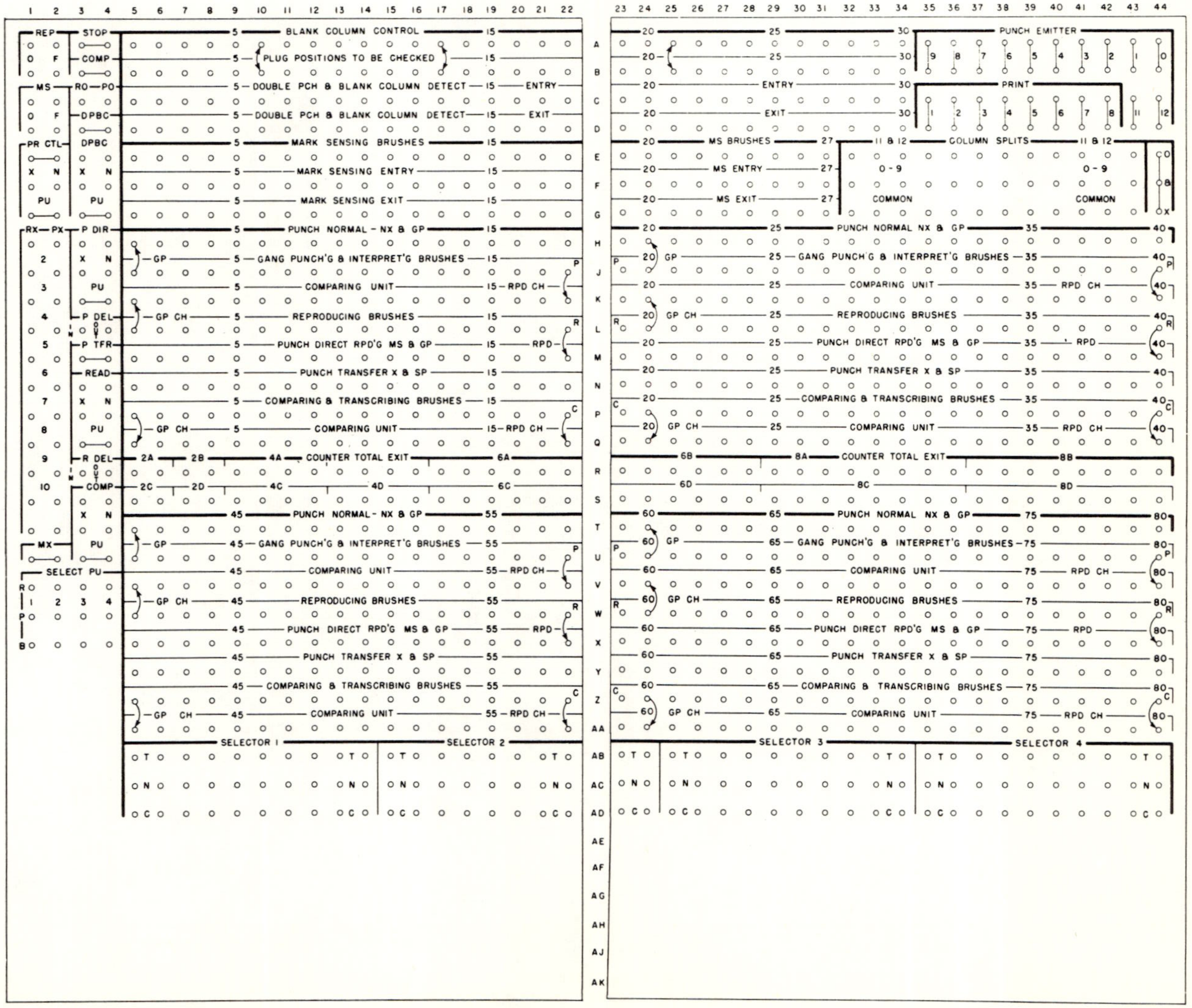